CUPPER JAMES
PUBLISHING

This book is dedicated to the
memory of my parents
Berta "Beti" Revah and Hayri "Zeki" Çağrı

Love birds.
Trail blazers.

Library of Congress Cataloging-in-Publication Data
ISBN: 978-0-615-45901-1

Tile Motif: Iznik Tile, XVI-C, from Takyeci Ibrahim Mosque, Istanbul, Turkey

Printed in Canada

First Printing 2012

The Ottoman Turk
and the
Pretty
Jewish Girl

 REAL TURKISH COOKING

BEYHAN ÇAGRI TROCK

Contents

Acknowledgments

This book could never have happened without the kindness and support of an exceptional group of people. Thank you to: Dr. Barry Kiracofe for generously allowing me to use your beautiful photographs, and for sharing your passion for history. Professor William Bechhoefer for awakening the true Turk in me, teaching me about regionalism, and for your unfailing guidance and support. Toğrul Mehmet Ergene for sharing your unique perspective, vast knowledge, excitement, curiosity and wisdom. Bonnie Loper for lovingly gathering up our family tree and keeping the photographs and records for so many years. Çaya Conger for sharing your detailed memories, loaning me your freshly-ironed table-cloths, your loving perspective and unfailing support. Ida Dana for sharing your recipes, your kitchen, your home, and your sage advice about marriage. Matilda Revah for the many years of dinners and barbecues, for showing me how to make *Agristada*, *Gato Salam*, and Yogurt. Your *Iç Pilav* is the best in the world. Amalia Levi for eloquently translating Turkish text, generously sharing your historical expertise, and loaning me all those books on Turkish and Jewish history. Sara Rahnama for your terrific editing, wisdom, and honest appraisal of what does and doesn't belong in a book about family. Paul Roochnik for kindly giving me your father's copy of Max Dimont's *Jews, God, and History*. Dulcie and Brielle Dana for sharing the recipes you collected over the years. Ilhan Çağrı for being my first and best teacher. Kemal Çağrı for your loving support and for sending me a hundred e-mails of internet links about our ancestry. Younos Mokhtarzada for generously sharing your thoughtful analysis of the teachings of the Qur'an, your clear intellect and unwavering integrity. Can Demir for patiently editing the historical sections of this book and translating the Turkish for me with honesty and generosity; yours was a labor of love. Gwen Zuarez for your support, terrific insights, and stories about Egypt; what an inspiration you are. Sheilah Kaufman for your friendship, critical eye, and limitless generosity. Suzy Menase, Viki Alhale, Viki Plihal Diaz and Marc Tinaz for keeping family memories alive. Robin Levien for being willing to taste strange foods any time of day with exuberance and thoughtful commentary. Elizabeth Levien Eitan for sharing your passion for growing your own vegetables and for the use of your wonderful book *Cooking the Sephardic Way*. Ismet Odabasio of *Ayar Rug and Kilim Company* for your hospitality in Istanbul. Gretchen Alexander for kindly beta-testing my recipes on your dubious husband. Tory for sharing your passion for food, trying out recipes you couldn't pronounce, and making the best baklava in the family. Isaac for your critical and artistic eye for graphics and fonts; your opinion means a lot to me. When I took on this vast project, you two surely made the greatest sacrifice, and I'm so grateful to both of you for not complaining about the many times I was at the keyboard instead of spending time with you. Shanie and Neely Gal-Edd for affirming me by raiding our refrigerator late at night looking for "Beyhan food," and for making me believe that there are indeed young people interested in cooking, after all. Naomi Felsenfeld for affirming my culture and traditional values, for loaning me books on Sephardic cooking, and for teaching me a thing or two about world history. And of course, my husband Bruce Trock for tasting every dish and making me feel like the best cook in the world, for never complaining that months were going by and I was still not earning a penny as an architect, for understanding my need to write this book, and for being my best friend.

Forward

My name is Beyhan, and I am the third daughter of *Hayri (Zeki) Çağrı* and *Berta (Beti) Revah*. He was a Turk, she a Sephardic Jew. In 1940, while working down the street from one another in Istanbul, their paths crossed and my parents fell in love. Because there were enormous cultural taboos surrounding interfaith relationships, theirs was a forbidden love which forced them to turn their backs on their communities, friends, and most painful of all, their families. When Zeki met Beti two worlds collided; their ancient and distinct traditions, cuisines, and religions became suddenly embroiled in a dance both passionate and heartbreaking. Yet, they held fast to their crazy love, despite all the ill will directed at them and obstacles set before them, and defied the odds by remaining lovers until the end of their lives. Their love produced four children, three girls and a boy. Their life dramatically took a new course in 1957 when my father retired from his job as chauffeur for the American Embassy in Ankara. He was given the choice to receive either a pension or a Green Card, Permanent Residence in the United States. He chose the latter. Soon after, the six of us immigrated to the United States, hoping to grasp every opportunity and chase every dream.

I was three and a half years old when we settled in Washington, DC as pioneers. Not long after, our whole extended family followed; my mother's brother first, then her sister, along with their own spouses and children. In the early 1960s, the Turkish population in D.C. was tiny. My parents, always thrilled to meet other Turks, invited practically every newcomer to dinner. Many of these Turkish immigrants became life-long friends and our "aunts and uncles." We eventually grew into an "extended family" of 30 to 40 people, with cousins, aunts, uncles, grandparents, and nephews living a traditional Turkish life nestled in the shadow of the nation's capital.

Figure 1: Beti Revah and Zeki Çağrı in Ankara, Turkey circa 1941. Though her decision to leave her family for my father had been painful, she refused to entertain regrets. Beti used to always say, "You can never go back."

Throughout those early years, we gathered for all-day American Turkish Association (ATA) picnics, leisurely family breakfasts where sometimes twenty of us would sit for hours around the table, and scrumptious dinners at each other's homes or at the fabulous Turkish Embassy parties. Every social gathering was centered on foods from home. Fabulous foods. Turkish staples like *börek*, eggplant, grilled lamb and *kebabs*, stuffed vegetables, and yogurt; Jewish and Passover dishes with strange Spanish names like *agristada* and *burmuelos*. Our food (like our language, music, and customs), had been handed down from one generation to the next. Whatever was "familiar" was comforting, and tied our family to our ancestors and to the world we had left behind.

My parents are both gone now. Their generation is rapidly disappearing. I find myself seated near the head of the table on Passover. My siblings and our cousins are all middle aged now. As I look around, I wonder, is it possible that one us will not be here next year?

Though my children have seen Turkey, prayed in mosques, and attended many a Passover Seder, I worry that they are outsiders to "my" culture. They don't speak Turkish, save a few greetings and choice curse words. And though they grew up with Turkish food, they don't really know where the dishes came from, or how they are prepared. I fervently cling to my receding Turkishness, all the while watching my children drift further out into the stew of the proverbial "American Melting Pot."

I worry that "our ways," our foods, traditions, and memories, will fade away, and that the children of my children will never have the chance to know where they came from. This is why I am writing this book. I'm one of those people Claudia Roden refers to when she says that the drive is still strong for Ottoman Sephardim to preserve family identity, the memory of parents, and an old life that was happy. I am one of the last of that generation of Turkish Sephardim who immigrated in the 1950's when Turkey was still "Turkish." I'm aware that the traditions, foods, manners, language, religions, history, and values my parents brought with them from the old Turkey still live within me. Dear reader, if I don't tell their story, who will?

So, in the spirit of Turkish Hospitality, I welcome you and invite you into my home, to meet my family, to sit at our table. You honor me with your presence. Pleasing you with an interesting story, delicious food, and pleasant company would be my sincerest joy.

TWO BOOKS IN ONE

The book you hold in your hands is divided into two parts: Part 1 is the story of our family. Part 2 is the recipes we brought with us from Turkey.

PART 1 - THE STORY

The narrative describes the dual histories of my parent's ancestors. First comes "The Turkish Muslim Side" which traces my father's family from its Central Asian beginnings. I talk about the Turkic people, nomadic horsemen, their lifestyle and how it influenced modern Turkish cuisine. You will read about how the Mongol Hordes were responsible for my family's appearance on the Black Sea, how there were Byzantine princesses in our ancestry, and even how my fez-wearing mustachioed grandfather rescued a kidnapped American actress in Istanbul.

The second section, "The Turkish Jewish Side," traces my mother's family from their Jewish origins in Palestine through their fleeing the Spanish Inquisition and arriving in the Ottoman Empire. I talk about Jewish life in the Ottoman Empire and about how strict social religious doctrine can be a double-edged sword when it comes to preserving families.

The third section, "Coming to America," describes life after our arrival in the U.S.A. a half-century ago. My parents built their life here in fits and starts, by trial and error. I talk about what Washington, DC was like then, and what it feels like to grow up an immigrant. I include anecdotes about trying to fit in, and also about the more difficult task of preserving Middle Eastern culture and traditions as the years go by.

PART 2 - THE RECIPES

I've tried to talk you through the recipes as if you were in the kitchen with me, and have included lots of pictures, so that even if you've never seen the dish, you can prepare it. I've drawn you a "blueprint" (if you'll forgive the architectural metaphor), to help you faithfully re-create the cooking and eating experiences of at least 25 generations of my family.

My father, whose ancestry traces back to Central Asia, delighted in the Turkish dishes that originated in China, Iran, and Central Asia, and were then perfected by the celebrated chefs of the Sultan's palace. These scrumptious foods were essentially the only kind of food he cooked.

My mother, though more eclectic and adventurous in the kitchen, enjoyed preparing the traditional Judeo-Sephardic recipes passed down through her family since the Spanish Inquisition in 1492. Many of these dishes still have Judeo-Spanish (Ladino) names. My mother also modified Turkish recipes to accommodate Jewish religious dietary restrictions, especially the one about meat and milk being kept separate. Mom did not keep Kosher, but she prepared the dishes as her own mother had.

These are recipes for the foods my family had known in Turkey include both classical Turkish and traditional Sephardic food. The symbols on the bottom of each page allude to the recipe's origin. A crescent and star means traditional Turkish, a Star of David means Sephardic or Judeo-Spanish. Certainly, there is a great deal of overlap, since many Ottoman dishes are perfectly acceptable to the Sephardic Jews of Turkey. After all, both communities exclude pork, and both cuisines are dependent on local ingredients. Many wonderful dishes from both cuisines have not been included in this book. I felt it important to limit myself to only those which I remember, the foods served at our table.

When I started writing this book, I only intended to include a general overview of the history of my ancestors, just enough to orient you to the times and environments through which they travelled. I accumulated almost a hundred pages of fascinating history, maps, charts, and stories going back a few millennia. As wonderful as that history is, a cookbook may not be the right venue for it. That's why I cover history only in a general way in Part 1, just enough to relate the origins of my ancestors, provide a context for the major historical events that affected their lives and forged the trajectory of their progeny.

Cooking the "Old Way"

In these recipes I have purposely tried to relay the cooking techniques and methods of my parents' generation in Istanbul in the 1950's. Much like my spoken Turkish, an almost comically archaic version of the Turkish spoken today, these recipes are "frozen in time." I illustrate how to prepare these foods "the old way," without many of the shortcuts now taken in the modern Turkish kitchen. Don't worry; I am certainly not suggesting that you will grow your own grains or milk your own goat. But much of the pleasure of cooking the Turkish way is derived from the tactile pleasure of handling fresh ingredients. Chopping, grating, and kneading by hand is just more satisfying than packets, cans, and noisy machines. The "old way" also assures fresher ingredients, better control and often a superior texture. But more than that, a "hands-on" approach makes the cooking experience more sensuous, exciting to the eye, the nose, and the touch.

Although the ingredients for these recipes call for specific quantities and measurements, you should know that traditional Turkish cooks didn't use recipes or "standard measures." Measuring a half teaspoon or a quarter cup would be comical. To the Turkish cook, the best unit of measure is the eye, a measuring device honed by years of observation, instruction, and trial and error. Careful measuring is distinctly un-Turkish. So, providing meticulous measurements for ingredients in these recipes is a bit oxymoronic, I admit. Still, it is the only way I could think of to ensure the flavors the way I remember them.

On the other hand, you may be confounded that sometimes I am not specific enough. I do not, for example, specify egg sizes. If you see a recipe that calls for 3 to 4 eggs, use common sense; four if you have small eggs in your fridge, three if they're large. Turkish cooks are just not that fastidious. In fact, carefully measuring ingredients detracts from the artistry, spontaneity, and fun of cooking. Get used to pouring salt into your hand and getting a feel for what a teaspoon of it actually feels like. Smell spices before you add them to a pot, and imagine what flavor they might contribute to the dish. When a pot of stew or soup is simmering, smell it. Admire it. Use your beautiful serving dishes to present the fruits of your labor. And for God's sake, enjoy the process. My aunt Ida used to dance to Turkish Disco music while she cooked, throwing in a little of this, a handful of that, all the while shimmying her hips.

I've translated certain Turkish measuring devices into their American counterparts for you in a chart called Units and Measurements (page 342). For example, I use ¼ cup when the Turkish recipe calls for the commonly used Turkish Coffee Cup. Another Turkish unit of measure, the "glass," actually measures about 4/5ths of a cup. To avoid this strange unit, I have adjusted the recipes by calling for a cup instead of a "glass" and increasing the other ingredients in the recipe accordingly.

While you're busy cooking, I hope you will occasionally slow down and allow yourself to feel connected to the long line of cooks who developed and perfected these ancient dishes. I hope you will enjoy preparing these wonderful foods the same way they did; handling the fresh ingredients, admiring the rich colors and textures. And when your kitchen fills with the wonderful smells of these foods, I hope you will remember that these are the very same aromas that still waft through Turkish homes.

And most of all, I hope the delicious flavors of these age-old recipes will bring your loved ones eagerly to the table, and bind them together with the memories you create.

Researching this Book

Researching my family roots and cuisine, albeit in a semi-rigorous way, was an enormously rewarding experience, and I recommend it to everyone. It allowed me to develop close ties with new-found relatives in Turkey, Venezuela, and Israel - strangers who were suddenly willing to share their pictures and memories with me. I uncovered recipes that were first made in Bulgaria, and brought to Turkey by my grandmother. I learned a great deal about world history and how political events impacted my ancestors' lives. I collected every recipe I remembered, and cooked every one of them, sometimes making several attempts before settling on the formula that tasted most like what I remember from my childhood. In fact, you may see two or three versions of the same recipe, depending on which aunt was cooking.

Best of all, I got to spend private time with my *tants* (aunts). In the process of interviewing them, I was blessed to gather not only recipes, but memories and anecdotes about their lives; stories that I would never have heard otherwise. For example, I never knew that in the early days of the Turkish Republic, Tant Mati's father was forced to do hard labor in a work camp. I learned this tidbit while we discussed tricks for reducing oil in fried eggplant. Tant Ida and I actually belly danced together in her kitchen while she showed me how to make *börekitas*. Cooking with them in their kitchens gave me the opportunity to notice idiosyncratic habits that they would never have mentioned if they had simply related their recipes to me. Subtle habits, like knowing which utensil is best to scoop the pulp out of a zucchini squash, or how to catch the seeds when you squeeze a lemon.

Turkish-ness in Cooking

When the Ottoman Empire disintegrated at the end of World War I (1914–1918) the Turkish Republic was established to preserve the last vestiges of a Turkic state. With the westward leanings of the new Atatürk government and a drive for modernization, decidedly un-Turkish foods and sauces like Bechamel, Mournay, Hollandaise, Béarnaise (*Beşamel, Mourney, Hollanda, Bearnez*), became fashionable and swept through the cosmopolitan areas of the young republic. Famous cookbooks like Ekrem Yegen's *Yemek Öğretimi* presented proper European table settings with modern, minimalist furniture. While visiting Istanbul in the 1970's, I was horrified to see fast food chains like McDonalds sprouting up and McBörek making its way into the modern Turkish diet. Today the glorious basilica that houses the head of the Greek Orthodox Church in Istanbul is hidden by a Burger King billboard.

Turkish culture is now a "defensive culture." It is no longer balancing innovation with tradition, but defending its values against what Bert Frager calls, "irresistible waves of Western civilization." My friend Sheilah Kaufman refers to westernized Turkish cuisine as "fusion food," not western, but not quite Turkish either. I worry that traditional Turkish cooking will continue to fade away. Fortunately, you and I are now engaged in something called "culinary conservatism;" I, by writing this book to preserve and share these recipes, and you, by reading this book, trying out these foods, and remembering where they came from. And we are not the only ones reaching into the past! The internet is loaded with recipe-blogs and Youtube videos of Turkish food, presented to a new generation of Turkish cooks. Perhaps the world is finally losing its fascination with fast food, coffee-to-go, and eating in the car. Perhaps we can look forward to a renaissance of traditional eating. In the mean-time, dear reader, if you can't find a particular Turkish recipe in this book, email me at beyhantrock@gmail.com and I will see if I can help.

At the end of each recipe you will find the Turkish phrase *Afiyet Olsun*. It's sort of like saying *Bon Appetit* in French or *B'te avon* in Hebrew, in that it is said by the cook when food is served. In Turkish, *Afiyet olsun* simply means "may it be satisfying for you." It expresses my most sincere wish about this book and the food prepared from its recipes.

One last note: When it comes to interpretation of the many historical events mentioned in this book, I generally present them to you as they were explained to me. Almost all of the conflicts, especially those between the Greeks and Turks, are presented with a Turkish bias. Since this entire book is based on oral tradition, I hope you forgive me for not being more concerned about a "fair and balanced" presentation. This is a book about my family, after all, and I try to present their lives as they lived them and from their point of view.

Pronunciation of Turkish

You will come across many Turkish words in this book, so here are some tips on proper pronunciation. The Turkish alphabet has 29 letters. It has all the letters of the English alphabet, except "q", "w", and "x." In addition, it has the characters *ç, ğ, ı, ö, ş* and *ü*.

Turkish is always read and pronounced phonetically:

a   pronounced "ah" as in "father". (There is no sound in Turkish like the "a" in "bat".)

e   pronounced "eh" like in "bet".

i   when dotted, is pronounced "ee" like in "pizza"

ı   an "i" without a dot is pronounced like "little" or "bill"

c   pronounced like the English letter J. "Coca Cola" would be pronounced Joja Jola

ç   "c" with a cedilla is pronounced "ch." My sister's name Çaya is pronounced like China without the n.

ş   "s" with a cedilla is pronounced sh. Shish Kebab is Şiş Kebab

ğ   a "g" with a breve (curvy bar) on top is sounded very lightly, almost not at all. Eğer, for example, is pronounced almost like a "y". "İğor" would be like the Pooh character Ee-yor.

ö   pronounced like the first e in "perfect" or the u in "purple."

ü   pronounced very tightly, like in the French "Jut alors!" Try this: pretend you have a ping-pong ball in your mouth. Now, without moving your pursed lips, say "ee." Try it!

Accent   Almost invariably, the accent in Turkish words is on the last syllable. The phrase I mentioned before, *Afiyet olsun* would be pronounced "ah-fee-YET ol-SOON."

Titles   Turkish names are rarely said without a title, meaning your position in society or family:

Bey   Mister or sir

Hanım   Ms. or Lady

Ağabey   older brother

Hala   Aunt - sister of your father

Teyze   Aunt - sister of your mother (or older woman)

Yenge   wife of someone's brother, *dayı* or *amca* (by marriage)

Dayı   Uncle - brother of your mother

Amca   Uncle - brother of your father (or older man)

Enişte   Husband of someone's sister, *hala* or *teyze* (by marriage)

Baba   Father

Anne   Mother

Introduction

AN ALL-AMERICAN GIRL IN ISTANBUL

Okay. I am going to admit something embarrassing. Even though I was born in Turkey, (arriving in the USA when I was 3 years old), I spent most of my life essentially ignorant of Turkish history. How ignorant? Let's put it this way; until last year, I thought the Byzantine Empire and the Ottoman Empire were essentially the same thing. I apologize to anyone who just fell off their chair.

It's just that I always figured I didn't really need to learn about Turkey since I was born there. This misguided notion irritated my father to no end. He spent years trying to get me to appreciate my Turkish ancestry. Anything I did that was remotely Turkish made him incredibly happy. As children, my parents would dress us up in colorful baggy pantaloons, silky vests with tiny mirrors sewn into them in intricate floral patterns, and Aladdin-type slippers with the curled-up toe and the pom-pom on the end. These village costumes were always topped with a colorful *Şile Bezi* scarf tied around our heads. In this get-up, we were hauled off to perform with other kids at Turkish-American galas, dancing onstage holding little candles in our hands. My father's eyes welled with tears when he saw us like this. Occasionally we would wear our headscarves while cleaning house, just because it tickled my parents so much. But I never really appreciated just how much staying connected to our Turkishness meant to my father. How could I? We were living in suburban Maryland, and I was a typical teenager interested in basketball, boys, and ironing my hair to look like Cher.

Every time dad started one of his lectures on the "Glory Days of the Ottoman Empire," or how Santa Claus was actually Turkish, or how Noah's Ark was in Turkey, my eyes glazed over.

I did finally begin to appreciate my unique ancestry, but not by choice. I was fifteen and my father had caught me holding hands with a very handsome African-American boy from the neighborhood. Dad's Ottoman sensibilities had no use for such carryings on, and three days later I was on a plane with him heading to Istanbul for the summer.

What a shock! With predictable teenage rage I spent the first two days of my "kidnapping" in self-confinement; emerging from my bedroom in Muzaffer Hala's (*hala* means aunt on the father's side) apartment only to eat. When I met my two half-brothers Turhan and Orhan, some twenty years older than myself, I never wondered how it was that I had brothers in Turkey. I purposely drowned out the *Müezzin's* calls to prayer by playing my beloved 45 record of *American Woman* by the Guess Who at maximum volume on a cheesy, antique record player.

I covertly recruited my *ağabey* (big brother) Turhan to mail a letter to my boyfriend in the States. He pleasantly agreed. The next day my father presented the opened letter to me with nothing more than a glance of disapproval. You can imagine the feelings of betrayal, rage, and helplessness I felt in this strange world where young women seemed to have no privacy, power, or real say in their lives.

THE GREAT THAW

Eventually, my resentment subsided and I began to explore my new world with trepidation. First obstacle - language. Though my parents spoke Turkish to us at home, it didn't take long for us kids to begin responding only in English. It had been years since I had actually been expected to converse in Turkish. Now I found myself sitting awkwardly silent in a room full of my Turkish family who spoke no English at all. There was a lot of nodding and fidgeting where pleasant conversation normally would have been. For weeks I felt like a complete social failure.

Worse yet was the indifference of adults toward a willful teenager. Unlike in the U.S. where kids enjoy being the center of attention, Turkish adults expect (and receive) sobriety, respect, and obedience from young people. It didn't take too long to figure out that the more maturely I behaved, the more people would bother to notice me.

Figure X: View of Hagia Sofia in Istanbul. Photo courtesy of Dr. Batty Kiracofe

That's not to say I wasn't taken care of. Every morning, Muzaffer *Hala* made me *kahvaltı* (breakfast) of soft-boiled egg served in a delicate egg holder, with a slice of bread, some cheese, homemade preserves, and tea. After my hot shower, a luxury attained only by burning wood under a small water tank hanging over the tub, I would find my hand-washed hippie-style bell-bottom jeans carefully folded on my bedspread, smelling wonderfully fresh from being hung out on a line to dry.

I imagined that this was the same line from which the honeymoon bed-sheet of my newest *yenge* (aunt by marriage) had been hung for the neighbors to confirm her chastity. Muzaffer *Hala* was her new mother-in-law and, like most Turkish brides, the bride had moved into the home of her in-laws. The couple shared her husband's bedroom in the tiny apartment we were all now sharing. My Turkish was getting strong enough to understand her, and late one night *Yenge* and I lay together on my bed chatting. She recounted the story of how, after three mornings with nothing to show on the honeymoon bed sheet, and with the family facing rumors of impropriety, the couple became more and more anxious that the marriage would not be accepted. Her doe-like brown eyes welled with tears as she explained to me how her loving husband comforted her with the promise that he would dribble ketchup on the sheet to assuage the neighbors, and that he would accept her as his wife, no matter what. Thankfully, the ketchup wasn't needed, the stained sheet was hung on the line, and my cousin had proven his genuine and deep affection for his bride through his gesture.

It was my first introduction to late-night girl-talk, Turkish style. Imagine her fascination with my stories of how I used to sneak out my bedroom window at night to meet my boyfriend. She held her hand tightly over her mouth as I told her how I would climb up a grand oak tree with him to make-out. It had been a perfect hiding place; when my father came looking for his wayward daughter with our dog in tow, the boxer couldn't pick up my scent. The boy and I would stand breathless on a thick limb, hearts pounding as we watched them pass below.

That part of my life was slowly fading in my imagination. The *müezzin's* call to prayer began to sound strangely comforting to me, as did the rooster scratching outside my window. My father began to take me on outings. We rode in a refurbished 1955 Ford station wagon, the same car my father and brother would one day drive to Afghanistan. Somewhere in the mountains near Kabul their radiator would spring a leak and they would use camel dung to fix it.

We rode with all the windows down, jostling and maneuvering perilously close to people and other cars on the winding cobblestone Istanbul streets. We were part of a circus of cars, animals, children, vendors, beggars, and diesel exhaust. Throngs of men squeezed past a new Mercedes Benz parked halfway on the sidewalk. Four or five people climbed into an antique Studebaker fitted up as a large taxi called a *dolmuş*. Horses and donkeys pulled and carried wares alongside men and women heavily laden with bundles of sticks, pots and pans, or clock radios. A bony cat scuttled ahead of a rickety, hunchbacked woman with a cane. She made her way carefully between cars, hauling bales of sticks piled six feet high on her tiny frame. A young man with no legs had tied himself firmly to a makeshift skateboard. With hands heavily wrapped in rags, he wheeled himself on his knuckles down the street. Occasionally he stretched out his leathery hand for a coin.

We crossed the *Galata* Bridge to *Eminönü* and arrived at the foot of the glorious mosque *Yeni Cami*. Here was the entrance to *Mısır Çarşısı*, the famous Spice Bazaar. Immediately upon disembarking, I noticed all eyes on me. I was obviously a spectacle to society with my striped, fringed bellbottoms and wild hippie afro-wannabe hair. It bothered me how much I stuck out. It wasn't just my clothing - it was the way I carried myself. I was not yet versed in the correct "body language" of young women in Turkey, and was unaware that locking eyes with a boy was an "invitation." Within minutes I had inadvertently signaled my "availability" to quite a few young men. My father fretted at all the boys he had to ward off with harsh glances or a shove. Each incident was followed by a cruel glance of disgust directed at me, as if to suggest that I knew exactly what I was doing. Maybe I did.

Yeah, I did.

My father would wake me in the mornings and tell me to get ready to go out, not bothering to explain where. One day we crossed a little bridge and climbed a rather steep hill, seemingly in the middle of nowhere. He stopped, and I watched him brush thistle and debris from a sad unmarked grave. He stood there silently, pondering it. Or maybe he was praying, a very private act for my dad. Then, without even looking at me, he started his descent. I sheepishly followed, feeling unworthy of an explanation.

I spent time with a whole world of nieces and nephews, astonished to hear them call me by my own title *Hala* (sister of your father), even

Fig. 2 - One of my favorite places in Istanbul is Eminönü. It's a transportation hub for ferries, buses, and taxis, and the main destination for tourists who come to visit Yeni Cami (the New Mosque), Kapalı Çarşı (the Grand Bazaar), and shops along Galata Bridge.

though some were ten years my elder. I also met my Turhan *Ağabey's* wife Semiha *Yenge* (wife of your brother), the first person in my life to utter anti-Jewish sentiments. When she and I were alone she shamelessly threw open my luggage and closely inspected the many gifts I had brought for the extended family, claiming some for herself. She whispered insinuating questions about my Jewish mother. Being married to my half-brother Turhan, Semiha had obviously heard stories about the Jewish girl who had stolen Dad from his mother Zehra. I felt myself blush. It was all too complicated for me. Looking back, I see that she was the only person in Turkey who behaved even mildly aggressively toward me.

Semiha *Yenge's* marriage to Turhan had been arranged. She had been a widow of some wealth, and as I understood it, he was a handsome ex-sailor with too many loose women floating around in his private

Figure 3 - My devilishly handsome half-brother Turhan Çağrı in Istanbul circa 1950

social sphere. The time had come to tie Turhan *Ağabey* down, to keep him out of trouble. I began to understand that rules of social conduct were not solely applied to impetuous teenage girls.

By the fifth week, the kindness and hospitality of my Turkish family had melted my rage and I suddenly began to speak Turkish in full sentences. It was as if a faucet had been turned and all the Turkish I had forgotten came pouring back into my head. The trips to *Topkapı* Palace, the Blue Mosque, the tea gardens along the Golden Horn, the green plums in the fruit carts, and the harrowing excursions

INTRODUCTION

across the glorious Bosphorus strait in rickety rowboats patiently pulled along by leathery old men, all began to feel strangely familiar.

Dad took me on a ferry to *Büyük Ada*, the largest of the Princess Islands which was, at the time, mostly occupied by Istanbul's Jewish families who summered there. Unlike Istanbul proper, the Jewish girls on *Büyük Ada* were very much part of public life. They could be seen in the latest European-style bikinis, sitting with other young people, boys and girls together, at tea houses on the waterfront, playing *tavla* (backgammon), listening to music, just enjoying life. It seemed like we had left Turkey altogether. There are no cars on *Büyük Ada*, so we took a beautifully decorated horse-drawn carriage up the hills to the bright and airy apartment of my *Onk Rıfat Menase*. (Notice I didn't call him *Amca* or *Dayı*. My Jewish uncles are referred to as *onk* from the French *oncle*.) His wife *Öjeni* (Jeni) had prepared a lovely lunch of brain salad, fried eggplant with tomato sauce and garlic yogurt, and a delicious poached fish in lemon egg sauce called *pişkado Agristada*. Oddly, the Menase's had no problem with their son Loni, also my age, showing me his awesome record collection. We sat alone in his room for some time, playing guitar together while my father and *Rıfat Bey* enjoyed *rakı* (an anise-flavored liqueur) on the patio. On the ferry ride back to *Eminönü*, I came to appreciate how my parents had grown up so differently in the same city. My Jewish relatives seemed to live in a future Turkey. They were modern, enlightened, with a *joie de vivre* that I had not seen in the Muslim side of my family. They also seemed to have money.

It was almost time to return to America. One day, as my father and I waited in the car for Turhan, I fell deep in thought, looking at the city, the people, the newness of the oldness. Between my thoughts, I sensed I was being watched and turned to find my father looking at me with a smile on his face. He said he was happy to see my eyes "bright" again. Turhan returned with a large package and gave it to my father. Handing it to me, he urged me to pull apart the paper. Inside I found the most fabulous embroidered sheep fur and suede vest, a fashion item that had become all the rage back home. He watched me run my fingers through the fleece trim and across the colorful stitching. When I realized it was for me, I looked at his face and saw that he was crying. I kissed my dad, and felt incredibly loved.

DISCOVERING MY HISTORY

By the time I returned to America, I had changed; I'd been outside the "fish bowl" and there was no way to jump back in. Trying to fit in with my Langley Park friends seemed silly. I was finally beginning to understand that there was a reason I had never fit in, and that it wasn't necessarily a bad thing. Best of all was the realization that there really wasn't anything wrong with me; I wasn't a "weirdo" as I had feared. I was just an immigrant.

IMMIGRANT

When you immigrate to another country as a child, you have a pretty good idea of what you are not. Having arrived in the United States at the age of three and a half, I realized pretty early on that we were not like other kids. All children spend a great deal of time confused and searching. But my siblings and I had to make sense of a culture that even our parents struggled to fathom. In school we had weird names that our teachers couldn't pronounce. We produced weird food from our lunch boxes. At home we listened to funny music, and danced with our hands in the air.

Here's an example of just how "immigrant" we were. My parents had taken us four kids to the Takoma Park Cinema for a Sunday matinee. Rather than buying popcorn and candies, my mother had packed a picnic lunch. As opening credits rolled she gingerly began peeling the hard-boiled eggs for each of us, passing them down the row in a napkin, along with a wedge of tomato on a slice of Italian bread. The salt shaker was passed back and forth as the cartoons and News Flashes beamed from the large screen. You can imagine the smell of those eggs in that theatre. We probably cleared the place.

My sisters once had the glorious idea of opening a jar full of fireflies in the movie theatre. It was like being in a magical forest, watching a film while tiny lights gleamed in the night sky.

My immigrant family was wonderfully and painfully complicated. Outside of the house, I was an American girl. But inside, I was living in a microcosm of not one, but two, Middle Eastern cultures; an extended family, with Jews on one side and Turks (Muslims), on the other. One week we'd celebrate Eid, the other Purim. At home there were two sides to every story, two points of view, and neither one seemed to have much to do with American society at large. It finally dawned on me that my American childhood would have to make room for two more sets of traditions, two religions, two histories.

I've been back to Turkey half a dozen times since that first visit to Turkey with my father; sometimes as a student of architecture, sometimes as a relative, once as a bride. But it wasn't until I started writing this cookbook that I began to seriously research my amazing family. I discovered that my ancestors and relatives not only lived through incredible historical times and events; in some cases they actually played dramatic and important roles in shaping them.

By interviewing family, reading journals, letters, diaries, and history, I found that my father's accounts of Anatolian battles, which I used to greet with a yawn, suddenly became real and fascinating. Why hadn't I paid more attention? His stories were not at all like the abstract events and tedious lists of dates we had to memorize in 11th grade World History class. He had tried to open my eyes to tangible events more astonishing and compelling than any video game developer could create.

Dad had talked about Mongol hordes, stolen princesses, battles and conquests, secret alliances, bravery and treachery, Khans and Kings, nomads and slaves. He had always said, for example, that we were descendants of a Greek princess. Here was her name! And Tamerlane's conquests? They brought our family to Trabzon on the Black Sea coast. Dad had said "We are Turks. We have Turkish blood in our veins." On the other hand, Tant Ida spoke to me about the Jewish blood in my veins. "We are Sephardic Jews," she would say proudly. "We left Spain, we left Bulgaria, we even left Turkey, but through all of it we preserved our Jewishness."

At that point which occurs in everyone's life when it is important to define oneself, I came to accept myself as a conglomeration of Turk and Sepharad. It then became my mission to tease apart a knotted tapestry of culture, symbolism, language and religion so that I could get a clear picture of their geneses.

Our house was a linguistic melting pot, and I became interested in how the languages spoken in our home served as a highly accurate cultural compass, pointing me down the various roads of my ancestry. Names were important clues. On my mother's side, they were Latin based: names like *Mari, Merih, Ida, Sara, Suzanna, Leon, Jak, Aron, Yehuda, Bulisa, Bella, Silvio*. On my dad's side, they were Muslim and Central Asian; *Mehmet*, (from the name Muhammad), *Ali, Hüseyin, Lütfiye, Fehmi, Haydar, Gökhan*. My mom's fluency in Ladino, Greek, and French revealed the existance of robust and interwoven non-Turkish communities in Istanbul. I began to appreciate the cultural soup that was the Ottoman Empire.

Language gave other clues. The fact that mom spoke Turkish without the strong Jewish accent of her siblings indicates the young age at which she left the Sepharad community. The way my grandmother pronounced my name *Beyhan* with a slavic '*kh*' pointed to her Bulgarian background. My father's knowledge of Arabic and Farsi points to the influx of Muslim and Persian culture in his Turkish ancestry.

My father's family has spoken Turkish for many, many generations. It was a safe assumption that at some point in history, his people resided in the mountainous Eurasian Steppe of Central Asia, domain of nomadic Turkic peoples since antiquity. This is where the story of the Ottoman Turk and the Pretty Jewish Girl begins.

Part 1
The Story

❖ **The Turkish Muslim Side**

❖ **The Turkish Jewish Side**

❖ **Coming to America**

Figure 4: Tile detail from Rustem Pasha Mosque in Istanbul by the architect Sinan. Photos courtesy of Dr. Barry Kiracofe

CHAPTER I

THE TURKISH MUSLIM SIDE

Figure 5: My grandfather Uzunoğlu Hüseyin Ibrahim in his uniform as Cavass (guard) at the American Consulate General in Istanbul, standing with my father Zeki in 1910. (Photo from the American Foreign Service Journal, October 1937, Library of Congress)

TURKISH BEGINNINGS IN CHINA

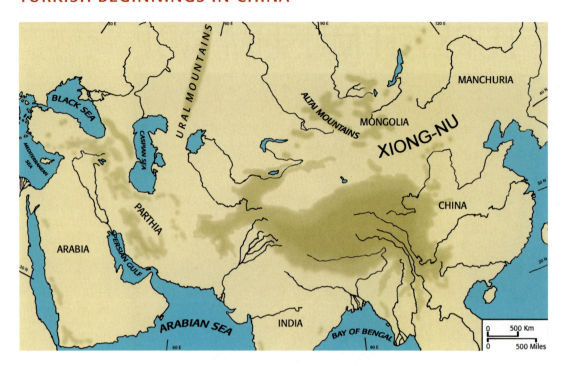

Figure 6: Map of Asia showing Mongolia, the Altai mountains, and the Xiong-Nu territory

Most of what we know about Turkish origins comes not from archaeology or anthropology, but from incredibly intricate linguistic theories that look more like math formulas than language. That's because it isn't race that makes Turks a unique people, but language. Turkish is an Altaic language, from the Altai Mountains at the crossroads of Southern Siberia, Mongolia, and China. I am no linguist, archaeologist, or even historian. My personal research on my ancestry is not meant to be taken as true "scholarship." This *is* a cookbook, after all. But the oral tradition in our family is strong, and there is enough written about the Turks that I can make a "best guess" about where my father's family came from.

I like to tell my kids they're Asian. They look at me like I'm crazy. But if you're Turkish, chances are pretty good that your earliest ancestors were living somewhere in China. In fact, the "original" habitat of the first people to bear the name "Turk" was the mountains of Siberia in Northern Asia. They were known to the Chinese as the *Tujue* (meaning combat helmet), perhaps because of the conical shape of the Altai Mountains, their homeland. These pre-Turks emerged from the forests onto the East Asian steppes north of China and eventually mixed with the livestock-breeding nomads on the move from the plains of Eastern Europe to the shores of the Pacific.

Nomadic people lived a lifestyle aligned with the rhythm of the seasons and the lifecycles of their animals and livestock. Their society and culture developed as a response to inter-tribal rivalries for sparse resources in extreme climates. It is no wonder that the nomadic horsemen cultivated a combative spirit, elegant equestrian skills and unusual dexterity on horseback.

Home for the nomad was anywhere he could feed his animals and pitch his tent or *yurt* (a small round structure, so beautifully suited to its environment, it can be called a masterpiece of regionalist architecture). Made of lattice and felt held together with horsehair straps, the yurt served as the nomad's spiritual microcosm, a respite from life's physical extremes.

Much of modern Turkish cuisine has its roots in the foods prepared sustainably and innovatively over the small fire in the Central Asian nomad's yurt. Stews and soups, kebabs and fruit condensates, flat breads were staples. Milk from the nomad's sheep, goats, yaks, and camels became yogurt, cheeses, curds, and even an alcoholic beverage called *kumis*, and all were prepared with the most primitive utensils over the yurt's single central fire. The flattened bread cooked in a skillet and then alternately layered with cream was later brought to a level of "high art" in the Ottoman Sultans kitchens, where it evolved into elegant and delicate pastries made from layers of paper-thin sheets of *yufka* and filled with sweets or savories. In modern Turkish cuisine these dishes are known as *baklava* and *börek*.

The Turks (6th-8th C)
1: Türgish 'tarkan' champion
2: Gök 'Blue' Turk armoured cavalryman
3: Eastern Turk tribesman

Figore 7: A rendering of the Turks in Transoxiana (6th-8th centuries) by Angus McBride from David Nicolle's Osprey Military Elite Series book "Atilla and the Nomad Horses."

The nomadic social body was held together by alliances of kinship and marriage. This early social structure, where status was based on age, gender, blood relationships, and then relationships via contract, continues to define the social order in modern Turkish society, as well.

Significantly, wealth and material possessions were of less concern than social cohesiveness. And marriage, which facilitated tribal allegiance and loyalty, made these nomadic confederations of tribes behave almost as extended families.

Around 2000 BCE, small tribes of these pastoral nomads formed a confederation known as the *Xiongnu* (Hsiung-Nu or "Ferocious Slaves" in Chinese, and pronounced shee-ung-noo). We don't know if the ruling class of the *Xiongnu* were Turks themselves, but the pre-Turkic *Tujue* tribes were certainly among them. These non-agricultural people raised their horses in the barren Mongolian highlands and migrated with

their animals from pasture to pasture along the rivers in the steppes of Outer Mongolia. When resources were scarce, they used their excellent equestrian skills to raid villages and townships on the border they shared with the Chinese.

Throughout the 4th and 3rd centuries BCE Northern China wasn't a single entity. It was more like a loose collection of warring states, (Qin, Zhao, Yan, Qi, Lu, Wei, Han and Chu), which the *Xiongnu* took every opportunity to invade. The nomads created so many problems for their neighbors, in fact, that Chinese warlords had to construct fortifications to keep the *Xiongnu* out. When China finally unified, the Qin Dynasty Emperor decided the best way to protect his empire from the Xiongnu was to connect all these fortifications with a wall. You guessed it; this huge structure would later become known as the Great Wall of China.

I'm thinking these are pretty auspicious beginnings for my family.

TURKISH BEGINNINGS IN CHINA   15

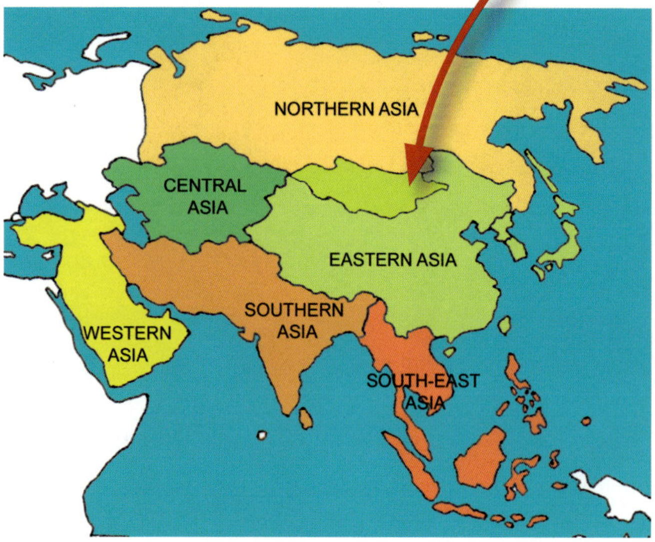

The European Hunnic Empire remained a chronic irritant to both the Western Roman and Eastern Roman (Byzantine) Empires for half a century. Their confederation, which had been governed by individual chiefs, gradually coalesced under central leadership; first under King Rugulas, and soon after under his nephew the infamous Attila the Hun. Atilla pushed into the Eastern Roman empire as far as Constantinople and in 447AD was stopped only when the Byzantines agreed to pay the Huns an annual tribute of 2,100 pounds of gold.

At its zenith, the Hunnic Empire stretched from the steppes of Central Asia into modern Germany, and from the Danube River to the Baltic Sea. They ransacked Gaul (now France) as far as Paris and Orleans. But Atilla suffered a military defeat in Gaul in 451 AD, was driven from Italy by plague and famine, and died in early 453. When the Huns were decisively defeated in 455AD, their hordes disbanded and moved back toward the north and the Black Sea where they were eventually absorbed into the general population.

In terms of tracking my personal ancestry, I found that the history of the Huns took me down a trail that quickly grew cold. Luckily, my father's brother *Bahri Ergene*, a true historian, had written letters regarding the appearance of our family on the Black Sea. I decided to follow his lead and backtrack a bit to explore another Turkic group in China; a fascinating ancient tribe named after a she-wolf.

Figure 8: When one talks about Asia it's useful to divide it into six distinct regions.

THE HUNS

At the same time the Xiongnu were threatening the borders of China, another group of proto-Turks appeared at the other end of the Eurasian continent on the plains of south-east Europe. Known as the Huns, these people may have incorporated Xiongnu who had spread westward. The Huns gradually worked their way westward from the steppes, across the grasslands of Central Asia, conquering tribes and pillaging everything in their way. They were outstanding warriors whose skills as mounted archers astonished and inspired great fear and wild rumors among the Romans and Europeans. People believed the invading Huns cut the cheeks of their male babies to teach them to endure pain. They claimed the Huns were cruel, dirty people who never changed their clothes. The undeniable truth is that the Huns were feared because they were unstoppable. They were fierce warriors whose iron swords and stirrups gave them a huge advantage over their enemies. In 375 AD they crossed the Rhine into the territories of the East Germanic tribe known as the Goths. They overthrew the Ostrogothic Kingdom in Ukraine and the Visigoth tribe on the western shores of the Black Sea (modern Romania), a year later. These victories would set off a desperate flight of Eastern Europeans toward Western Europe, leading to the Great Invasions of Europe and ironically, the expulsion of my Jewish ancestors from Spain. I'll tell you more about that in the next chapter.

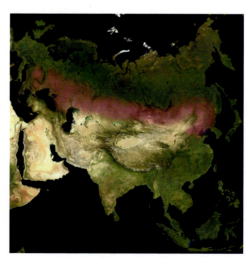

Figure 9: The Eurasian Steppe, (in pink) extending from Hungary through the Ukraine and Central Asia to Manchuria.
Image from commons.wikimedia.org

THE ASHINA

Somewhere around the late 4th century, a large group of horse-riding Mongolian (not Turkic, not Chinese) nomads known as the *Xianbei* migrated from their lands in Manchuria and eastern Mongolia to Northern China where they set up various kingdoms. But one federation of the *Xianbei* remained behind in the Mongolian steppes. By the late 5th century, these war-like people called the *Ruan-Ruan* (Juan Juan or Rouran) had subdued and dominated all the tribes of the Mongolian steppe, Central Asia and parts of Siberia and Manchuria. The vanquished tribes, referred to as vassals, were permitted to use *Ruan-Ruan* land in return for rendering homage, fealty, military service or whatever the *Ruan-Ruan* needed. One group of these vassal tribes living in the Altai Mountains were also *Tujue*, (Turkic). Chinese texts as early as the 6th AD century tell us that the *Tujue* (also known as *Tu-Kiue*, *T'u-chueh* and *Türük*), originally came from a place called Qiansichuzheshi Mountain, which is unknown today. They had been allied with a large Turkic confederation in upper Asia known as the *Tolesh*.

Between 265 and 460 AD the *Tujue* people left the *Tolesh* and moved north of modern Xinjiang Province, to a legendary place called Ergenekos located in the inaccessible southern hills of the Altai mountains. There, the *Tujue* became well-known for their iron-working, and served as

blacksmiths for the *Ruan-Ruan* leader. Called "Blacksmith (*Duannu*) Slaves," they produced many kinds of weapons, first from horn and wood, and later metal, (once they had learned to cast bronze and iron). These were tough people. They lived in severe climates, primarily raising livestock in a nomadic-warrior style. They spent most of their lives on the backs of their horses, and all of them, including the women, were armed. Their reputation with a bow and arrow was unequaled, as was their speed during attacks.

The mightiest entity within the *Tolesh* confederation was a group of ten tribes known as the *Ashina*. The *Ashina* were named after the tribe whose ruling family was considered the legitimate source of its leader (*khan*). Of the many stories surrounding the mythical origins of the *Ashina* tribe, the most impressive is that *Ashina* was one of ten sons whose father was the sole survivor of a tribal massacre, and whose mother was a blue/grey she-wolf (*Kök Böri*) named *Asena*. The tribe's totem was therefore a wolf.

In 521, as the Tolesh Empire dissolved, a charismatic leader of the *Tujue* emerged to establish the *Gök-Türk* federation of tribes. This leader, Bumin Khan, whose name means "Commander of 100,000" is said to have been himself born of wolf-mother Asena.

The individual tribes of the *GökTürk* confederation were small and nimble, able to move quickly and often, to reach fresh grasses. But when Bumin Khan, ordered a military campaign, the warriors of the tribes would coalesce and raid the frontier as one enormous and devastating army. The *Gök-Türk*, the first empire to use the name "Turk" (which means solid or strong), demonstrated their fortitude and warrior skills in raids along the western frontier of China. In 546 they compelled the Chinese Western Wei (who had recently separated from the Northern Wei dynasty) to negotiate a truce, and thereby establish a commercial relationship.

Bumin Khan, still very much in the service of the *Ruan-Ruan* over-lords, was obliged to also fight other Turkic people, including the six tribes of the Turkic group known as the *Tiele* (Chile). Nicknamed *Gaoche* or "high wheel" by the Chinese (because of the high, many-spoked wheels of their wagons), the *Tiele* were also known as (and I'm not making this up) the Dinglings. When the Dinglings tried to revolt against the Ruan-Ruan, they were put down by none other than Bumin Khan. The *Tiele* became subservient to the *Gök-Türks* and since they were not so different culturally, a quarter million of them were incorporated into the *Gök-Türk* army. Subtle cultural distinctions between the tribes are interesting.

Figure 10: The Importance of Blue: Jean-Paul Roux writes in "Turkic Peoples of the World" that the oldest known word in the Turkish language is Tengri which meant both the name of God and "sky." The word Gök also means "blue sky" or "blue heaven." The color blue is ubiquitously important in the Middle East as it is still believed to ward off evil. Window and door frames are painted blue for that purpose. Ironically, the color also seems to ward off flies.

In 552 the Gök-Türk army launched a revolt against the *Ruan-Ruan*, defeating them and the beheading some 3,000 people. The remaining *Ruan-Ruan* fled across the Mongolian steppes and into China, where they were absorbed and disappeared forever as an entity.

So we see that four hundred years after the collapse of northern *Xiongnu* power in Inner Asia, the *Gök Türks* had destroyed the *Ruan-Ruan* state, subjugated their other nomadic neighbors, and become uncontested masters of the Mongolian steppe. Bumin Khan bound the nomadic Turkish tribes together and moved them into the Orkhon Valley in Central Mongolia.

In 552, from the sacred Mount *Ötüken*, (Otukan, Utukan) Bumin Khan proclaimed the *GökTürk* (Blue Turk or Sky Turk) khanate, with himself its *Illiğ Khan* (Great Khan or King of Kings). Thus was created the first Turkish empire.

Unlike the *Gök-Türk*, a *Tiele* man would move into his wife's home after marriage and would not bring his wife to his own home until the birth of a child. The *Tiele* also had different funerary rites, burying their dead underground.

Bumin Khan, after having demonstrated military bona fides as well as loyalty to the Ruan-Ruan, felt he had earned the right to ascend to the status of the ruling family. This was normally done through marriage. He made a request for the hand of a *Ruan-Ruan* princess to the *Ruan-Ruan* Khan who replied to the proposal thus, "You are my blacksmith slave." The response had been insulting enough for Bumin Khan to kill the unfortunate messenger and then organize his own revolt against the *Ruan-Ruan*.

Still determined to marry into a family of higher status, Bumin Khan requested the hand of another princess, this time from the Chinese Western Wei. The Emperor gave his permission, sending the young Princess "Changle." (Yes, I'm afraid to say he married Changle of the Dinglings!) The marriage accomplished its political purpose, and the two rulers grew quite close; so much so that when the Wei Emperor died in 551, Bumin Kahn sent 200 horses to the Wei in Tribute.

Fig 11: Transoxiana, home of the Oğuz Turks in western Uzbekistan, is literally across (trans) the Oxus River. Oxus was the Greek name for the Amu Darya River, so for the Greeks, reaching that area would have meant crossing over the river.

THE FIRST TURKIC EMPIRE

THE GöKTÜRK (BLUE SKY TURKS)

Just as arteries carry fresh blood and nutrients from one part of the body to enrich and nurture another, so did the Silk Road deliver products and goods from China to the Mediterranean, Africa and Europe. Silk, more valuable than gold in the 6th century AD, was carried from it's sole source in the Far East on the backs of camels plodding slowly across deserts, grasslands and snow-covered mountains to the markets of Byzantium. At the same time, there were two types of people living in Central Asia; the settled people who built their towns, fortresses and agricultural centers along the trade routes of the Silk Road in the south, and the pastoral nomads who routinely swept down from the north to rob them. The *GökTürk* or Blue Sky Turks were the latter.

The three communities of early Central Asia, (the mobile nomad, the settled farmers and villagers, and the traders along the Silk Road), were all part of one symbiotic economic system. Though the nomads lived separately, they depended on settled communities for their survival. Their's was a "trade or raid" mentality; what they couldn't get by trade with their neighbors, they would simply take by force. The merchants, who would need the settled people for food, rest stops and markets along their route, often enlisted those same nomadic warriors to protect the settlements and Silk Road.

I mentioned earlier that tribal allegiance made nomadic confederations of tribes behave like extended families. Sometimes these "families" became too large to manage. In 583 AD the *GökTürk* Empire split into two khanates. The western group, known as the *Oğuz Turks*, left the Altai mountains and the Siberian Steppe to settle east of the Aral Sea in a place called Transoxiana (now Uzbekistan, Tajikistan and southwest Kazakhstan). The *GökTürk* arrived in the Orkhon Valley (the Ural-Altai

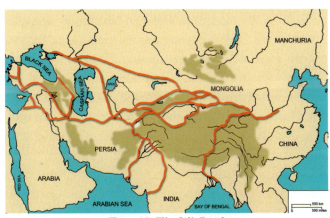

Figure12: The Silk Roads

Figure 13: Orkhon Valley in Mongolia. Photo courtesy of World Heritage Sites on i.images.cdn.fotopedia.com/flickr-166014932-original

region of Central Asia) under their leader Bumin Khan and gradually built a vast confederation. By 745 they had assimilated all the other sub-tribes to create an empire so immense it spread from the Volga in the west to the Yellow River in China. It was the first time so great an expanse of Asia had been controlled by a single ethnic group.

Around the middle of the 6th century one of the largest confederations of tribes in the Orkhon Valley emerged as leaders within the Gök-Türk empire. These were the the 24 tribes known as the *Oğuz* (Oghuz) Turks.

PRE-ISLAMIC TENGRI-ISM AND THE ETERNAL BLUE SKY

Like most of the early *GökTürk*, the *Oğuz* Turks had been specialists in iron works under the Chinese, and had mostly lived in the area surrounding Mount Khan Tengri, a sacred site on the Kirgiz-Kazakh border. This mountain, deified as "Ruler of the Sky," one of more than 90 gods deified by the Shamanistic population. The greatest god for the *Oğuz* Turks was *Gök Tanrı*, the "Sky God," creator of the celestial universe, the supreme awe-inspiring entity which appeared before anything else and ruled the fates. The mountain-dwelling *Oğuz* Turks embraced a faith, Tengri-ism, where living in harmony with the surrounding world was the meaning of life itself.

We will see later that Tengri-ism has not been thoroughly eradicated from the collective psyche of my father's family. Dad's explanations of Allah (God in Arabic) were as closely aligned to a Tengri-ist reverence for nature as they were to Islamic tradition.

ISLAM IN CENTRAL ASIA

THE RASHIDUN CALIPHS, DYNASTIES AND THE SPREAD OF ISLAM

The first four caliphs of Islam are known collectively as the "Rightly-Guided Caliphs" (*al-khulafa al-Rashidun*). They expanded the reach of Islam by first unifying the Arabs against the Byzantines in Syria and the Sassanids in Persia. There was a period of enormous upheaval as dynasties and nations vied for global domination. The leadership of Ali was disputed by Mu'awiya of the Umayyad (centered in Damascus). When Ali (pbuh) died at the hands of an assassin in 661, the Umayyad claimed the caliphate. They gradually established the largest Arab state in history.

But anti-Umayyad sentiment ran hot in Shi'a Iran and Iraq. A descendent of the Prophet, Abu Al Abbass al-Saffah led a Shi'a supported revolt against the Umayyad and overthrew them and killed almost the entire Umayyad aristocracy. Only the talented Umayyad prince Abd ar-Rahman escaped; fleeing to Al-Andalus, (the Iberian Peninsula, Spain) where, in 756, he established the Umayyad Caliphate of Córdoba.

Meanwhile, the Turks of Central Asia, who had witnessed a growing Chinese presence in their lands, allied themselves with the Arabs against China. The powers fought it out in the Battle of Talas in 751 to determine which of the two civilizations, the Celestial Empire or the Muslims, would dominate Central Asia. With the help of the Turks, the Arabs prevailed and the Chinese were defeated.

Conversion to Islam had already begun among the Turkish-speaking tribes of Central Asia, especially where contact with the Arabs was most prevalent, namely along the Silk Road. A major stretch of the trade routes ran along the region south of the Aral Sea known as Transoxiana. This is where the *Oğuz* had established the Western *Gök Türk* Empire. The teachings of the prophet, brought to them by the Arab traders from the south, and the concept of a single God, Allah, rapidly superseded Shamanism and Tengri-ism. Islamic customs, traditions, and law took firm root, and soon there were mass conversions of Turks to Sunni Islam.

If you've ever wondered how it is that Turkish culture, especially in this region, has so much Persian influence, the presence of a new dynasty, the Abbasids is the answer. The Shi'a Abbasids from Persia conquered the Sunni Umayyad and annexed most of the West Turkic Empire of Central Asia, including the *Oğuz* Steppes. From the 7th though the 10th centuries Arab influence in Central Asia gave way to Persian, and Central Asia became one of the world's most verdant and influential cultural centers.

When the Prophet Muhammad (pbuh, or peace be upon him) died in the year 632, the Arabs had extended their influence past their homelands in Arabia to Central Asia where they came into contact with the Turks. By then, there were two super-powers in Central Asia. One was the enormous Persian Sassanid Empire. The other the Roman Empire, which was divided into the Western Empire (mired in the "Dark Ages") and the Eastern Empire, known as Byzantium. Both the Persians and the Romans were earnestly monitoring the Muslim threat to their dominions.

The prophet's successors ascended to the Caliphate with varying degrees of popular support. The rift between Shi'a and Sunni Islam in fact, stems from passionate disagreement about who should have succeeded him. The Shi'a, who comprise 20% of the world's 750 million Muslims believe that Ali, the prophet's son-in-law should have been the first Caliph. The disagreement persists today and is a chronic source of tension.

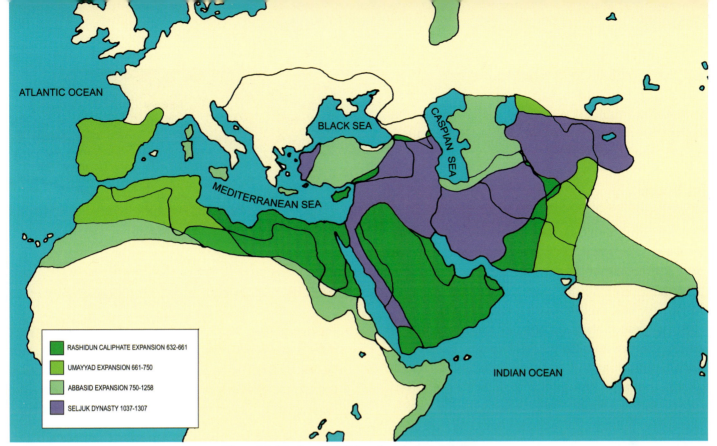

ATLANTIC OCEAN

BLACK SEA

CASPIAN SEA

MEDITERRANEAN SEA

INDIAN OCEAN

RASHIDUN CALIPHATE EXPANSION 632-661
UMAYYAD EXPANSION 661-750
ABBASID EXPANSION 750-1258
SELJUK DYNASTY 1037-1307

Figure 14: The Spread of Islam through the Seljuk Dynasty.

And while many strong traditions of pre-Islamic Turkic culture were stubbornly preserved, Islam became the only religion, and the Turkic peoples in Central Asia had become its biggest champions.

The Abbasids allowed the small and scattered Turkic emirates to rule independently. As the tribes fanned out across the steppe, several grew to become kingdoms and empires by fighting one another for territory. One such tribe was the Seljuks. It's eponymous leader, an *Oğuz* Turk warrior chief, renounced Shamanism and embraced Islam. Seljuk marched his people from their ancestral homelands on the Black Sea and settled his newly converted tribe on the left bank of the Syr Darya River in Transoxiana.

As part of the Abbasid constellation, Seljuk and his descendants raided the Muslims in the province of Khorasan (Khwarazm) in Persia and eventually conquered all of northern Iran and most of Azerbaijan, and established Isfahan as their capital.

As rulers, the Seljuks were known for mixing with local populations and their presence in Khorasan explains the strong Persian influence on the language, ethnicity, and culture of primarily Turkic Transoxiana.

The Seljuk Turks introduced Islam to Christian Anatolia by establishing relations with the Byzantine populations living there: the Greek-speaking Christians and the Armenians. Frequent inter-marriage between the Turks and Byzantine princesses as well as trade agreements with the Genoese and the Venetians widened the cultural exchange between Christians, Arabs and Persians.

Meanwhile, the Abbasid umbrella was fraying. In 1055 their Caliph in Baghdad, beleaguered by internal revolts, appealed to Seljuk leader *Toğrul* for help. The Seljuks arrived, bringing order to Baghdad, and *Toğrul* declared himself protector of the Abbasid caliph. He was honored in return with the title "Sultan and Sovereign of the East and West." Thus the Seljuk Sultanate became centered in Baghdad and included both Iran and Iraq.

If anyone ever asks, the Christian Crusaders were driven from Muslim soil not by the Arabs, but by the Turks. In 1071 the Seljuk Turks under Alp Arslan defeated the Byzantine army and captured its Emperor Romanus IV Diogenes. The Battle of Malazgirt (Manzikert) north of Lake Van was a stunning military victory that originated the slow decline of Christianity in Asia Minor and the rise of Muslim Anatolia.

Seljuk power reached its zenith under their new leader Alp Arslan (1063-1072) and soon after the empire separated into two branches: the Great Seljuks in Isfahan (Iran, Iraq, Syria), and the Anatolian Seljuks, also known as the Seljuks of Rum (Byzantium, also known as the Eastern Roman Empire).

THE MONGOLS

Aside from the constant pressure from the Byzantine Crusaders to their west and the Arabs to the south, the Seljuks faced another and deadlier enemy from the east; the Mongols.

Like the Turks, the Mongols started out as a group of nomadic warrior tribes in northeastern Mongolia. Under their leader, one of the most infamous characters of Central Asia, Genghis Khan (1162-1227), they grew into a marauding army, a swarm on horseback, which raided and looted their way across the plains of Mongolia. By 1204 these "people of the felt walls" had become "The Great Mongol Nation," a vast and culturally-diverse dynasty that ruled all of Central Asia. The Mongol Empire stretched from the Pacific to the Danube, and from Siberia to Burma. *Temuçin* (Genghis Khan's name at birth) and his successors ruled the empire with considerable skill. Focused on economic expansion, the Mongols were diligent patrons of trade and commerce who introduced Europe to Central Asia by encouraging merchants, pilgrims and travelers like the Venetian Marco Polo.

In the winter of 1242-43, Genghis Khan's third son *Ogedai* put an end to the Seljuk Sultanate of Rum in a battle which took place in a narrow gorge between the mountains at *Köse Dağ*. Even with the aid of the Byzantines in the Black Sea region of Trebizond, as well as Frankish mercenaries and Georgian nobles, the Seljuks and their allies were overwhelmed by the Mongols. Trebizond and the Seljuks became Mongol vassals.

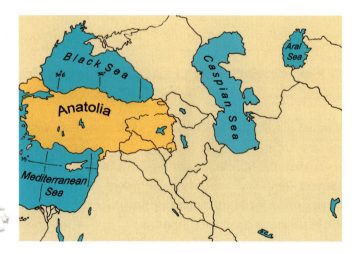

Figure 15: The Seven Regions of Anatolia

ANATOLIA

The word Anatolia comes from the Greek word *anatole* meaning "break of day" or sunrise. This is because the first Greek navigators to make their way north through the Bosphorus saw the sun rising over the land in the east. (The word Europe may come either from the Akkadian *erubu*, meaning "sunset," or the Greek *europa*, meaning "eyes wide apart.")

Known to the Greeks and Romans as Asia Minor, Anatolia refers to what is 93% of modern Turkey. The other 7% of Turkey lies in Europe, across the Dardanelles, the Sea of Marmara, and the Bosphorus Strait. It is mostly a plateau 3,000 to 5,000 feet above sea level surrounded by a fringe of low-lying coast. The region is bounded by the Black Sea to the north, Georgia to the northeast, Armenia to the east, Mesopotamia to the southeast, the Mediterranean Sea to the south, and the Aegean Sea to the west. The Sea of Marmara forms a connection between the Black and Aegean seas through the Bosphorus and Dardanelles, separating Anatolia from Thrace. South and east of the highlands lays the "Fertile Crescent," known as the dawn of civilization and the place from where agriculture spread onto the central plateau in the Neolithic era.

After the Seljuk Empire dissolved, Turkmen tribes (Western *Oğuz* Turkic nomads in Central Asia), began spreading out all over Anatolia, establishing their own independent emirates. Faced with fierce resistance from the Turkmen, the Mongols decided to forego conflict in the west, and concentrate instead on the profitable trade routes which passed through northeast Anatolia and Trebizond. Anatolia, albeit fragmented, remained the "Land of the Turks."

Myriad Turkish emirates had claimed their own parcels of Anatolia and were at varying times each other's allies and enemies. One particular emirate in northwest Anatolia, bordering what remained of Byzantium, draws our attention. This was the emirate of Osman, Khan of the Osmanli. Known today as the Ottomans, this small Turkmen tribe was destined to rule more than three continents for six centuries as one of the greatest empires in history.

Figure 16: I had bought this plate in Turkey a few years back and recently asked my cousin Mehmet Ergene if he could tell me anything about it. "It is a lousy ceramic plate, probably manufactured recently. Whoever is responsible for the 'caligraphy' should be publicly flogged; it is an abomination. The bastard obviously has no notion of Arabic script. It imitates the tuğra of an Ottoman Sultan and is a very lousy depiction of the very first pillar of Islam, (there are five of them). In Turkey it was known as 'Kelime-i Şehadet' (words of witnessing) and translates as 'There is no one but Allah, and Muhammad is his prophet.'" That's Mehmet for you.

The Ottoman Empire, which lasted from 1302 through World War I was one of the greatest empires the world had ever seen. At its zenith in 1683 it controlled more than 7% of the world's population (39 million people and more than two million square miles of territory. My father was 15 years old when the Ottoman Empire disappeared from the face of the earth. He viewed its end not only as a geopolitical event of huge proportions, but as a personal tragedy. How can I not be curious about how my family ended up being a part of that vast empire, and what it meant to us when it finally evaporated? Wouldn't you be?

We know that Anatolia (Asia Minor) had been part of the Roman Empire but became known as Byzantium (or the Eastern Roman Empire) after the Roman Empire split into East and West. When the Byzantine emperor Constantine came to power in the year 324, he founded his capitol, Constantinople, on the Bosphorus (the strait connecting the Black Sea

to the Sea of Marmara). Nine hundred years later, a prince of the Turkic *Kayı* tribe (*Kayıhan*) named *Osman* entered northwestern Anatolia along with other *Oğuz* Turkmen nomads migrating from Central Asia. By that time the holdings of the Byzantine Empire had been reduced to basically the capital city, Thrace, Macedonia, and Greece.

Osman, son of *Ertuğrul*, whose lineage has been traced directly back to Noah, (yes, Noah), became the new Khan of the *Kayıhan* when his father died in 1281. Like most of the *Oğuz* Turks, the *Kayıhan* had been vassals to the Seljuk Sultanate of Rum. But when the last Seljuk prince of the dynasty died, Osman declared independence and established a small *beylik* (principality) whose main goal was to take territory from the Byzantine state.

With the allegiance of *Ghazi* (Holy War) warriors, mercenaries, and the flood of Muslim refugees fleeing the westward drive of the Mongol invasions, *Osman* spent much of his life conquering one Christian city after another. His son *Orhan Gazi* continued the march and extended *Kayıhan* control from their center in the Marmara region all the way to the northwest corner of Anatolia.

Figure 17: Map of Istanbul showing Bosphorus Strait which separates the Sea of Marmara from the Black Sea, as well as the Golden Horn

Fig 18: Shehzade Cami in Istanbul was commissioned by Sultan Süleyman I in memory of his eldest son Mehmet who died of smallpox at the age of 21, in 1543. The building was architect Sinan's first major commission. Photo courtesy of Dr. Barry Kiracofe

As the Byzantine Empire declined and the Ottoman Empire (Empire of *Osman*) grew, the two states occasionally found it expedient to assist one another in conquest of common enemies, so that when the Ottomans under Orhan expanded into Europe, they did so, not as conquerors, but as mercenaries in the service of Byzantium.

Infighting between the Christian emperors, as well as alliances forged through marriage, opened the door for the Ottomans to invade the Balkans and finally Constantinople itself in 1345. Subsequent *Kayıhan Khans*, now being referred to as Ottoman Sultans, expanded the empire further, leaving Constantinople to be administered by the Byzantines while the Ottomans set up their own capital in Adrianople (Edirne).

Under Sultan *Murat I* they conquered the Bulgarian capitol, Sofia, where my grandmother Sara would be born a half century later. The fourth Sultan, *Yıldırım* (Thunderbolt) *Beyazıt* widened Ottoman suzerainty over the Turkish *beyliks* in Anatolia and expanded Ottoman possessions eastward. Ankara in central Anatolia, the city where I was born, was taken by the Ottomans in 1385.

Conquest eventually brought the Ottomans up against the infamous Muslim/Mongol warlord from Transoxiana, *Timour Lenk*, (Timour the Lame or Tamerlane 1335–1405). Allied with the Byzantine Emperor Manuel III, *Timour* had also been recruiting warriors from the Central Asian *beyliks*, but his purpose had been to wrest control of Central Asia from the Ottomans. (Many of the Turkic nomadic warrior tribes who had been vassals to the Ottomans were more than willing to switch sides in these affairs since their main motivation was personal enrichment from the spoils of conquest.)

One such *beylik*, which had been in Anatolia since 1340, was the *Ak Koyunlu* or White Sheep tribe. My father used to tell me that our ancestors were *Ak Koyunlu* Turkmen who themselves were descendants of *Bayındır Khan*, the great folk hero described in the "Book of Dede Korkut" as the leader of one of the original 24 tribes of the *Oğuz* people. (You may recall that these *Oğuz* were the blacksmiths who had served the Chinese and made their way to Asia Minor as part of the Seljuk conquest.)

In 1399 the *Ak Koyunlu Khan, Kara Yülük Osman,* who had recently conceded lands to the Sultan's forces in Sivas, pledged allegiance to the Mongol *Timour*. Together they began invading the Turkish provinces to drive the Ottomans out.

Sultan Bayezit had conquered almost all the European provinces in the west and was pressing ahead to the Byzantine capital Constantinople when news of *Timour's* growing threat came to his attention. Luckily

Figure 19: Interior of Hagia Sophia in Istanbul. The building was originally a Byzantine (Eastern Roman) Basilica before Mehmet II conquered Constantinople in 1453 and converted it into a mosque. (Photo courtesy of Dr. Barry Kiracofe)

for *Timour's* ally, the beleaguered Emperor Manuel III, *Sultan Beyazıt* was forced to abandon his quest for Constantinople and redirect his forces eastward to confront the Mongol army in Anatolia.

The vast armies of Mongols and Turkmen clashed bitterly in the renowned Battle of Ankara in 1402. By the end of the fighting, *Sultan Yıldırım Beyazıt* was reportedly seen standing alone on the dusty battlefield swinging his axe wildly at anyone who dared approach. The Ottomans were beaten badly and their devastated Sultan was ultimately captured.

One would have expected the entire empire to collapse after the defeat that overthrew the Ottoman state. But *Timour* had not come to Anatolia to rule it. His main objective had been to secure his western flank to free him up for further conquests into India. After his victory in Ankara he restored sovereignty in Anatolia to the various Turkmen *beys* who had joined him in battle. Perhaps *Timour* reasoned that a divided Anatolia

ruled by small *beyliks* would be less of a threat to his ambitions than a unified empire. So in 1402, after *Beyazit's* defeat, *Timour* granted *Kara Yülük Osman* of the *Ak Koyunlu* all of Diyar Bakir in northern Iraq/southeastern Turkey.

When my father told me our ancestors were *Ak Koyunlu*, he also noted that we were descended from a Greek Princess. You can imagine how fascinating it was for me to learn that after the Battle of Ankara, the *Ak Koyunlu Khan, Kara Yülük Osman*, did in fact, marry a Byzantine princess, a common practice at the time. Is it too far a stretch to wonder if she was the one my father meant?

And the defeated Ottomans? After a number of years of sibling rivalry on steroids, one of *Beyazit's* seven sons, *Mehmet I*, emerged as Sultan and began the arduous process of re-unifying the empire and formed alliances with his former enemies; the Byzantines in Constantinople.

Figure 20: The Byzantine Church Hagia Sophia above was converted into a mosque after Constantinople was conquered in 1453 by Sultan Mehmet II, whose protrait appears on the right. (Photo courtesy of Dr. Barry Kiracofe)

In 1405, after his army of Mongols and Turkmen conquered Persia, sacked Delhi in India, invaded Syria, and then Baghdad, Timour died, and Asia Minor descended into a chaotic power grab. As it turned out, Timour's strategy of divvying up Anatolia into beyliks had been an astute maneuver that hindered Ottoman efforts to restore the empire. But the Ottomans did gradually unify, and in 1453 their seventh sultan, *Mehmet II* renewed the quest to conquer Constantinople. The siege was one of the greatest in history and involved building fortresses on either side of the Bosphorus and transporting huge ships over land to circumvent an enormous boom chain which the Christians had stretched out across the Golden Horn. In the end, the city fell to the Ottoman army.

Mehmet II (from then on called *Fatih Sultan* or the Conqueror Sultan) entered his new capital not as a victorious barbarian, but as a cultivated and enlightened king with grand plans for his new capital; plans which included re-populating the city. Whole communities of Greeks, Muslims, Armenians and Jews from Anatolia and the Balkans were uprooted and resettled in Constantinople to suit the economic needs of the Empire.

Byzantine Constantinople was no more, and the remaining Christian dominions prepared themselves for an inevitable showdown with the Ottomans. To the north, Alexius IV, emperor of Byzantine Trabzon on the Black Sea, was making alliances with the fearsome anti-Ottoman Turkmen tribes whom Timour had left behind to rule. To cover all his bases, Alexius gave one daughter in marriage to the ruling family of the *Ak Koyunlu* and another to their arch enemy the *Kara Koyunlu*.

Trebizond interests us primarily because its location on the Silk Road at that particular time in history explains how it was that my ancestors finally arrived on the Black Sea from their lands in Transoxiana and the Aral Sea. Trabzon is also important to us because it is where my father's parents were born and our love story will soon begin.

THE TURKISH MUSLIM SIDE

BYZANTINE TREBIZOND AFTER THE FALL OF CONSTANTINOPLE

Now, about the Byzantine Empire of Trebizond. Genoese and Venetian merchants who had established trading posts in the Seljuk and Persian empires had long since negotiated with the Byzantines for the right to ship their goods through Trebizond to their colonies in Constantinople. Trebizond was therefore the maritime outlet for trade from Tabriz, (Iran), the capital of the *Ak Koyunlu* tribal federation. When *Timour* left Central Asia, it was with the understanding that Trebizond could continue its trade arrangements independently, as long as it paid tribute to the Mongols. Collection of this tribute was to be administered by *Timour's* allies; the *Ak Koyunlu* Turkmen.

Meanwhile, back in Constantinople, *Fatih Sultan* had embarked on grand plans to rebuild his new capital. The two-month siege had left the city under-populated and dilapidated; little more than a cluster of desolate villages. The sultan, who had run out of funds, heard that Trebizond, the lone Christian outpost on the Black Sea, was enjoying a renaissance of culture and commerce. Trebizond was said to be plating its domes and churches with gold. After the fall of Constantinople, the Byzantine Emperor of Trebizond from 1429 to 1459, John IV Komnenos, had insulted the Sultan. He had welcomed the wealthy Christians from the vanquished city of Constantinople who, no doubt brought their wealth with them, and were now living like royalty on the southern shores of the Black Sea. To the sultan, the food and supplies he needed were "ready for the taking."

The Ottoman sultan became increasingly aggressive, imposing heavy tolls on the city's Venetian shipping and demanding what can only be described as an unreasonable annual tribute from the Byzantine emperor. John IV resisted, and as his father had done, began promoting anti-Ottoman alliances with both the Europeans and his Turkmen neighbors. In 1458, just five years after Fatih Sultan took Constantinople, Emperor John IV and the new *Ak Koyunlu* leader and now *Padishah* (king) of Persia *Uzun Hasan* had recognized their common interests. As usual, the hand of a pretty princess came into play during diplomatic negotiations, and John IV's daughter Katerina, (Theodora Megale Komnene) was promised to the khan. (She would later change her name to *Despina Hatun* and play an important role in the *Ak Koyunlu* court.) By 1460 the *Ak Koyunlu* were prepared to openly defend Trebizond against the Ottoman Sultan.

No doubt *Khan Uzun Hasan* had intended to honor the agreement. But when Fatih Sultan's forces overwhelmed his in Koyulhisar in 1461, the Ak Koyunlu leader withdrew, leaving his mother with Fatih Sultan

Figure 21: Author's Sketch of Çakırağa Konak, Birgi Izmir, 1761

as assurance that he would refrain from further assisting Trebizond. The Ak Koyunlu army departed toward Georgia, while the sultan, (taking Uzun Hasan's mother *Sara Hatun* with him as collateral), began the arduous trek over steep, snow covered mountains toward the Komnene lands. With the Ottoman army approaching, and no allies in sight, Trebizond's newest Emperor, David Komnenos, quickly reconsidered his personal attachment to the city. Surrender was arranged and the 250 year Byzantine Empire of Trebizond was no more.

UNFINISHED BUSINESS WITH UZUN HASAN

Fatih Sultan continued to see *Uzun Hasan* as a threat; especially because the King of Persia had strong allies; the powerful Turkmen *Karamanoğlu* tribe and the Ottoman Empire's arch rival at the time- the Republic of Venice. In 1471, the sultan successfully neutralized the Turkmen and with greater confidence moved his forces deeper into Anatolia where he met *Uzun Hasan* in battle near Erzincan. In true irony, the Venetian support he had counted on failed to materialize and in the summer of 1473, King of Persia was forced to face the Ottoman forces alone in Tercan (near Erzurum) to fight the famous Battle of Otlukbeli.

Uzun Hasan was badly defeated. Routed, in fact, and it was truly the end of his relevance in central Anatolia. In less than noble fashion, the King of Persia literally abandoned a large portion of his defeated army on the battlefield and retreated rather hastily to Azerbaijan where he died in 1478.

MAÇKA

MY FAMILY ARRIVES IN MAÇKA

After the battle of *Otlukbeli*, the surviving Turkmen soldiers of *Uzun Hasan's* army found themselves defeated by the Ottomans and abandoned by their Khan who had fled to Persia. These troops, new arrivals from Central Asia, regrouped on the battlefield and soon stood face to face with the forces of Fatih Sultan Mehmet II. One can only imagine their astonishment to find that the Ottoman soldiers with whom they had just battled were much like themselves; Turkmen of the same faith, the same sect, even speaking the same language. The *Ak Koyunlu* were so moved to find an army of their own people, they offered their services and allegiance to the sultan on the spot.

Figure 22: Houses in Trabzon (photo courtesy of Professor William Bechhoefer)

Fatih Sultan, intent on rebuilding Constantinople, uprooted 1,500 of Trabzon's Greek residents and shipped them there (as well as to Crete, and Peloponnesus), where they were re-settled in the Fener and Balat districts of the city. Trabzon's abandoned Byzantine villages were then re-populated with 258 Turkish families, thus making the port city entirely Muslim. Fatih knew he needed an authority to manage the traders and merchants making their way from China and Persia to the Mediterranean. The *Ak Koyunlu* who had pledged allegiance to him fit that bill.

And here's where things get interesting. According to the memoirs of my Uncle Bahri, Fatih decided to send these Ak Koyunlu soldiers to Trabzon (Turkish form of Trebizond). An *Uzun Hasan* prince named *Uzun Oğlu* (meaning "son of Uzun") was made leader. Under his command, a group of *Ak Koyunlu* mercenaries were sent north to settle among the heavenly green slopes of the Zigana Mountains in the villages overlooking the southern shores of the Black Sea.

Some of these soldiers stayed within the town of Trabzon, but most were sent to the small town of *Maçka*. Their mission was to protect the Zigana mountain pass, (*Zigana Geçidi*), an important travel way and trade route between Turkey and Persia. The *Uzun Oğlu* prince had his men build a *kale* (a large and imposing building were travellers spend the night) directly in front of the pass, which also served as a fort-like outpost for the Ottoman sultan. From that position the soldiers collected a toll or *baç* from travelers in exchange for protection from bandits

and enemies of the Ottoman State. This was a unique and profitable arrangement for Sultan Fatih. He had essentially set up the army of a defeated enemy as a self-sustaining fiefdom - a security force for his eastern front - which would be paid for by the traders whom it protected.

The strategic location of the *konak* proved to be hugely profitable for the *Uzun Oğlu* clan. Because the Crusades had been disrupting trade and endangering merchants traveling the Silk Road to the south, trade routes were diverted north to the Black Sea. One passed directly in front of the *konak*, thus providing an enormous financial advantage to the family and the clan. The soldiers did their job well, and under Ottoman rule, the *Uzun Oğlu*, *Maçka*, Trabzon and the Black Sea coast enjoyed peace, tranquility, and most of all, prosperity. Ownership of the castle was handed down from one generation of *Uzun Oğlu* princes to the next for hundreds of years, until it finally became the property of my great grandfather *Uzunoğlu İbrahim Ağa*.

Something else happened over those centuries. As the Ottoman state continued to develop and evolve, the fiefdom of the *Uzunoğlu* clan eventually became obsolete. Government became more centralized, and the Sultan's army became more integrated, organized, and streamlined. Recruitment of a regular army became the norm. By the 19th century, the arrangements of independent lords and mercenary armies who charged their own taxes and fees were rescinded. Such was the case for the *Uzunoğlu* khan, whose privileges of *ayan*, as it was called, were permanently invalidated. The modern age had caught up with the

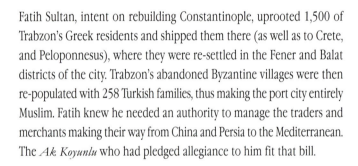

Turkmen warrior. The title *Khan*, which had once meant being leader of a powerful nation with its own flag and subjects, had come to simply mean ownership of a mansion which had become both idle and impractical.

The last *Uzunoğlu* prince, still a man of considerable wealth, abandoned the *konak* for village life in *Aşağı Hacavera* (Lower Hacavera) where he built himself a formidable, thick-walled mansion (also referred to as a *konak*). *Uzunoğlu İbrahim Ağa* came to own this *konak*.

True to his lineage in the *Ak Koyunlu* or "White Sheep" clan, *Uzunoğlu İbrahim Ağa* continued to make a profitable living raising livestock. We know that at one point he lost a good deal of money exchanging gold for Ottoman paper currency (which in turn lost its value and ultimately evaporated). From this transaction we can estimate *Uzunoğlu İbrahim Ağa's* date of birth to be somewhere around 1840. We know he lived in *Maçka* where he married a woman named *Güllü Hanım* and that in 1871 she gave birth to two sons. One was Osman. The other was my grandfather *Uzunoğlu Hüseyin*. The *Uzunoğlu konak* in *Aşağı Hacavera* was passed down from *İbrahim Ağa* to my grandfather *Hüseyin*. According to local land deed records, it still exists, is still the property of my family, and is known as *Uzunoğlu Hüseyin's konak*. I hope one day to travel to Trabzon to see it.

MY GRANDFATHER HÜSEYIN BEY

Hüseyin is said to have been a beautiful child. He grew to be tall, narrow in the waist, with a sparkle in his eye, thick hair and a blond moustache. They called him a *şehleben* or good looking youth. I guess these days you would say he was "hot." Perhaps if he had been born centuries earlier, when young men led lives of adventure on horseback in the open plains, *Hüseyin* would have been a great warrior. Unfortunately, nomadic days were a distant past for the *Uzunoğlu* family, and a settled life left young men few outlets for their over-abundance of testosterone. I wish I could rave about my father's father, but the truth is that *Hüseyin* was not particularly industrious, barely learned to read or write, and preferred instead to spend his days leisurely riding his horse. Villagers even remarked that the bow-legged way he walked was a result of all the time he spent on horseback. Having no skill or trade to speak of, the young Turk relied on his father's wealth for his everyday needs. Never one to back down from a fight, the headstrong and insubordinate *Hüseyin* accumulated quite a few rivals, and on more than a few occasions got into fights which left him pretty badly beaten up.

Hüseyin was 16 years old when, in another village in the township, Upper Hacavera, the *Müftü* (cleric) of Maçka; *Karahasanoğlu Hoca Mehmed Ali Efendi* and his wife gave birth in 1885 to a daughter, my grandmother *Lütfiye*. Before I tell you about how *Lütfiye* met my grandfather and came to be his wife, please permit me to say a bit about my grandmother's illustrious family, the *Karahasanoğlu*.

LÜTFIYE HANIM'S FAMILY IN MAÇKA

The *Karahasanoğlu* family, also of nomadic Turkmen roots, probably arrived in Maçka with the Muslim families who were settled there by *Fatih Sultan Mehmet II* after he conquered Byzantine Trebizond in 1475. Unlike most of their neighbors who occupied themselves with animal husbandry and agriculture, the *Karahasanoğlu* were educators.

What precious little we know about the family comes from carefully protected records pertaining to their career of *hocalık* (master or teacher). In Turkey, as in most of the East, a teacher is still highly revered. The name of one's teacher was therefore honored and carefully recorded. My great, great grandfather *Karahasanoğlu Hoca Osman Efendi* (1803-1866) was a certified imam and teacher, as was his son, my great grandfather (*Lütfiye's* father) *Karahasanoğlu Hoca Mehmed Ali Efendi*. In fact, *Mehmed Ali* began his lessons under the tutelage of his own father. The records are incredibly precise; upon the father *Osman Efendi's* death, the responsibility for training the 15 year-old went to *Müderris Kolezade Haci Süleyman Efendi* at the *Hatuniye Medrese* (religious school). Two years later, in 1868, upon his new teacher's death, the young *Mehmed Ali* went to *Of* (the name of a town) to study under *Müderris Velizade Haci Osman Efendi* at *Khospera-i Ulya Medrese*.

Mehmed Ali was 23 years old and married with children when he received a diploma to be *Müftü* (official in charge of Islamic affairs) in 1874. Because polygamy was common in the Ottoman Empire until its collapse after World War I, *Müftü Mehmed Ali Efendi* actually had two wives and eleven children. *Ilve Hanım*, bore him six; a son Mohammad, (whom records show was "lost," which I assume meant died in infancy), four daughters named *Havva, Nuriye, Güllü* and *Fatma*, and then a son named after his father, *Osman*. The second wife, my great grandmother *Asiye Hanım* (affectionately called *Ne-Ne*, short for *anne-anne* or mom-mom) bore three sons (*Fehmi, Haydar,* and *Neşat*) and two daughters (my grandmother *Lütfiye* and her sister *Aliye*).

The years passed slowly, as they tend to do in the villages of *Maçka*, and *Lütfiye* grew into a lovely girl. In fact my grandmother's beauty was renowned; her long and beautiful hair legendary. Hüseyin, living in the Lower Hacavera village nearby, was surely not the only young man taken with her. But he was the only one who somehow managed to arrange clandestine meetings with her. At this time, single men and women meeting, especially before they were engaged, was absolutely taboo. If a boy had not publicly stated his honorable intentions to marry a young girl he couldn't even look at her without risking a beating at the hands of the men in her family. Occasionally, if a girl was walking with her friends or relatives, a boy might have been able to steal a glance at her, but that was it. And that glance would have kept a pulse racing for weeks on end. Even after being promised (*sözlü*) or engaged (*nişan*), young people could not "hang out" together. They didn't "date." In fact, unless a grandmother or aunt accompanied them, they could not even walk together, and there was certainly no physical contact. None. Virginity and family honor were paramount, and a girl whose reputation had been compromised was at best, un-marriageable, and at worst, in mortal danger for dishonoring the family.

To give you an idea of how seriously all this was taken, allow me to digress a minute and tell you what happened to me when I was fifteen years old and had returned to Turkey for the first time with my father. Keep in mind, this was 1970. Our family had been invited to a *Sünnet* party, a circumcision celebration which looks much like a wedding except that the "guest of honor" - the unfortunate 7 or 8 year-old boy - sits on a throne-like bed and receives gifts and gold for his ordeal and coming of age. We were sitting at our family's table among perhaps 200 guests and as I gazed across the room I noticed a cute guy, about my age, also seated at a table, also wedged between older relatives. After a couple of minutes, I realized that he was looking at me. Like any red-blooded American girl, I looked back, with a slight smile. It was then that I felt the fingers of my older half-brother Turhan firmly grasping my ear and twisting it mercilessly. When he finally let go, I glared at him in defiance. He didn't even bother to return my burning gaze.

I felt more angry than embarrassed, but the message was clear; I wasn't in Kansas anymore. Adrift in my hyper-hormone fantasies, I had failed to realize that acceptable behavior in Turkey was nothing like the free-love hippie culture of the United States. My brother's warning had been quick and concise; any misguided attempt to interact with someone of the opposite sex would be met with a swift and painful disciplinary action. I suddenly realized, in horror, that there was something called body language in Turkey, and it was sophisticated. Articulate. And everyone was fluent in it. I felt blood rush to my face as I became aware that the whole table had been well aware of my antics. A few moments later, schooled in the ways of the East, I stole a careful look back across the room and saw that the boy was now laughing at me. The little shit.

Imagine the risks *Hüseyin* was taking at the end of the nineteenth century, to actually meet with the young *Lütfiye*. And she was young indeed. *Hüseyin* was at least in his mid-twenties, but she had barely reached puberty. For me, the idea of a man that age being interested in a child was very difficult to swallow. It's clear that *Lütfiye*, like Shakespeare's 13 year-old Juliet, was much younger than today's image of a romantic heroine. In those days, girls (and boys for that matter), married very, very young. Islamically, the rule was that she had to have had her first menstrual cycle before she could be married. For some girls, that was as young as eleven years old. The Turkish civil code establishing fifteen as the minimum age for girls to marry would not be written for another thirty years! But life expectancy in the Ottoman Empire at the turn of the century was only 49 years. Children took on adult responsibilities, contributed to society and became productive citizens much earlier than they do now. Still, Lütfiye's family would have been outraged that a 26 year-old man with dubious intentions had contacted their beloved girl.

Clearly *Hüseyin* would have been the mastermind, the one handling the logistics. I cannot imagine that the Müftü's young daughter could wander far from home without someone noticing. It would have been dangerous, if not impossible, for her to set up a clandestine tryst with a man. When the two did meet, (which was more than just once or twice), it was with help. A friend of *Hüseyin's*, known only by his nickname *Genç Ağa*, was instrumental in setting up the place and time for each rendezvous.

THE CHERRY ORCHARD

One day, *Hüseyin* and *Genç Ağa* were on their way to meet *Lütfiye* at a mill between the Upper and Lower Hacavera villages. The men were unaware that *Lütfiye's* older brothers had caught wind of the plan. The brothers, armed and on horseback, had hidden themselves in the cherry orchard belonging to their father the *Müftü*. Clearly intent on protecting the honor of their little sister, they waited patiently until my grandfather and *Genç Ağa* came riding through the orchard. *Lütfiye's* brothers, whom *Hüseyin* would later describe as "barbaric," attacked them. At some point during the clash *Genç Ağa* urged *Hüseyin* to flee. It was not in *Hüseyin's* character to run away from a fight, but his friend convinced him that if he were to kill one of *Lütfiye's* "uncouth" brothers, there would be blood between the families and he would never be able to marry the girl. Thus, *Hüseyin* abandoned the fight and rode off.

News of the young man's scandalous behavior and the subsequent violence it caused spread throughout both villages, and both families faced gossip and disgrace. The offense was serious enough that *Hüseyin* could no longer stay in Lower Hacavera. There was no place left for him even in Trabzon 36 kilometers to the north. He had no alternative but to leave the Black Sea altogether.

Hüseyin packed his belongings and went to Constantinople, the enormous bustling capitol of the empire. There, he fell into the type of work most young men from *Maçka* did at the time; he became a laborer; a *hallaç* in fact, working cotton fibers into pillows and blankets.

Back home, *Lütfiye* was kept under wraps. By all rights her father could have cast her out or worse. But the *Müftü* would never have done that; he loved her so. In fact, years later Lütfiye's father gave her the cherry orchard as a gift. It is still our family's property.

Figure 23: Galate Bridge in Istanbul ca. 1880 -1900 (Abdullah Freres) courtesy of Adem Ozkul Doocumentarist.com

Hüseyin didn't work as a laborer for long. Unfortunately, his number came up, and at age 26 he was drafted into the army and sent to Greece to fight. The Greeks living on the island of Crete had rebelled against Ottoman rule and the Greek government had sent a fleet to the island to protect the Greek citizens from potential massacre by the Turks. It was only when Greek ships began to open fire on Ottoman vessels, and Greek soldiers landed to occupy the island that *Sultan Abdulhamid II* moved into action. He sent an army of 140 battalions, 27 squadrons and 36 artillery batteries to Crete to restore order. Greek raids and efforts to instigate revolt continued, however, and drove the Ottomans to declare war on Greece.

Figure 24: Ottoman Soldiers during the Battle of Domokos 1901, by Ottoman Court Painter Fausto Zonaro (1854-1929)

The Greco-Turkish war of 1897 (also known as the "30-days war") was fought on two fronts, Epirus and Thessaly, (south of Salonika). *Hüseyin* was sent to the latter. On April 23, after suffering significant defeats in the Meluna Pass, Mati and Tirnova, the panicked Greek inhabitants fled by the thousands. The Ottomans pursued them southward toward the Aegean coast where several more towns quickly succumbed. In early May, the Greek forces withdrew to Almyros and *Dömeke* (Domokos). On May 14th when *Hüseyin* marched with the Turks under *Edhem Paşa* to *Dömeke*, Greek defeat was inevitable.

The Greco-Turkish War of 1897 ended, and *Uzunoğlu Hüseyin*, who had only served a few months, was discharged. No doubt he considered returning to his village in the beautiful green mountains of *Maçka*, but that door, at least for now, was closed to him. Still my grandfather's luck was finally changing. Upon returning to Constantinople Hüseyin found a terrific job as the *kavas* (cavass or security guard, sergeant at arms) for the American Consulate. The respectable, steady work and good salary gave him both security and confidence. The handsome ne're-do-well who had been run out of *Maçka* could now be found standing proudly at attention in front of the American consulate wearing an impressive gilded uniform.

Figure 25: Greeks defending three Turkish blockhouses at the head of the Pass as the Turks advanced and ultimately prevailed at the battle at the Meluna Pass near Mati. Image by artist W.T. Maud from the British weekly newspaper the Graphic, dated 1897.

Figure 26: My grandfather Uzunoğlu Hüseyin Ibrahim would make a name for himself as the cavass of the American Consulate in Constantinople, (1910)

Figure 27: The Black Sea region of the Kackar Mountains. (Photo Courtesy of Professor William Bechhoefer)

Life had changed for *Lütfiye* since the shenanigans between her and *Hüseyin*. Her brothers (whom *Bahri Amca* later described as "rough and ill-mannered"), had not forgotten the cherry orchard incident. It had left them feeling angry and humiliated. With society's tacit approval, the brothers treated their wayward sister harshly. Not in a physical way, of course, but by severely restricting her comings and goings, and deciding for themselves with whom she would be permitted to socialize. She had, after all, disobeyed her father and made her family fodder for the rumor mill. Had the family quietly married her off, her reputation may have been restored. But this was not done. Instead, her brothers became her keepers, Don't think they were being cruel. When my brother *Turhan Ağabey* twisted my ear that night at the circumcision party, he was not trying to be cruel. In his mind, I was his little sister and he needed to keep me out of trouble. Similarly, there is no question that *Lütfiye's* brothers loved her dearly and were trying to do the same.

Matters were complicated by the fact that they also loved *Hüseyin*. In the small villages on the Black Sea everyone knows everyone and young people grow up in a tight-knit community. It's reasonable to assume that *Hüseyin* regretted the impetuous behavior. It had certainly impugned his dignity as well as *Lütfiye's* honor. More than that, it may have nullified any chance he may have had to marry the girl. There is reason to believe that *Hüseyin* therefore stated his intentions to earn the right to marry her before he left Trabzon. It's also possible that the *Karahasanoğlu* men considered giving him the chance to make something of himself while

Lütfiye's reached a more reasonable age for marriage. Perhaps this was why her brothers refused proposals by other suitors. Young men would have come with their mothers to the *Karahasanoğlu* house ostensibly for tea, but actually to inspect the potential bride. As was customary, *Lütfiye's* parents would have sat with the guests and engaged in the requisite polite conversation as she demurely served them tea; her movements small and her head lowered. Typically, this would have been the only chance a young man had to get a close look at the light-eyed girl with the lustrous hair. If she had given gave the hint of a smile, the adults could have negotiated terms for a marriage. But *Lütfiye* offered no such smile. There were many families in Maçka who did request the beautiful *Lütfiye's* hand in this manner, but all were rejected. One can imagine how fervently she beseeched her father through tears to let her wait for her beloved to return.

One cannot say whether it was kindness or machismo that kept the brothers from revealing *Hüseyin's* whereabouts to their sister. For after *Hüseyin* left Maçka, *Lütfiye* heard no more about him. None of whatever knowledge they had of him reached her ears, and for years the *Müftü's* daughter had no idea where he was or what he was doing. Imagine her fortitude. Here was a young woman, cloistered at home, pining for years for a man she had seen only a handful of times and who had left abruptly with no goodbyes or promises. And though she heard nothing from him, she refused to marry anyone else.

Three years passed. In 1899, *Lütfiye's* father *Müftü Mehmet Ali Efendi* travelled to Constantinople where he took and passed the important certification exam of the *Şeyhul-Islamlik Ders Vekaleti*. He became certified to preach Islam in two very prestigious mosques in the capitol; the *Bayezit Cami* west of *Topkapı* Palace and the fabulous *Yeni Cami* (New Mosque) in front of the Galata Bridge in *Eminönü*.

Uzunoğlu Hüseyin had been in Constantinople a few years when he learned that the *Müftü* was living in the same city. He went to visit *Mehmet Ali Efendi*, and in a cordial manner appropriate to the seriousness of the occasion, the humbled *Hüseyin* knelt to kiss the hand of the *Hoca* (master). What could he have said? Surely *Hüseyin* would have spoken about his time in the military and about his position at the American Consulate, presenting himself as more mature, more serious about life. He was no longer the carefree and careless *Hüseyin*. He had indeed made something of himself. And he had come to *Müftü Mehmet Ali Efendi* to formally request the hand of the *Hoca's* 16 year-old daughter *Lütfiye Elif Karahasanoğlu* in marriage.

As is always the case in a proud family, the *Karahasanoğlu* patriarch was not about to give his precious daughter away cheaply. It would take *Hüseyin* another five years to prove himself worthy of the *Hoca's* daughter. And in accordance with Middle Eastern tradition, *Lütfiye* stoically waited. *Bahri Amca* said she kept her pain hidden, but physically wasted away from worries and sadness. The years crept by until finally, in 1904, the family in Trabzon received word from Constantinople that the *Müftü* had granted *Hüseyin* permission to marry his daughter.

A victorious *Hüseyin* returned to the Black Sea to fetch his bride. With a certain disregard for practicality, and obviously caught up in romantic notions of noble pursuit and attaining unreachable goals, the proud and handsome *Hüseyin* returned to Trabzon in quixotic style. Bow-legged, mustachioed, with the lightest blue eyes, he proudly entered her village, (now called *Yeşil Yurt*) driving a horse-drawn carriage. The scene was quite emotional. After seven years the Turk had made good on his promise and cleared his name. In tears, the formerly thuggish *Karahasanoğlu* brothers embraced him, with large hands clasping him behind the neck, looking deep into his eyes, as if searching for a boyhood friend - long lost and suddenly rediscovered. The hard feelings of the past were forgiven. *Hüseyin* received his bride *Lütfiye*, now a young woman so beautiful he couldn't bear to look at her. With shyness and heart-pounding happiness, the couple finally stood together in plain view, and the fairytale marriage ceremony was performed.

Figure 28: Author's sketch of traditional half-timber houses typical of the villages of northern Turkey. (Safranbolu, Karabük Province)

Figure 30: View of Süleymanie Cami (mosque) circa 1900 Photo Courtesy WIlliam Bechhoefer

NEWLYWEDS IN CONSTANTINOPLE

Hüseyin Bey and *Lütfiye Hanım* returned to Constantinople and moved into a small house on the *Keşfi Osman Efendi* cul-de-sac in a neighborhood called *Kulaksız*. The couple's first son *Mehmet Bahri* was born in that house on May 15, 1905 and the new family was very happy indeed. Three years later, on August 15, 1908, a second son, my father *Ali Hayri* was born. Broad faced with bright inquisitive eyes, the baby was clearly intelligent, even analytical. He was so smart, in fact, he immediately picked up his lifelong nickname *Zeki* (clever). The two brothers *Bahri* and *Zeki* most assuredly enjoyed the attentions of their grandfather the *Müftü*, as he would have spoiled the children of his beloved daughter *Lütfiye*. Unfortunately, that same year, *Mehmet Ali Efendi* became ill and decided to return home to *Yeşilyurt*.

Perhaps it was better not to be in Constantinople; the city was rife with political unrest. The Young Turk revolution, a nationalist movement favoring a modern Turkish identity, threatened the ultra-conservative old guard of the Ottoman Establishment. In particular, the Janissary army, those older soldiers who started as captured children and rose through the military ranks (*alaylı*), were being replaced by a professional army of *mektepli* officers (those trained in elite military academies). *Hüseyin's* cavass uniform nearly got him killed when, on March 31, 1909, the embittered *alaylı* revolted in front of the *Divan Hane* (government building) and literally started roughing up and even killing any military officer in sight. Unaware of the brawl, *Hüseyin* had started walking down the hill in front of the *Divan Hane* Circle wearing his uniform which closely resembled those worn by officers of the Ottoman Navy. Fortunately, just as he was about to enter the fray, an astute coffee shop owner grabbed a coat, threw it over *Hüseyin*, and spirited him away.

Figure 31: Süleymanie Street Scene 1995 (Photo Courtesy Professor William Bechhoefer)

My Uncle Bahri, whom I've often mentioned, was an educated man with a love of history. He kept journals his entire life. His son Mehmet shared with me a few pages of Bahri Amca's notes regarding our ancestors. These documents were graciously translated by my dear friend *Can Demir* and proved to be full of fascinating clues and stories about my father's parents.

In one passage, *Bahri Amca* described an incident involving a kidnapped American actress in Istanbul. This story had been part of our oral history for many years but remained somewhat suspicious until Bahri Amca cited an actual article written about it in "The American Foreign Service Journal" (Volume 14, No. 10. October 1937), written when my grandfather *Hüseyin* was almost seventy years old. After a few minutes of online research, I learned that copies of the American Foreign Service Journal were housed in the Library of Congress, just twenty minutes from my home. I decided I had to find the article about the kidnapping.

The cherry blossoms were in full bloom the day I became an official Library of Congress Researcher, having acquired the I.D. card by simply filling out a form. Card in hand, I gained access to the Adams Building and patiently waited in line to pass through the tight security. I walked down ancient halls, rode a disturbingly old elevator with dark wood paneling to the fifth floor and entered a gigantic reading room with what seemed to be 25 foot-tall ceilings. An imposing Central Desk loomed in front of me. I approached it and filled out a small request form. I was directed by the stern clerk to wait at desk number 6.

Authentic researchers (unlike the poseur I felt myself to be) were sitting around massive desks, hunched over ancient books, yellowed pages perfectly lit by a heavy brass lamp centered on each table. I waited about an hour. Finally an enormous musty book was laid in front of me.

Too excited to sit, I got to my feet and stared down at the volume for a few moments. I began to sift through it, looking for the year 1937 and then the correct page. Suddenly, there it was; the article my uncle had described, along with a 1910 photograph of my grandfather *Hüseyin*, resplendent in his cavass uniform, saber and fez. His hand was resting on the shoulder of a toddler standing on a chair next to him. The boy peering back at me from the page was my three year-old father. The find literally took my breath away.

Figure 32: Detail of 1912 photograph of my grandfather Hüseyin in uniform, with my father Hayri (Zeki). Photo was taken 26 years before the article was written.

Figure 33: "The American Foreign Service Journal" (Volume 14, No. 10. October 1937 – Caption pp. 602-603 – Title "Istanbul - Hussein Ibrahim Completes 35 Years of Service" from the Library of Congress

Here was the chance to learn more about my mysterious grandfather. The article was titled;

Istanbul- Hussein Ibrahim Completes 35 Years of Service
Hussein Ibrahim, cavass (guard) at the American Consulate General
1902-1937

It stated that *Hüseyin* was born in Trabzon on the Black Sea in 1870, but mistakenly noted that he belonged to the Laz people. (The Laz are descendents from an ancient colony of Greeks who settled on the southern shores of the Black Sea.) But of course, we are not Laz; as I've said all along, we are *Ak Koyunlu* from Central Asia. But who wouldn't want to be Laz; the tough, fierce race, renowned in Turkey for their intelligence, energy, and honesty? A funny thing about the Laz; ask any taxi driver in Istanbul to tell you about them and he will invariably say that the Laz are so smart they routinely finish a full day's work by noon.

Apparently *Hüseyin* was a faithful observer of the *Kuran* (Qur'an). He never missed prayer time, and always took his annual leave during *Ramazan* (Ramadan, the holy month of fasting when devout Moslems fast from dawn to dark for thirty days). It said my grandfather felt "he could not remain on active duty during this period and successfully 'deliver the goods' on an empty stomach." The article talked about how he always managed to be useful and cheerful. "If his job for the moment is only to call a taxi, he does it as if he were off to raise a siege or to bring first aid to his stricken mother." I was reminded of how my father *Zeki Bey*, a relaxed and quiet man, detested laziness. If he instructed us to do something, we were expected to rise quickly. If we dawdled getting up from our seats he'd shout *Koş!* (Run!) That always got us moving.

The article describes how Americans whom my grandfather assisted had the impression that he had "Aladdin's lamp" under his coat. "Supremely courteous and considerate, he strives to give those he serves the illusion that they are potentates." *Hüseyin* was "well-connected, with a friend in every government office and police station in Istanbul. On more than a few occasions these friendships helped Americans in Istanbul by making fines for certain minor infringements go away."

When I read this, I thought of my brother Kemal. He's the "go-to" guy if you're in a hurry to get a passport or visa in Washington. Written up in *Who's Who*, Kemal is able to work "magic" when others fail because of the cordial relations he has established over the years with personnel from every embassy in town. These international friends are often willing to expedite a particular visa as a personal favor to him.

Now I was reading the part about the kidnapping. Once, in the old days, a *paşa* (Pasha, a favorite in the Sultan's court), took a liking to a young American actress and kidnapped her, taking her to his villa on *Büyük Ada* (Prinkipo), the largest of the nine Prince's Islands in the Sea of Marmara. It was evening and *Hüseyin* was one of the few people present at the Consulate when he received a smuggled message of distress from the lady. Deciding not to waste time seeking his Chief's instructions, he hastened to the island and rushed to the Pasha's villa. Challenged by the guards at the gate, he knocked them aside. Then, drawing his revolver, rushed into the villa. *Hüseyin* "seized the terrified lady before the eyes of the astonished Pasha, made a whirlwind escape, and brought her post haste by carriage and boat safely back to the city."

I could see that my illustrious grandfather was still as daring as he had been in the cherry orchards of *Maçka*. And just as in his early days, there were times when *Hüseyin's* boldness got him into real trouble. In 1916, for example, a Russian national attempting to defect had been hiding in Istanbul. One day he made his way to the American Chancery to seek asylum. Not quite appreciating the sensitive nature of the situation, *Hüseyin* wouldn't let the Russian in. When a group of Turkish civil police arrived on the scene to straighten things out, the hyper-vigilant *Hüseyin* refused to grant them entry, as well. My grandfather's indomitability obviously ruffled some feathers because he was consequently court-marshaled and put into a military prison where he remained for a short time until the American Consulate straightened things out. Thankfully he was acquitted and released.

Clearly, *Hüseyin Ibrahim* was less imposing a man when he retired. He had served from 1902 through 1937. According to the article, he kept his well-worn prayer rug in the cubby-hole of a guard room off the entrance corridor of the Consulate General. His magnificent old uniform with the Sultan's decorations he wore on it, the sword, and gold braided cap were carefully locked in the drawer of an old "armoire" in the consular library. He would take it out once or twice a year when a sympathetic person had time to listen to his reminiscences.

We've jumped ahead quite a bit to the end of *Huseyin's* life, when he was living with one young daughter and three grandchildren in a house near the Golden Horn. My father was performing his military service then. Dad's brother *Bahri Amca* held an important position with an American Automobile company in Egypt. Surprisingly, my uncle *Seyfi*, *Huseyin's* third son wasn't even mentioned. And where was *Lütfiye*?

A LIFE CUT SHORT

It is possible that by the time my grandmother *Lütfiye* was pregnant with her third son Seyfi (born December 1, 1911), she was already losing weight.

Consumption, which we now know as tuberculosis, had no cure in those days. Having had it myself, I can tell you that it is so indolent, so insipid, that by the time you notice it, it has already drained most of your life out of you. At first you may have just a mild, tickly cough, and a general feeling of fatigue. You may not even be aware that you are sleeping more hours every day, or that you never wake feeling rested. But soon, others begin to remark that you are too thin. I was 27 when I contracted TB (possibly while traveling to Afghanistan). I was sleeping 12 to14 hours a day by the time my sister *Çaya* finally aired her concerns. A pulmonary x-ray presented the shocking image, a nickel-sized tubule 3 inches long through my right lung. The doctor likened a TB lesion to a bruised spot in a tomato; it gradually gets softer until it becomes mushy and fluid. Luckily, here in America the Public Health Service has been providing treatment, the medicine INH (Isoniazid) since 1952. Within weeks of starting the regimen I was regaining my strength and putting on some weight. Thankfully, it's completely gone now. But there was no such medicine for my grandmother.

When the lovely *Lütfiye's* health began to deteriorate, the family discussed their options. Her father Müftü Mehmed Ali Efendihad returned from Constantinople to *Maçka* and had taken up the newly vacant position of *Maçka* Township *Müftü*.

Having personally benefitted from the curing properties of fresh mountain air for his own illness, the *Müftü* thought it best she follow him home to the mountains where she could rest. He had a summer house in the highlands, a *yayla ev* which they called the *keliv* on the cooler plateau. When *Lütfiye* arrived, they took her there. While 5 year-old *Bahri* and the infant *Seyfi* accompanied their mother, her 2 year-old son *Zeki* remained behind in Constantinople with his father. This is the reason only *Zeki* is the only who appears with his father in the photograph on the previous page.

The mountains on the Black Sea are enchanting; so different from the choked atmosphere of İstanbul. In the highlands, *Lütfiye Hanım* could watch the sky for falcons and sparrow hawks. Perhaps she could hear the wild rivers rush through the landscape, and enjoy the countless varieties of alpine flowers that dot the fields. *Bahri* remembered those days at the *keliv* and how he ran and played in the meadows around the

house. He spoke of the day his mother had asked him to spread a red blanket on the grass on the south side of the house where the sun shines best. In his mind's eye he recalled seeing himself running in the fields, watching his dear mother sitting on that blanket in the grass, caressing his baby brother *Seyfi's* head as she cried. This was an image that my uncle could never erase from his mind.

And then the night came, sometime in 1912, when she couldn't draw another breath, and *Lütfiye Elif*, 27 year-old mother of three, died in that house in the highlands. The grief-stricken family immediately sent word of her passing down to the village, and the *Karahasanoğlu* brothers rushed through the dark to be with her.

The next day they cut down a hazelnut tree. They trimmed and planed it into lumber from which they manufactured a coffin for their sister. Then in the Muslim way, the women washed *Lutfiye's* body, the final ablution. Perhaps she was washed by her mother, *Asiye Nene*. Perhaps her younger sister *Aliye* helped. We don't know. But we know they wrapped my grandmother in a white cloth and laid her tenderly inside the unadorned coffin. They loaded it up on a horse and brought her back down to the village. The grave had been dug under the hazelnut tree between her brother *Fehmi's* and the *Müftü's* houses. When they laid her in, they turned her to her side, facing Mecca. They prayed, and finally covered her with the earth from which she came. Thinking back on this sad event, her son *Bahri* wrote that his mother had died too young; "still hungry for life."

Word of *Lütfiye's* death was sent to her husband in Constantinople, and when *Hüseyin* heard the bitter news, he had a headstone made. With my father accompanying him, he went to *Maçka* with the stone. Then together with her brothers, he placed it at the head of my grandmother's grave, where it remains today.

ORPHANED

The three orphaned brothers *Bahri, Zeki* and *Seyfi* remained for a time in the village; cared for by their grandmother *Nene Asiye Hanım*. So little is known about those days that every tidbit of information carries great significance. (Remember this with your own children; at every opportunity, talk about your own family history!) *Bahri* remembered, for example, how he had been playing on the second floor of the house where someone had set out apples to dry. He took a bad fall and landed on some stone

Lütfiye's two older sons *Bahri* and *Zeki* would be raised by her younger sister, *Aliye*. The infant *Seyfi* would remain with his grandmother who wanted to raise him. And so it was that the young and inexperienced second daughter of *Hoca Mehmet Ali Efendi*, married to her late sister's husband *Hüseyin* and left with him and two sons for Constantinople.

Three years later, on December 12, 1914 (*A.H. 12 Kanunuevvel 1330*), *Müftü Mehmet Ali Efendi* also died. He was interred next to his daughter *Lütfiye*. In the 1930's *Bahri Amca* went back to *Maçka* to take a look. He said he cleared the graves which had become wildly overgrown with plants. But the father and daughter were resting under the hazelnut trees *koyun koyuna* (a Turkish phrase which literally means "sheep-to-sheep" but the idea is more like "in each other's arms, or "held to one's bosom.")

May God's mercy be upon them both.

Figure34: Grave of my grandmother Lütfiye Karahasanoğlu in Maçka, Trabzon (above). Her father Müftü Mehmet Ali Efendi was buried next to her (right). (Photos Courtesy M.T. Ergene

steps below, injuring himself so badly his left side felt "like a bag of bones." He attributed his speedy recovery to *Nene's* loving care as well as the many delicious foods she prepared for him through his convalescence. He especially loved her delicious fried eggs in butter which he recalled fondly until the end of his days.

A final decision had to be made about what to do with *Lütfiye's* children. Sororate (a specialized version of polygamy where a man may marry his wife's sister if the wife dies, or if she is unable to bear children), was agreed upon. The arrangement was, and still is, commonly practiced in the Middle East and other societies with a strong clan structure. Traditionally, the practice (and its male counterpart levirate), helped maintain and reinforce family connections and political alliances. But in this case, the thinking was that *Lütfiye's* sister would love her nephews more than a woman from outside the family. She also shared her sister's sensibilities for child-rearing, religion, and family traditions. So they agreed that *Aliye* was the sensible choice to replace *Lütfiye* in those crucial roles.

A teaching Family of Strong Character

Is the ability to teach inherited? Is there a genetic reason why my sisters and I are all teachers? Consider the following. The literacy rate in *Maçka* has consistently been the highest in Turkey. And for the last century, education in the *Maçka* region was continuously under the province of my grandmother's family, the *Karahasanoğlu*. *Lütfiye Hanım's* brothers *Fehmi Bey* and *Haydar Bey* were both prominent educators; teachers, school superintendents and inspectors. They were also *hafiz*, meaning they had memorized the Kuran from beginning to end.

But just because they were educators doesn't mean the *Karahasanoğlu* led quiet lives of scholarship. *Hafiz Fehmi*, who served as head of the Red Crescent (Muslim version of Red Cross), was no bookworm. He flaunted his social status by dressing ostentatiously and riding atop his expensive horse with his gun in full view. Unfortunately, *Fehmi's* conspicuous carriage bred enough resentment that one day, while out riding, he was ambushed by his enemies. He had come upon an old woman lying in the road, and when he dismounted to help her, was attacked. His body was found sprawled out in the road, riddled with more than 30 bullet holes.

Fehmi's son *Neşat*, a well-mannered, sophisticated man, served as both Superintendent of Education for Trabzon Province Eventually *Neşat* built an impressive High School in Maçka, served as mayor of Maçka, and head of the *Maçka* branch of Atatürk's "Republic's People's Party."

Hafiz Haydar (the other brother) was principal of Maçka High School. He was well known for his severe teaching style which primarily relied on the frequent use of a hazelnut stick to bend behavior to his liking. To this day the whipping stick is sardonically referred to as the "*Hafiz Haydar* teaching method."

Lütfiye's youngest brother, *Hikmet,* was an Education Inspector who, unlike his brother *Neşat,* would have little tolerance for the single party authoritarianism of the Young Turks nationalist movement. During the earliest days of the young Turkish Republic (which I will tell you about shortly), men like Hikmet, unafraid to voice opinions or forfeit their principles were often sent off to work in the miserable provinces in the East. *Bahri Amca* remembered his *dayı* (uncle on the mother's side) *Hikmet* as a thinking man who took him aside to teach him about oxygen and carbon. *Hikmet* was also passionate about his family history, and researched the *Uzunoğlu* ancestry in detail. In fact, most of what I've learned about my grandmother's family came to light through my great uncle's research. His son *Subutay Maçkalı Karahasanoğlu* (who died in 2006) was also a well-known author and poet in Istanbul.

The Black Sea Personality

Unlike the dour fatalism of the Anatolian interior or the easy-going lifestyle on the shores of the Mediterranean, the independent and assertive spirit of the people of the Black Sea (*Kara Denizli*) has been documented by historians as far back as the Greek writer Xenophon 2400 years ago. The first time I read about the "Black Sea Personality" it was like I was reading about my family. Territory and honor gave *Kara Denizli* people a highly developed sense of clan and community loyalties. From this sense of community came an equally strong sense of open, friendly hospitality. The people of the wild mountain tribes are also known for their self-deprecating wit; telling great stories is practically a regional specialty.

While researching this book, I enlisted my good friend *Avi Levi* to help me establish contact for the first time with any remaining family in Trabzon. (Avi, a native speaker, can understand the heavy Black Sea accent). We placed a call to the closest thing we could find to a Census Bureau in Maçka, the *Nufus Müdürlüğü* (Directorate of Population) and learned that all the birth and death records were lost in a fire in 1969. Sensing our great disappointment, the elderly gentleman on the other end of the line asked why we were calling all the way from America. When Avi explained that we were trying to contact *Karahasanoğlu* relatives from the *Upper Haçavera* village, the gentleman, *Mr. Odabaşı*, said he just happened to be standing next to a man who was visiting from *Upper Haçavera,* and that this visitor said he knew someone from there named *Karahasanoğlu*. Before we even knew what was happening, the visitor had placed a call to his friend *Barış Karahasanoğlu* via cell phone, who within seconds gave us the cell phone number of his father, *Sabahattin Karahasanoğlu* in *Upper Haçavera* who just happened to be my grandmother *Lütfiye's* nephew.

(Wow. Welcome to Turkey.)

At first confused, the elderly *Sabahattin Bey* became excited when we said we were calling from America and that I was writing a book. Avi mentioned I was doing research and was planning to come visit. "What for?" he asked. The quick-witted Avi, realizing how complicated it would be to explain, answered with quintessential diplomacy. "We want to come and kiss your hand and pay our respects." This must have pleased *Sabahattin Bey*. "*Gelin, gelin!*" (Come, come!) he said in a very warm and welcoming pure Trabzon accent.

That's about as close as I got to my living relatives in Maçka until late 2010 when serendipity stepped in again. My cousin *Mehmet Ergene* told me that we were related to the famous Turkish singer *Volkan Konak* who was coming to D.C. for two concerts. Mehmet and I decided to go meet our cousin for the first time. It turns out *Volkan Bey* is a fabulous singer and musician. His long hair and stylish clothes bely the traditional, wonderfully poetic, often nationalistic themes of his music. He brought the crowd to tears with songs full of Black Sea rhythms, and instrumentation, often singing with that unique accent. Young people ran to the back of the hall, joined hands and danced side-by-side with high steps and jiggling shoulders, the way young people have danced in Trabzon for hundreds (if not thousands, of years). *Mehmet* and I were in heaven.

After the concert, armed with charts and graphs of our common lineage, we were escorted past the backstage door and up steep, narrow stairs by black-suited security guys. In the middle of the room where the "band" and entourage had gathered with refreshments stood *Volkan Bey*. He rushed to Mehmet, and I could instantly see those familiar hazel eyes. The two men spoke hurriedly and the first thing Volkan said was that our family tree chart was wrong. "You have to fix these! Come look, come look." We huddled around a table. Still energized from the concert, he began to quickly strike through some names, adding others. So *Lütfiye's* brother *Fehmi* had the son named *Neşat*, whose daughter *Saynur* (one of nine children) had 15 daughters of her own, (yes, fifteen) before she finally gave birth to a son, *Volkan*.

Figure 34: Volkan Konak's Washington, DC 2010 concert poster, "Son of the North in America!"

Pausing for a moment, Volkan Bey inspected my face. *Mehmet* told him who I was, and he hugged me. Turning, he called for a tall nice-looking youth to come forward. He put his arm around the young man's shoulder and told us, "This is my sister's son, *Akin Bahçekapılı*." Oh my God, another cousin!

We could only stay a few more minutes (the crowd outside was anxious to meet the musicians), but we were able to exchange email addresses, and we all hugged one another warmly, taking long last looks with moistened eyes.

People of the Black Sea are intense and proud, quick to respond to any perceived attack on their territory, honor or freedom – even if it means taking the law into their own hands. The manufacture and use of guns is a passion. And the divvying up of highland meadows has traditionally given rise to serious hostilities among villages and clans that sometimes last for generations. We've already seen some of this temperament in my grandfather *Hüseyin*. Here's another example.

In the mid-nineteenth century there had been a simmering feud between several of the villages attached to the small town of Maçka; the problem being disagreement about the property boundaries on the large plateau. (During the hot summer months people moved with their animals to the highlands for cooler temperatures and fresh grasses.) The men in the four villages had been arguing about where the property lines dividing the highlands were actually located.

The disagreement finally got so bad that groups of men armed themselves with guns and set out to claim their territory by force. My great grandfather, *Hoca Mehmet Ali Efendi,* grabbed his wooden staff and rode up to the highlands. No one would dare shoot the *Müftü* who came galloping wildly into the middle of the fray, hitting the ambushers from each village over the head with his stick until the men finally receded. He then rode to a natural boundary and, motioning to it with his staff, called out to the men, "This is the border!" The boundary drawn that day in the highlands by my great grandfather bears the *Müftü's* name and is still conventionally accepted as the legal boundary between the villages. Thus a border dispute between rival clans was reconciled, and a law was enforced purely by the strength of one man's character.

I know that most people are not particularly interested in war. And I'm aware that one doesn't normally open a cookbook to read up on the subject. But politics and war, as we've seen, have huge consequences for families and can forever alter the future course of their lives. If the *Oğuz Turks* had not fought the *Xiongnu*, and if the Ottomans had not fought Timour, my grandfather's family could still be living somewhere in China. And as we'll see, if the Huns had not forced mass migrations of Europeans westward, the Visigoths might not have re-conquered Spain. If the Crusades had not forced the Muslims and Jews from Córdoba, my mother's family might still be living in Spain. But these wars did happen, and the culture of my family, including the languages we speak and the foods we eat, can be directly attributed to them.

Three years after *Lütfiye's* death, war came to Maçka. On October 29, 1914 the Ottoman Empire entered the First World War on the side of Germany and the Central Powers. Four days later, Russia, the vast empire to the North, declared war on Turkey. Within a month, Trabzon was bombed by Czar Nicholas II's warships. Great Britain's Admiral Churchill devised a plan to quickly knock the Ottomans out of the war so that the allies could occupy Istanbul and send supply ships from the Bosphorus to the Black Sea to support Russian troops. We know now that his plan failed. In fact, World War I, the "Great War," became the catalyst for widespread rebellion in Russia, resulting in the 1917 communist Bolshevik overthrow of the Czar. But not before 35,000 young Turks who resisted Russia's Caucuses Campaign and lay dead in the frozen mountains of *Sarıkamış*. The Russians occupied Trabzon, took Maçka, and in the meantime arrested my granduncle *Hafız Haydar*. He was sent into exile to *Batum* on the Black Sea coast. His brother *Fehmi* took his rifle into the mountains from where he waged a personal war against the invaders. One story about the renegade *Fehmi* relates how some anxious villagers tried to block Russian efforts to build a road through *Haçavera*. It was the rational *Fehmi* who sent word from the mountains that the Turks would benefit from the Russians spending their time and money building the road. "When they leave," he argued, "it will be ours to use." And that's what happened. As far as I know, the Russians never did capture *Hafız Fehmi*.

Figure 35: Turkish Cafe ca. 1880-1900

Figure36: Galata Bridge, Istanbul Abdullah Freres 1880-1900(Photo courtesy of Adam Ozkul)

In 1912, war was not the first thing on *Hüseyin's* mind; his interests lay more in making love. Over the next few years, a number of women of varying ages and stations in life would appear and then evaporate from *Bahri* and *Zeki's* young lives. Women would seem to simply show up out of the blue. They would stay for a while and then one day, the boys would wake up and they would be gone - forever. Polygamy was still legal in the Ottoman Empire in the early 20th century, and *Hüseyin* would be married three more times, sometimes with two wives at the same time.

After *Lütfiye's* death, *Hüseyin* returned to Constantinople with two sons and his second wife, *Lütfiye's* sister *Aliye*. The sororate arrangement between the ex-siblings-in-law was ill-fated. *Aliye* could find no happiness living as the wife of her sister's husband. They were divorced within a year.

It's possible that *Aliye's* desertion of her husband and nephews was precipitated by the appearance of another woman; one named *Asiye*, but known by her nickname *Hanımcık* (little woman). One day, *Hanımcık* simply showed up at the house the family rented at *#320 Kasımpaşa*, in the neighborhood of *Küçük Piyale Paşa*. She moved her belongings in, along with her mother. We don't know for sure if *Aliye* left before, or after, *Hanımcık* arrived. All we know is that within the span of a few months in 1912, *Hanımcık* (wife #3) was in, and *Aliye* (wife #2) was out. *Aliye* returned to *Maçka* and later married a man named *Ismail*. (We know she never had children of her own, and that she lived a long life, and died in Istanbul.)

Some women in *Huseyin's* life were more willing than others to take on the role of surrogate mother to his sons. *Hanımcık* was not one of them. After *Aliye* left, *Bahri* and *Zeki* were again essentially orphaned. Zeki was sent to *ana okul* or nursery school with about 15 to 20 other children. They lived in the home of a woman who provided both child care and lessons. By then *Zeki*, not yet four years old, was proving himself to be both precocious and brilliant (already reading the *Kuran*).

Then, in 1914, The Ottoman Empire entered the "Great War" (World War I), and *Hüseyin* was again taken into the military. The boys were moved back from the *ana okul* to the house in *Kasımpaşa*. By then *Hanımcık* was pregnant (with her daughter *Muzaffer*), and was even less inclined to care for the two boys. She and *Hüseyin* tried to enroll them into a government-sponsored boarding school for orphans, but the school refused to take them since they weren't true orphans; their father was absent, not dead.

The couple then decided to send them off to a *medrese* (religious boarding school). Aware that *Zeki* was too young, they altered the date on his birth certificate and enrolled him as an eight year-old when he was actually only six.

These were tumultuous times. Money became tight as taxes were raised to support the Turkish military. Families were anxious about whether or not their men would return. Orphaned children fell through the cracks. Though small for his age, *Zeki* was street smart and learned to take care of himself in a bad situation. Still, his everyday needs were met only when a kind-hearted stranger took pity on a child in need of care. Luckily, a mother and daughter living across the street from his home were kind and looked out for him. It was this daughter, in fact, who sewed the white shirt-dress my father is wearing in this photo.

Conditions at the *medrese* were no better than at home. Food was scarce. Even the most resourceful

Figure 37: My three-year old father in 1910, just months before his mother Lütfiye died. By this time, he was already reading the Kuran (Qur'an) and had acquired the nickname Zeki (clever).

students, those lucky enough to find their meals at church charities, had to eat the most awful food; stale and full of worm holes.

Dad studied for three years as lessons at the *medrese* continued through the war years. He failed the first year because the Arabic was very difficult, but soon caught up with the older students. The principal and religious teacher (who also served as the Imam of *Büyük Cami* (Big Mosque) in *Kasımpaşa)*, recognized my father's talent and intelligence, and put him in charge of a dozen or so other students. At the age of seven, my father was teaching math to a classroom of children. Again, the *Karahasanoğlu* genes for teaching.

GETTING AN EDUCATION

After leaving the *Medrese*, *Hüseyin's* two sons began their new school (*mektep*) within the walls of *Rumeli Hisar*, a fortress located on a hill on the European side of the Bosphorus. This was the fortress built by *Fatih Sultan (Mehmet II)* between 1451 and 1452, to control the Bosphorus during his conquest of Constantinople. Within the walls of this fortress, there was a school, and both boys were sent there to take up the third year of *Kuran* classes.

Zeki was still a year and a half younger than most of his classmates. He did not pass the first year's lessons but again soon caught up. In the second year he was moved up to the secondary school, *Üsküdar Tekke*, on the other side of the Bosphorus, near the insane asylum. By now, the nine-year old orphan had become resistant to authority and mischievous. He recounted that while the other boys crossed the street to the *Validiye Cami* for prayers, he would steal away and explore the gardens, sometimes hiding amid the turbaned headstones in the mosque cemetery, fingers purple from eating mulberries.

During roll call one particular day, my father was caught peering down from the roof at the children

Figure 38: Rumeli Hisar (Zeki's elementary school). From a very young age Zeki exhibited artistic talent. Unfortunately he was forbidden to draw pictures; medrese hocas insisted that only God may create. A stifled artist his entire life, Zeki would occasionally allow himself to sketch an idea. He'd then dismiss his drawing as a pitiable.

lined up in the courtyard. He defiantly refused instructions to come down until a combination of hunger and a sweet-talking *hoca* convinced him he would not be punished. As promised, he was fed. But the next night the teachers caught him and subjected him to the dreaded *falaka* (foot whipping), a common form of corporal punishment during the Ottoman Empire. They tied a rope around his legs, twisting it tight with a long stick. The stick was then raised up from both ends by two of the other students. The soles of *Zeki's* feet, thus prominently displayed, were then repeatedly slapped with a long switch by the *hoca* while the younger students were made to watch.

The only thing worse than school was coming home. Bahri by and large refused to make the weekly trip to do laundry on the grounds that "she" (as he referred to *Hanımcık*), would, no doubt, be there. So *Zeki* made the trek across the Bosphorus by himself. Of course, there were no bridges crossing the strait at that time, and he didn't have money to pay for the small row boats that shuttled people back and forth between

DAD'S CLOSE ENCOUNTER OF THE THIRD KIND

Though he was a capable child, Zeki was very much alone. Those early war years were filled with certain minor, but to him significant, events that haunted him his entire life. As a child, for example, he saw the young woman from across the street popping corn in a skillet. A kernel flew out and became embedded in the girl's neck. He admitted to me how strange it was that he never forgot this event.

Without a mother or caring adult to care for him, many of life's events remained unexplained curiosities. If tragedies were explained or resolved in his young mind, it was only by way of his own fertile imagination. The most fascinating story he recounted occurred one night in the religious boarding school. He had gotten up from bed and was crossing the courtyard toward the toilet area. The howling wind and creaking sound of the trees made him uneasy. As he passed the rooms of other students, he peered into one doorway and saw what looked to be two children, about his height, standing there staring back at him. Zeki stood for a moment. He greeted them with a shy hello. When they didn't answer, it dawned on him that these children were not children at all. In fact, he surmised, they were not even human. The terrified boy ran back to his room screaming. With everyone in the school awake and rushing to see what had happened, Zeki had jumped into his bed and pulled the covers up over his head, convinced that extra-terrestrials were abducting children.

My father told me this story many times, always insisting that, though they were about his size and weight, and dressed in the white smock children wore, "They were not us," he would say. "It was dark, and they were looking right at me. I let out such a scream. *Ne patırdı!* (What a ruckus!) Everybody got up!"

One might say that neglected children are prone to such magical thinking, but you could never have convinced *Zeki* that this event was anything different than what he said it was. For the rest of his life he was fascinated by science fiction programs about alien abductions. Shows like "Chariots of the Gods" mesmerized him. He always claimed he was marked by them, and showed me a red circle the size of a fingernail on his left hip. "My brother *Bahri* has one, too," he would say.

Europe and Asia. Luckily, there were always moored boats at the port of *Üsküdar;* large sailboats which transported sheep and other livestock across the strait. The resourceful boy would jump into one of these boats just as it pulled away from the dock. It was wartime, and no one bothered with a skinny child who seemed to be doing no harm. He would sit quietly among the animals, arms wrapped around his small bundle of clothes which he'd neatly wrapped in a square patch of old sheet. (Until the end of his life, *Zeki* kept his clothes wrapped this way, with the sheet folded like an envelope; the flap held together with a rusted diaper pin.) Once on the other side of the Bosphorus, he would walk the remaining 5 to 6 miles to the house in *Küçük Piyale Paşa.*

Hanımcık, who had her hands full with her two-year old daughter *Muzaffer,* was more irritated than ever when *Zeki* showed up hungry and dirty. She never much liked him anyway, and could be mean and vindictive. She teased him, and called him names like *Tatar Yüz* (Face like a Tatar or Mongol) because his face was hairless.

Like most boys whose fathers had been drafted, *Zeki* and *Bahri* were expected to fend for themselves and provide for the family as best they could. My father remembered that the Red Cross located in the American Embassy gave out salted fish and bread. The Swiss Embassy also provided rations of rice, sugar and bread to American dependents. He was often so hungry that he would nibble like a little mouse at the edges of the bread he was sent to fetch. One day, he couldn't help himself and what began as a nibble ended with him eating the entire loaf. The beating afterward was particularly painful.

SERVET HANIM

When *Hüseyin* returned home from the war, he took up his position as cavass at the American consulate. I'm proud to say that the American diplomatic corps always looked out for their Turkish staff. When the Consul General returned to the United States, he offered his empty residence for *Hüseyin* and the family to live in, in exchange for guarding it in his absence. The house was wonderful. My father remembered it had a huge garden with six or seven ponds full of fish and turtles. Just when it seemed that the family would enjoy some comfort and security, things again became "complicated." *Hüseyin* came home one day with yet another woman. Yes, while still married to his third wife *Hanımcık* with whom he had a daughter, *Hüseyin* married a fourth wife, *Servet Hanım.* This was a fairly easy thing to do back then, since there really were no official papers to sign.

I'm fairly certain that *Hanımcık* was not pleased with these developments, but the children, especially *Zeki,* finally saw a glimmer of warm light pierce the gloom of their home. *Servet Hanım* was different. She was kind, loving; the only real mother my father ever knew. Now, when he returned home from school with laundry, she would welcome him, wash his clothes for him, and feed him. She treated *Zeki* like the child she had always wanted. He always said that this lovely woman took care of him in a way no one else ever had, and he grew very fond of her.

Unfortunately, *Servet Hanım* stayed only a year. It couldn't have been easy for her, living under the same roof with *Hanımcık.* But I believe

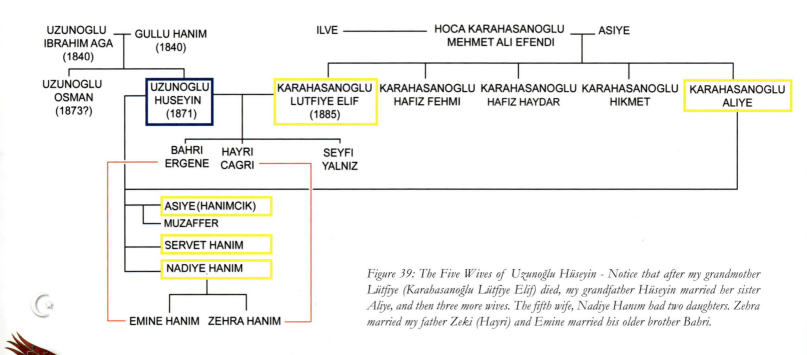

Figure 39: The Five Wives of Uzunoğlu Hüseyin - Notice that after my grandmother Lütfiye (Karahasanoğlu Lütfiye Elif) died, my grandfather Hüseyin married her sister Aliye, and then three more wives. The fifth wife, Nadiye Hanım had two daughters. Zehra married my father Zeki (Hayri) and Emine married his older brother Bahri.

Servet Hanım did right by her husband and his children. She was also awarded alimony when she divorced *Hüseyin*. And *Zeki* cried bitterly when she moved away. Only nine years old, he had lost a mother again.

The family soon moved again, which meant a new school for *Zeki*. He was enrolled at *Fatihe*, the school associated with the *Fatih Cami* (Mosque), where he studied for two years. Then it was on to *Rüstem Paşa* for a year, and then *Sultan Ahmet Medrese* for two more years before passing onto *Hağia Sophia*. In 1924, the *Hağia Sophia* school was closed, and at 16, my father's formal education came to an end. He found a job in a *bakkal* (grocery) and began to earn some money.

NADIYE HANIM

Could it be that *Hüseyin* couldn't stand peace and tranquility, or was he just easily bored? I ask this because it is amazing to me that my grandfather would bring home yet another wife. He had seen *Nadiye Hanım* selling groceries, fruits, oils and soap on a street corner, and marveled at her business savvy. She always had a crowd of customers around her very successful produce stand. Perhaps her success was due to the fact that she was a single mother with two daughters; people may have bought her wares out of pity. Then again, she was a clever, self-made woman; a novelty in those days. Or perhaps *Hüseyin* was attracted to her because she, like himself, hailed from Trabzon. For there was indeed an attraction, and *Hüseyin* decided to keep this woman. At first he put *Nadiye Hanım* and her two daughters up in their own house, which he would visit from time to time. My father, a strapping teenager at the time, remembered accompanying him there. That was when he met the elder daughter *Zehra*, a pretty young thing, all of 15 years old. Soon, *Hüseyin* decided, unilaterally I'm sure, to consolidate the family and bring *Nadiye Hanım* and her two daughters home. His other wife *Hanımcık*, their daughter *Muzaffer*, and his two teenage sons lived on the first floor, while *Nadiye Hanım* and her two daughters *Zehra* and *Emine*, took the upper floor.

One can only imagine the awkwardness and pent up hostility between the two wives. *Hanımcık* started a campaign to purge the interlopers. Zeki would spy her fervently "reading curses" to force *Nadiye Hanım* out. She even tried to enlist his help in these superstitious rituals, but he refused. She insisted that *Hüseyin* send the other woman away, but he ignored her protests. This was not a home where feelings were talked out. People were stoic in those days, proud.

Figure 40: My grandfather Hüseyin Uzunoğlu with his fifth wife Nadiye Hanım around 1924. The couple arranged the marriages of her two daughters to his two sons.

Finally *Hanımcık* decided she could no longer tolerate the living arrangements. My father told me she "chose freedom." I was never sure what he meant by that until I realized that when she eventually moved away, *Hanımcık* left her own daughter *Muzaffer* behind to fend for herself in the most disagreeable circumstances.

At first, having emerged victorious from the rivalry between wives, and satisfied with her new status as the "woman of the house," *Nadiye* behaved well toward *Muzaffer*. The girl's new stepmother encouraged her with sweet words, assuring *Muzaffer* that she was a true daughter just like her other daughters. But these words of affection rang hollow, and as days and months passed *Nadiye Hanım* became increasingly hostile toward the daughter of *Hüseyin's* good-for-nothing ex-wife who had left her this burdensome child. *Muzaffer* wasn't getting along with her new step-sisters Zehra and Emine either. She once told me that in the beginning, her father had been aware of the tension in the household, and had even made some attempts to mediate the family disputes. But there was no remedy for all the feelings of resentment, abandonment, and jealousy.

Feeling ineffective and perhaps even bored with the discord, the "man of the house" removed himself from the fray, as if the arguments didn't much matter to him anymore. Perhaps my grandfather reasoned that "when Mama ain't happy, ain't nobody happy" because *Hüseyin* eventually left it completely up to *Nadiye Hanım* to resolve disputes. One always hopes that a step-parent will strive to do what's best for the all the children. And to be fair, it is especially difficult to raise step-children when one is on bad terms with the biological parent. But the capable *Nadiye Hanım* showed little patience for her step-daughter and was more than willing to "lay down the law" with a certain prejudice. It was three against one, and *Muzaffer* was blamed for everything. For years she suffered from neglect and harsh treatment. Abandoned physically by her mother, and emotionally by her father, the kind, shy, and polite *Muzaffer* patiently endured her predicament.

Before we leave *Muzaffer* I would like to tell you that finally, in 1939, at the age of 24, she left her father's home to marry the soft-spoken *Mustafa Açıkalın*, twelve years her senior. It was a peaceful marriage, respectful. The two settled in a small apartment and raised two sons together. Years later, she would learn that her mother *Hanımcık*, from whom she had been estranged since the day she left, had been sent to the *Darulaceze* (Institution for the Destitute), a shelter for homeless children living on the streets or people found living in the mosque courtyards. And because my *Hala* (aunt) *Muzaffer* felt so bitter toward her mother, she couldn't bring herself to visit her. Many years later still, *Muzaffer Hala* would receive the bitter news that her mother had died with feelings of ambivalence and curiosity. The little girl had grown into a wise, generous woman, a giving wife and loving mother. Her two sons were a source of great pride and her home was always filled with family around the dinner table, singing, and playing cards together. When her son *Ulvi Açıkalın* married a beautiful doe-eyed girl named *Ferhunde* and brought his shy bride home, it didn't take long before *Muzaffer* welcomed an adorable, doe-eyed grandson *Gökhan* to shower with all the maternal love and closeness she herself had missed. (As I write this, my *Muzaffer Hala* is 95 years old, *Maşallah* (Praise God) and living with her son and *Ferhunde Yenge* in the suburbs of Istanbul.)

So, in case you got confused about all the wives and kids, let's do a short re-cap. My grandfather *Hüseyin Uzunoğlu* married four more times after the death of his first wife, my grandmother *Lütfiye Hanım*. First came her sister *Aliye Hanım*, then *Asiye Hanım* (*Hanımcık*), then *Servet Hanım* (my father's favorite), and finally *Nadiye Hanım*. Of these four, only one, *Hanımcık*, bore him a child; a daughter *Muzaffer*. The last wife, *Nadiye Hanım* already had two daughters. *Hüseyin and Nadiye* decided to marry the two sons to the two daughters, so my uncle *Bahri* married the younger daughter *Emine* and my father, the younger son, married the older daughter, *Zehra*. On that day, my father's stepmother *Nadiye Hanım* became his mother-in-law, and his step-sister *Zehra* became his wife. And in a complete irony, one might say that *Zeki's* own father became his father-in-law.

By the way, to reward *Hüseyin* for his loyal service at the Consulate, the Americans purchased the rented house in *Küçük Piyale* and gifted it to him. The family lived there for some time. In fact, *Bahri* and *Zeki* married *Emine* and *Zehra* in that very house.

BACK TO THE ARMY

In 1917, Turkey was in the midst of World War I and the Ottoman government was drafting everyone from age 7 to 70. My 46 year-old grandfather, well past military age, was called up again. At first he had been able to avoid military service by paying a *bedel* (fee), but toward the end

Figure 41: Family photo taken in Istanbul around 1925, not long after Hüseyin married Nadiye Hanim. Front row: Hanımcık's daughter Muzaffer, her oldest half-brother Bahri, and the two new step-sisters Zehra and Emine. Soon Bahri would be married to Emine, and my father to Zehra. The boy standing is unknown.

of the war, even this was not possible. The document shown here is *Hüseyin Bey's* draft card, written in *Osmanlıca* (Turkish as it was written before the new Republic replaced the Arabic alphabet with the Latin. Next to it is Bahri Amca's translation). So *Hüseyin* returned to the army and was stationed in the *Kağıthane* neighborhood in Constantinople as part of the Fixed-Balloon Division. Luckily, the general ceasefire was declared shortly after. The Great War was over, and *Hüseyin* was discharged for the last time.

PAPERS IN TRABZON

Emine knew *Hüseyin's* history very well. She once went with my uncle *Bahri* to the family *konak* (mansion) in Lower *Haçavera*. On the first floor in a big room on the left hand side she showed him a small closet. Bahri opened it and pulled out a cylindrical container and papers from within it. "Look," she said. "This konak is your father's, and these papers tell the story of his family and who you are. One day, come and read it. Don't forget." They then went with *Asiye Nene* to the nearby cemetery nearby cemetery to read the *Kuran* for their grandparents.

Figure 42: Hüseyin's Military I.D. Card, the second time he served.

Figure 43: Family picnic behind the house in Kasımpaşa near the Piyale Paşa Cami in Ok Meydani (literally meaning "Archery Field"). Clockwise from the tall woman at the left: Fatma Hanim (married to man with hat), "Hanım Yenge," Nadiye Hanim's brother Ahmet Karpak, Emine (my cousin Mehmet Ergene's mother), Mehmet's sister Nurhan, my grandfather Hüseyin Bey, my half-brother Turhan (back to us), and his mother Zehra (back to us). (1936)

Sadly, the container disappeared during the Russian invasion of *Maçka*, though the cupboard remains. The *konak* is currently occupied by the sons of my father's *Hüseyin's* brother *Mustafa Osman*, Arif and Abdi. Bahri said that these very old men had lived in Istanbul for a long time, but could never be gentrified, and returned to village life. (By the way, props to my dear friend Can Demir for painstakingly translating this information from Bahri Amca's notes.)

HÜSEYIN EFENDI'S DEATH

Hüseyin retired from the American Consulate in 1937 with a modest pension. And to the last, he remained vital. My uncle *Bahri* wrote, *Ne elden ayakdan düşer oldu* (he was never incapacitated nor incapable of caring for himself). My grandfather remained mentally acute to the very end. On May 1, 1946, he was laying in his death bed in a house the family was renting on *Bakrac Sokak* in *Cihangir*. *Bahri* remembered the day clearly. The family needed him to endorse his last pension check. Just minutes before he died, he held it in his hand, and noticing its dampness, remarked, "you've put this on something wet." He slipped away quickly and in complete peace. May God bless his soul.

BREAKING UP THE EMPIRE

EMPIRE IN DECLINE

In 1914, the six year old *Zeki* watched the British forces enter Constantinople to occupy the Ottoman Empire's seat of power. One would think that World War had ended the Empire, but its dissolution began long before the Treaty of Versailles officially partitioned it. Nationalism was always brewing in the subject states, particularly when their economies begin to decline or when ethnic passions ran hot. As far back as the fall of Christian Byzantium in the 1500's, Greek revolutionaries were spoiling for independence. There was the Greek War of Independence beginning in 1821. Then the Crimean War of 1854, followed by the Russo-Turkish War of 1879. There were Serbian protests to Ottoman rule in Bulgaria. Then in 1885 Greek and Bulgarian Christians battled

Figure 44: The Süleymanie Mosque from the Bosphorus, circa 1900 Photo Courtesy of William Bechhoefer

Ottoman forces in Macedonia. The Empire's response to insurrections was often ugly. By 1894, reports of Turkish atrocities toward the Armenians were making their way into the Western press. By that time, the three Great Powers (Russia, United Kingdom and France) were circling the wounded empire, "the sick man of Europe," like vultures. They maintained a safe distance while it was in its death throes, while at the same time keeping a watchful eye on one another.

Increasingly isolated from Europe, Ottoman *Sultan Abdül Hamid II* cozied up to Germany. In 1902 Germany began to invest heavily in the Ottoman economy and was given permission to build the Berlin-to-Baghdad railway. By then, reformers calling for modernization from within the Empire were becoming more vocal in their opposition to imperial rule.

In 1907 the sultan's repressive policies had fostered enough serious disaffection that progressive intellectuals and artists began to gain traction in their call to end the absolute monarchy and reinstate a constitution. Several nationalist reform organizations, collectively known as the Committee of Union and Progress (CUP) or "Young Turks" openly

revolted. In 1908, the sultan was forced to approve parliamentary elections which CUP overwhelmingly won.

Unfortunately, the most authoritarian elements of the Young Turk movement usurped its leadership. Their hawkish leader *Enver Paşa* staged a coup in 1913, and the CUP became a military dictatorship. Power became concentrated in the hands of a triumvirate, with Minister of War *Enver Paşa* its acknowledged leader. The pro-German *Enver* then convinced the sultan to secure a secret alliance with Germany.

Then came a seminal moment in history. Three young Serbians, angry that Austria-Hungary had annexed Bosnia-Herzegovina, got caught up in the romantic notion of political change through assassination and martyrdom. On June 28, 1914, Austrian Archduke Franz Ferdinand, who had been sent by his father the emperor to observe military maneuvers in the newly acquired Bosnia was riding with his wife in a motorcade in a convertible sports car with the top folded down. The car passed the first assassin who failed to shoot his pistol. The second one threw a bomb which bounced off the convertible cover, rolled off, and detonated under the car behind, wounding twenty people. The motorcade sped up, confounding the third assassin. At a town hall reception later in the day, the archduke read from a speech that had been bloodied from the bombing. The royal couple decided to visit the day's wounded in the hospital. En route, the third assassin came out of a delicatessen and fired two shots, fatally wounding both the archduke and duchess.

The Allies (Britain, France and Russia) became embroiled in the aftermath of the assassination of their Austria ally, forcing the Ottomans to abandon their ambivalent neutrality and declare war on France, Russia and Great Britain. The "Great War" had begun.

WORLD WAR 1

You would think that after the devastating military setbacks, the Ottoman's suffered in the quarter century leading up to the war, they would avoid military confrontation, or at least "circle the wagons" - assume a more defensive military posture. Unfortunately, the ambitious *Enver Paşa* envisioned German industrial and military power as the road to a renaissance of Ottoman imperial glory; an opportunity for the Ottomans to regain lost territories and incorporate new lands and peoples into the Empire. The sultan ordered general mobilization of the Ottoman forces. Every man capable of fighting was called up, including the fathers of both my parents. They would become part of an ill-prepared Ottoman army of about 800,000 men which would soon be engaged in global conflict fought on four fronts. The Turks fought the Allies in the Caucuses, in Persia, Sinai and Palestine. They fought bravely in Gallipoli and Mesopotamia. But the states of the Empire fell like dominoes as the Allies converged on it. The Arab lands, Mesopotamia, Syria, Palestine; all gone. Past the Black Sea the Armenians and Georgians were establishing their own states. One after another Ottoman states became untethered from the centuries-old Empire.

Figure 45: "Tezkere-i Osmaniye" was the common identification document issued by the Ottoman Government. This one belonged to my grandfather and states that the holder, Çağrı Hüseyin, is the son of Uzunoğlu Ibrahim. The language is old Turkish (Osmanlıca) the language of the Ottoman court prior to its dissolution in 1923. It is Arabic script with some Persian letters thrown in to get certain sounds (like "p") that you find in Turkish but not in Arabic. The number of people who still know Osmanlıca is dwindling. My uncle Bahri, a scholar and historian, was able to read it. He once took me on a tour of Topkapı palace and read out-loud the beautifully caligraphed ceramics along the Topkapı Museum walls. We were being eagerly followed by a group of curious tourists who marvelled as my mustachioed uncle, with his open palm motioning proudly in the air, dramatically "proclaiming" the inscriptions with a proud, booming voice. (Photo Courtesy of Mehmet Toğrul Ergene)

Early in October 1918, Ottoman resistance was exhausted. The hawkish government resigned, and the Young Turk triumvirate - *Enver, Talat,* and *Cemal* - fled to exile in Germany. The new sultan *Mehmet VI* and a government headed by liberal ministers sued for peace. (A strange way of saying they gave up since, on October 30, 1918, the Ottomans signed an armistice which was essentially dictated by the Allies.) Two weeks later, on November 12, the day after the end of the war in Europe, Allied warships steamed through the Dardanelles and dropped anchor in the former Ottoman capital, Constantinople. The insulting, often cruel British occupation had begun, and most Turks (including my young father) learned to suppress their feelings of outrage and resentment.

THE PARTITIONING OF THE OTTOMAN EMPIRE

After the war, partitioning of the Ottoman Empire created a new map of Europe and the Middle East. Central Europe was completely redrawn into numerous smaller states. France recovered the provinces of Alsace and Lorraine, and controlled Syria and Lebanon. The United Kingdom maintained the independence of Belgium, and took control of Mesopotamia and Palestine (which would later become Palestine and Transjordan). Parts of the Ottoman Empire on the Arabian Peninsula became parts of what are today Saudi Arabia and Yemen. My father always spoke bitterly about how Europe had taken advantage of the vulnerability and attractiveness of the Empire's vast treasures. After all, he had observed it firsthand. This may explain the insatiable appetite my parents had for history and politics. They read the paper religiously, and dinner time was the forum for illuminating and lively discussions about politics and global affairs, all of which were taken very personally.

Figure 46: British officers interrogating Turkish prisoners at Cape Helles at Battle of Gallipoli, 1915. Photographer: Lt. Ernest Brooks (Australian War Memorial)

THE TURKISH REPUBLIC

Figure 47: Cover of Time Magazine March 24, 1923 with the title "Mustafa Kemal Pasha -Where is a Turk his own Master?"

While the Sultan in Constantinople signed treaty after treaty partitioning the Empire, former Ottoman officials outside the capital, in Anatolia in particular, were setting up outposts (*Karakol Cemiyeti*) as part of the "resistance." These Turkish Nationalists, under the leadership of *Mustafa Kemal Paşa*, waged a four year War of Independence (*İstiklâl Harbi* or *Kurtuluş Savaşı*) against the Allies to keep Anatolia and Eastern Thrace. They mobilized their resources to successfully keep the Greeks from claiming Western Anatolia (Smyrna) in the Greco–Turkish War of 1919–1922. They fought the Turkish-Armenian war, and the Franco-Turkish war. In March 1920, Turkish revolutionaries openly accused the sultan of being usurped by the European powers, and asserted that the only true Turkish government was the new parliament they had established in Ankara. The "Grand National Assembly" assumed full governmental powers and declared *Mustafa Kemal* the Turkish Republic's first president. By October, 1922 the Allied forces and the Ottoman sultan had been expelled. The Turkish revolutionaries were able to force the Allies to abandon the Treaty of Sèvres. Then on July 24, 1923, after eight months of arduous negotiations, the Lausanne treaty which would preserve Anatolia and Eastern Thrace to form the Republic of Turkey, was signed. The independence movement which coalesced under *Mustafa Kemal* had culminated in the founding of the Turkish Republic which was recognized as the successor state to the defunct Ottoman Empire.

By October 2nd 1923, all the British troops in Istanbul had been given orders to leave the newly recognized republic. My father was 17 years old that year. He stood in the crowd which had formed in front of the mosque and quietly watched the evacuating British soldiers march past him to their boats.

Fig. 48: No, this 1928-ish photo is not a "Jail break." This rag-tag crew of freshly head-shaved recruits is off to do their military service in the New Republic. The only one not going is my father, (standing second from the right), presumably because he suffered from bronchitis. The men are holding satchels of their belongings. The newspaper is a sports gazette announcing the start of the Galatasaray and Fener Bahce Soccer League. If you can tell me what the Dunce Cap is all about, please write me at beyhan@trockworks.com

It was the dawn of the new Turkish Republic. The "Kemalist" government intended to bring Turkey into the modern age at break-neck speed. The Ottoman millet system of semi-autonomous subject states gave way to the birth to a modern, secular Turkish state.

If you had been living in Constantinople at the turn of the century, the changes proposed by the new government would have seemed impossible to achieve. At that time, secular institutions were all subordinate to religious ones. Your religious affiliation determined who you were in society. Your clothing identified your religion, and your headgear in particular (fez, turban, bonnet, etc.), established your "sex", "rank" and "profession" (both civil and military). The pinnacle of this ranking system was the *Ulema*,

the educated class of Muslim scholars and arbiters of *Sharia* law (the moral and religious code of Islam. They were considered knowledgeable and pious, and therefore had the right to run state affairs.

But the new government disassembled this entire construct. The Republic was to be a secular, representative democracy with a new constitution and European-style laws. Zealous Kemalists considered the religious community of the *Ulema* "non-scientific" people, essentially superstitious and *gerici* (backward). In 1925 the new government passed a law forbidding the use of religion as a tool in politics. And despite the predictable backlash, the government moved ahead. Secular public education was quickly

Figure 49: When Zeki was drafted in his early twenties, he had not yet been circumcised. The military had its rules, and performed the surgery without fanfare or anesthesia. Zeki often related the story of how he lay in a nearby ditch to recover. Still, the military introduced my father to one of the great joys in his life; horseback riding. While in the Turkish Cavalry he proved himself a very good rider and judge of horses. Later in life, one of my father's few prized possessions was a pair of stiff, black riding boots. As children, we helped him take them off by straddling his foot with our backs to him and holding on to the heel while he pushed us away with his other foot.

established, as were state enterprises and state banks. Professions which had previously been in the hands of the *Ulema* were secularized, leading to a new breed of lawyers, teachers, and also doctors.

The Ottoman "dress code" which had stratified society was also abolished. Beginning in 1923, traditional religious clothing and other overt signs of religious affiliation were outlawed. The Hat Law of 1925 required that every male use Western-style fedoras instead of the turban (worn by teachers), fez (worn by civil servants), etc. (My grandfather *Hüseyin*, who intensely disliked Ataturk's modernization policies) refused to wear the fedora. The American Embassy created a unique hat made for his guard uniform to appease him.) In 1934 religion-based clothing such as the veil and turban were banned altogether. Women were given the right to vote and education for girls became compulsory.

I'm sure that men like my grandfather also didn't appreciate that polygamy was also banned.

Mustafa Kemal introduced the Western Alphabet, ordering all Turkish newspapers, books and street signs to be printed in the new script. Can you imagine? In 1934 the Turkish Assembly gave Mustafa Kemal the name Ataturk, "Father of the Turks." That year it was also decreed that everyone in Turkey had to have a surname, a family name. No more "Ali the son of the blind carpet-maker."

CHOOSING A LAST NAME

"Modern Turkification" was a vast, unpredictable undertaking; a very rough ride on an uncharted road, with only one headlight and myriad potholes. The government's ambitious rush to modernize often forced a generally compliant Turkish population into untenable and frustrating situations. Let me give you one very small example of how rocky those early days were in the new Republic.

My own last name, by rights, should have been *Uzunoğlu*. When it was decreed that every citizen had to register a "real" last name, my grandfather *Hüseyin* went together with my father to the packed courthouse to register. When his turn came, *Hüseyin Bey* informed the clerk that his last name was *Uzunoğlu*. After shuffling through God knows how many pages of names, the clerk replied that the name had already been taken by someone else. The fact that it had been taken by *Hüseyin's* uncle was irrelevant to the clerk. No amount of explaining or reasoning could budge this obviously overwhelmed yet fastidious civil servant.

Hüseyin Bey thought up another name, and upon offering it, learned that it, too had been taken. Frustrated after trying a third time, he glanced around the packed courthouse. He glanced down at the hundreds of scraps of paper strewn all over the floor; the used call numbers. He noticed a young man calling out the next number to be served. "*Çağrı*" he yelled, and then the number. Literally, *Çağrı* (pronounced Chah-ruh) means "calling" - as in "calling number 47, calling number 47." At his wits end, *Hüseyin Bey* impulsively said "Alright, enough of this. I'll take that name; *Çağrı*" So it was that my grandfather, my father, and his half-sister Muzaffer were given the same last name, *Çağrı*.

It's funny that all my life I thought my name had a much more auspicious origin; more akin to "a higher calling." After learning the real story, I am just grateful that the guy calling out numbers that day in the courthouse wasn't peddling eggplant instead.

My dad's two brothers also tasked also had to find a name for themselves. The eldest *Bahri*, was in Iran at the time and wrote to Istanbul with instructions that he wanted the name *Ergenekon*, (a mythical valley in Central Asia from which the Turks were led out by Asena, the Grey Wolf). Unfortunately, the court in Istanbul mangled the message. They dropped the "*kon*," leaving the name *Ergene*, which is the name of the plains and a small river near the city of *Edirne*. This state of affairs was highly disconcerting to *Bahri Amca*, (uncle on father's side), because he said Edirne is "Rum" or Greek territory, and has nothing to do with "our people." Giving someone named *Uzunoğlu* the name *Ergene* is like giving Jose Sanchez the new name Timothy O'Boyle. *Bahri's* son *Mehmet* has spent his life convincing people he is not of Greek descent, despite his name.

ZEHRA HANIM

The war had ended and soon after *Zeki* married his sweet step-sister *Zehra*. They had two sons, *Turhan* and *Orhan*. The family, by outward appearances, was happy. They vacationed on the beach, strolled along the Bosphorus, and joined the extended family on outings and picnics. But *Zeki* was not happy. After 8 years of marriage, he suddenly left his wife and abandoned his sons. The three were left unsupported and had to rely on the generosity of the extended family, who cursed *Zeki* and insisted that *Zehra Hanım* divorce him and build a new life for herself with another man. They tore up every picture of him, and refused to speak his name. But *Zehra* could not imagine a life without *Zeki*. He was her one true love, the only man she'd ever known. She spent the rest of her life waiting for him to return.

It's difficult to talk about *Zehra Hanım* because I have always been acutely aware that if my father had not abandoned her, I would never have been born. If my mother had not bewitched my father, *Zehra* may have been able to hang on to him, and he would have been there to help raise their two young sons. *Zehra Hanım* had a generous spirit; she was kind, loving, and selfless. She was also shy. In later years she walked with a limp, and had either a cataract or eye injury which made one of her eyes look somewhat cloudy.

I visited her home in the early 1970's with my father. It was a basement apartment in *Cihangir*, Istanbul which she shared with her son *Orhan* and his two children *Gulcan* and *Ercan*. *Orhan* divorced his wife when the children were quite young, so they were essentially raised by their grandmother *Zehra*. She knew who I was, what I represented, but she never held it against me. I remember she welcomed me warmly, despite the fact that my mother had stolen her husband 30 years prior. Thankfully, she saw me as an innocent child, another victim of my father's indiscretions.

Figure 50: My father and Zehra Hanım taking their sons Orhan and Turhan on vacation to the beach, around 1934

Figure 51: In Kabataş, Istanbul 1930 (From left to right) Emine Hanım, Nadiye Hanım's brother Ismail, my father Zeki, and his wife (Emine's sister) Zehra. Emine's daughter Nurhan Ergene Ertem is behind the wheel of Emine's Model A Ford!

She spent most of her life in the tiny kitchen of that apartment. That kitchen! There was barely enough room for two people to stand side-by-side in it. The small sink sat directly next to the stove, with precious little counter space to prepare food. Yet she somehow managed to produce fabulous meals there. She'd make fried *börek*, fish, meats, rices, and desserts for her family (my two older half-brothers *Turhan* and *Orhan*, and her two grandchildren).

Each night at dinner time, the family gathered into the small dining room. *Zehra's* mischievous grandson *Ercan* who had been playing soccer in the streets would have to be dragged in, often by his ear, to eat. He would restlessly call out through the open window to his friends while he ate, and in a matter of minutes his skinny frame was scurrying out the door.

I noticed that *Zehra Hanım* brought out dish after dish from the kitchen to men who barely looked up as they voraciously ate her food. *Gülcan* (perhaps 7 years old), could barely take her eyes off me, her mysterious aunt from America. That little girl has grown into a gorgeous woman, nurse, wife and mother. Her grandmother Nadiye Hanım, (my father's ex-mother-in-law) had passed down her good cooking, first to her daughter *Zehra*, and from *Zehra* to *Gülcan*. (The Artichoke Bottoms, Celery Root in Orange, and Lentil *Köfte* recipes in this book come to us this way.)

SEYFI, THE THIRD BROTHER

My father's younger brother *Seyfi* was an infant when his mother *Lütfiye Elif,* sick from tuberculosis, returned with him to Trabzon. When *Lütfiye* died soon after, *Seyfi* was left under the care of her mother, my great grandmother *Nene* who loved and cared for him like a son. Unfortunately, when *Seyfi* was about 8 years old*, Nene* died as well, at which point *Seyfi's* life became a living hell. His uncles, *Lütfiye's* brothers, harbored old resentments against his father *Hüseyin,* and abused *Seyfi,* treating him like the family slave. They were harsh with him, and made him do all the chores. When they went up to the highlands to collect wood, they would pile it all on his back to be carried down.

When *Seyfi* was fifteen years old, he left Trabzon alone and made his way westward, showing up he showed up in Istanbul around 1925. All we know is that his father *Hüseyin* summarily shunned him and sent him on his way. It is no wonder then, that when it came time for *Seyfi* to choose his last name, he decided on the moniker *Yalnız,* which sadly, in Turkish, means "alone."

The family had no further contact with their outcast brother *Seyfi* until the day when *Bahri,* my father, and their two wives were out on a picnic. It was a serendipitous encounter. Looking up, *Bahri* spotted a man who looked very much like my father, selling *simit* (a roasted bagel-like ring coated with sesame seeds). *Bahri* remarked, "Hey, this is my brother," and apparently called him over. What an awkward conversation it must have been when the three brothers were re-united after so many years. After all, they barely knew one another. They talked for a few moments, and that was it. *Seyfi* simply left.

Bahri did remain in touch with *Seyfi* over the years. Oddly, it took another 25 years for *Bahri* to inform his own son, my cousin *Mehmet,* that another uncle even existed. *Mehmet's* parents had driven him from their home in *Cihangir* to old Istanbul where they introduced him to a gentleman who looked, again, just like my father. *Mehmet,* in fact, assumed he was my father. Of course the man turned out to be *Zeki's* brother *Seyfi,* a policeman who had been living in *Samsun* (on the Black Sea coast). *Seyfi* had a wife, *Dürriye,* and three sons. *Hikmet* the youngest is also a police commissioner who has since retired from the force and lives in Istanbul. The middle son, *Ünsal,* passed away. The oldest son, *Ünal,* 2 years older than Mehmet, is a free spirit, who spends much of his time fishing on his boat in the Sea of Marmara. The sons are estranged and no longer speak to one other, even though they live near one another east of Istanbul in a place called *Kartal. Mehme*t last saw *Ünal* at my half-brother *Turhan's* funeral.

Seyfi had been a fingerprint expert working with the police in the southern city of *Adana.* In the early 60's he was offered a post in *Balıkesir* as head of the traffic police, (which is funny because *Seyfi* never learned to drive). His marriage to *Dürriye* ended strangely; she had a government job with only two years left until she qualified for her pension. He wanted her to quit her job to move to *Balıkesir,* but she refused. So he divorced her. *Seyfi* went to *Balikesir* alone, and later married a woman named *Zülfiye* with whom he had one more son, *Asım.* Unlike my half brothers *Turhan* and *Orhan* who continued to love my father, even after being abandoned by him, *Seyfi's* sons hated him for leaving them and their mother.

Figure 52: 1936 Photograph of Hüseyin's family. From left to right; Emine, her daughter Nurhan, Emine's mother Nadiye Hanım, Nadiye's mother Asiye Hanım with her own grandaughter Shükran (Ismail's older daughter). Standing in back is the author's father Zeki. Zeki's father Hüseyin Efendi holding Zeki's sons Orhan (seated) and Turhan. Beside Zeki is his half-sister Muzaffer (meaning "Victorious") and to her right Zeki's wife (Emine's older sister and the mother of the two boys) Zehra. (A clean-shaven Zeki was probably going to or had just come back from the military).

Seyfi Amca ultimately retired in Istanbul, where he maintained a very good relationship with, of all people, his father *Hüseyin's* fifth wife, *Nadie Hanım*. It was a strange relationship, given that *Seyfi* was the abandoned son of her husband. Worse still, he was also the brother of the much maligned *Zeki*, her no-good son-in-law who had abandoned her daughter *Zehra*. *Nadie Hanım's* family was so bitter about my father leaving *Zehra Hanım*, that instead of calling him by his real name *Hayri Zeki* (*Hayri* meaning charitable), they called him *Hayırsız* (rascal or scoundrel) *Zeki*.

In 1968, my sister *Çaya* accompanied my father on her first return trip to Turkey and was the first of my siblings to meet our long-lost uncle *Seyfi*. When she first saw him, *Çaya* was convinced that he and my father were twins, they looked so much alike. He had the same modest demeanor, and shy smile with a closed mouth like my father's. His hazel eyes and neat moustache were identical to my father's, as was his proud nose.

ZEKI'S GOODBYE TO NADIYE

I told you that the first time I returned to Turkey I was a fifteen year-old in need of a serious attitude adjustment, so my father had taken me to Istanbul for that purpose. During the first few weeks when he wasn't speaking to me at all, he would occasionally take me out of the house to run an errand with him. One such day we had been driving for a half hour or so. (I had no idea where I was in Istanbul, so I can't really say where we ended up). We got out of the car and he led me down a small hill and through a simple courtyard to a cottage no bigger than a single 8 x 8-foot room. I immediately sensed that he was nervous. He hesitantly pushed open an unlocked wooden door to reveal a stark, white-walled room. In the corner an old woman was resting on a thin mattress spread on top of what looked to be a wooden table. As she struggled to a sitting position, she modestly adjusted her white house dress that had risen up around her thighs. She squinted as her eyes adjusted to the sunlight that now bathed the room from the open door, and her thin, pale hand checked the position of the white *Şile bezi* scarf wrapped loosely over her white hair. My father bowed somewhat to peer through the small door. Finally recognizing her long-lost son-in-law, she thoughtlessly remarked, "Oh, it's you."

Using only body language, he asked permission to enter. She warily obliged. I watched him lower his head to kiss the hand of this ancient woman whom, I would learn years later, was *Nadiye Hanım* herself. She had not seen my father in many years, but her disapproval was still fresh in her expression. She looked me over with a dismissive air, as if she had noticed one of the bastard children from that Jewish girl. I imagine my father had gone to pay his respects to his father's last wife; not to seek forgiveness from the mother-in law who never stopped hating him. No matter. Each believed what they needed to believe. She permitted him to kiss her hand, holding it out for him as he bent down, placed his chin to it, and raised it to his forehead, in the age-old custom of deference. All was not forgiven, but society's conventions had been observed.

As we ponder the life my father lived in Turkey so long ago, it occurs to me, dear reader, that I have not even introduced you to my mother. It's true she was not even born when *Zeki* married *Nadiye Hanım's* daughter, the heady times of the New Turkish Republic. Yes, while the 17 year-old *Zeki* was hearing speeches on Istanbul's streets about *Mustafa Kemal* and the modern Turkish Republic, a Bulgarian woman in the Jewish sector of Istanbul was giving birth to a little girl who would become the love of his life.

In 1930 the name Constantinople was officially changed to Istanbul. Greeks often claim the new name was derived from "stin poli" or "to the walled city." When I was a kid my football coach Mike Folstein used to tease me about being Turkish by singing the popular Kennedy/Simon song about the name change:

Istanbul was Constantinople.
Now it's Istanbul not Constantinople.
Been a long time gone, old Constantinople
still has Turkish Delight on a moonlit night.

Every gal in Constantinople
is a Miss 'Stanbul, not Constantinople
so if you've a date in Constantinople
she'll be waiting in Istanbul.

Even old New York was once New Amsterdam
Why they changed it I can't say
(People just liked it better that way!)

Take me back to Constantinople.
No, you can't go back to Constantinople.
Now it's Istanbul not Constantinople.

Why did Constantinople get the works?
That's nobody's business but the Turks'
'stanbul!

Figure 53: 1936 From left to right; Turhan Ağabey, Nurhan Ergene, the author's father Zeki Bey, his sister-in-law EmineErgene and wife Zehra. By the time this photo was taken, Zeki was already feeling squeezed out as head of his family.

CHAPTER II

THE TURKISH JEWISH SIDE

Fig 54: The Revah family 1938. Clockwise from top left - Berta (Beti), Granmama Sara,
Granpapa Kemal, Merih, Ida, and Nesim (Niso)
(Photo courtesy of Barry Kiracofe)

We've traced my father's ancestors from China through Central Asia, through Anatolia, up to the Black Sea and then to Istanbul in the early 1940's. Zeki, the proud Muslim Turk in his early thirties, was married with two children and had his life pretty well laid out in front of him. He would one day take over the job his father held at the American Consulate, live close to his extended family in Istanbul, and ultimately get a reasonable pension which would keep him comfortable through his retirement years. All this changed when Zeki met Beti.

The pretty Jewish girl who worked at the dry-cleaner near the Consulate was extraordinary. She was clever, talented, irreverent and worldly. No. She was *other* worldly. Living as a Jew or any other minority in Istanbul was literally like living in another universe altogether. The Jewish community lived apart from the Turks (Muslims). They had their own schools, their own places of worship, their own languages and neighborhoods. Turkish men rarely had the opportunity to see, much less talk to Jewish girls. Yet here she was. Everything about her was different. He was more than charmed by her; he was caught in her shimmering web.

I always knew that Beti's background was very different from Zeki's. But I never really appreciated how remarkable it was that she was in Istanbul in the first place. When I started writing this book, I realized I didn't know the answers to the most basic questions about the Jewish side of my family. Who are the Jews? Why are the Jews in Turkey so different then the Jews in America? How is it that Jews were living in the capital of the Ottoman empire? Why did they come? When did they come? And where did they come from?

Sometimes strange things are so pervasive, they don't seem strange. Growing up, for example, I thought all Turks spoke Spanish. That's because my mother and her relatives spoke more Spanish than Turkish to one another. It was only when I learned that my father couldn't speak Spanish at all that I became aware that my parents did not share the same religion. Confused? Let me break it down.

The language my mother and her family were speaking is *Ladino*, the Spanish spoken in Spain in the 15th century. My mother's family was Jewish, and had lived in Spain until 1492 when the Spanish Monarchy forced all non-Christians out.

We learned the song of Columbus' discovery of the New World in elementary school. It went like this; "In 14 Hundred and 92, Columbus Sailed the Ocean Blue." Of course, I was too young to know then that 1492 was also the year the Catholic Monarchs of Spain, Isabella I of Castile and Ferdinand II of Aragon, issued the Expulsion Edict that forced my ancestors to flee Spain. The edict, known as the "Alhambra Decree," gave Spain's Jews and Muslims exactly four months (March 31 to August 31) to either convert to Christianity or permanently leave the Kingdom of Spain and its territories and possessions.

Because my mother's family speaks Ladino, we can be sure that not only had my family once been in Spain, but also that they left before the language evolved into its current form. Spanish speakers are tickled pink when they hear my family speak Ladino. It's so archaic it's like someone speaking Shakespearean English complete with the "thine's and thee's." Ladino is also sprinkled with loads of allusions to Christianity Just as we might say "Oh my God! Or Jeezus!" my aunt Ida says *Atyo!* (short for *Ay Dios Santos Piodosos* or "Oh God and the Pious Saints.") This comes out of the mouth of a Jew from Istanbul.

By all oral accounts, my ancestors fled Spain at the time of the Grand Inquisitor Torquemada. We will get into that subject and how they were welcomed into the Ottoman Empire very soon. But first, we must ask the important question, "Where did the Jews come from, and how did they get to Spain in the first place?"

THREE RELIGIONS - ONE GOD

There was a time when there was no Torah. There was no Qur'an. No Bible. There was no concept of prayer. Or after-life. Or "God." You made sense of the world by what you could personally experience; the sun, the sky, the seasons. Transformative events like birth and death were part of a living mythology, stories and rituals which somehow included us as participants. There was time when we believed our behavior could affect a solar eclipse, the first buds in springtime, or the return of the moon to a full circle. We believed if we were grateful enough, we could bring about a bountiful harvest, a successful hunt, a healthy child – all we needed to do was show our appreciation through sacrifice. Passionate rituals grew up around our offerings of food, children, virgins, even our sexuality, to either invite or ward off the awe-inspiring natural world.

Undeniably, the way people understood the world, the way we explained life's existential questions, came to define us, and eventually separate us from one another. Today, almost half of the world's population adheres to one of only three primary monotheistic faiths, Islam, Christianity, and Judaism. The earliest, Judaism, began in the first and second millennium BCE in the ancient lands of Israel and Judah, during which time the Hebrew Bible (the Old Testament), was written. About 1,500 years later, Jewish followers of Jesus of Nazareth (peace be upon him) gave birth to Christianity which is based primarily on the New Testament. Then, in the 7th century AD Islam, the fastest growing religion in the world, appeared, based on the *Kuran* (Qur'an) as it was revealed to the prophet Muhammad (peace be upon him).

Figure 55: The Dome of the Rock mosque in Jerusalem is the third holiest site in Islam, and from where the prophet Mohammad ascended to heaven. It is also the site of the Jewish temples of Solomon and Cyrus the Great. It is also the site of the church of the Holy Sepulchre, where Christ was resurrected. (Photo courtesy of Dr. Barry Kiracofe)

ABRAHAM AND THE COVENANT

What most people choose to ignore is that the sacred narratives of all three religions include many of the same historical figures, stories and places. Noah, Moses, Daniel, Aaron, David, and Solomon are not only known to all three faiths, they are even considered prophets in all three. In Islam, all the prophets of Judaism and Christianity are considered Muslim, including Jesus Christ. This is because Muslims believe in only one God. Jehovah (more appropriately written YHWH), is God, is Allah.

The reason the histories and beliefs of these three religions have been so intertwined is that they have a common root: Abraham. He was born in Sumeria, a part of Mesopotamia, or ancient Iraq in 2018 BCE (only 352 years after the Great Flood), and is said to be a tenth generation descendant of Noah. Abraham is referred to as "father" of the Jews and Christians through his son Isaac from his wife Sarah. Abraham is also "father" of Muslims through his other son Ishma'il, born to Sarah's handmaiden Hagar.

THE COVENANT

In 2100 BCE, when King Hammurabi united the kingdoms of the Babylonian empire, the Jews was non-existent. The story of the Jews begins when Abraham's family left their home in Ur. The act of crossing over the Euphrates River and travelling 600 miles to southern Turkey would indelibly mark his family as the first people in the Bible identified as *Ivrum* (Hebrews), the people "from the other side of the river." Thus the word *Ivrit* in Israel, the name of the Hebrew language.

It was in Turkey, in the land of *Haran* (Charan), that Abraham received a revelation from God, who introduced Himself as Jehovah or Jahweh (YHWH). Like Adam, Noah and others before him, Abraham was chosen to deliver a message to humankind. Abraham was told that if he followed God's commandments, God would make Abraham's descendants His "Chosen People" and place them under His protection. Abraham was given a single commandment and a single promise. The commandment was that all males were to be circumcised. The promise? God gave Abraham the land of Canaan.

Abraham's revelation is understood as a covenant, a solemn promise, between Jehovah and Abraham's people. In a subtle way, it gave them a reason to survive "as a people." Historian Max Dimont in his wonderful book *Jews, God and History*, points out that Jewish history can be read as a succession of ideas designed to perpetuate this singular aim.

In Canaan, Abraham's barren wife Sarah offered her Egyptian handmaid Hagar to him to bear their child. Abraham's first son Ishma'il was born. One would think that Ishma'il and all his descendants would then be considered the Chosen People. But Jews and Muslims disagree about what it meant when Sara, who was well into her eighties, then gave birth to Abraham's second son, Isaac. Which son was the rightful heir?

Jews believe God promised Ishma'il twelve sons who would multiply to become a future nation, but made it clear that the "covenant" would be with Isaac. Muslims believe that God's covenant was intended to be a covenant with Abraham's descendants who are obedient to Him and follow his command. Thus Muslims are also Chosen People. Both faiths agree that when Sarah asked Abraham to cast Hagar and the boy out, Abraham complied. He left them in the desert with a few dates and a skin of water. The child was overcome with weakness and would surely have died had it not been for a spring of water that seeped up through the ground under his feet. That spot where the water first appeared is in Mecca and is known as the Spring of Zam Zam, a place to which Abraham returned many times. According to Islam, when Abraham left Mecca and the house he built for Hagar, he prayed for all mankind, asking that Allah not leave mankind without prophets for guidance. The house he built for Hagar and the black rock he placed near it are still there. Today it is known as the Ka'ba, destination of the annual Muslim pilgrimage called Hajj. The fact that Islam's holiest place was built by the first Jew certainly gives one pause.

MOSES

For 400 years the Chosen People lived in the land of Canaan, spiritually isolated. They didn't worship idols, they circumcised their sons, and refused to take part in sacrificial rituals. They refined a concept that the invisible, incorporeal God was separate from their bodies as well as their sexuality. They began to adopt an inner discipline (rather than a law) to control sexual impulses and keep those impulses within the realm of procreation to fulfill the mandate to "go forth and multiply." Abraham sired Isaac, who sired Jacob (*Yakub*), who then had twelve sons, the youngest of whom was Joseph (*Yusuf*).

In the 16th century BCE Joseph was sold into slavery by his jealous brothers and taken to Egypt. He became a favorite of Pharaoh Hyksos and eventually got permission to invite the Hebrews to live in Egypt. But the Hyksos pharaoh was overthrown (by Egyptians from Thebes in the south). When the Pharaoh was enslaved, all his "guests," including the Hebrews, were enslaved, as well.

We don't know a whole lot about the Hebrew slaves in Egypt (then called Israelites) until Moses led them back out in the 12th century BCE. And just as the Prophet Muhammad is never named in the *Kuran*, Moses is barely mentioned in the *Passover Haggadah* which recites the very exodus he led. In fact, Moses was never able to set foot into the Promised Land himself. He bid his people farewell and ascended Mount Nebo to set his eyes on the distant land of Canaan before he died.

When the Israelites entered Canaan, they had to fight various kingdoms for the right to live there. Joshua led them across the river Jordan in conquest, and when the walls of Jericho came tumbling down, Canaanite culture was no more.

The reintegration of the people of Moses and their "brethren" who had never left Canaan was less than perfect. As the Israelites settled in the land, their leader Joshua warned them to avoid local practices (like human sacrifice, sexual orgies, and sacred prostitution). A system of Jewish judges and elders managed to maintain a certain cohesiveness, but the story of Samson losing his power to the seductress Delilah speaks to this issue of temptation and how serious it was at the time.

PALESTINE EMERGES

By 1000 BCE, the twelve tribes of Israel which had settled into villages and towns in the strip of land known as Canaan. Unfortunately, the emerging nation that would be Palestine found itself tragically located. The armies of Egypt, Assyria, Babylon, Persia and Rome would each pass through the Canaanite "bridge" in conquest of one another, and would wreak havoc on the inhabitants in their way.

Facing powerful enemies, the tribes united to form the Kingdom of Israel with Saul from the tribe of Benjamin their first "king." King David, a warrior during Saul's reign, defeated the Philistines and expanded the Hebrew kingdom into an empire five times the size of modern Israel. He made Jerusalem the political capital of Palestine and earmarked the Temple of Jerusalem to enshrine the Ark of the Covenant (a chest containing the stone tablets on which the Ten Commandments were inscribed). Being a warrior, David was not permitted to actually build the Temple of Jerusalem. This task fell to David's son, King Solomon.

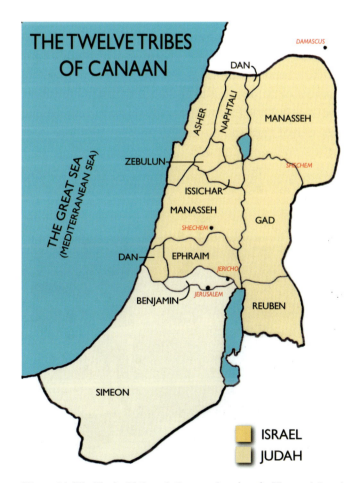

Figure 56: The Twelve Tribes of Canaan: Israel or the House of Joseph in the North, and Judah to the South.

Solomon unified the "dual" kingdom of Israel in the north and Judah in the south, and industrialized Palestine. Agrarianism was converted into urbanism by virtue of one project; Solomon's Temple. Copper and gold from the Phoenicians, vast quantities of cedar from Lebanon, huge blocks of quarried stone and thousands of craftsmen and architects were paid for with heavy taxes and forced labor. Solomon assumed so much debt building the Temple he was forced to pay the Phoenicians with twenty towns in the Galilee, thus creating a new "landless" class of Hebrews who then had to migrate to the commercial centers to find work. The crowds arrived before the jobs did, and massive unemployment (coupled with a small and oppressive aristocracy), bred widespread corruption, unrestrained vice, and passionate discontent. The fact that Solomon also had 700 wives and 300 concubines (most of whom were pagan) was also a source of discontent. The breaking point was reached when Solomon died around 922 BCE. Israel, comprised of the ten northern tribes (or Ten Lost Tribes), split from the two southern tribes of Judah.

In the 8th century BCE, the powerful Assyrians invaded Palestine and subjugated the ten northern tribes of Israel. Its citizens were forcibly resettled to cities in modern Iraq and Iran. Some of these exiles continued to move along the Silk Road as far eastward as Afghanistan, Pakistan, and even China. By 720 BCE almost all the people of the Ten Lost Tribes had been resettled. Israel was no more.

Figure 57: Group of Jewish children with teacher in Samarkand modern Uzbekistan (1910) (Prokudin_Gorskii Collection_LOC)

BABYLON

And what of the two remaining tribes of Judah? A new power emerged in the Middle East; Nebuchadnezzar II. The king of the new Babylonian empire raised a fearsome war machine which conquered the Assyrians in 612 BCE and Jerusalem along with it. When Judah then conspired with Egypt to gain her independence, Nebuchadnezzar's armies tore down the walls of Jerusalem, and set fire to Solomon's Temple. The Babylonians caught the last Davidic king Zedekiah and killed his sons in front of him before tearing out his eyes. The city was looted, and the entire population of Judah was deported to Babylon.

This could have been the end of the history of the Jews. We know from history that when the Assyrians dispersed the population of the Israelis of the north, the Ten Lost Tribes disappeared as a distinct ethnic group. But it was different for the two tribes of Judah. The Babylonians who conquered them had a policy of keeping exiled peoples together. Thus, the Jews living in Babylon were able to maintain their ethnic and religious identity.

As it turns out, Jewish captivity in Babylon wasn't too shabby. The conquered people from Judah frequented the many Babylonian libraries and acquired a taste for learning. They became interested in manners, grace, and refinements. And the trade routes through Babylon took these Jews to every corner of the known world, making them men of commerce and international trade.

DIASPORA AND THE UNIVERSAL JEW

During this time, important ideas were developing within Judaism that would significantly affect my ancestors who managed to hold onto their religion and traditions despite being tossed from one empire to the next until we finally settled here in the United States. At issue was man's relationship to God, especially the idea of forging an inner discipline to obey the authority of the "Book."

Jews adopted a revolutionary concept that humanity, justice, and morality served God better than "ritual." As sacrificial rites disappeared, the need for a venue to perform them, the Temple itself, also receded. Religious observance became free of the confines of both place and time. Dimont wrote that Judaism was became an "exportable commodity," which meant that re-settlement, dispersal, even diaspora no longer doomed the religion. Untethered from a single temple for rituals, Jews began to build synagogues, a new building prototype, for religious assembly. And instead of offering sacrifices at the ritual altar, they offered something else that was very new: prayers.

Also, for the first time, Jews were hearing the prophecy that the message of Judaism was no longer the exclusive religion of the Jewish people, but meant for all mankind to hear. And prayer, not ritual sacrifice, was emerging as the universal symbol for devotion to God.

A noteworthy event occurred in 629 BCE. During the renovation of the Temple of Jerusalem the scrolls of a book written by Moses were discovered. King Josiah, recognizing the unifying potential of the manuscript, proclaimed it was to be read aloud. Jews flocked to Jerusalem to hear the book of Moses, now known as Deuteronomy.

FROM BABYLON TO PERSIA

In 540 BCE, the small kingdom of Media south of the Caspian Sea defeated Babylonia. The Jews who had been exiled to Babylon became part of the Persian Empire. They were returned to Palestine, became prosperous, and filled Median King Cyrus' coffers with tribute. In Jerusalem, the priestly class quickly began reversing years of assimilation to forge a national and religious Jewish character. They reconstructed the Temple of Jerusalem, forbade interfaith marriage, and added Four Books of Moses to Deuteronomy. In 444 B.C. Jews from everywhere came to Jerusalem to hear the five books of the Pentateuch (Genesis, Exodus, Leviticus, Numbers, and Deuteronomy), read aloud. Palestine rivaled Babylon in its love of books, and the synagogue took on a new function; in addition to being a place of assembly (*knesset*) and a place of prayer, it became a place of study (*midrash*). The Arabic word *medrese* (educational institution) comes from this Hebrew word which means "investigate."

ENTER THE GREEKS

While Israel was being defeated by the Assyrians in the Near Seat, the Greeks were building their own empire, establishing city states like Sparta, Athens and Corinth. In 334 BCE, a young Macedonian warrior (and pupil of Aristotle) named Alexander put together an army of 32,000 men and shattered the Persian armies. When Persian King Darius III surrendered, the Jews who had lived under the Babylonians and then the Persians then came under Greek rule. Hellenization (cultural exchange with the purpose of creating a universal Greek culture) dominated the Near East for 600 years, and soon drove a wedge between Hellenized and non-Hellenized Jews.

Alexander (*Iskender*) had achieved his Pan-Hellenic Utopia when he died at the tender age of 32. But almost immediately, his top three generals dismantled his enormous empire. Antigonus claimed Greece. Seleucus grabbed up Asia Minor and Syria, founding the Seleucid Empire, and Ptolemy took possession of Egypt and the Jews in Palestine. The kings and queens of the Ptolemaic Empire (including Cleopatra) left the Jews pretty much alone as long as they paid their taxes.

The Jews prospered, not only as farmers but also in commerce. Because they travelled and traded all over the Hellenistic world, it's impossible to say where my Jewish ancestors had gone. Every Greek city in Asia Minor had a considerable Jewish population, after all. My people could have gone to any number of places; Antioch (*Antakya* in southern Turkey), Alexandria in Egypt, Ephesus in Asia Minor, Olympia and Sparta in the Peloponnese, Syracuse in Italy, Attica and Ithaca in Greece, even Troy near the Dardanelles. But I persevere, hoping that there will be more clues.

SELEUCID HELLENIZATION

The Seleucids wrested control of Palestine from the Ptolemies and Hellenization soon penetrated Judaism through language, manners and customs. At first, the Greeks saw the Jews as uncouth barbarians, while Jews considered Greeks immoral heathens. Certainly, the cultural divide between the two peoples was vast. A Jewish historian once said, "The Greeks believed in the holiness of beauty, the Jews believed in the beauty of holiness." Hellenized Jews began to wear Greek tunics, speak Greek, and name their children with Greek names. Jewish youth were attracted to anything Greek: nude wrestling, cabarets, and especially hedonism (the philosophy that the pursuit of pleasure was man's only goal since God didn't meddle in man's affairs and morality was a myth). Anyone who has teenagers can understand how the pervasive doctrine of pleasure-seeking swiftly corrupted Jewish youth at the time.

The Seleucids hit a snag when Hellenization entered the Temple. When the Hellenizing Jewish aristocracy opened the Temple to pagan rites and brought Grecian statues into the holy sanctuary, simmering resentment erupted into a political movement. The anti-Hellenist Hasmoneans massacred the king's appointees in the Temple, throwing them, and anything else Greek, over the 100-foot high Temple walls. In reprisal, Seleucid king Antiochus Epiphanes slaughtered 10,000 Jews. Greek statues were re-installed in the Temple. Pagans were encouraged to settle in Jerusalem to dilute the Jewishness of the city. Finally, when Antiochus outlawed the Sabbath and circumcision, even moderate Jews were compelled to join the resistance.

Figure 58: Destruction of the Temple of Jerusalem by Frencesco Hayez (Wikipaintings Encyclopedia of Paintings)

THE MACCABEES

The spark that set the Jerusalem tinderbox aflame came in 167 BCE when an aging Temple priest named Mattathias, refusing to sacrifice to the Greek gods, killed a Seleucid official. King Antiochus' reprisals led to an all-out revolt by Mattathias' five sons and their followers, known as the Maccabees. The bitter war between the Seleucids and the Maccabees lasted 25 years. Failing to see that even if he killed every last man, he could not be victorious over a religious ideology, the King continued to fight until 164 BCE when the Jews finally prevailed and recaptured Jerusalem. They purged the Temple of all idols and re-dedicated it to God, giving birth to the celebratory holiday Hanukkah.

The Maccabees gradually pushed the Seleucids out of Palestine altogether and re-established the Jewish Kingdom of Judah.

ENTER THE ROMANS

JEWISH WARS WITH ROME

When Roman Caesar Octavian annexed Judah into the Roman Empire at the dawn of the first century BCE, it was for a specific reason. A new empire made up of remnants of the Babylonian, Assyrian, and Persian kingdoms, had been shaping up in the East. The Parthians, as they were called, were a constant threat to the Romans, and Judea (as they called Judah) was seen as their most logical point of potential incursion into the Roman Empire. The Parthian threat is perhaps why the Romans ruled Judea with an iron fist.

Repression in Judea was so severe that by 66 AD a political party bent on war with Rome called the Zealots, revolted. They had the support of three factions of Jews (the Pharisees, the Sadducees, and the Essenes) as well as a new group of Jews: the Christians. Rome used its full military might to suppress them, but Jerusalem remained unconquered. There was a difficult and protracted siege of the city (with Romans outside the city walls, Zealots within, and thousands caught in the middle dying of starvation). Finally, the Romans starved the Zealots by ensconcing the city within a huge earth wall. The end was inevitable. In 70 AD the Romans stormed the walls, torched the Temple, and slaughtered the starved inhabitants. Hundreds of thousands of Jews were killed, sold into slavery, or marched to Rome where they were executed.

Masada, the last Jewish stronghold against Rome, fell in the Autumn of 72 AD when almost all of the 967 inhabitants killed themselves rather than being taken by the Romans. After such a protracted effort to dominate the Jews, Dimont wryly notes that the Roman Triumphal Arch built in honor of Titus' victory could just as easily have been built in relief that the wretched siege had ended.

Jewish resistance in Egypt, Antioch, and Cyprus did weaken the Romans enough to force them to abandon their conflict with the dreaded Parthians of northwestern Iran. Jews attempted rebellions two more times; during the Kitos War and then in 132 under the "military messiah on horseback," Simon ben Cozeba. They were almost wiped out by 35,000 troops under Hadrian's best general, Julius Severus.

Judean Palestine was then made "off-limits" to Jews and Jewish Christians. Many survivors, physically defeated but morally victorious, fled to Parthia and were warmly welcomed by the Jewish community which had been there since the 6th century BCE, when the Babylonian Empire settled Jewish exiles there.

THE DIASPORA

By the second century AD, most of the world's Jews were stateless and dispersed throughout the Roman Empire, over three continents and dozens of nations. The term diaspora (Greek for "the scattering"), came to mean the body of Jews scattered outside the boundaries of Israel. But they didn't disappear, as populations in exile do. The inner core of each Jewish group remained distinctly Jewish, although, as Dimont says:

> "Each took on the dominant traits of the host civilization... When a civilization was philosophical, like that of the Greeks, the Jews became philosophers. When it was composed pre-dominantly of poets and mathematicians, like that of the Arabs, the Jews became poets and mathematicians. When it was scientific and abstract, like that of the modern Europeans, the Jews became scientists and theoreticians."

We've seen that throughout history, the Jews have adapted when they could, or remained distinct when they couldn't.

PRESERVING JUDAISM

One event more than any other has prevented the world's Jews from assimilating and disappearing altogether. It happened in the year 68 AD when Jerusalem was under siege by the Romans. The rabbi Jochanan ben Zakkai, realizing that no foundation had been laid for keeping Jewish learning alive, predicted that an imminent Roman victory would disperse his people and end Jewish history. Zakkai (disguised as a corpse in a coffin) was able to escape Jerusalem with his disciples and soon obtained permission from the Roman general Vespasian to establish the first Yeshiva (school of Jewish learning).

He and the rabbi's after him had the daunting task of ensuring that the religion wouldn't vanish in the diaspora like scattered ashes. How would you have held together a fragmented people who had no country and were relocated to other lands with different religions, languages, and cultures? How would you maintain the identity of a people who were mostly being sold as slaves and took nothing with them but their ideas?

Between the 2nd and 6th centuries, rabbis and their students sought to provide guidance and enable Judaism to thrive despite the destruction of the Temple - the focal point of religious activity and observance of the laws of the Torah. In order to do this, they codified the oral law into the Mishnah and Gemarah. These laws, which became part of the Talmud (the collection of Jewish law, philosophy, history, and traditions), were exceedingly practical. They ranged from having to be your brother's keeper (so that any Jew sold into slavery could be ransomed and freed), to writing dictionaries to preserve the Hebrew language. Social organization was dictated by these laws as well. Ten Jewish men (above the age of thirteen) constituted a Jewish community (*minyan*). Every community had to tax itself to provide money for education and charity. Boys had to go to school, and girls could not be denied school. Teachers had to be paid well. All charity had to come from within the community, and had to be provided with dignity. Girls were given dowries to promote marriage and children. Intermarriage was prohibited. Laws of the host country had to be respected, and Jews had to fight in defense of the country in which they lived, even if they had to fight against Jews.

One law, in particular stunned me. Jews had to abandon the idea of reconquering Palestine and of establishing another Jewish state there. It wasn't until the 20th century and political Zionism that Jews took up arms to fight to restore their ancient homeland.

One last note: Dimont mentions that the popular assembly and senate of Jews in Israel and Judah were democratic institutions which predated Greece. The concept of a "president," a charismatic leader whom God would send to unite the twelve tribes in times of trouble, was a natural outgrowth of their system of judges who relied on God to provide centralized leadership. The belief was that God would send leaders for specific purposes. Take Moses, Deborah, and Noah, for example. They were "deliverers" of the people who arrived for a specific crisis. When the crisis was over, the deliverer would leave, and the people would wait for another to arrive for the next crisis. You can see that the concept of a "messiah" sent to deliver us from evil, is very much congruent with Jewish history and beliefs.

CHRISTIANITY, SPAIN, AND THE ARABS

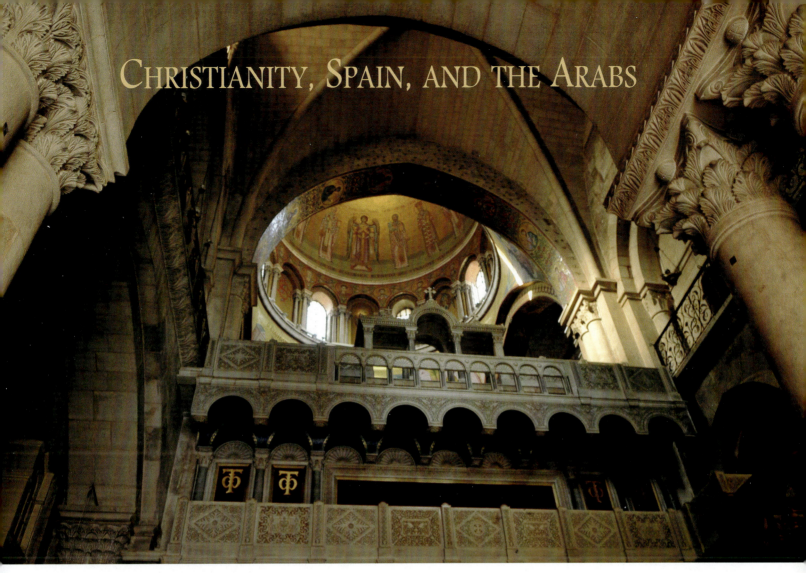

Figure 59: Church of the Holy Sepulcher within the walled Old City of Jerusalem on the purported site of the resurrection of Jesus. Construction began under Roman Emperor Constantine in the year 325. (Photo courtesy of Dr. Barry Kiracofe)

Christianity first arose as a reform movement within Judaism, and spread through the primarily urban Jewish communities of the Roman Empire. It grew significantly among the pagan population when it was made easier to convert; mainly by dropping Jewish dietary laws and the requirement for circumcision. Lynn Nelson, Professor of Medieval History at the University of Kansas tells us that the early Christians steered clear of the Roman government, creating overseers (bishops) of their own communities instead. Early Christian enclaves communicated with one another through letters (epistles), held secret meetings (councils) and kept records of the faith through secret books (bibles). Early Christians were intolerant of other faiths, believing that Jesus was the only saviour and the only way to God. The Roman majority (primarily rural, traditional people who tended to cling to old ways), resented the Jews, whom they considered isolationist intellectual elites. The "pagans" (as the rural Romans came to be known), became increasingly hostile toward the aggressively proselytizing Christian sect, as well.

What started as mob violence and stonings gradually evolved into statewide persecution of both the Christians and Jews. Then, in 313 AD a Roman general named Constantine, using a Christian symbol as his banner, gained control of the Empire and decreed that Christianity would be lawful, but that Christians were to have nothing to do with the Jews. Marriage between a Jew and a Christian, for example, was punishable by death. In 325 AD Emperor Constantine set about unifying the Christians by calling a council of bishops (Church Council of Nicaea) which sifted through the many gospels, and kept only those in line with their formula for the Christian faith (the Nicene Creed). Those texts became part of the list of books of the New Testament or the Bible, while all others were banned. Finding it increasingly difficult to rule the vast Roman Empire from Rome, Constantine moved the seat of government to the shores of the Bosphorus where it became known as Konstantinoupolis (city of Constantine), or Constantinople. When Theodosius became emperor in the late 4th century, Christianity became the official religion of the Roman Empire.

At that time, the empire was facing another huge threat. The "warriors on horseback" known as the Huns had been squeezed out of China and were squatting in north India, southern Russia and the Balkans. Unfortunately for Rome, East Germanic tribes known as Goths and Vandals, who had been living in those lands, were forced to flee across the Danube and invade the Roman Empire. These invasions weakened the empire so much that when Emperor Theodosius died in 395 AD, the empire was split in two. Theodosius' son Arcadius moved to Constantinople, making it the capital of his Eastern Roman Empire (also known as Byzantium), while the other son Honorius took the western part of the Roman Empire, keeping Rome as his capital.

The Goths, many of whom converted to Christianity, continued to invade the Western Roman Empire throughout the 4th century and sacked Rome in the 5th. But the Huns, by then a huge military machine riding under the banner of Attila, were right on their heels. When the Huns got as far as France, the Goths and Vandals came to Europe's defense and in 451 AD stopped the Huns. Attila fell back to Italy where he suddenly died. I've heard it said that the Goths and Vandals essentially prevented Europe from becoming an Asian colony under the Huns. But in doing so, they also condemned it to centuries of medieval feudalism; under the Christians, Europe would descend into the gloom of the Dark Ages which would last more than 500 years.

> "BEHIND THE ROMAN ARMIES CARRYING THE IMPERIAL EAGLES MARCHED THE JEWS CARRYING THE BANNERS OF FREE ENTERPRISE." - MAX DIMONT

JEWS AFTER THE FALL OF ROME

When Rome fell in the 5th century, the Jews found themselves to be very little fish afloat in a sea of three giant civilizations, Byzantium, Islam, and Feudal Europe.

Remember when I said we were on the trail of my ancestors to find out how they got to Spain in the first place? That trail just warmed up. That's because we know that the Jews throughout history moved when they were forced to move, either because they couldn't make a living where they were, they were re-settled prisoners, or they were fleeing persecution. They fled slavery in Egypt, were resettled by Babylon and Persia, were forced out of Jerusalem by the Parthians. The Jews followed the Romans into Europe as traders; Italy in the 2nd century BCE, France in the 1st century BCE, and Spain at the dawn of the 1st century AD, each time taking advantage of new markets for trade and commerce. The question for Jews in the 5th century would be the same as it had always been, where could they go this time to be safe?

The one thing I know for sure about my Jewish ancestry - the one irrefutable fact regarding where my ancestors had been - is that my mother and her mother spoke Ladino, the language spoken in Spain at the time of the Inquisition in 1492. The question is, when did they go to Spain?

It's possible my ancestors followed Rome's conquests into Spain in the 1st century AD. In that case, they would have settled mostly in the east and south, and in the Balearic Islands. If they had remained in Spain after the fall of Rome 400 years later, they would have been subjected to almost a thousand years of Christian persecution under the Visigoths. That doesn't seem likely.

Christian Europe also seems unlikely. After all, it was repression on steroids. The new faith spread like a blanket over Europe, suffocating every population it covered with ignorance, fear and intolerance. Illiteracy and stubborn anti-intellectualism would soon swallow up Spain, France, Germany, Italy, and England. And Europe would remain in the Dark Ages until the 1400's. Jews were actually the only minority to *not* be exterminated in the Middle Ages in Europe, primarily because Christian doctrine required the presence of Jews for the second apparition of Christ to occur. Still, Europe was no place for Jewish families who had been pursuing a serious intellectual path toward enlightenment.

Returning to Palestine where the Byzantine Empire was at war with the Sassanids would have been dangerous. For many Jews, the only choice was to head eastward to a place where their co-religionists seemed to be doing pretty well; the land of the Arabs. If that is the case, it is possible that the Jews in my family made their way to Spain on the coattails of the Muslims.

THE ARABS

We know that by the time of the Prophet Mohammad (peace be upon him), the Jews had been engaged in commerce in Arabia for many years. Their book, the Old Testament, was familiar to the Arabs, including the prophet himself, who spent many hours talking to Jewish traders along the caravan routes about their faith and prophets. The Muslims were comfortable with the Jews whom they considered people of the Book (*Ahl al-Kitab*) who also recognized the God of Abraham as the one and only God. Similar to Muslims, Jews followed a revealed scripture, were devoted to their families and to education. The Jews had no sexualized rituals or idols which would have been offensive to Arab culture. The commerce-savvy Jews helped the coastal Arabs build villages into cities, founded the city of Medina, and gave Mecca a more "cosmopolitan" flair. The Jews also joined the Arabs in war, helping to defeat their common enemy, the invading Christian armies. Soon after the Prophet's death in 622 AD, both the mighty Roman and Persian Empires also fell to them.

The Jews flourished in the Arab world. During its formative years the Arab empire was a wonderfully fertile environment for intellectual discourse, scientific research and innovation. It became a repository of knowledge for fields as widespread as philosophy, mathematics, medicine, architecture, and agriculture. And Muslim principles of equality and fraternity enabled non-Arabs, even conquered races, to take part in government as well.

But you're asking, what does this have to do with Spain? Well, while the Arabs and people in North Africa were prospering under the Umayyad Muslims, the people up north in neighboring Spain were suffering under the tyranny of the Gothic king, Roderick, (Rodrigo). Spanish farmers and peasantry (both Christians and Jews) were moving in huge numbers to the Arab Maghreb (northwest Africa) to escape the heavy taxes and constant harassment by their hated king. A ruler in North Africa named Count Julian sought Umayyad help to overthrow Roderick, the Muslims obliged. In May 711 A.D., Governor of Tangiers and former Berber slave *Tariq bin Ziyad* crossed the strait between Morocco and Spain with a Moorish army of 7,000. They landed on a hill which took his name "Rock of Tariq" (*Jabal-ul-Tariq* or Gibraltar). The Umayyads routed the Gothic forces in 711, A.D. and Spain and Portugal quickly fell into Muslim hands, becoming the biggest European territory the Muslims would ever hold.

It didn't much matter if my ancestors were already in Spain or if they accompanied the Arab conquerors. In either case, the Jews of Spain welcomed the Muslims with open arms. For eight centuries the Muslims in Iberia held a bright torch of learning and civilization that dispelled the gloom that had enveloped Medieval Europe.

Figure 60: In Moorish Spain, Visigoth churches were converted into masterpieces of Umayyad style Muslim architecture. Here is the Great Mosque of Córdoba (Mezquita-Catedral) (784 AD).

Even though the Moors conquered almost the entire Iberian Peninsula (except for the Kingdom of Asturias in the North), the Visigoths never stopped resisting the "occupation." By 722, the Reconquista (re-conquest) began to succeed and the Muslims were eventually pushed back to southern Spain, which they called *Al-Andalus*. The Muslims and Jews lived mainly in the Andalusian cities of Córdoba, Grenada and Sevilla until 1492, when they finally surrendered the region to the Catholic monarchs King Ferdinand and Queen Isabella and were expelled.

But during those 800 years under Arab rule, Spain reached a height of incredible prosperity. They covered the land with palaces, mosques, hospitals, and bridges. Enormous aqueducts with lofty arches swept across valleys and through mountains. The Arabs created huge irrigation projects and imported tropical fruits and vegetables from their homelands. They mined precious metals and manufactured silks, cottons, and

wool which they shipped to Constantinople. The fabulous goods from Spain were then diffused throughout Medieval Christendom. I love how William Winwood Reade described it:

> "At a time when books were so rare in Europe that the man who possessed one often gave it to a church, and placed it on the altar *pro remedio animae suae*, to obtain remission of his sins; at a time when three or four hundred parchment scrolls were considered a magnificent endowment for the richest monastery; when scarcely a priest in England could translate Latin into his mother tongue; and when even in Italy a monk who had picked up a smattering of mathematics was looked upon as a magician, here was a country in which every child was taught to read and write; in which every town possessed a public library; in which book collecting was a mania; in which cotton and afterwards linen-paper was manufactured in enormous quantities; in which ladies earned distinction as poets and grammarians, and in which even the blind were often scholars; in which men of science were making chemical experiments, using astrolabes in the observatory, inventing flying machines, studying the astronomy and algebra of Hindustan."

But the Arabs were not exactly liberators. Expressions of Judaism took a back seat to the exciting developments in Arab culture. Just as Jews in Palestine became Hellenized under the Greeks, the Jewish minority in Andalusia gradually became more and more "Arabized." Arab poetry, music and culture filtered out to both the Jewish and Christian communities. My friend *Roufat Esquenazi* once showed me how the typical Arab musical scale of A-minor can still be heard in the Flamenco music of Spain, and in the Sephardic synagogues of the world as well. To the untrained ear, a Sephardic Hazan's recitation of the Torah sounds much like an Imam reciting the *Kuran* (Qur'an).

By the way, when the Italians began to navigate the Mediterranean, a line of ports was opened to them on Spain's eastern shores. This Italian sea connection would be important to Spanish (Sephardic) Jews fleeing the Inquisition and making their way to the Balkans by way of Italy.

A "Sephardic Civilization"

There are clearly cultural differences between Ashkenazi Jews from Europe and Sephardic Jews from Spain. While the Jews of Europe persevered through the Dark Ages, the Jews in Spain were basking in the warm light of enlightenment. The Arab quest for knowledge threw open the doors for Jews to study their own history, and Córdoba became an important hub for Jewish scholars. As they came from the east and North Africa a uniquely "Sephardic" culture began to take shape; an Arab/Muslim/Spanish Judaism different from the rest of the world's Jewish communities.

As I firmly believe, the similarities between Jews and Muslims far outweigh the differences. I have been admonished by friends and family for refusing to choose Islam over Judaism or vice versa, as if the two are polar opposites. But there are many examples of religious people who have successfully merged these two cultures and religions. *Samuel ha-Levi ibn Nagrella ha-Naqid* (father of Jewish secular poetry in the Middle-Ages), for one, was able to integrate Islam into Judaism without abandoning the principles of Jewish religious traditions. He was prominent in the court of Granada as both *Vizier* (deputy to the Caliph) and *Nagid* (leader of the Spanish Jewish community). In the 10th century, many Jews played a prominent role in the Jewish diaspora while at the same time attaining social prestige, cultural leadership and economic power in the small Muslim kingdoms of Andalusia.

Reconquista

Not all Jews felt safe with the Arabs. When the zealous North African Almoravids seized control of southern Spain, many Jews fled north to the relative safety and protection of the Christian kings. They enjoyed equal treatment under Alfonso VI and many thousands fought with the Christians against the Muslims. Regrettably, when the Arabs defeated Alfonso VI in 1108, anti-Jewish riots broke out in Toledo, and many Jews, with no king to protect them, were slain by disgruntled Christians.

It can be said that during the 12th and 13th centuries Jews in Christian Spain benefitted from the Christian re-conquest of Moorish Andalusia. Christian kings protected Jews who lived in walled communities near the royal palace. The key to the main entrance gate to these communities, the *Puerta do los Judios*, would be ceremoniously offered to the king as a symbol of the Jews relinquishing their autonomy in exchange for his protection. Thus the practice of a visiting dignitary being given the "key to the city."

As the Christians regained territory and the Muslims receded, Jews were encouraged to populate the re-conquered towns in the south, including Mallorca, Valencia, Córdoba and Seville. Mosques were converted to synagogues, and Jews were given farms, vineyards, orchards and estates. Jews in the cities worked in many trades, as weavers, cobblers, chemists, butchers, silversmiths, doctors, shopkeepers, grocers, jewelers. Women, however, were mostly restricted to jobs which kept them out of the public eye, especially the Christian public. They were mostly weavers, midwives and laundresses.

Jews were also the majority of financiers and tax collectors, and often served in high positions in the Royal Court. The stereotype that Jews are adept money handlers can be attributed to the fact that in medieval Europe, many governments actually restricted money handling and lending to Jews and Arabs, believing the practices to be inappropriate for Christians. Furthermore, European Jews were subject to expulsion at the whim of the political class. Jews therefore learned to consider themselves resident-aliens in the sense that they needed to develop skills and professions which could be taken up wherever expulsion landed them. These professions generally provided scarce and valuable intellectual talents and skills, such as teachers, doctors, lawyers, accountants and money lenders.

Money-handling, tax collecting and intellectual skills often gained favor with political power holders, which meant protection and security for the Jewish community. But these professions also drew enmity from enemies of the regime and made Jews obvious targets if the regime were overthrown. Thus, for much of European history, it was dangerous for Jews to appear prosperous. The need to flee at a moment's notice also made it a bad idea to invest in immovable things (land, factories), and more sensible to have in gold or jewelry which could be taken with you. Dealing with money was a trade, and was handed down through generations of a family dynasty, as so many other trades are. Once the trade was learned, it became the family inheritance.

JEWISH GHETTOS AND SEPHARDIC CULTURE

Inexplicably, as late as the mid 1490's some Sephardim were still celebrating the Christian conquest of Granada and liberation from Muslim rule. Some even took part in festivals where the prophet Muhammad was burned in effigy. They told themselves that they were better off than Jews in Europe, and ignored the signs of a distinct shift in official policy toward them and other non-Christians. Anti-Judaism incited by the Catholic clergy began to spread, and the engine of bigotry began to pick up steam.

In large cities with significant Jewish populations, officials dictated where Jews could and could not live. Jewish quarters called *Judería* specifically isolated Jews from Christians. In 1412 the vicious Queen-regent Catherine (Dona Catalina) ordered that the *Puerta de los Judios*, the only gate to the Jewish quarters, could only be used by Jews and Muslims. Even windows and doors of Jewish houses had to face the perimeter wall so that they couldn't be seen from Christian areas.

For a while, life in the *Juderia* felt fairly normal. Aside from a mezuzah placed above the door, the houses within the walls were much like typical Muslim and Christian middle class courtyard houses, with lush gardens, marble terraces and fountains. But because Christian and Jewish communities lived separately, their shared public institutions began to adopt segregated policies. Public baths had separate days for each community; Friday and Saturday allocated to the Jews, with one day for women, the other for men.

Christians began to resent sharing the public baking ovens with Jews who had specific requirements for leavening. Butcher shops became more segregated, and those which practiced *Shechita* and *Dhabiha* slaughtering techniques (see box), were considered "the dirtiest of the dirty." In some cases Christians who sold Jewish meat were punished.

Jews were made to wear special clothes and hairstyles to prevent co-mingling between the Jewish and Christian populations. Jewish women at that time had been wearing make-up and adorning themselves with strings of pearls across their foreheads, decorative headdresses, silk cloth with long trains, enameled brooches, and gold rings with gemstones. Even men were in the habit of wearing a ring on every finger. But now Jewish women were told to wear long mantles down to their feet and folded over to cover their heads like the Muslim women did. In the male-dominated society of medieval Spain the status of Sephardic women was already much more in line with that of Muslim women than Christian. Women were in a secondary position; less educated, confined mostly

RELIGIOUS LAWS ON BUTCHERING MEAT

Both Jews and Muslims discern between "clean and unclean" meat. Only certain meats are permissible. Animals with parted hoofs, (cloven footed), and that chew cud are permitted for consumption. (A camel chews cud but is forbidden because its hoof is not parted. Pigs have cloven feet but don't chew cud, so they too are unclean.)

The way an animal is slaughtered is also strictly observed in both faiths. "*Dhabiha*" the Islamic method and "*Shechita*" method based on Jewish law are similar in many ways. *Shechita* requires that an animal be conscious at slaughter; so electrical stunning before slaughter is forbidden. Muslims also forbid the use of electrical stunning. Both require the animals neck be cut across with a non-serrated blade in one clean cut to sever the main vessels. The spinal cord must be avoided during slaughter. Both require draining the blood. Also, any sane adult Jew who knows the proper technique can perform *Shechita*. Similarly, *Dhabiha* can be performed by any adult sane Muslim who first says *Bismillahu Allahu Akbar* (in the name of Allah, Allah is Great). Some Islamic authorities allow *Dhabiha* to be performed by Jews.

Today there is plenty of evidence that any slaughtering method that reduces stress on the animal and kills it swiftly is not only more humane but also healthier, since the meat contains fewer stress-induced chemicals and hormones.

to the home and seated separately from their men in the temple, a practice that is still found in Sephardic synagogues around the world.

In fact, Sephardic Jews have customs much more akin to Muslim customs than modern Ashkenazi. Personally, I like that our synagogue still separates the men and women. I get to catch up with my female relatives and friends, while my husband does the same with the men. And, as is the custom, when he goes up to read the Torah, I stand as well. It's a beautiful thing, really, when a man's family stands for him as he reads in front of the congregation. (I also like sitting separately from him because poor Bruce is sort of tone deaf when he recites Hebrew so it's actually a blessing that he's sitting way over there.)

SEPHARDIC FAMILY

Until very recently Sephardic marriages in Turkey were still arranged as they were in 15th century Spain. Girls began to collect their trousseaus from a very early age. Brides were contractually obligated to be virgins. The couple's roles were very specific; he would work and provide, she would keep the home. Man and wife were expected to relate to one another in ways that nurtured the marriage. A mother would teach her daughter not to irritate her husband, or be critical of his lovemaking. She was taught to speak softly to calm her husband's anger, cook his favorite foods and pretend to love him as much as he does her. A wife was never to get drunk. She was to keep his confidence, obey his orders, not be jealous, and not ask for things that were difficult for him to give.

Though I fought it tooth and nail, traditional values were drilled into me. Of course my mother was a free-spirit who couldn't care less about what society expected. But almost everyone else, on both sides of my family's religious divide, had the old-world belief that marriage was crucial. An adult without a spouse and children could have no status in the community. In a society where personal relationships, especially kinships, made the world go 'round, unmarried adults were pitied if they were women, and viewed suspiciously if they were men. People did whatever they could to get married and build a solid family.

Society was committed to keeping marriages together. A boy was taught to read the Torah, to learn a trade, and to lead his family. A girl was taught subservience, not to oppress her, but to ensure her successful marriage and happy home life. Weddings were solemn occasions where the entire community promised to help a young couple stay together. The typical arrangement of several generations living in the same house may have evolved out of necessity, but its by-product, the passing of wisdom and social skills from one generation to the next, was critical to preserving family harmony. Parents and in-laws got into their kids "business," not only to console and advise, but even to threaten their children to stay together for the sake of family honor and survival. Is it any surprise that in Turkish there is a word for the unique relationship between the couple's parents, but no such word exists in English? By the way, the word does exist in Yiddish; *Machuten* is the father of your child's spouse, *Mechetayneste* is the mother.

RAISED IN A TRADITIONAL WORLD

Even though my cousins and siblings were raised here in America, we had to sit through countless hours of advice concerning how to make a successful marriage. My Tant Ida, for example, said that it was important

that I not be more educated than my future husband for fear that he might be threatened. I was also told I must never marry a younger man because I needed to be pretty for him in later years so he wouldn't stray. Any "girl" things I did, like cooking and sewing were rewarded with smiles and approval, while skills like being able to sink a three-pointer from half-court were dismissed with worried glances. As a young adult I was constantly reminded to wear lipstick and make myself more appealing. I definitely caught hell in the 70's during my bra-less phase. And though my education was certainly a source of pride for my parents, they worried it would reduce my marriageability quotient.

My mother Beti, a very independent woman, told me that we women had to "work the system." She counseled me to feign a subservient role to keep the peace. I can see her standing by the kitchen door modeling the correct behavior. "Yes dear, yes my Pasha" she'd say as she mimed patting a husband on the back as he left the house to go off to work. Then she would kick the invisible man in the seat of his invisible pants. Slamming the door, she would turn to me and "Would it kill you to do this? It makes him happy!"

Granted, my mother had issues. But it's not as if anyone thought women were weak; it was kind of understood that women needed to protect the fragile egos of their men. In return, women got a secure home to raise children, and a man could always feel like a man. *Macho* is not a derogatory term in Sephardic culture. Clearly, no woman wanted to be married to a wimp. Yes, today women can get high-paying jobs and support a family, but there was a time not that long ago when a woman who wanted a strong, secure family needed a strong, hard-working, responsible, educated, and most of all, kind man. Bruce will tell you that this is exactly the kind of husband he is. And one thing Beti was right about; Jewish men make the best husbands.

And two pieces of advice I received about marriage are brilliant and noteworthy. One, never go to bed angry. Talk it out, even if you're exhausted, so that you can wake up happy. Two, always have respect for your partner. "Respect!" Ida would say, with her finger held high in the air. She likens marriage to a room surrounded by curtains. If you say something disrespectful, it's like pulling a curtain back and seeing what's behind it. Once you've seen what's back there, you cannot close that curtain again. You'll always remember what you saw, and something in your relationship will have died. So always have respect.

Now, let's get back to Spain.

SPANISH RECONQUISTA AND INQUISITION

SPAIN 1300

Figure 61: The Reconquista of Christian Spain left only Granada in Muslim hands by the 14th century.

In the beginning of the 14th century, the small southern region of Granada was the last remnant of Muslim Spain. Intolerance of all things non-Christian, and open hostility toward Jews especially, were commonplace. In large cities violent mobs attacked the residents of the *Juderías*. Pogroms in 1391 were especially bloody: hundreds of Jews were killed, synagogues were destroyed.

By 1391 up to half of the 600,000 Jews in Spain were baptized as part of the mass conversion of Jews and Muslims alike. A new social group called *Conversos*, (converts or New Christians) was established. And among them were people who continued to practice their religion secretly while publicly professing to be Christian. The Crypto-Muslims were called *Moriscos* (from the word Moors) while the Crypto-Jews were known as *Marranos* (Spanish for pigs).

The Catholic monarchs of Spain, Ferdinand II of Aragon and Isabella I of Castile publicly held that Crypto-Judaism was a serious threat to the religious and social life of Spain. However, it is widely believed that their real reason for seeking out and expelling non-Christians was to confiscate their property and wealth. In either case, the monarchs decided that the Iberian Peninsula needed to be "ethnically cleansed."

This belief was shared by Isabella's confessor and adviser Tomas de Torquemada. Torquemada, the Grand Inquisitor, whose own grandmother was a Jewish convert, established tribunals to expose the *Marranos* and *Moriscos*, and determine their crimes of heresy, sorcery, sodomy, polygamy, blasphemy, and usury.

Torquemada literally "wrote the book" on how to torture people to get them to admit that they were not really Christian; methods which included both the "water cure" (now sardonically referred to as the "enhanced interrogation technique" of water-boarding), and burning at the stake. So grotesque were Tomas de Torquemada's methods that his name has since become synonymous with horror and cruel fanaticism.

THE EXPULSION EDICT OR ALHAMBRA DECREE

On March 31, 1492 Ferdinand and Isabella issued the Alhambra Decree expelling all non-Christians from their dominions. The edict to expel the Jews had an almost apologetic tone, as if the monarchs were themselves victims. They claimed that their early attempts to isolate the Jews had failed, and that after 12 years of inquisitions the Jews were still doing "great harm" to the Christians. They claimed that even by conversing with Jews, Christians were being subverted and drawn away from their holy Catholic faith, pressured to circumcise their children or read prayer books that dishonored the holy Catholic faith. The Jews were therefore to be punished for spreading their "contagion." The monarchs ordered all non-Christians to leave Spain within three months. They could take all their possessions, except gold, silver and money. And they could never come back.

It was an incredibly sorrowful time. A time of mourning with tears, hair-shirts, and ashes. Passover in 1492 was no doubt a bitter reminder of another time when Jews fled their homeland for an uncertain future.

Jews and Muslims had only three months to sell their properties (for a fraction of their worth) and exchange their money, (at exorbitant rates). Priorities shifted; a house was sold for a mule, a vineyard for a little cloth. Gold and silver coins were sterilized and then swallowed; carried in the bellies of women passing checkpoints. (Each person was advised to swallow only 30 coins at a time. Can you imagine swallowing a single quarter? Just one quarter?)

It's hard to imagine how sad it is for people, any people, to be forced from their homeland. They left on foot, on mules, donkeys, and in carts, along roads and through fields toward Portugal or the ports. Some fell ill, some died. In the novel *Farewell Homeland*, Fuat Andic describes the feelings of a Jewish Doctor in Granada who is taking stock of what he left behind in Spain. He writes:

Figure 62: Beyazit II Mosque, Istanbul. (Photo courtesy of Dr. Barry Kiracofe)

BEYAZIT'S WELCOME

"But it wasn't just his beloved books that he had abandoned; he also left behind his garden full of pomegranate, fig, pear, and apricot trees; the marble sprouting fresh water that came from the Sierra Nevada; and the white and purple lilac trees around the fountain. Within the house, he had left behind the silver candelabras, the rooms covered with carpets woven In Fez and the curtains woven in Damascus. He would miss more acutely still the voices of his friends who gathered in the house every Saturday night to discuss philosophy and poetry; the monthly gathering of musicians in his garden; the snow-capped mountains that looked like a sea of molten gold when they reflected the red and golden rays of the rising sun; the sound of his wife's footsteps; the laughter of his children running in the corridors; his patients; the graves of his parents and of their parents before them."

When the last Jews left Spain in 1492, many thousands fled to Portugal, the Netherlands, Italy, North Africa and the New World. But the biggest lot, about 150,000, went to the Ottoman Empire, by way of invitation from the Sultan himself. Sultan Beyazit II reasoned that the Sephardic Jews were the *crème de la crème* of Spanish society and would bring to his empire something much more precious than the material wealth they left behind. They had an impressive collective knowledge of science and the arts, as well as creativity and insatiable curiosity. Surely an influx of so much talent would be like a shot of adrenaline into the Ottoman body. Sultan Beyazit's official decree inviting the Jews ridiculed the Spanish monarch; *"It is said that King Ferdinand is a wise man. He is not wise at all. Let us bring to our land every Jew who wants to come. Spain's loss is our gain."*

Convoys of Ottoman ships picked up desperate Sephardic refugees stranded at Spain's ports and brought them aboard their vessels under Ottoman protection. The refugees were taken to Constantinople, Izmir, and Salonika where they were re-settled. It had been more than 60 years since the Ottomans had ransacked the Greek port city of Salonika, and it now stood as a "beacon on the hill" to an entirely new population.

It's interesting to note that just a few days after decreeing the expulsion of the Jews, Isabella's favorite explorer Christopher Columbus sailed out with three ships to discover a new route to Asia. His voyage was financed by the confiscated wealth of the Jews driven from Spain. Also, interesting is that the Christian King of Bohemia invited Sephardic Jews to come to Prague after 1492 where he had built for them what is today the oldest surviving Synagogue in Europe.

The Sephardim were not the only Jews coming to the Ottoman Empire. At least 50,000 Romaniot, Karaite and Ashkenazi Jews were already living there. Jews had also followed Alp Arslan to Anatolia following the collapse of the Khazar Jewish communities which had existed in the south-east since ancient times. Jewish families had also been living in Salonika throughout the Byzantine era, as well. There were Greek-speaking Jews still there from Byzantine Constantinople, and Anatolian Muslim Turks who had only recently been re-settled there after Mehmet II conquered Constantinople in 1453. When Portugal exiled its Jewish population in 1497, a large majority of them also found refuge in the Ottoman Empire. European Jews fleeing the ghettos in Northern Spain, Portugal, Venice, Sicily, and Genoa had also arrived. In 1501 Jews from France arrived. The migration would last several decades.

LIVING UNDER OTTOMAN RULE

Most of my Jewish relatives feel indebted to the Ottoman Empire for protecting the Jews, starting with Beyazit II. He was right. Jews did make a terrific contribution to his empire. They served the Sublime Porte as diplomats to Europe and brought significant technological innovations to the empire, including the first printing press. But the sultan's position was not necessarily a pro-Jewish one. The Ottoman millet system was based on the idea that all minorities within the empire could rule themselves with very little interference from the Ottoman government. All that was required was that they remain loyal to the empire.

Figure 64: Map of the Crimean Peninsula and Bulgaria. My grandmother's family left Sofya (as it was called by the Ottomans), in the early 1900's and made their way to the Ottoman capitol Constantinople.

When my mother's ancestors left Spain, they made their way to the Balkans. We know this because my Granmama *Sara Gerşon* was actually born in Sofya, Bulgaria. It is my belief that, like many Sephardim, they first travelled to Italy, and then, after the subsequent expulsion from Venice in 1550, continued north to the Crimea and Balkans.

JEWISH LIFE IN THE BALKANS

The Crimean Peninsula has a mixed history when it comes to its Jewish populations, and there is even disagreement within my family about when my grandmother's family actually arrived there. No doubt there were other Jews who had been there as early as the 10th century; Ashkenazim, Sephardim, Mizrahim and indigenous Krymchak Jews in the Crimea. Also in the early mix were Jews from the Caucasus and from the Italian colonies settled by maritime republics Genoa and Venice.

In the 15th century, Crimea was the western-most post of the Silk Road for trade between Asia, the Mediterranean, and the West. Everybody wanted to control it. In 1475, as things were heating up for my family in Spain, the Ottomans conquered the southern coast of Crimea and made its Tatar Khanate a protectorate of the Ottoman Empire.

Figure 63: Istanbul Skyline (Photo courtesy of Dr. Barry Kiracofe)

It was a powerful and productive alliance which enabled the Tatars to manage a massive slave trade with the Ottoman Empire and the Middle East for 150 years. Some 3 million Slavic people (typically blonde haired, blue-eyed) were captured, one of the most famous being Roxelana (*Hürrem Sultan*), the future wife of Süleyman the Magnificent. There's one account that in 1650, 300 Jewish pogrom survivors from the Ukraine were captured by Crimean Tatar slave traders and it was the Istanbul Ashkenazi community who paid the ransom to free them. (Again, the pragmatic Jewish law about "being your brother's keeper" was still having significant effect in preserving Judaism.)

Sephardic Jews who settled in the Balkans no doubt mixed with Jews known as Ashkenazim who had been continuously migrating there from Germany since the 11th century Crusades forced them out of Western Europe. The Ashkenazi had escaped to the relatively peaceful Slavic countries and spread their Germanic customs and language (*Yiddish*) among the Romaniot and Karaite Jewish populations already living there.

Another Jewish population living in the area since the 8th century was an independent group of Turkic people, (successors of the *Western Göktürk*, actually) known as the Khazars. They became a Jewish state when their ruler, *Khagan Bulan*, converted to Judaism. The Khazars did not firmly adhere to Judaism and possibly kept Shamanist customs from their Turkic past. I only mention them to discount them as possible ancestors, since we arrived in the Balkans more than 500 years after they disappeared as a distinct people.

At first, the Sephardim arriving from Spain shared precious little in terms of traditions and cultures with the Balkan Jews, and were as foreign to one another as they were to the non-Jewish population. They certainly looked different from one another. The 19th century historian Konstantin Irecek noted that Bulgarian Jews were "mostly fair-haired, a temperate, modest, industrious and kindly people" who, like the general population, wore standard European dress and the fur cap. The newly arriving "*Espanoles*" were darker in complexion and hair color, and "arrived wearing the fez and Turkish ankle-length padded jacket."

There is little doubt that my grandmother's family did mix with Balkan Jews, because her family members were tall, with broad bones, fair skin and blue eyes. I'd even guess that it was the women who married non-Sephardic Jews. As Tant Ida always said, Jewishness is passed down by the mother. Clearly Spanish customs, language and especially foods would most likely have been passed down from mother to daughter.

We know that my Grandmother's family (the *Gerşons*) lived in the Balkans for more than three hundred years. We also know that my grandmother arrived in Constantinople in the early 1900's. What made them leave Bulgaria? Nothing in the oral histories gives a clue. Perhaps a look at what was happening politically could shed some light.

BALKAN NATIONALISM AND SLAVISM

In 1853, Russia had attempted to claim Ottoman territory in the Crimea and was stopped by an alliance of the French, British, and Ottoman empires. Revenge for this Crimean War (as it was known) became Russia's main foreign policy goal. So Russia backed the nationalist movement in Bulgaria, hoping that if the Balkans could be freed from Ottoman rule, Russia could maintain her fleet in the Black Sea. The Slavic Christian people of the Balkans did ultimately free themselves from the Turks by winning the Russo-Turkish War of 1877–1878, and after almost five centuries of Ottoman domination, the Bulgarian state was re-established with a Christian government and its own army.

The Ottoman troops were supposed to pull out of Bulgaria, while a Russian military occupation force was to come in. Unfortunately for Russia, the European Great Powers and the Ottoman Empire met in Berlin in1878 to reorganize the countries of the Balkans. Unbelievably, the resulting Treaty effectively disavowed Russia's recent victory the Russo-Turkish War and, among other things, took Macedonia from Bulgaria and gave it back to the Turks. Why? Because they wanted to deal a fatal blow to the burgeoning movement of "pan-Slavism." Just stay with me on this for a minute.

London and Paris were nervous that if the decaying Ottoman Empire got too weak, Russia would be able to expand to the south, where both Britain and France were poised to colonize Egypt and Palestine. An autonomous Bulgaria, along with Macedonia, could have given Russia access to the Bosphorus Straits which separate the Black Sea from the Mediterranean. The British Empire considered Russian access to the Mediterranean a grave threat to its power.

Even before the Treaty of Berlin, the British Prime Minister (and Sephardic Jew) Benjamin Disraeli had signed a secret alliance with the Ottomans against Russia. Britain would occupy the strategically located island of Cyprus. In exchange Disraeli would threaten war on Russia unless Russia complied with the Ottoman demands. Can you believe that?

BULGARIAN JEWS CAUGHT IN THE MIDDLE

Not everyone in the Balkans had wanted to be free of the Ottomans; most of all the Bulgarian Jews. My grandmother's family (the *Gerşon's*) were living in Sofya and like most Jews, had remained patriotic and ever-loyal to their benefactors, the Ottoman Empire. In fact, the family found their niche selling supplies to the Turkish military, providing brushes that the Ottoman army used to clean tents and groom horses. The *Gerşon* family had apparently amassed considerable wealth in the endeavor. Unfortunately, Bulgarians who had been loyal to the Ottomans were now considered "the enemy." And since most Bulgarian political parties were already steeped in anti-Semitism, treaties meant to secure equal rights for minorities did little to keep the Bulgarian government from introducing anti-Jewish legislation. The Bulgarian peasantry also resented the Jews and prevented them from buying land. From time to time there were blood libels.

Turkish rule over Christian Bulgaria eventually gave rise to protests which were brutally put down by the poorly organized and undisciplined Turkish irregular forces known as the *Başı Bozuk*. Worldwide condemnation of the atrocities committed by the *Başı Bozuk* fueled the insurrection so that when the Turks retreated from Sofya in 1878, general rioting, robbery, and arson broke out. The Jews had to form their own militias and fire brigades to prevent Christians from setting fire to their towns. Even Rabbinic appeals to the Russians for protection were not enough to prevent the looting of Jewish property in places like Vidin, Kazanlik, and Svishtov, where the local population regarded Jews as supporters of the Turks.

Many Jews were forced out and most of them, including my grandmother's family, fled to Adrianople and Constantinople. Luckily, the *Gerşons* left Bulgaria a decade before the national uprising in 1923. Anti-Semitism in Bulgaria continued to intensify through World War II when anti-Semitic nationalist associations structured on the lines of Hitlerite organizations sprang up.

Cuisine as Tradition

Traditional Judeo-Spanish cuisine has been handed down through perhaps fifty generations of my family since the Spanish Inquisition. Each generation has no doubt modified the recipes to accommodate the particularities of whichever country it occupied. Much like words from the myriad languages my family will parse together to construct the perfect sentence, ingredients were added, deleted or modified to best suit the local climate, produce, culture, religion, and even available technology of the region. The Passover Haroseth is a good example, since it is slightly different among Sephardic Jews in Turkey, Morocco, Israel, Iran, and Egypt. The Haroseth with dates, sultanas and walnuts found at the Seder table in Cairo is very different from the Afghan version containing apples, raisins, and bananas. The hazelnuts in Moroccan haroseth are not found in the Greek or Turkish versions. (You can find the Turkish Haroset recipe on page 172)

Bulgarian Jewish cuisine bears a strong resemblance to the cooking of Sephardic Jews in Greece and Turkey. The Bulgarian *borekitas*, small pockets of dough filled with savory cheese and spinach or sweet pumpkin and spice, are similar to the Greek *spanakopita* or Turkish *börek*. Greek and Turkish Sephardic cooking is loaded with spinach, peppers, eggplant, and squash, which are also widely used in Bulgaria. The same goes for honey and sugar syrups scented with rosewater over delicious light pastries. Similarly, Bulgaria's *agristada*—a tart egg and lemon sauce—strongly resembles Greek *avgolemono* sauce. The meat dishes of Bulgarian Jewry, however, are not flavored with the sweet spices indigenous to Turkish or Greek cuisine; they contain the onion, garlic, and pepper or pimentos more reflective of their Spanish roots.

Luckily, Jewish women in Turkey found many similarities between their cuisine and that of the Ottoman/Muslim kitchen; the ban on eating pork being the most obvious and most important. Without the pork issue, modification of recipes often involved little more than using vegetable oil rather than butter (dairy), in dishes that contained meat. Jewish cooks might substitute matzo meal for dried bread or bread crumbs during Passover. They would simply not place yogurt (which Ottomans use as a garnish for many meat dishes), on the table. Pretty basic stuff. It's interesting to note that even isolated Muslim communities made similar modifications in cuisine. In Kashmir, for example, there are Muslims who not only refuse to eat milk with meat, they also extend the restriction to include no fish with milk as well.

THE BEN BASSAT AND GERSON FAMILIES

The "oral history" of the Jewish side of my family, meaning history based on actual memories that were told directly to someone with whom I have spoken, begins around 1900 in Sofya, the capitol of Ottoman Bulgaria. A young Sephardic Jewess named *Bulisa Mari Ben Bassat,* my great grandmother, married a man named *Yehuda Leon Gerşon,* and together they had five children; *Buka, Jak, Sara, Elisa,* and *Albert.* The third child, *Sara,* was my grandmother; my mother's mother.

When the youngest son *Albert* was about a year and a half old, tragedy struck. His young mother *Mari* fell ill, and it became clear she would not live long. Laying in her death bed, and fearing for the future of her children, *Mari* sent for her little sister *Bella* (pronounced Beya). Mari told her sister, "You will marry my husband so that my children will not be left alone."

This situation will sound familiar to you because it's the same thing that happened to my father's family on the Black Sea when his mother *Lütfiye* died and her sister took on her role as wife to her husband and mother to her children. Here in Bulgaria, *Mari's* request for sororate was also commonly practiced, especially among the Jews, who forbade marriage outside their a close knit community.

It was not just women who had to marry their sister's husbands; levirate (from the Latin "levir" or "husband's brother") required a man to marry the widow of his dead brother. The arrangement made sense in ancient societies where women never worked outside the home, and a widow (especially one with children), would need immediate support. Who better than the brother of the deceased husband to step in, protect and raise his children? The arrangement is still practiced today, not only if the first wife dies, but sometimes also if she is unable to bear children.

Figure 65:
Granma Sara's sisters Elise and Marie Gerşon visiting Paris. "Affectionate memories from your dear sisters Elise and Marie Gerchon the 27th of April 1923. Note the French spelling of the name, Gerşon.

BELLA'S PROBLEM

Of course arranging marriages is never as simple as it sounds, especially in *Bella's* case. When *Mari* asked (actually instructed) her sister *Bella* to marry her husband, *Bella* was already engaged to, and very much in love with, a young Rabbinical student at the Yeshiva. *Bella* was also much younger then her sister *Mari.* In fact, she was only two years older than *Buka,* the eldest of her sister's children. Can you imagine?

Despite these critical obstacles, the arrangements were made, and when *Mari* died, *Bella Ben Bassat* had no alternative but to accept her familial responsibilities. She broke off her engagement to the young student and became the second Mrs. *Leon Gerşon.* She then moved into her late sister's house and stepped into her new role as mother to her five nieces and nephews.

One can assume that her new husband *Leon* was at least twenty years older than his new bride. It is known that *Bella* showed him the proper respect as her husband and provider, but it is also clear that she never grew to love him. And although *Bella* bore three children of her own with *Leon,* a son *Mordo,* and two daughters *Mari* and *Rejina,* she carried her ex-fiancé's picture with her until the day she died.

I wish I could say that Bella had been a wise and patient woman, but such was not the case. Whether it was the bitterness of having been denied her own husband, or the stress of having to raise five step-children, one can't be sure. What is sure is that Bella Gerşon was an authoritarian woman. There are stories that she treated her sister's children differently from her own. Having been a step-mother myself, I can feel compassion for a woman in Bella's situation. As much as you can love your step-children, it is a different love than the one you feel for your own. In my case it might have been this way because I always saw their biological mother when I looked into their faces, and she had never been particularly nice to me. I like to think that if one of my own sisters had died, *Allah korusun* (God forbid), I would have had much more loving feelings toward their children because of how much I love my sisters. But it's easy to judge. In any event, when I was 17 years old, I did not have five children and a new husband like little Bella did on her wedding day.

The *Gerşon* house in Sofya was obviously very crowded, with children ranging from 1½ to 15 years in age. There was also the issue of a young girl suddenly facing her "wifely" responsibilities with a former brother-in-law. Not a unique situation for the times, but in hindsight almost impossible to imagine. It's also known that the family struggled financially for a time, so the early years were difficult, indeed. But they persevered. Leon got into the hotel business and the family began to amass some wealth. However their relative prosperity would not last long.

By 1912 the only way Bulgaria could pay its debts was to confiscate property and wealth from its most vulnerable minority citizens. The *Gerşons* were among thousands of Jewish families in Bulgaria who had become destitute, and their distress was indescribable. The businesses and hotel which *Leon* and *Bella* had owned were confiscated. The family was no longer permitted to own property and had gone through all their savings trying to survive. In bitter irony, my impoverished great-grandfather *Leon* was ultimately forced to scrape a living by playing violin for tips in the lobby of the very hotel he had once owned.

Rabbis throughout the empire were appealing for assistance and protesting Bulgarian anti-Jewish atrocities. In conformity with the Treaty of Bucharest, whole towns were being reverted to Bulgaria, and were no longer under Ottoman protection. Mob attacks had become the norm, as were protests that Jews were conducting ritual murders of fallen Bulgarian soldiers. Blood libels had returned. The Jews, following the example of the Muslims, Greeks and Armenians, abandoned whatever they had left, and headed for Ottoman or Greek territory. It was time for the *Gerşons* to go.

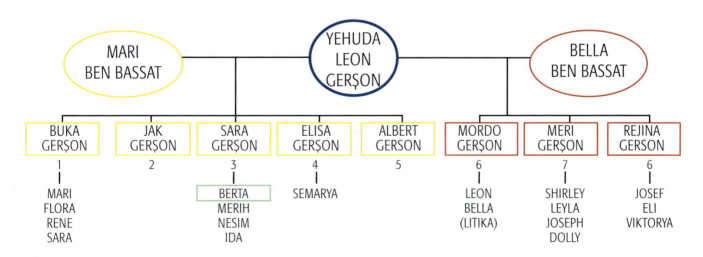

Figure 66: Family Tree - *When my great grandmother Mari Ben Bassat died, her sister Bella married her husband Leon, raised her five children, and had three children of her own. Sara Gerşon was my granmama Sara. Berta Revah was my mother, Beti.*

Leaving Bulgaria for Constantinople

Unable to support the family, *Leon* and his wife Bella took their seven children south, and settled in the Ottoman capitol, Constantinople. Their youngest daughter *Rejina* (Bulisa) was born soon after, in 1913.

The eldest daughter *Buka* (married to her cousin *Buko Ben Bassat*) left Bulgaria with the rest of the family. The couple had also owned a hotel in Sofya which was confiscated. In Constantinople they were able to buy another hotel called the *Çankaya Palas Otel* on Prinkipo(*Büyük Ada*), the very island where my grandfather *Hüseyin* saved the American actress.

Unfortunately *Buko* made the decision to move to Paris. During World War II he was caught by the Nazi's in France, along with his son *Rene's* wife, *Ester*. The two perished in the ovens. Had *Buko* stayed in Turkey, the family would have remained under the protection of the Turkish

Figure 67: Buko (Bohor) Ben Bassat

government which considered Turkish Sephardic Jews full Turkish citizens and refused to turn them over to the Nazi's. As far as I know, *Buko* and *Ester* are the only members of our family to have been sent to concentration camps during World War II.

Bella's family settled in *Sirkeci* and took over a shop and factory in the *Tahtakale Bazaar* District. Can you imagine what it must have been like to start life anew in the capitol of the Ottoman Empire? The children, now young adults, certainly walked through the Grand Bazaar. I like to imagine my grandmother heading downhill along *Uzunçarşı Caddesi*

Figure 68: Prince's Mosque, Istanbul (Photo courtesy of Dr. Barry Kiracofe)

through the *Tahtakale* district to the Golden Horn and the *Mısır Çarşısı* (Spice Bazaar). Who knows how many times she stopped to admire the exquisite *Rüstem Paşa* Mosque, one of Istanbul's finest architectural sites. Then again, women at that time rarely lingered on the streets. They kept their eyes toward the ground and, clutching the arm of their mother or sister, quickly made their way to their destinations. The *Gerşons* would have to work fast to make connections with other Jewish families in order to marry off the daughters while they were still of marriageable age.

FAMILY DYNAMICS

The fact that the *Gerşon* children were so close in age to their aunt/step-mother led to complicated and often painful family dynamics. For example, *Bella* was pregnant with her youngest,

Figure 69: Rejina Gerşon (Alhale) left, and her mother Bella, above.

Rejina at the same time her eldest step-daughter *Buka* was pregnant with her own daughter *Flora*. When the girls were born, *Buka* was said to have occasionally nursed them both; her daughter as well as her half-sister. *Rejina* was only three years old when my granmama Sara gave birth to my mother, *Berta (Beti)*. Aunt and niece grew up together, played together, and shared many happy memories and heartaches. Still, *Rejina* never let *Beti* forget that she was of the elder generation, and *Beti*, in turn, always afforded *Rejina* her due respect.

Rejina Gerşon (whom I knew as *Tant Rejina*) always mourned the fact that she never met her father *Leon*, being only a month old when he died. She often said she never "tasted the meaning of father." She never mentioned how he died and insisted on not talking about him because it was so painful. But *Rejina* always spoke lovingly of her mother *Bella*, whom she adored. Throughout their lives the two consulted intimately with one another almost daily.

Bella had had some sort of accident with a tramway or cable car that ran over her foot, so she walked with a limp. That's how my cousin *Litika* (*Bella's* granddaughter via her son *Mordo*) remembers her. *Litika* (actually named *Bella* after her grandmother) lived with her grandmother when *Bella* came to live with her family in Istanbul. *Litika* insists that in her youth, *Bella* had been a beautiful blonde woman with fair skin and clear blue eyes. But she was an unlucky, sad woman with few friends, who never recovered emotionally from the enormous sacrifices she made for her family.

Clearly unhappy and alone, *Bella* sought solace from the four year old *Litika* who became her grandmother's unwitting confidant. She would listen for hours to *Bella's* laments and regrets. "She would tell me that everyone comes to this world with her own *kismet* (destiny), and that you can't change your *kismet*," *Litika* (now a grown woman living in Israel) tells me. "She always talked about how unhappiness and tragedy seem to haunt a family from one generation to the next. Being unhappy herself, she couldn't help but make everyone around her unhappy, as well." Profoundly affected by her grandmother's depression *Litika* struggles at times to accept her own *kismet*. "I am carrying her name," she says. "And I too have not been happy in my life."

Rejina didn't divulge the truth about how her father had been married to two sisters until her daughter *Viki* was 12 years old. It was a very sore subject and any suggestion that some of the eight siblings might have been treated better than others was quickly dismissed. Still, there did remain in *Bella's* family a certain malaise regarding the right to marry. It's as if you had to feel shame for having what was denied your mother, the right to marry for love.

GRANPAPA KEMAL AND GRANMAMA SARA

The second *Gerşon* daughter, my *Granmama Sara*, was an exceedingly patient and proud woman, with a great deal of dignity. Surely, if her mother had survived, if the family had remained in Bulgaria, if times had been better, she would have married well. Unlike her half-sister *Rejina* who enjoyed the warmth of a loving mother, *Sara* had been very unhappy at home with her step-mother *Bella*. Her situation was made worse when *Granmama Sara* fell in love with someone and *Bella* firmly refused to permit her to marry. Again, the harsh reminder that obligation to family comes before love and happiness. So instead of starting her own life and family, the young *Sara* spent her days in the house doing laundry, which had become the family business. She would sometimes tell *Litika* about how the harsh soap and relentless washing and wringing of the clothes made her hands constantly red and chapped.

A chance for a new life came when the young and industrious entrepreneur from Edirne, my grandfather *Kemal Revah* asked for Sara's hand in marriage. For some reason, *Bella* was willing to accept the proposal. When he asked for *Sara* he surely must have offered more than love. Though *Sara* didn't love him, she saw this marriage as a means to escape her bitter life.

Grandma Sara had a breathy voice, and spoke *Ladino* almost exclusively, with a little Bulgarian, and even less Turkish. Tall with fair skin and blue eyes, she carried herself with dignity and had an almost regal appearance. As a wife and mother, she worked very hard at preserving the honorable reputation of her family. This was no easy task given the cruel nature of her husband. *Grandpa Kemal* was a small abrupt man with a moustache

cut in the style which was so much in fashion that even Adolph Hitler adopted it for himself. Perhaps the early years of their marriage were pleasant, as *Kemal Bey* seemed to have some money. But he turned out to have no patience for children and ruled the roost with a harsh and domineering personality. A demanding man, he worked his wife and children with a heavy and unforgiving hand. Sara was never happy in her marriage with *Grandpa Kemal*. And although he adored her, *Kemal* could not, or would not, overcome his miserly and selfish nature.

No one really wants to say bad things about family, but the truth is, *Granpapa Kemal* was cruel. He set the children to work in his dry clean-

Figure 70: Granpapa Kemal and Granmama Sara soon after their marriage. One can assume that he was already a man of means, given the stylish attire and beautiful furnishings.

ing business at a very early age. (Perhaps *Granmama Sara's* family was already in the laundry/dry cleaning business, which Kemal then bought into as part of the marriage agreement.) Washing took place in the family kitchen, in the lower level of the house, opening out to the garden. My mother's little brother *Onk Niso* told me how he would come home from elementary school every day and find piles of laundry waiting for him on the table. He'd wash clothes in soapy barrels until his hands were raw. Like his mother had always done, he would first scrub them with very strong soap, then rinse the clothes in three consecutive barrels of water, twisting them hard after each dip. Only after he'd finished his work would he be permitted to go across the street to the municipal music conservatory for his beloved piano lessons.

Sara knew the unhappiness of her son all too well. When *Kemal* was away from the house she would sometimes come into the kitchen and take over *Niso's* washing, shooing him outside for a few minutes of play.

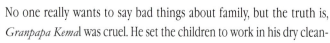

I'm sure it was her mother's merciful sacrifice and *Niso's* love of music that inspired *Beti* to work extra hours so that her little brother could play piano. The talented *Niso* had waited years for a piano and was 17 years old when his father finally bought an un-tuneable, dilapidated one. *Niso* would sing in German as he played Schubert on those clackety keys with fingers that were and swollen from hours of harsh detergents.

My mother *Beti* had been a brilliant student. By the time she started second grade she was well ahead of the class and clearly enjoyed learning. But *Kemal* removed her from school to work in the family business. She was a very bright seven year-old, and her teacher actually came to the house to beg her father to let her stay in school, but he refused. He needed someone to work, and my mother was not only capable, she came free.

One summer morning, my mother had been ill, and my grandmother made her two eggs instead of one, to help her regain her strength. When *Kemal* saw the extra portion, he took it off his daughter's plate and placed it in his own. "One is enough for you," he said.

As I said, *Granmama Sara* was a proud woman who was able to hide the family strife from the community. Friday dinners were always served in elegant style, with beautifully embroidered cloths and linens, dishes served decoratively on elegant platters. She would greet her guests with a tender smile, and serve inexpensive cuts of meat prepared in the best possible way. She never confronted her husband, especially during his fits of rage. Instead, she cleverly balanced her dual and often conflicting roles of dutiful wife and nurturing mother. She made clothes for her four children with the material garnered by taking apart *Kemal's* old suits. She gave food on the sly to her children when they were sick. *Sara's* sacrifices did not escape my mother's watchful eyes. When *Grandpa Kemal* insisted it was time for *Niso* to begin working full-time for the family business, it was my mother, who offered to work twice as hard so that her younger brother *Niso* could continue his studies.

Figure 71: Three Photos of young Beti. Left:. By her eighth birthday Beti (circa 1930) had been taken out of school to work in the family business. Center: Granpa Kemal's mother Ida (Dudu) with Beti (circa 1934) Right: Identification photo of Berta Revah around 1935, when she would have been 12 or 13 year's old.

Figure 72: Onk Niso's (Nesim Revah's) elementary school class. He is standing in front of the teacher. The early 1930's were lean times in Istanbul, and sending children to school was a luxury many families could ill afford.

LIFE IN THE REVAH HOME

SEPARATE COMMUNITIES

Romance between Turks (Muslims) and Jews was unheard of in Turkey in the 1930's. Minority communities (including Jews, Greeks and Armenians), had always lived segregated from the Turks. It wasn't a government dictate that kept the communities apart; the Jews, after all, had been welcomed into the Ottoman Empire and enjoyed an acceptance rarely seen in the rest of the world. Still, minorities had their own neighborhoods where they maintained their own schools, churches, synagogues, police forces, and banks. It was just the way it was.

Jewish women, in particular, were completely isolated from Turks. First of all, they didn't even speak the same language! Whether they arrived from Bulgaria, Italy, or Greece, Sepharads in the Ottoman Empire spoke Ladino, the language of 15th century Spain.

In Istanbul's Jewish communities, a family's survival hung on its reputation. The social sphere of Sepharad women was limited to home, their friends' homes, their own schools and businesses within the neighborhood, or their synagogue. Marriages within the community; Jewish men to Jewish women, were arranged very early, often in childhood. In a society where everyone was into everyone else's business, damaging gossip about a family could seriously impact a daughter or son's chances of marrying at all. That's why a young Jewish woman rarely, if ever, left the neighborhood without an escort, explicitly to prevent her exposure to outside men and to prevent gossip. Because gossip was different then. It wasn't just an inconvenience. With little by way of government-sponsored social services to count on, a family with un-marriageable daughters and aging parents could quickly slip into poverty.

That's why families rarely, if ever, aired their "dirty laundry." Arguments

occurred, but in hushed tones, so the neighbors wouldn't hear. A child with disabilities was kept hidden at home, for fear that the family carried unsuitable "seed." When leaving the house, one always dressed well. Even if you had only one pair of pants, they would be clean and pressed. One always had impeccable manners. Girls were expected to walk with grace, know how to maintain a home, and obey their parents. Boys were *Paşam* (my king) at home, but were expected to be men outside, especially to be able to withstand the hostile competition and bigotry from the Turkish community at-large.

In return, a family in good standing was welcomed in the synagogue and enjoyed the security and benefits of community life. With invitations to weddings and dinners came critical opportunities. Business deals could be made, jobs could be found, anxious young men sitting next to their mothers could catch a glimpse of their prospective brides, products could be advertised, partnerships could be arranged, and one could lean on friends when times got tough.

LIFE IN THE REVAH HOME

In 1938 the Revah family (my mother's family) were living in a part of Istanbul known as *Aynalı Çesme*. The house was *Alhatun Sokak #19*. My father *Zeki* was working at the American consulate (now known as the *Palazzo Corpi*) just a few minutes walk south in *Beyoğlu*, next to the Pera Palas Hotel. He became interested in the tiny dry cleaning business set up in Revah house just a few minutes walk north. The girl working inside was different from anyone he'd ever met. She was a pretty little thing, with wavy brown hair. But what made her special was the way her hazel eyes danced in a kind of flirtatious manner that was unheard of in those days. Perhaps he said a few words to her here and there. But no more.

Certainly he could not have known she had been pressing and ironing the suits of Istanbul's gentry for seven of her fifteen years. He had seen her father, her boss, and he could sense that he was a driven man who liked the finer things in life, including the opera, theater and art. But *Zeki* would not have known that her father *Monsieur Kemal* could be a cruel man, who took her out of school after the first grade because he was simply too cheap to pay a worker to take her place. She was brilliant even then. Her teacher had come to Monsieur Kemal, pleading with him to let little Betina continue her education. She showed spark, and an insatiable curiosity. He would hear none of it. Preposterous, he thought. Educate her for what? So that she would become unmarriagable? Uppity? She was a girl after all. He knew she was capable of handling the heavy workload, and he relied on that capability. The great tragedy was that, rather than nurture his daughter's brilliance and talent, and possibly direct it toward a higher calling, he preferred to exploit it, for profit. Anyway, she had made a deal with him; he would permit her younger siblings to attend the musical conservatory and the French Lycee, if she would work their shifts.

And work she did, with that industrious, Old World ethic. Washing shirts by hand, pressing the new western style jackets and pants that had just come into style with the new Republic. Those jackets looked so dashing on the diplomats and staff who worked behind elegant iron security gates. She imagined the gentlemen who wore these suits as she pressed, smelled the cologne left on their collars, or secretly laughed at their fine undergarments.

50 years later, pressing would still be somewhat of a fetish for Beti. She would begin early Saturday mornings, sitting on the couch in her nightgown, old à la Turka records playing on the phonograph, my father singing from somewhere in the kitchen. The ironing board would be set up in front of her, wrapped in blankets and then covered with an old sheet; the assembly held taut by ancient safety pins that surely came from diapers from our early days in America. She'd empty the basket of clean laundry, dipping her hand into a bowl of water and lightly splashing the cloth with flicks of her fingers. She'd then twist the dampened shirt into a loose ball, and lay it onto a pile of balls on the dining room table. The steam would hiss from the hot iron as her licked finger tested the temperature with an expert flash. She'd shake out the first white shirt, spray it with starch, and spread it onto the board, all the while singing to *Zeki Müren*. First came the collar, then the sleeves, both pressed with plenty of steam and pressure. A small towel bunched in her hand filled the shoulder which she deftly pressed all around while holding it up in the air.

Figure 74: Granpapa Kemal and Granmama Sara walking with their daughters Merih and Berta in Eminönü, Istanbul. This picture was taken around the time Beti met Zeki, and was surely keeping it a secret from her family.

To the end of her life, Beti's linen cabinet was a masterpiece, a shrine to neatly folded scarves, elegant folded tablecloths and napkins, and hand-crocheted doily.

Beti had been ironing like that for fifty years, and in those early days Granmama Sara had been aware her daughter was unhappy. She had tried to convince her to be nicer to her young suitor Jak Alhale who had asked permission to marry her. She had begrudgingly accepted the engagement weeks before, but now her feelings had changed. She had already been spending time with my father and could think of nothing but finding a chance to slip out of the house to meet him somewhere. What a dangerous game she was playing, secretly running around with a Turk; a married man, 17 years her senior.

You could ask yourself, what was she thinking, but of course we know she wasn't thinking. She was so much in love. And she was a renegade, irreverent, irrepressible. Her father's *joie de vivre* had worn off on her, and she was unstoppable. And that day in her father's laundry the ironing seemed less tedious because she was busy fanticizing about her lover. Perhaps she had already heard that Zeki's wife had thrown his belongings on the sidewalk. Perhaps he had already gotten word to her that he had rented an apartment and that she should meet him there when she could get away.

Figure 75: Beti and Zeki on a stroll, probably in Ankara 1940.

BETI TAKES OFF

Dad was more worried about mom in the trunk than about the flat tire. The American Ambassador was waking up in the back seat as Zeki Bey steered the hobbling limousine over to the side of the dirt road. Ankara had been designated capital of the Turkish Republic in 1923, and the functions of the embassy in Istanbul were gradually transferred there. The last American ambassador residing in Istanbul, John Van A. MacMurray, moved to Ankara in 1937 and my father was most likely the chauffeur who drove him. This particular trip from Istanbul to Ankara had been uneventful. At least that's the impression Zeki had been hoping to give. But now, as he brought the car to a gradual stop, he saw that the Ambassador was gathering himself up. "I'll help you change the tire," he said. A lovely gesture, a living example of American democracy and egalitarianism. Even in the best of circumstances my proud father would never have accepted this breach of diplomatic protocol and Turkish custom. The idea of an American Ambassador helping his Turkish chauffeur with a tire change would be shameful. But today, it would be catastrophic.

"No, no, sir. not problem," he said in broken English, smiling nervously as he put the car into park. Quickly glancing in his rearview mirror to check for any trucks coming up from behind, Zeki stepped out. He removed his uniform jacket, folded it across his arm, and laid it on top of his chauffeurs hat. "I have spare in de trunk," he said with a nod and a slight wink. His Excellency began to open his door. Zeki was imagining what would happen if the Ambassador opened the trunk for the spare. He would surely find the pretty Jewish girl tucked neatly inside.

It had all been her idea. Zeki had told her that the embassy was being relocated to the new capital, Ankara, and that the Ambassador needed to be taken to his new residence there. But Beti refused to be left behind.

"How can I take you? What am I supposed to say to His Excellency? Oh, do you mind if I bring my girlfriend along? She's only 17 but she's very clever; you'll love her?"

Zeki leaned into the limousine. "Please, sir. I do this alone." He thought he heard rumbling coming from the back of the car. Surely it was his imagination. "I can help, Zeki," came the reply. "Oh no, sir. No," said my father reassuringly. "You will get grease on your clothes. Let me take care of it."

Zeki quickly ran to the back of the car and threw open the trunk. Her hand covered her eyes as she blinked from the sudden brightness. She was fresh and lovely. Wavy brown hair arranged fashionably, though tousled now, around a delicate face. Her platform shoes lay beside her suitcase, pocketbook and hat. She had carefully selected her shoes to complement her fashionable outfit, perfect for the evening she had envisioned; they would promenade on the grand streets of Ankara, arm in arm, she with her handsome Turk. Her shaded hazel eyes looked up at him with surprise.

"Get out!" He whispered urgently. He quickly gathered up her things as she struggled to pull her shoes on. "Hurry up before he sees you!" He helped her out of the trunk and she watched him circle around the car to the ambassador's door. As he assured his passenger that it would not take long, his hidden hand motioned for her to make a run for it. Beti quickly rushed into the woods at the side of the road and hid among the shadows.

From her spot behind a tree the girl watched, heart pounding, as the diplomat and chauffeur retrieved the spare from the trunk. They jacked up the car, and without a word between them, replaced the tire. She gathered her belongings into her arms. She watched as Zeki laid the flat into the trunk. The American stood behind him, wiping his dusty hands together. After an awkward moment, the chauffeur pulled the trunk shut with a heavy thump.

He dared not look around for her, and she knew better than to present herself. The Ambassador had gone to his side of the vehicle and waved the chauffeur off as Zeki attempted to hold his door. It may have felt silly to the American, re-establishing strict decorum so soon after being crouched in the dirt together. Zeki briskly walked to the driver's side, and as the Ambassador lingered, he opened the door, pulled his jacket back on, and got in.

She held her breath.

A moment later, the heavy V6 motor started up, and as the black limousine with the fluttering American and Turkish flags pulled away, she realized she was alone, a Jewish girl deserted on a highway somewhere between Istanbul and Ankara.

Such was the unconventional, unpredictable, and wildly passionate life of my parents, Hayri (Zeki) Cagri and Berta (Beti) Revah. From the very beginning, the two were renegades, on the run from all things conventional. Most women in my mother's position would have been terrified standing there by the road. But Beti was not like most women. The girl was hungry for life, for excitement, for love. She was clever. So clever. And incredibly charming; able to talk herself out of any situation with lies so convincing she believed them herself as soon as they escaped her lips.

It had been several hours since Zeki had rudely abandoned his precious cargo. He had delivered his passenger to the new American Embassy, unloaded the Ambassador's belongings, and without even stopping for tea, rushed back to the spot. Incredibly relieved to see her sitting politely on a small suitcase at the edge of the woods, he picked her up. Riding this time in the front seat, she jokingly badgered him for mistreating her. He smiled as she teased that he was lucky she hadn't accepted the many offers for rides by handsome truck drivers and cabbies. They sat together in the limousine, she happily enjoying the newness of her life, and he the pleasantness of her voice.

Figure 76: Beti and Zeki around 1940. If either of them felt regret for having left their families, it doesn't show on their faces. For many years, it was all love and happiness.

It was up to *Sara* and *Kemal* to protect their children from the fallout. Their daughter's sudden departure was not simply a matter of embarrassment for the family. It was disaster. *Sara* would have a difficult time showing her face to the community. Neighbors would certainly gossip about their daughter who ran off with a married Turk. They would wonder about the morals of the other children, especially the daughters. *Sara* surely understood that her daughter *Merih's* reputation was compromised, and that no one wanted to be associated with scandal.

Figure 77: When Beti ran off with Zeki, Kemal Bey cast her out. Her siblings Merih, Niso, and Ida were not permitted to see or speak to her, and her own mother would have no contact with her for more than twelve years.

So imagine the gossip when it was learned that *Mr. Revah's* talented daughter *Berta* had run off to central Anatolia with a Turk, and that she had stowed away in the trunk of the American Ambassador's limousine, and had been abandoned on the side of the road near Ankara. I can hear my grandmother Sara's voice as she pats her forehead with a lace handkerchief. "*Ay que me morier ayo, no!*" Ladino for "Oh that I could die, but no!"

And when her father heard about it he called the police and *Zeki* was arrested. A court date set and *Zeki* found himself facing not only the magistrate but also his wife *Zehra Hanım* and the father of the Jewish girl with whom he had been having "relations." Clearly, *Zeki* was in a great deal of trouble, with his wife hoping for an end to his affair and the father hoping for a prison sentence for statutory rape.

No one could have predicted that a lone seventeen year old Jewish girl would dare walk into a courtroom, much less ask permission to speak. Certainly the blood must have drained from the faces of *Zehra Hanım* and *Granpapa Kemal* when the judge allowed Beti to approach. She simply told the judge that no one had forced her to do anything, that she had gone to be with my father on her own volition. The judge had no alternative but to dismiss the case. One could say that it was a day when "all Hell broke loose" or a day when all the stars aligned, depending on your point of view. That day, Kemal Revah knew that the reputation of his family had been destroyed and that his daughter had made herself a pariah in the Jewish community. That day, *Zeki* realized what this crazy girl had sacrificed for him, and knew he could never abandon her. That day *Zehra Hanım* went home to an empty apartment knowing she had lost her husband forever. And that day, Beti left her home and family to move in with the man of her dreams.

Let's not forget that while the *Revah* family was in upheaval, the status of Jews throughout Europe, the Balkans, and Turkey were very much in flux. Politics would once again determine the trajectory of the lives of the *Revah* children.

Once Turkey became a Republic, the Ottoman "Millet" system which had given non-Muslims full citizenship and equal rights was replaced with one where they became a minority with treatment based on the Lausanne Treaty of 1923. Education became unified under a national organization, Turkish became the national language, and population exchanges were made between Greeks in Anatolia and Muslims in the Balkans. These reforms aimed at homogenization and support for an authentic "Turkish state" in the face of a splintered and disappearing Ottoman Empire had the effect of putting pressure on minority populations to adapt to new reforms and policies.

Figure 78: Revah Family minus Beti - (From left) Ida, Granmama Sara, Niso, Granpapa Kemal and Merih. The family's reputation within the tightknit Jewish community was in deep peril. Merih would have a difficult time finding a suitable husband. This was one of the reasons she left Istanbul for Israel.

The Ottoman/Turkish public school system had actually been inferior to the education provided by the Alliance Israelite Universelle (the Paris-based international Jewish organization whose mission was to advance the Jews in the Middle East through French education and culture). It, along with B'nai B'rith became the schools of choice, and Turkey's Jews paid to send their children to these schools which conducted high level classes in French.

It should be mentioned that the Alliance was an anti-Zionist organization which frowned on emigration to Palestine, teaching instead that Jews should be integrated into the lands in which they settled. In fact, most prominent Jews in the Ottoman Empire felt the need to demonstrate loyalty to the Ottoman Empire in exchange for its protection. The Young Turks felt comfortable with the ideology of the Alliance, and made its protegé Haim Nahum the *Haham Başı* (Chief Rabbi) of the Ottoman Empire.

Still, the "homogenization" mentioned earlier, and incidents like the Thracian massacre and the 1942 Capital Tax or *Verlık Vergisi* led to an even stronger impetus for non-Muslims to leave. It can be said that

Turkey's process of nation building had the effect, perhaps unintentionally, of pushing minorities out of the new Republic.

Meanwhile, the Nazi rise to power in the early 30's reinforced the idea that Jews needed Palestine as a safe haven. As Jews from Central and Eastern European countries fled for Palestine, Turkey became the main legal/illegal transit site for their immigration.

Unfortunately, the wave of Nazism did get a foothold in Turkey among some of the Nationalists, which caused even Turkish Jews to join the migration to Palestine. After the Thracian incidents in 1934, (which Mati believes was not officially sponsored or even condoned) there was a significant rise in emigration to Palestine. Between 1934-5 about 2,000 Turkish Jews emigrated to Palestine, with the help of the Jewish Colonization Agency and the Palestine Aliya Anoar Organization which both had offices in Istanbul. When WWII broke out in 1939, Jews fleeing the holocaust with Palestine as their destination were permitted to use Turkey as a transit country en route. Some 37,000 Europeans made this trip between the years 1934-1944.

MERIH

I'm not sure when my mother's younger sister *Merih* got the idea to emigrate to Palestine herself. Perhaps it was *Beti's* scandal that limited her marriage prospects; *Merih* was well into her twenties and still single. She was a small dynamo, generous of spirit and always laughing. But she wasn't as naturally pretty or charming as *Beti,* and had lived somewhat in her sister's shadow. At that time, there was a great deal of excitement surrounding a new state for the Jews. *Merih* had been spending her spare time (if there was such a thing in the *Revah* household) active in youth groups helping European Jews emigrate through Turkey to Palestine. The sense of hope and adventure among young Jews at that time was infectious. Bright, with more energy than she knew what to do with, *Merih* embraced the dream of creating a Jewish nation and decided to go. How she managed to go is not clear; permits for Turkish Jews immigrating to Isreal were limited by British policy. But somehow Merih got to Palestine and ultimately settled in Haifa near the Bahai Temple. She was almost thirty when she married *Ruben Baruch*. They raised two daughters, *Tamar* and *Sara*, who still live there with their families. *Merih* always longed to be re-united with her family, but once the *Revahs* moved to America, she was only able to see her siblings a handful of times before she died in 2010. Still, *Merih* is remembered for her love of life, her warm smile, and the joyful way she danced all night at weddings and parties.

Figure 79: Merih Revah with Aliya friends in Istanbul crice 1943. By the end of World War II, Jewish emigration to Palestine had subsided. Still, Merih would soon make the decision to leave Turkey to start a new life.

Figure 80: Mati Eskenazi, on right, with her sister Ida and brother Moris, known as Onk Mimi. Mimi was a brilliant man and prolific poet who suffered from intolerance and bigotry because of his minor birth defects and disabilities. Born without a thumb on his right hand, Mimi was forced to write with that hand in school because using the left hand for "clean activities" like writing, eating, or shaking hands is culturally taboo in the Middle East. His was a potentially magnificent life stifled by ignorance and bigotry, but a life lived with quiet dignity, nonetheless.

MATI AND THE VARLIK VERGISI – THE WEALTH TAX

Before my aunt *Matilda Eskenazi* met her future husband, my mother's brother *Nesim*, she was living the life of most smart Jewish girls in Istanbul. *Tant Mati's* mother *Suzanna* was well-educated (unlike *Granma Sara* who came to Turkey very young, not knowing much about Bulgaria and never having gone to Turkish School). *Suzanna* had gone to a German school and learned French as well. Her children were all getting a good education and looking forward to prosperous futures.

All that changed in 1940, when the Turkish government passed the National Protection Law which allowed it to closely regulate economic activity and resources in case Turkey were to enter the war. At that time, non-Muslim minorities were also being blamed for profiteering and smuggling. It was in this atmosphere that the extraordinary Wealth Tax (*Varlık Vergisi*) of 1942 appeared. The government divided the population into four groups which were each taxed at a different rate; Muslims at 5% of their circannual income, Greeks 156%, Jews 179%, and Armenians 232%. The idea was that, since Muslims were already required to pay a religious tax, non-Muslims should pay their fair share of taxes, too. But the taxes were not fair. Commissions of Turkish businessmen set up in each city to assess each family's worth, were often made up of competitors to non-Muslim entrepreneurs. They put together wildly inaccurate estimates of what these families owed. The foreign embassies protested the tax and helped their nationals pay it, but for the Jews, there was no such homeland to help pay the absurd sums.

Tant Mati told me the story of how her father, *Aron Eskenazi* was unable to pay the Wealth Tax and was therefore sent to the *Askale* labor camp to work off the family debt. *Mati* was 17 years old when she went to the barn in *Demirkapı* with her mother *Suzanna*, her sister and brother to say goodbye to her father. They took coats and food for him, knowing how dire the conditions would be for him in a labor camp. *Mati's* family huddled and cried together that day, wondering if they would ever see their father again. We now know that the 4,000 to 5,000 non-Muslims sent to the camps at *Askale* for "defaulting" on their taxes were cramped into filthy living quarters, fed poorly, harassed and given little access to medical care. *Mati* confirms a report I found, filed by British Colonel named Binns in February 1943 describing the heart-wrenching scene of men being taken from their families to go to *Askale*:

"... some forty merchants, lawyers and others have been imprisoned for the last ten days and are being dispatched this evening to Askale to join the 32 already there. The room in which they are imprisoned is some fifteen yards in length by eight yards in width ... There was not a stick of furniture of any kind with the exception of one stove. The room was full of weeping men, women, and children who had come to say goodbye, and to bring deportees odd parcels of food and clothing. A most depressing and wretched picture."

Mati remembers that on that day, two very wealthy Jews were also being sent. She was astonished that their wives had brought expensive fur coats which they had laid on the grass to sit on. Mati and many others felt angry seeing this, because it was exactly this kind of ostentation that perpetuated the rumors that Jews were war profiteers, hence the Wealth Tax.

After their father was sent off, *Mati*, her sister, mother, and disabled brother *Moris* had to fend for themselves. In an attempt to recoup the unpaid tax, the authorities came to their house and confiscated everything they owned. They took the china, the linens, even pulled the lamps down from the ceiling. All tthat was left in the house for the mother and three children were four chairs, one table and three beds. When *Mati's* sister *Ida* protested, insisting they leave a bed for her father, they harshly told her she shouldn't be so confident that he would ever return.

In fact, many did not return from the Turkish Siberia, as *Askale* came to be known. While serving his sentence, *Aron Eskenazi* sold coffee on the side and was able to make enough money to survive. But the family was left with nothing.

It was only by a twist of fate that my mother's family was not similarly impoverished. My grandfather's name was *Samuel Kemal Revah*. When the taxing Commission saw the name *Revah* they assumed it was simply a mis-spelling of the word *Refah* which means prosperity in Turkish. The family was therefore taxed at the Muslim rate of 2,000 Lira rather than 80,000 for Jews.

Figure 81: Wedding of Matilda (Mati) Eskenazi and Nesim (Niso) Revah in 1953. Back row (left to right) my grandparents Kemal Revah and Sara Gerşon Revah, Onk Niso, Ida Revah (Tant Ida) and her future husband Yehuda Leon Dana.

Fig 82: Beti had not been invited to her brother's wedding. It had been almost twelve years since she had seen her mother. But a new arrival, my sister Ilhan Merih Çağrı (shown in December 1952) would soon soften hearts and begin the mending.

Niso and Ida

As young people do, Niso and Ida found love, and both of them were lucky in it. Finding Mati was maybe the best thing that ever happened to Niso. His childhood had been tough and Monsieur Kemal was very hard on his only son. As I've already told you, his love for music was used as a bargaining chip, a way of getting obedience and work from a child who couldn't wait to get his fingers on a piano. I always wondered if the way he stammered was a result of the unpredictable temper of his father. When Niso found the beautiful Matilda Eskenazi, he found a woman of intellect, patience, and compassion. There was a level-headednessabout her, a calm. And best of all, she adored everything about him. When he asked her to marry him, it was a cause for real celebration for the Revah clan. Granmama Sara was so happy she went to inform Beya (whom she called Nona Granma). By then her stepmother's health was failing, so Sara put a small piece of candy in her mouth and whispered that her grandson Niso was engaged. Beya died a week later, in April 1953.

The youngest *Revah* was born ten years after my mother and barely remembers the time when *Beti* lived with her. *Ida* was, afterall, only seven year's old when *Beti* left. Back then, the only time she saw her estranged sister was when Beti would wait outside the gate of *Ida's* elementary school for a chance to call her over for a quick chat during recess.

Compared to *Beti's*, *Ida's* childhood was charmed. Ida always says her feet never touched the ground as a child because she was so loved she was passed from "lap to lap." Her outlook has always been positive, traditional, and pragmatic. Unlike my mother who was always at the center of high drama, *Ida* preferred stability. The most meaningful event of her youth was her courtship with the incredibly handsome *Leon Dana* whom she met while still in her early teens.

Rapprochement

By that time *Beti* and *Zeki* were considered a done deal. Still, there had been no contact with the lost *Revah* daughter for twelve years, until she gave birth to her first child, my sister İlhan. Living in Ankara at the time, she sent a telegram to her mother in Istanbul. It was short and sweet. "You have a granddaughter. Would you like to meet her?"

For the first time in their marriage, *Granmama Sara* actually stood up to her husband. "We are going," she said. *Sara* and *Kemal* did go to Ankara to meet their first grandchild, and though all was not forgiven, especially between the two men, there was a detente, of sorts. For the women it was the happiest of family reunions and set the stage for many future visits. *Ida* would finally have a relationship with her long-lost sister. *Leon*, in fact, would escort her to visit *Beti* and *Zeki* in Ankara.

Figure 83: Nesim (Niso) Revah (above) and his future brother-in-law Yehuda Leon Dana. The two would become business partners in the USA, and open their record store, Serenade Records, just down the street from the White House.

Figure 85: After so many years apart, it's hard to say what the relationship was like between Monsieur Kemal and his estranged daughter, Beti. But my grandmother was thrilled to have grandchildren. In this 1954 photo we see Beti, her father Monsieur Kemal, my sister Ilhan standing, and my other sister Çaya.

Figure 86: It pains me to say that if we had stayed in Turkey, I would have had many more years with Granmama Sara. I was only three and a half when we left Turkey, so my memories of her from that time are vague and rudimentary. In fact, one of those earliest memories is of a time I her in Istanbul. I was holding the hem of her dress while she prepared sütlaç (rice pudding) for me.

Here is Granmama Sara with three of her grand-daughters, Ilhan on the left, Çaya on the right, and the sweetie in the middle is one of her name-sakes, Sara Revah, the daughter of Mati and Niso.

Figure 84: The three Revah sisters were finally re-united after Ilhan was born and Granmama Sara convinced her husband to visit their first grandchild. Here we see Beti, Ida, and Merih. The baby on the left is Ilhan. On the right is Merih's older daughter Tamar.

THE TURKISH JEWISH SIDE

Figure 87: Bulisa (Rejina) Gerşon Alhale and Jak Alhale

Figure 88: Beya Benbassat Gerşon and her son Mordo pressured her daughter Rejina to break off her engagement to the man she loved to marry the man her mother preferred.

TANT REJINA

If my mother had not met my father, I wonder if she would have gone through with the marriage to her fiancé *Jak Alhale*. He was a gentle fellow, very Slavic looking, even though his family had once lived in Egypt (hence the Arabic name). If *Beti* had married him, I think she would have driven him crazy. She'd be the first to admit that. Jak was a quiet man, kind and centered. I can't imagine him with someone as highly charged, and irreverent as my mom. I do know that the two of them argued when she cancelled the engagement. And that *Jak's* mother *Madam Viktorya* had always preferred *Rejina* for her son over *Beti*. When the opportunity arose, *Viktorya* pushed him to ask for *Rejina*.

This turned out to be a very big deal. *Rejina* was already engaged to a doctor with whom she was very much in love. I mean, crazy love. *Rejina* at first refused to break her engagement, but the family insisted. Even her brother *Mordo* pressured her to break it off. When *Rejina* finally conceded and broke her engagement, the incredulous young doctor argued vehemently. What right did her brother have to deny his sister's marriage? Could he have known that *Mordo* was also being denied permission to marry his beloved *Simone*? Could he have known that *Rejina's* own mother had given up her true love? This was all part of *Rejina's* family obligation, and the poor thing had no choice. The doctor finally gave up, storming out of the house and breaking a window on the way. Soon after, two simple white roses were left on the doorstep. Incredibly, *Mordo* and his love *Simone* waited nine years for permission, and realizing it would never be granted, the two finally eloped.

Meanwhile *Rejina's* mother was counselling her to not miss the chance to marry the eligible *Jak*. So in the end, my mother's aunt *Rejina* married *Monsieur Jak* and together they had three children, *Josef (Jojo), Eli,* and *Viki*. If you ask *Viki*, she will tell you that her mother never stopped loving the young doctor. But *Jak* loved *Rejina* and was a won-

derful husband with a clean heart. Every Monday night he would bring home the Park Hotel chocolate cake she loved so much. Every holiday he brought flowers. A true gentleman, he never used a harsh word. Gradually, *Rejina* grew to love him, as well.

Tant Rejina was a very intelligent and interesting woman who unfortunately inherited her mother *Beya's* fierce need to keep her children too close. With loving kindness and a firm will, she raised two sons and a daughter who were so devoted to her that they lived with their parents well into adulthood. Independence was hard to come by in such a close-knit family, and although *Eli* and *Viki* came close to it, none of *Rejina's* children married. Well, at least not yet.

Figure 89: Four Siblings - İlhan, Ayhan (Çaya), me, and Kemal held by a servant in Ankara 1956

TRAGEDY IN ISTANBUL

In 1986, a great tragedy befell Tant Rejina's family. It was summer and our group of Turkish friends had gone to Turkey for a short *Mavi Yolculuk* (Blue Voyage). We rented a small boat with a crew of three and traveled around the Aegean, stopping every day at another little port town. It had been a wonderful way to explore the southern coast of Turkey, but after ten days at sea I was looking forward to a few days in Istanbul where I would visit *Rejina's* family and get in some shopping. When we arrived in Marmaris I called the USA and *Çaya* answered the phone;

"Are you alright?" she asked.

"Yes, it was fabulous, we had a great time."

"Oh my God, haven't you heard?" I sensed the tension in her voice. "There was a terrorist attack in Istanbul!"

"Oh no, I'm fine," I said, somewhat relieved. "We're here in the south."

"Beyhan, there was an attack on a synagogue in Istanbul and terrorists went in and killed a whole bunch of people! *Jojo* was killed!"

There were all kinds of people milling around the pay phone and I pressed it tightly to my ear trying desperately to hear more clearly. "Our *Jojo*? *Tant Rejina's Jojo*?"

"Yes! " she said. "They went in and killed everyone while they were praying." I suddenly felt very faint. "It's all over the news here," she continued.

"I am supposed to go to *Tant Rejina's* today," I said, trying to make sense of it. "They're expecting me for dinner tonight."

"Oh my God, Beyhan."

I told *Çaya* I would call her as soon as I knew more, hung up, and went across the street to the news stand. It was all over the front pages, and I am sorry to tell you that my cousin *Josef* was indeed killed in the September 1986 terrorist attack on *Neve Shalom*, Istanbul's largest synagogue. *Jojo* had gone there to mourn the recent death of his father *Monsieur Jak*. *Jojo* was killed with another 21 people who had gone there for Saturday services. Every single paper at the stand was plastered with full color photographs of the horrific scene. The bullet-riddled interior of the synagogue. The bloodied bodies. I saw a front page photo of my cousin Viki, stricken with grief, being supported by other women as she passed through the synagogue doors. There were worse photos.

Somehow I made it to Istanbul. It was evening and a young woman sharing the cab from the airport worried about me. As she got out, she leaned back into the driver's window. "She's a stranger here, brother. Be her eyes and ears. Don't leave her on the street somewhere. Find the house and make sure she gets in." Turkish hospitality. God bless her. We toured the neighborhood looking for the apartment. The driver stopped several times to ask directions. He even left the car to go into a tea house to ask. We arrived and he helped me out and carried my suitcase up the dark marble stairs. I don't know if I even paid him.

Viki let me in. Pale. An attempted smile. "He was so excited you were coming." she said. "He asked me what I was going to cook for you." *Rejina* sat in the living room, looking out the enormous window into the darkness. *Onk Niso* had arrived from Washington. *Eli* had arrived. There were family members talking in hushed voices. It was an awful night of trying to make sense out of something senseless. *Tant Rejina* was lost somewhere in her own mind. She sat by that window all night, and all the next day. The day of the funeral was blisteringly hot. Onk *Niso* and I stood huddled in the crowd of people pressed against the Synagogue doors, waiting for them to open. I read the sign, *Neve Shalom* (Oasis of Peace). Along that tiny cobblestone street twenty-two drab green military hearses sat ready. There were police and news media everywhere. We waited quietly and when the doors slowly opened we walked in. The grisly scene had been purposely left uncleaned for the international news media to see.

I wasn't sure what to feel. I'm not sure I was feeling at all. Cameras clicked as somber men spoke. Afterwards, Niso took my arm and we got into cars that followed the convoy of coffins in the procession to the cemetery.

My cousin *Mehmet* happened to be watching the news here in America and noticed that the Turkish woman being interviewed on World News Tonight with Peter Jennings spoke English very well. He suddenly realized he was watching me.

A reporter had been looking for an English speaker and asked if I would speak with him, "My father is Muslim and my mother is Jewish, and it's like we have our own mideast crisis at home every night. But this attack is not a Muslim attack. This is not part of the Muslim faith."

Thinking back on that day 25 years ago, and remembering that *Jojo* had been so excited about my coming to visit, I think about my two religions. Their beauty. Their poverty.

Of course, *Rejina* never fully recovered from the loss of her oldest son. When she arrived in the USA to start over with her children *Viki* and *Eli,* she had lost much of the strength and humor for which she was known. She passed away in 2007, may God bless her soul.

Funeral for victims of terrorist attack in Istanbul, Turkey

Fugire 89: Top Left: Tant Rejina on the day of her son Jojo's funeral. She sat at that window for days, just looking out, trying to make sense of the senseless death of her eldest child. Soon after she, Eli and Viki immigrated to the United States to join the rest of the family.

Figure 90: Top: The funeral procession from Neve Shalom Synagogue. The attack drew widespread condemnation from the Turkish people as well as from others around the globe.

Figure 91: Photo from Insight Magazine, October 20, 1986 at the cemetery. Onk Niso and I can be seen standing behind the fourth coffin.

COMING TO AMERICA

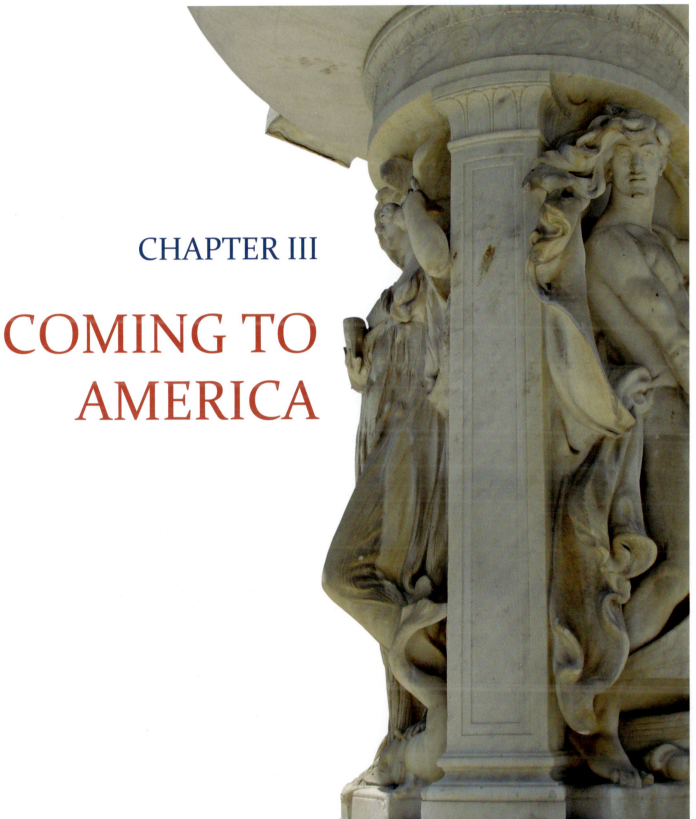

CHAPTER III

COMING TO AMERICA

Figure 93: A growing family in Ankara. Having children out of wedlock, especially with a married man was enough deterrent to keep my parents childless for more than a decade. But once İlhan arrived unexpectedly, the flood gates were opened. Çaya, Beyhan, and Kemal quickly followed.

A Growing Family

For twelve years Beti and Zeki enjoyed their freedom and romance. But when İlhan Merih was born in April of 1952, their lives changed dramatically. Not only did they welcome a much loved child, but the occasion had mended ties with Beti's family. Beti also realized she loved being pregnant. Ayhan Sara followed just eighteen months later. They were going to call her Sara, after Granmama Sara, but İlhan's pronunciation of Sara sounded like Taya, so the name Çaya stuck. Twelve months later I came along, and then just fifteen months after that my mother finally had a son, my brother Kemal, named after her father.

At the time both of my parents were working; my dad still with the American Embassy, and my mother with the Embassy of Mexico. In 1958, my father turned 50 years old and was eligible for retirement. When the Americans offered him his choice of either a pension or a Green Card for permanent residence in the United States, he chose the latter. This was a seminal decision that he often regretted in his later years. But at the time, a chance to live in the United States of America was a dream come true. It's still hard to imagine how Zeki had the

fortitude
to restart his life
when most men his age
were preparing for retiring. And
it's not as if he or Beti had any work
lined up. They really had no idea what they
were getting into. They just believed that America held promise, not only for them, but for their bi-religious children. I'm sure my parents believed that in America you could be anything you wanted to be, and they simply chose to believe in the infinite opportunities that lay ahead.

Of course the issue of getting a mistress and four bastard children out of Turkey would need to be handled delicately. They hid the fact that they weren't married even from us, until we were teenagers. When we asked about her wedding dress, she would always say it was beautiful and that she gave it to the gypsies. We were so impressed with her generosity and imagined some poor gypsy girl in a lovely lace and pearls gown. Marriage had been out of the question for Zeki. It wasn't even so much the two religions issue; by that time we had had no formal religious training to speak of. The fact of the matter was, he was still married to his step-sister Zehra, and she was still waiting for him to return to her.

The idea of contacting the family again after having deserted them twelve years earlier, and not for reconciliation but for divorce, was unthinkable. Though Beti had no legal status as his wife, my parents had the foresight to give their children his last name. And with World War II still recent memory, she decided to list us as Muslim on our birth certificates, a decision he was more than happy with. So my parents arranged for passports for each of us.

My father came to the United States a couple of months ahead of us, to scope things out. For as long as he could remember he had wanted to

Figure 94: Passport photo of Beti and her four children in 1958. Left to right: Me, Beti, Kemal, İlhan, and Çaya

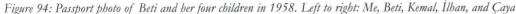

Figure 95: Me and my sister Çaya having just arrived to the United States, standing in DuPont Circle.(1958)

He remembered that a visiting official had once instructed him to purchase a shirt for him, which my father dutifully did. The American was dissatisfied with the shirt and told my father to return it. Of course, reurning merchandise was not done in Turkey, where a deal is a deal. My father couldn't bring himself to go back on his word to the merchant, so he refused the official. "I am happy to buy you another shirt," he had said, " but you bought this one so you must keep it." The American was so angry at my father's insubordination, he demanded that Zeki be fired, which he was. He was re-hired some time later and stayed on long enough to accept the offer for permanent residency in the United Sates.

It was June, 1958. The plan was for Zeki to come first, and the family to follow. He arrived in New York, traveled to DC to make contact with people he knew at the Embassy. The next step was to continue on to San Francisco where his friend Taki, who had also worked at the American Consulate, was waiting to offer support. But he never made it to California; two months after my father's arrival, my mother flew into JFK with the four children. With no "officially sanctioned" relationship with my father other than being the mother of his children, the best she could do was get a tourist visa to Canada. In typical Beti style, which is to say "flying by the seat of her pants," she decided to take advantage of a one day layover in New York to fly down to the nation's capitol to see my father. My sister Caya remembers that we landed at National Airport in a propeller plane and walked down the steps onto the tarmac. My father was waiting there for us, and when he saw us running toward him shouting "Baba, Baba!" he bent down on one knee and swooped the four of us into his strong arms. In his hands he had four of the biggest Hershey's chocolate bars we had ever seen.

come to America. After all, he had been around Americans his whole life and knew them to be honest people. His father had worked for years at the U.S. Consulate in Istanbul. Zeki took his father's position and worked at the American Consulate in Ankara. Still, when he reached retirement age (which was 50 then) he had to carefully consider the Green Card offer for his years of service. To him, America was certainly the land of opportunity, where anything was possible, where a forward thinking person could live an unconventional life and even be rewarded for it. Zeki also liked how straightforward Americans were, direct in their conversation. What you see is what you get. He could relate to that.

Many previous ambassadors and statesmen had been kind and generous to his family. But then there was also the other type: the Ugly American.

That very same day, my parents took us to Dupont Circle, sight-seeing. As my mother sat on a bench a man happened to sit next to her, whom she immediately recognized as Turkish. They struck up a conversation and it turned out that the man worked at the Turkish Embassy just down the street from Dupont Circle. I'm sure she laid on the charm, and after impressing him with her experience at the Embassy of Mexico in Ankara and her five languages, she suggested they could probably use her skills at the Turkish Embassy in Washington. She was hired that day, thus receiving diplomatic status. As part of the diplomatic corps, my mother no longer needed a visa or work permit since she would be working inside the embassy which was considered the Republic of Turkey. So we got to stay here. I like to to tell people that when I came to America I was an illegal immigrant for about 6 hours.

Figure 96: Beti and Zeki often took us out to explore our new city, Washington, D.C. where we visited the national monuments, like the Lincoln Memorial pictured here in 1960. Just two years after arriving in the USA I had already forgotten how to speak Turkish. I could understand my parents most of the time, but could only respond to them in English, much to their consternation. Like most immigrant children, we learned English faster than our parents did, and in the early years helped translate for them when we were in public.

Having left Istanbul just weeks earlier, the "Old City" of Washington, D.C. was still brand new. DuPont Circle was the center of my little universe, its central fountain my *axis mundi*. My earliest recollections of America come to me only as snippets of occasions, places, smells, tastes. But I remember Dupont Circle. It's a hot August afternoon. I'm holding tight to my father's enormous hand as we walk along New Hampshire Avenue heading toward DuPont Circle. I have a towel slung over my shoulder, flip flops on my tiny feet. I see that my brother and sisters are up ahead, also holding hands, waiting at the street light. We've been warned about the mad rush of traffic circumambulating this landmark fountain. The cars slow and finally stop for the light. We cross to the first median. Pigeons scuttle around our feet as my father instructs Ilhan to hold on to my little brother Kemal. The rush of cars in the inner circle of traffic finally subsides and we rush to the safety of the park.

I couldn't possibly have known then that this part of the District had only been developed since the large influx of new residents after the Civil War. I would learn in architecture school that the genius of Pierre Charles L'Enfant's master plan for Washington D.C. is most observable here, where three large avenues converge on this one traffic circle. The memorial statue of Admiral Samuel DuPont was no longer there. In its stead stood the fabulous white marble fountain landscaped with exotic flowers and ornamental trees. The powerful statues with the flowing hair that form the trunk of the fountain inspired me somehow, and made me feel protected when I first saw them as a child immigrant.

To most D.C. residents, that fountain is a national landmark. To us, it was the pool. On hot summer days like this one, my parents would strip us down to our underwear and let us frolic in the fountain under the loving gazes of the three alabaster figures. If we weren't swimming, we were running races around the inner circle; a course which at the time seemed Olympic. My father always set me on the outside lane since I was the fastest runner of the four of us. He would then sit on one of the benches at the perimeter of the inner circle, smoking a cigarette and chatting amiably with other immigrant fathers in their suits and skinny ties. *Bir, iki, üç!* And we were off, racing around the fountain, spurred on by their cheers and waving handkerchiefs. I remember falling and scraping my knees. Baba held me in his lap as one of the men carefully dabbed my scraped skin with the ashes from his cigarette. Old school medicine. A moment later, I was off exploring.

My sisters had found large green metal discs hidden inside circles of tall bushes. The discs sat on cylinders of grated metal which periodically groaned and rumbled beneath us when we climbed on top of them. They seemed monumental perches to us, and we would jump from them, hurl ourselves over the bushes and spill onto the grass, like paratroopers. Researching this book, I recently discovered that our secret castles were actually the fresh air intakes to the streetcar station and tunnels underground, part of the Capital Transit Project.

But we didn't care about all these grand plans then. We were just happy, living as so many other immigrant families did in Dupont Circle in the late 1950's. Lucky for us, the neighborhood had deteriorated after World War I so we newly-arrived foreigners (mostly Turks, Greeks, and Armenians) could afford the rent. My father had given up his plan to go to California, and managed to get a job as the embassy chauffeur. Busy with their new jobs, every morning my parents dropped us off at the Georgetown nursery school and went to work.

Figure 97: (Top left) Çaya and me on a Washington D.C. street with our father Zeki Bey a year after arriving. (Left) One of many times our parents dressed us in traditional Turkish outfits and posed us with one hand held at our waist. This time the honor was mine. (Bottom left) Granpapa Kemal and Granmama Sara came to visit us a year after we arrived. Ya gotta love the bathing suits. (Above) Beti lounging with the Sunday paper while Ilhan poses after a bath.

We learned important things there, like the fact that a black woman could be called Mrs. White and a white woman could be called Mrs. Brown. We learned that if you didn't know how to tie your shoes, you could be abandoned in a dark closet for an entire day. We learned that if you refused to change into a bathing suit in front of other children, a teacher could try to force you. And if you bit said teacher, as Çaya did, Mom would back you up and insist you be given a private corner to change your clothes. We learned English. And every afternoon, my sister Ilhan, aged 7, piled the three of us (ages 6, 5, and 4) onto a city bus to bring us home. We learned that if you went behind the Italian restaurant at the first bus transfer, people would set a small table for you, seat you on old wire spools, and feed you whatever extra food they had that day. We learned not to lock ourselves into our apartment or we'd have to throw our key down to a passerby again to let us out. Yes, with both parents working hard to start a life, we were left to our own devices. It's a terrible way to raise young children, but one could say we each benefited in our own way from this benign neglect.

Figure 98: We lived for a time in the basement of the Residence of the Ambassador of the Republic of Turkey

EMBASSY ROW

It wouldn't be long until the neighborhood began to acquire a certain Bohemian feel. By the early 60's the hippies had taken over DuPont Circle. These strange young people scorned the perimeter wood benches (symbols of the hated establishment) preferring to sprawl out on the grass in small groups, tossing their long hair around as they played guitar, smoking strange-smelling cigarettes, and throwing Frisbees to their bandana-collared dogs

We moved out of the one bedroom apartment on New Hampshire Avenue to live for a time in the basement apartment of the glorious Sheridan Circle residence of the Turkish Ambassador. Most of my time was spent in these cramped but not unkind quarters. The small apartment was sunny, and there were always embassy staff dropping in for tea and a smoke, or to play cards. Cooks in white jackets, housekeepers, and gardeners stopped in throughout the day, often sitting at the bottom of the driveway in small chairs set up by the garage door, to have a cigarette and listen to the latest gossip.

The Ambassador's residence has a terrific history. Apparently, this turn

of the century mansion was built in 1910 for a tenor opera singer who performed concerts in a large room on the second floor designed specifically for its acoustics. When the Turkish Republic came into being in 1923, Kemal Ataturk began looking for a place to house the Republic's Ambassador to the United States. A photograph of the building, then up for sale, was sent to him, and after only seeing the photograph Ataturk bought the building, It is the first piece of foreign property to be owned by the modern Republic of Turkey.

In 1934 the first Ambassador of the new Republic, Munir Ertegün, took his post and moved his family in. The name Ertegün should sound familiar; Munir was the father of Ahmet Ertegün, founder and president of Atlantic Records. Ahmet's passion for music started at a very young age when his older brother Nesuhi introduced him to jazz. The brothers hung out in jazz clubs in D.C. with musicians like Duke Ellington and Louis Armstrong, and convinced their father to allow concerts in the residence. The building became one of the few venues in D.C. where black musicians could play, and the shows were apparently attended by some very notable personalities.

Figure 99: Çaya, Ilhan, Beti, and me in D.C. around 1960. Ilhan's hair had still never been cut. My father loved it. Every morning they observed a sort of ritual where he would sit behind her and lovingly comb it with a tortoise-shell comb. He'd carefully arrange it into two long braids (like you see above); a style she wore until it was finally cut at age eleven. By then it had reached a length of 2 inches below her knees.

Ambassador Ertegün died in 1944 and was sent home to Turkey on the Battleship USS Missouri (a courtesy ordered by President Truman as a gesture of friendship but also as a show of force to the Soviet Union that Turkey was under American protection). The brothers remained behind to finish their education. Ahmet Ertegün, who only recently died, became an incredible record producer, record label executive, and composer. He helped define American music by developing the careers of acts like the Rolling Stones, Cream, Led Zeppelin, Ray Charles, Bobby Darin, Aretha Franklin, Bette Midler, the Drifters, Otis Redding, Wilson Pickett, and Abba. He backed Crosby, Stills, and Nash, and was actually the one who convinced them to let Neil Young join them on tours. Ahmet Ertegün was also Chairman of the Rock and Roll Hall of Fame. It tickles me to imagine that he and I grew up in the same house, although I'm sure his visits to the basement were as infrequent as my sorties to the fabulous upper floors.

Living on Embassy Row was a little like living at the United Nations. As we played hopscotch on the sidewalk in front of the embassies, members of the diplomatic corps would stroll by, dressed in their traditional national costumes, speaking every language imaginable. People were cultured, educated, and optimistic, or so it seemed to me at my tender age. The Ambassador (possibly Feridun Cemal Erkin) and his wife not only lived there, they also hosted elaborate dinner parties and receptions. We often accompanied my parents to these exclusive events. Changing from our school clothes to our nice dresses and shiny black patent leather shoes, we would walk out of our basement apartment, past the parked cars in the side lot, around the building and up the circular drop-off to the line of guests forming under the porte-cochere at the front entrance. I remember stepping into the white marble entrance foyer and breezing past the sharply dressed greeting staff in their black suits. Climbing the elegant grand staircase, I always paused to admire the huge bronze bust of Atatürk displayed in front of the stained glass window on the landing. I imagined he had claimed this place of honor just as he had claimed his place in history.

Of course we were only the children of the Ambassador's secretary and chauffeur (since my dad had gotten a job at the embassy as well), but once we stepped out to the glorious second floor reception hall, we

Figure 100: Our family in the back yard of the Embassy of Madagascar, another temporary home. From left to right, Kemal, Beti, İlhan, Zeki Bey, Çaya, and Beyhan kneeling. (1962)

meandered around feeling very much at home among diplomats sipping their cocktails. We politely smiled at military officers from both the USA and Turkey dressed in full regalia. We made our way around the bejeweled and fashionable wives and escorts (think the television show Mad Men to get the fashion sense), to find an opening in the crowd pressed up against the resplendent buffet table. There, we could take morsels of the finest Turkish dishes: *börek*, and *tarama*, *köfte*, rice, eggplant, and tender slices of beef, and withdraw to our own private dining area under the table. Our secret fort of linen table cloths and thick mahogany legs was the perfect setting for us to feast while we admired the lovely shoes and crisply pleated pant legs circling around us like some sort of magic carousel. When we got tired, we went to the coat room and laid out the softest furs on the floor to sleep on.

The main dishes at these parties were prepared by the embassy chef, but other members of the staff, including my mother, helped with the cooking. My mother was asked to prepare *yaprak dolması* for 150 guests for one of these occasions. *Yaprak dolması* (succulent, lemony, stuffed grape leaves wrapped around seasoned meat) takes some time to prepare.

First there's the filling, and then each leaf is carefully rolled, one by one. I've told you how Turks, especially from the Black Sea love to tell great stories. Well, the story about what happened when my mom was asked to prepare 300 grape leaves is referred to in my family as the famous "Grape Leaves Story," and you can find it along with the recipe on page 233.

We moved from the basement of the Turkish Embassy to that of the Madagascar Embassy around the corner on Massachusetts Avenue when Mom took a job there for a higher salary. As children, we figured this was a "step up" because the building had a small backyard with a pool. In the afternoons, we would walk the ambassador's standard poodle Lulu in front of the beautiful buildings on Embassy Row, and then play in the small pool. If my father got a free few minutes between runs he would sit with us in the yard. He always looked so chic in his chauffeur's uniform and neatly trimmed moustache. While he sat in a patio chair smoking a cigarette, we scrambled to impress him with our jump-rope prowess or swimming skills. We had long since learned not to pee in the ambassador's pool.

Granpapa Kemal didn't deserve Granmama Sara. She was really such a beautiful and kind wife, a woman often referred to as "an angel." Unfortunately, even though Kemal loved his wife, he could not find a generosity of spirit, even for her. He had amassed a small fortune in savings but still allowed her to suffer from asthma, refusing to pay for a doctor. I'm so sorry, Tant Ida. I know you asked me to not say sad things about our family. But I think families can be well-served by insight into generational patterns that we may then be able to break.

And I certainly don't want to give the impression that it was all bad in the Revah household. Grandpa Kemal could be demanding and impatient one moment, and then suddenly change his mood and urge his wife to gather up the children for an evening walk and an ice-cream. He loved music, poetry, and art. He would sit on the balcony on hot summer evenings, and have my mother sing "à la Turka" for all the neighbors sitting on their balconies to hear.

SARA REVAH 1898-1967

O Pasajeros
Desparesyo Mujer de valor
Atristo a todo su deredor
Ijo y ijas yóran kon dolor
Rogan por eya al Kriador
Sufrio munco en kama
Asus 69 anyos dyo su alma
De°ando su buena fama
Durme en pas madre kerida
A gan Eden seas meresida

Oh passers by
A woman of valor has vanished
Leaving her surroundings in sadness
Son and daughters cry in pain
They pray for her to the Creator
Bedridden, she suffered much
In her 69th year she gave her soul
Leaving behind her fine reputation
Sleep in peace dear mother
May you be worthy of the Garden of Eden

But Kemal, the talented man with joie-de–vivre, who loved to dance and sing, simply lacked a capacity for compassion. He didn't seem to notice that his beautiful daughter Beti with the lovely voice was standing in shoes that had not fit her feet in years. In fact, my mother's feet were permanently deformed; her toes were piled one on top of the other so rigidly that she could never walk comfortably. For the rest of her life she suffered with those feet, even when she was finally able to buy her own shoes.

I often wonder what hardships my grandfather must have suffered as a child to make him unwilling to buy new clothes for his children, even when he could afford it. But Sara was patient and she persevered. When he had no more use for an old suit, she would tease it apart and re-use the material to make outfits for her four children.

By the time Sara was in her early fifties, she was already struggling to breathe, especially when she got off the tramway and walked up the hill to their house in *Kurtuluş*. Everyone would beg Kemal to call a taxi for this gentle dignified lady, so she wouldn't have to struggle with the climb. But he refused to spend the money. He would bark at her to keep walking, "*Yürü!*" (walk!), he would say, "*Yürü!*" And she did as he said, not out of fear, but to diminish the agony her children felt watching her suffer.

One day in 1967, at the age of 69, my grandmother had a particularly harsh asthma attack . She didn't survive it. Ironically, her husband Kemal wrote a beautiful poem for her which is engraved on her headstone in both Ladino and Hebrew.

AMERICAN PIE

Then my parents bit off their first taste of American Pie; we bought a house. We moved into a bungalow on 6th Street in Takoma Park. Çaya and I were enrolled in Takoma Park Elementary School, the original two-story schoolhouse across from the church on Piney Branch Road. Ilhan attended Immaculata, the elite Catholic School for children of senators, ambassadors and presidents. Every morning she would leave the house in her neatly pressed jumper, and my father would drive her to school like royalty in the back of the embassy limousine. My brother Kemal, too young for school, was cared for at home by a sad chain-smoking couple who rented our basement apartment.

We kids were on our own from 7:00 in the morning to perhaps 7:00 every night. We got involved in everything we could. Çaya and I walked to school early to learn French. We proudly manned our corners as crosswalk patrols; standing proudly, arms akimbo, brandishing our sashes emblazoned with a silver shield. We made friends with the Naisbitt kids around the corner, whose father John would one day write the best seller *Megatrends*. We auditioned for the children's chorus, Community Singers. The aptly named director Mrs. Singer must have been politically connected, because we sang for venues like the Democratic Convention at the Mayflower Hotel, and the home of Oscar Roy Chalk, owner of the D.C. transit system. There was a small gathering at Mr. Chalk's house and I sang a solo for Robert Kennedy Jr., who patted me on my head. We did smart things like joining the Girl Scouts, and not so smart things like climbing up on the roof to see if we could touch the chimney. We got yelled at by neighbors a lot.

With four children all under 10 running amuck, the inevitable happened and the Takoma Park house caught fire. Thankfully, the only victims were my father's two parakeets. We had to move again, temporarily. This time to the garage of the Madagascar Embassy on Reno Road. At John Eaton Elementary School we were introduced to children of a "different" income bracket, a fact that became immediately clear from the way the teachers and other children looked down on us. Apparently not knowing how to tell time as a 6 year-old was a capital offense, because I was kept in from recess as punishment. Of course no one had ever actually tried to teach me how to tell time, but I never questioned authority.

After the fire, we stayed in the garage of the embassy - a horrid place. The six of us slept on two mattresses on the concrete floor. I laid awake at night listening to the rats scurrying around. When we excitedly told my mother about how the groundskeeper drowned a rat in the garbage can with a garden house, she took quick action, and we thankfully

ÇAYA WAS HERE!

moved from there to a small house in the neighborhood. We got a nanny; Mom had brought home another stray, a young French nun who was pregnant and spoke no English. We talked to her in French, and loved her for her skillet-size pancakes (ode to crêpes, I imagine) and the Mapo she gave me every day after school.

With repairs complete, we finally moved back to our house. Baba now worked as a guard in the Pan American building downtown, while Beti continued at the Turkish Consulate. My sister İlhan was again left in charge of us. We had always been instructed to obey her and call her *Abla* (older sister). The honorific was small compensation for the heavy load she carried as a young child having to keep the three of us safe and occupied. Ilhan was (and still is) brilliant. She was amazingly resourceful and got us involved in all kinds of projects in the long hours between the time school ended and my parents got home. She had us troll the neighborhood for items we could sell at our own yard sales. She had us set up lemonade stands. We put on carnivals in our front yard where we offered rides in grocery carts which we pushed up and down the street. We put on a Carnival for Muscular Dystrophy and made enough money to win a bicycle from Captain Tug on T.V. We all agreed that the poor boy down the street should have it. We put on plays in the garage, which every kid in the neighborhood paid a nickel to watch.

Ilhan was more our mother and teacher than sister. One summer, she decided to open a school in the garage, and taught me to read. Despite my protests, she also taught me that there was a number smaller than one and that there were these things called decimals. Here was a true *Karahasanoğlu*. She taught me so well I skipped first grade and joined my sister Çaya in the second grade (much to her chagrin) when I was only 6 years old.

Figure 104: Onk Niso certainly had the Revah joie-de-vivre (shown dancing in a restaurant in Istanbul in 1961). My mother sponsored him and he arrived in the US in 1962 with his wife Mati and their children Sami and Sara. On their way here, they visited Granmama Sara's sister Buka in Paris. It was Buka's husband and daughter-in-law who died in the German camps.

We spent many afternoons at the Takoma Park Library on Cedar Street, the first Neighborhood Library built in D.C. I'd follow Çaya through the main reading room to the children's area, a recessed alcove with a fire-place and raised platform. We'd sit on the floor with the other children and get lost in the magical stories the children's librarian read to us.

By then Çaya had become pretty independent herself and this "Abla" big-sister thing with Ilhan was wearing thin. Not only did the title give Ilhan clear authority, but my father had recently decided we should say it in English, which meant he wanted us to call her "Sister." Of course, he didn't realize that "sister" has a completely different meaning in America, and Çaya was mortified, especially when her friends called her out on this bizarre salutation. Çaya finally threw down the gauntlet and refused.

The sharp slap from Ilhan's hand across Çaya's face only galvanized the younger sister's resolve, launching Çaya's life-long struggle with Ilhan

for "self-determination." To this day, (and we're into our late fifties now), the two sisters maintain a certain détente, a fascinating dance between two cultures; Ilhan's Turkish world of respecting the dominion of the elder sibling and Çaya's American egalitarianism. Kemal and I, not wanting to be caught in the middle of this fray, have unfortunately vacillated back and forth through the years, with our feet tenuously planted, one on each side of the cultural and familial divide.

FRESH OFF THE BOAT

We had been in the United States three years, but were still very much "fresh off the boat." I've already told you about how my mom would crack and peel hard boiled eggs for us as the credits rolled, and how Beti would pull out her paring knife to slice cheese and tomatoes and hand them down the row. Can you imagine what other people in the theatre must have been thinking of this immigrant family happily munching away at dinner during the Music Man?

Speaking of movies, sometimes after school the four of us would walk down Butternut Street for a matinee. Never quite knowing or caring where we were going, I just followed Ilhan and Çaya wherever they went. This time it was to Sam's, a magical little candy shop, to stock up for the movie. We bought wax lips and wax pan flutes filled with syrup that you could drink when you bit into the wax. We bought straws filled with flavored sugar that we poured into our gaping mouths. There was Good and Plenty, and Bonomo Turkish Taffy which I can still spell because of their catchy advertising jingle. We picked up chocolate cigarettes coated with powdered sugar, individually wrapped in rolling paper, and placed 20 to a pack. (We were children of the "Mad Men" era, after all. Even the Flintstones advertised cigarettes!) We'd offer them to one another, "care for a smoke?" and then blew into the wrapper and watched the powdered sugar waft into the air just like real smoke. A Chunky chocolate bar cost a whole nickel, so we settled instead for 1-cent strands of black or red shoe-string licorice which the proprietor kept looped over nails on the wall.

Well-stocked with loot, we'd head back down the street to the theater, where Tant Mati sat smiling from her stool inside the ticket booth. She had landed the job quickly. Amazing really, since she had only recently arrived to the USA with Onk Niso. My mother had managed to sponsor her brother and his family, so they arrived and moved into our house with their two kids Sara and Sami. The Revah family stayed with us in our small bungalow at 6919 6th Street, N.W. for several months while Niso established himself. By then, he had excellent musical credentials and landed a terrific job at the Disc Shop on Connecticut Avenue near the Hilton. Niso's years of experience there paved the way for him and Tant Ida's husband Leon Dana to open the Serenade Record Shop which would support their families for decades. Onk Niso's knowledge of classical music was limitless, and Serenade records was the best place in D.C. to go for hard-to-find jazz, classical, and international recordings.

Mati has her own stories about adjusting to American life. After having been on the job at the movie theatre a few weeks a man had called the theatre to ask if it was "integrated." Not knowing what that word meant, Mati had to ask the manager. The 1954 Supreme Court decision on Brown v. Board of Education was supposed to have ended segregation, but in 1962 people were still unsure that businesses would respect the law. Many did not. Happily, the manager assured Mati that the Takoma Park Cinema in 1962 was indeed allowing blacks and whites to sit together to watch a movie. Mati never imagined this could be an issue.

In any event, Mati always made sure her little nieces and nephew paid the entrance fee; we never got in for free, even when the price went up from 10 cents to a quarter. We complained about it to Mr. George and his hand puppet, the theatre's live act before the cartoons. We often sat

Figure 105: Within months of their arrival, Sara and Sami were speaking English and had definitely learned how to dress "American Style." Here we are in the Takoma Park house. From left to right are Çaya, Kemal, Sara, Ilhan, Sami, and me.

through the double-feature (two movies for the price of one) because movies were short back then; unless it was Lawrence of Arabia.

My cousin Sara was all of 7 years old (6 months younger than me) and though I was speaking less and less Turkish, we became fast friends. Sara and I hung out in our secret clubhouse - the walk in closet off the upstairs hallway - where we excitedly giggled about our secret language that no one else in the world knew. It was called Spanish.

Clearly, by the time the Revahs arrived, we had already begun to acclimate to American culture; the differences between ourselves and our cousins were remarkable. We were stunned seeing little Sami for the first time, dressed in Lederhosen-style shorts and sandals. Sara was wearing a cute little dress her mother had made for her. Unfortunately, American girls at the time of the British Invasion were wearing poodle skirts below the knees, and Sara's dresses, all hemmed just inches below Sara's bottom, were scandalous. They elicited merciless jeering and mockery from my sisters until Mati put together a new wardrobe for her daughter. It was tough for Sara; the poor girl had gotten off a plane from Istanbul one day, and the next morning was off to first grade not knowing a single word of English.

Figure 106: My mother attended one ATA (American Turkish Association) or embassy party after another in the 60s. Her social circle grew quickly as more family and friends arrived in the United States. In this photo we see Richard Plihal, a captain in the US Navy, Tant Mati (who worked at the Moroccan Embassy), and her husband Niso (Washington's expert on classical music records at the Disc Shop), "Aunt" Ester who arrived in the US alone with her young son David, Marylene Tinaz, a French woman with an acerbic wit who married the Turkish jeweler Bedi, and my mother Beti who loved having chic friends. Missing at these parties was my father, Zeki, who felt uncomfortable in these crowds, preferring to stay home with the children.

MOUNTING TENSIONS OF THE LATE 60'S

Zeki and Beti were busy, busy, busy. They each worked long hours to make ends meet, and it took a toll on their relationship. Dad would get home in the late afternoon to find a houseful of children rushing around picking up couch pillows, dishes, stray animals, bicycles and anything else we had gotten into between the time school let out and he came home. On a good day, he would go out into the small front yard and mow the grass. Owning a house was next to impossible for him in Turkey, so having a piece of land, bushes to clip, and a driveway for his used white Pontiac was like a dream come true.

But even Zeki had to admit that the neighborhood was changing. President Kennedy, much loved and a friend of civil rights, had been

shot. We ran across the street to watch it at a neighbor's house, and didn't know what to make of it at all. My parents took it in the gut. Their vision of America, pristine and hopeful, was sliding back like an old boat into murky waters. This was when their fighting really started.

Both exhausted and feeling their dreams slip away, my parents started to take their frustrations out on each other. His old world vision of family life with a loving wife who would be home making dinner every evening was not at all in line with the cosmopolitan life Beti had embraced amongst the diplomatic elite. She often worked very late into the night either putting on or attending one diplomatic gala after another. She was also a founding member of the American Turkish Association, an organization he wanted nothing to do with. For more than ten years she served on its board. Parties, poetry readings, festivals kept her tightly knitted into the Turkish community while my father remained conspicuously absent. He was spending his evenings at home watching Westerns on a small black and white television with four children, mounting bills, and a growing sense of disappointment and resentment.

Beti, like her father, had an insatiable appetite for life. If there was laughter and music, she was there. And if there were cards, she was there until midnight. Beti loved to gamble. The friendly card games among friends in our kitchen using navy beans as chips gradually evolved into serious poker tournaments among a motley crew of hairdressers, divorcees, and newly arrived embassy personnel. She became less and less accessible, if that's possible. We'd call her at work and in mid-conversation she would change her voice to make it sound like she was talking to someone about embassy matters and then hang up abruptly. She'd come home tired, quickly feed us frozen TV dinners or pot pies from the poorly-stocked fridge and then change into glamorous clothes for an evening event at some embassy.

For my dad, who had lost his mother as an infant, seeing her leave the house was always painful. They would fight, she would cry. She would leave. Late night arguments became commonplace. Thank God for Saturday mornings, because they would stay in bed until noon while we watched cartoons and our favorite shows, My Friend Flicka, Sky King, Astro Boy, Mighty Mouse. When she opened the door, we would all run into their room and jump on the bed, throwing ourselves on top of my father while comics and newspapers flew this way and that. They'd be in love again, and they'd laugh at each other's jokes, tease each other, or dance in the living room to Perry Como.

Moving to the Suburbs

Unfortunately the gambling didn't stop and money began to get tight. At the same time racial tensions were running high. It was the Civil Rights Era with plenty of unrest. Takoma Park was experiencing "white flight." We were soon part of a very small white minority at school, which would have been fine, I think, were it not for the fact that when we were picked on, it was always by larger black kids. The situation made my mother nervous enough to convince my father to sell his beloved house. By the time of the 1968 riots, we had moved to a three bedroom basement apartment in the Maryland suburbs.

I can't say we liked the move. We found white children to be very unfriendly and provincial (to say it kindly) in their world view. We felt much more foreign among whites than we ever had in our African-American community. We tried hard to fit in, especially Ilhan, who was a teenager by then. She began to bring friends home after school, friends who seemed particularly keen on the liquor cabinet my parents kept unlocked in the living room. Being hospitable Turks, we felt very happy to offer these older kids as many drinks as they liked, which we served with nice glasses and a cocktail napkin. We certainly didn't expect the crowd of boys that showed up the next day, but by then we had run out of my father's best chocolate liqueur and Crème de Menthe.

By this time, Baba (Dad) had left his job at the Turkish Embassy and bought a taxicab. Though he was now a "hack," his Diamond Cab car #823 was kept as ship-shape as any diplomatic limousine, and he drove his fares as if he were driving an ambassador. Every evening, Zeki would come home and empty out his coin till onto his bed, and count the money he had made that day. An avid coin and stamp collector, he'd separate out the true silver dimes and quarters from the copper-filled, and set them aside. He later gave me this collection of silver coins which helped get me through my lean college years.

Picnics

In the early 1970s, by the time my mother and her brother Niso sponsored the immigration of their sister Ida's family (husband Leon, son Silvio, and daughter Suzy), the Turkish community was well-established in D.C. Several families, thirty to forty people, would get together regularly for picnics either at the Tidal Basin near the Jefferson Memorial, or sometimes driving out to George Washington's home in Mount Vernon. Kids would play soccer or volleyball while the men pushed picnic tables together and the women laid out pre-made dishes. Peeled tomatoes and cucumbers would be sliced and laid alongside cheeses and hard- boiled eggs. Small spiced meat patties called *köfte* were ready to be grilled, skewers were threaded with onion, green pepper, tomatoes and meat for *şiş kebab*. Someone would open a large Tupperware of a bean salad called *piyaz*, and someone would place whole watermelons into plastic bags and submerge them into a nearby stream to stay cool. My father and uncles would tie a rope between two trees and fold a blanket up and over to create a makeshift hammock. Not so expensive oriental carpets were laid out on the grass under a large tree, along with blankets and table cloths. Two or three games of *tavla* (backgammon) would start up while a group would set up in a small circle to hit around a light volleyball. The boys would challenge each other with a soccer ball, deftly trying to get past one another with a quick kick, sometimes back behind themselves and over the head of the opponent. My "cousin"

Dide Saracli, a tomboy like myself would play hide 'n seek with me while her mother *Tülin* sliced a homemade spicy sausage called *sucuk*. Her husband *Dr. Teoman*, one of my father's only true friends in America, was a really good *tavla* player. He would lounge around with the other men on blankets, a cigarette dangling out of his mouth and two tiny dice effortlessly flying out of his hand and ricocheting off the sides of the *tavla* board. Tea was brought along in a thermos and they drank it in little tulip-shaped tea glasses.

Figure 107: (Above) We girls got plenty of attention for our theatrics, which was hard on our little brother Kemal. Beti wrote "our animals" on the back of this photo. (Below) Left to right: Beyhan, Beti, Zeki, Sara, Kemal, Mati, Niso, Ilhan, Sami, and Çaya. In the late 60s we were all busy getting involved in our American lives. The Revahs embraced all things Americana, and being Turkish began to matter less and less to all of us - except my father. He tenaciously clung to the old ways and couldn't accept ideas like dating, or girls playing Rock and Roll or basketball.

My parents had settled into a sort of "detente." They still accepted their religious differences, but begrudgingly. Sarcastic comments about each other's faiths began to permeate conversations as a way to relieve tension. One thing that made my father very uncomfortable about Judaism, for example, was seeing women at the synagogue flaunting their jewelry and expensive hats. He couldn't square this with his Muslim concept of modesty and not drawing attention to yourself, especially at times of worship. It really irritated him to see people at the synagogue in "finery." My mother, on the other hand, couldn't stand how Muslim women seemed to hide themselves with *hijab* (the Muslim concept of modesty which has become somewhat synonymous with wearing a headscarf). To her, it seemed sad and oppressive. Their observations of each other's religions didn't cause fights really. They were just festering wounds which never seemed to heal. He would accuse her of being a pleasure-seeker because she loved to go to the Kennedy Center or to extravagant parties. He would impersonate her laughing by baring his teeth in a grotesquely exaggerated smile. My mother would call him a barbarian with no joy for life. He claimed that the Jews were indeed the chosen people, but sarcastically noted that we are not told exactly what God had chosen them for. She couldn't understand how he could expect her to sit home night after night like a dour Muslim housewife. He couldn't understand why she needed so much approval outside the home.

They never really fought about Israel, mostly because the topic was just too hot, too loaded. On some level she shared his outrage at the treatment of the Palestinians. But she was also unable to openly agree with him without feeling she had betrayed something at her core. So they would back off the issue and settle into less hazardous territory. He would scoff at her careless gaiety, she at his arrogance and inflexibility. Then they would turn on classical Turkish music, bring out the playing cards and make each other laugh.

Oh, and they did laugh! They were comfortable making fun of each other's ethnic stereotypes and would fall over laughing when we wrapped head scarves tightly around our faces like good Muslim girls. She loved his impersonation of "the pompous Jewish businessman." He would begin by sitting way back in his seat, floating one arm grandly over the back of the chair. Slinging out one leg over the other, and pretending to smoke a cigarette with one hand, he would slowly and dramatically thumb invisible worry beads one by one, with the other. He would tell us that these normally small beads (a Middle Eastern addiction for all the faiths) were, in this case, golf ball size and made of solid gold. My mother would fall over laughing as he absent-mindedly perused the ceiling, slowly flipping the beads while mimicking their sound, "shahk... shahk... shahk."

Beti and Zeki were forever in love. He was her Errol Flynn. Manly, strong and silent. He fixed cars, built things, rode horses. She was his seductress. He felt she had cast a spell on him. Like that scene in the 1924 film Metropolis, where a crowd of men are driven wild by the provocative dance of a scantily clad temptress, so was my Ottoman father mesmerized by that pretty Jewish girl.

frustrated, beaten down, yet undefeated by a callous world. In each other they found a kindred spirit and fellow warrior. She was the first person who understood his creative nature, his artistic talent, his acerbic wit. He was the man who took her away from her oppressive father and delighted in her uniqueness and capability. All they wanted in life was to love each other, and they were both willing to sacrifice everything for it. That was their bond. So again and again they wiped off their disappointments like gravel on knees after a tumble. They looked into each other's eyes, recognized themselves, and were comforted by the familiarity. So each morning was new, and they would wake up ready to give it another shot. Because they couldn't imagine life any other way.

She was young, vivacious, an unabashed flirt. She could charm anyone, a fact which he both loved and hated. She always wanted more. More out of life. She couldn't help but live it burning the candle at both ends. She was compelled to attend every single ATA event, even if it meant a huge argument beforehand and afterward. She attended every party, every Kennedy Center concert. She played poker like a con artist. She bet on the horses. She bet on the slots. She bet on him putting up with it.

Figure 108: Beti at an evening event in the early 1970s

Figure 109: When Beti and Zeki were in sync, they were a joy to be around. In this photo, Ilhan, Zeki, Beti, and Granpa Kemal are enjoying a family meal.

And as I said, in their darkest times, these issues would lead to horrible fights which left them both wounded and demoralized. They were bound together by a subconscious cognizance that they were both still surviving tragic childhoods. They had been clever capable children,

Figure 110: (Above) One of the many gifts Beti received for her service at the Embassy of Iran, a porcelain box with a picture of Shah Reza Pahlavi and the royal family. (Below) Beti preparing for one of the embassy's elaborate parties.

THE EMBASSY OF IRAN

Around 1966 Beti got a great job as receptionist and head secretary at the Embassy of Iran. The Shah was still in power and the Embassy enjoyed a very close relationship with the American government. Most people were and still are unaware of America's complicity in overturning Iran's democratically elected government and how we installed the Shah Mohammad Reza Pahlavi. The naked truth is that while Iran's dissidents were being imprisoned and tortured by the dreaded Iranian secret police (*Savak*) my mother was helping put together glorious parties for the Iranian Ambassador and his American guests. We attended more than a few lavish dinners at the embassy, strolled the gardens and sat in the immaculate room where hundreds of thousands of pieces of intricately cut mirrors adorned the underside of the dome. And Beti loved fielding the Ambassador's calls from people like Elizabeth Taylor and Jacqueline Bisset. She loved the embassy and they loved her. Of course no one there ever suspected that Beti, a woman who had her hand in almost everything that went on in that embassy, was Jewish.

Beti was "passing" as a Muslim and was so nervous about being exposed and losing her job that she made a point of observing Ramadan and speaking Farsi. When we visited the embassy she would pull us aside and remind us to keep our mouths shut. We used to threaten her that if she didn't let us go to such and such a party, we would call the embassy and tell them she was a Jew. She would always laugh, albeit nervously.

The incredible irony is that when the Ayatollah Khomeini headed the Islamic revolution against the Shah in 1979, everyone in the Embassy in Washington was immediately fired . . . except for Beti. There were two reasons she was kept on. One: she was the only one there who really knew how to run the place. And two: her son-in-law, my sister Ilhan's husband Younos had a reputation for being a devout Muslim with very leftist politics. This gave my mother credibility with the new regime. Who could have imagined that the Islamic Republic of Iran, which was holding several hundred Americans hostages, had an Embassy in Washington which was being run by a little Jewish lady from Turkey?

The new ambassador and staff came with a wholly different agenda. The great rooms of the building were divided into little cubicles, and the amazing dome room was closed off. Thousands of dollars worth of Dom Perignon were poured out onto Massachusetts Avenue as a symbol of rejection of the old regime's patterns of excess. Beti was not ashamed to admit she missed the grandeur and excitement of the old Iran. She stayed about a year and finally moved on, unceremoniously, to her next position at the Embassy of Tunisia.

ZEKI TAKES OFF

When my mother and father flew to Afghanistan to visit Ilhan and her husband Younos in 1974, Beti had no idea what Zeki was planning. Their stay in Kabul was uneventful, and Beti returned home with suitcases full of Afghan antiques to sell at the Georgetown flea market. She managed to pay for her entire trip with money she earned selling broken teapots and rings fashioned from British coins left over from England's ill-fated conquest. Kemal and I were living with Mom and Dad in yet another apartment, this time in Adelphi, Maryland. Çaya had moved out. Beti was rarely home, but we had all gotten used to that. Then one night she woke me up, crying. She had expected my father to follow her home in a couple of weeks, but it had been a month and Zeki had called her to say he was not coming back. He planned to live in Afghanistan with my sister Ilhan. Being a teenager, I couldn't grasp what had happened; that is until a memory quietly dawned on me. It was one afternoon a few days before my parents left for Afghanistan. I had come home from campus to find my dad laying on top of his bed. This was strange for a man who was always making himself useful. He seemed somber, glum. I laid down next to him and for some time neither one of us spoke. Then he petted my brow and told me he loved me. He told me he was sorry. When I asked him why, he confessed that he had not been a good human being. I tried to protest but he wouldn't listen. "I could have done things differently," he said, looking at the floor, shaking his head. "I regret so many things." Now Dad was telling Mom that he was going to stay in Afghanistan. I suddenly realized he had already said goodbye to me.

Mom was devastated. Convinced of a conspiracy, she came into my room night after night, sobbing inconsolably. The late-night drama was just too much for me, and being only 18 years old at the time, I did the only thing I could do and ran away myself. I quit school and took off for Washington State, as far as I could go without a passport. I had a girl-friend who put me up, and got a job working at a Dairy Queen. School was off my radar for the time being.

Ever resourceful, Beti tracked me down. She phoned me the night I left with a kind of tender, motherly voice I was unaccustomed to. Frankly I didn't want to have anything to do with her. Teenage angst and self-ishness, coupled with a healthy dose of resentment that she had finally noticed me. But she had a way of softening my heart. As months passed she began suggesting I visit relatives in California, and then maybe drop in on an aunt in Albuquerque. Gradually she convinced me to come share an apartment with my sister Çaya in Maryland. Within a year Beti had worked her magic, and I was home.

Meanwhile, she had recovered too. She had taken a free trip to Tunisia, paid for by the embassy as her retirement gift. She came back with a photo album full of pictures of herself, now in her 60's, joyously dancing alone in the center of a crowd of Arabs cheering and clapping. We were all receiving letters from my father, too. He seemed to miss us, but it almost didn't matter. We were doing okay.

Then one day, after living in Afghanistan for two years, we learned that my dad had gone back to Turkey. He was welcomed into the home of his ex-wife and step-sister *Zehra Hanım* who had been waiting more than 25 years for him to return to her. They lived together in her small apartment, and I really don't know what the living arrangements were. It was none of my business. My half-brothers Turhan and Orhan finally had both their parents together again. It was joyous for them, and they ate together every night as a family. Zeki and Zehra had known each other 40 years by then. They had been siblings, then spouses, then parents, then ex-es. Who could say what they were to each other now?

Figure 111: In Turkey, Zeki enjoyed his three grandchildren. Here are two of them; Turhan's daughter Nurcan and Orhan's son Ercan. Though he had told Beti that he was living with his sister, my niece Gülcan told me that during those days, the relationship between my dad and Zehra Hanım (still legally his wife) was much, much more.

Figure 112: Beti was always the first one on the dance floor, even if it was a dance floor for one. She brought life to every party, and light into every room she entered. Watching our mother so comfortable as the center of attention equipped us with public speaking skills and the ability to "work a room." But my father had grown increasingly irritated that his wife was getting more vivacious as she got older, not less.

When Zeki told my mother he was staying with his step-sister, his choice of words was meant to provide assurance and some comfort, an idea for her to hold onto after the rug had been pulled out from beneath her. But after Beti had a few weeks to mull it over, I believe she came up with her own story to cling to. She figured she was much younger than *Zehra Hanım*, and certainly more fun. She decided it would only be a matter of time until Zeki returned.

Anyway, she had gotten used to life without him; without the arguments, without the accusations. She had made new friends and was enjoying her freedom. She rented a pretty little apartment in the Willoughby and enjoyed entertaining friends there. At one time or other Çaya, Kemal and I crashed on her couch for a few months between jobs, or after our own breakups.

Part of the freedom Beti enjoyed during those years included running a "gambling den" of sorts in her Chevy Chase apartment. Just recently,

one of my dearest Turkish friends told me how he used to play poker there. It was a veritable casino. Maybe 20 to 25 people would show up on any given night; hairdressers, poets, widows and divorcees, jet-setters and housekeepers - all professional card sharks playing for some real money. They'd sit hunched over card tables set up in every corner of that smoke-filled one bedroom apartment while Beti held court, going from one table to the other serving tea, emptying ash trays and, of course, collecting the house fee.

Yes, Beti had survivor skills. She could put unpleasant thoughts out of her mind completely, and focus only on tomorrow and its possibilities. She still charmed and flirted, seemingly unaware of how old she was. There was always another show at the Kennedy Center, another French movie, and Beti still had a lot of living to do. Many months passed this way without incident, until the day Beti learned that Zeki had left Turkey and Zehra. But instead of coming home, he had returned to Kabul to be with my sister Ilhan. This is when her heart broke.

Zeki went to Afghanistan, and we didn't hear much from him for a few months. But there appeared to be a falling out with Ilhan, because he soon returned to Washington. Almost immediately, Beti forgave him and welcomed him home. They moved into a ground floor apartment in the residence of the Ambassador of Tunisia and enjoyed a second honeymoon, if that term can apply to people who were never officially married. I should mention that Beti always insisted that she and my father were, in fact, married under common law, which requires only seven years of cohabitation. But who cared about that now? They were finally together again! She didn't seem at all concerned that she could no longer compete for high-power positions like the one she held at the fabulous Embassy of Iran. In fact, the countries that now employed my mother were progressively less wealthy and less relevant to the global political landscape. Her duties were certainly less glamorous. Beti had made a deal with the Tunisian Ambassador. She and my father would live in his residence in exchange for my father working as his chauffeur and gardener while my mother wrote the occasional official letter and did the Ambassador's ironing. And the years they spent there on Arizona Avenue were very happy ones.

ZEKI TAKES OFF

Again, politics complicated our lives. When the Russians invaded Afghanistan in 1981, Ilhan's husband Younos was arrested for allegedly sympathizing with the *Mujaheddin* (freedom fighters). It should be made clear that at that point, 99.99% of Afghans were Mujaheddin sympathizers, and they were backed clandestinely by the U.S. Government. (The 2007 movie *Charlie Wilson's War* with Tom Hanks is about this period). It became clear that Younos would not be released anytime soon, and that the family was in jeopardy. So, while our government was funding Osama bin Laden to help him and the Taliban rid Afghanistan of the Godless Russians, Ilhan managed to escape with their four children. They endured many months in India while Younos languished in jail, trying to put together the appropriate bribe to get him out. A year later, The much changed but unbroken Younos was released. All the family's worldly possessions had been confiscated by the Afghan puppet regime, so when my sister's family moved back to Washington, D.C. they came with nothing to their names but a suitcase.

The tension between Ilhan and my mother quickly erupted, causing my father to move out altogether to his own apartment, launching a new phase in their tumultuous relationship. For the next ten years, Beti and Zeki would live in separate apartments but "date" each other. It was an arrangement that worked for them on several fronts.

First, there were the grandchildren, ten in all. Clearly, family gatherings could only work if they both attended. Sometimes they behaved like a couple who could proudly admire what they had accomplished. At other times they could only manage to be civil to one another. But we were grateful to them for that, because it at least allowed us to all be together for Thanksgivings, birthdays, and weddings.

Their living arrangement also worked because they often genuinely missed each other. They spent time together, sometimes sleeping at each other's apartments, often entertaining friends and relatives together. For all intents and purposes they were still a couple. But when they got on each other's nerves, they would go home. That way, she could stay out as late as she wanted without him wondering where she was, and he could turn up the radiator as hot as he wanted without worrying that she would immediately throw open the windows. She could leave her shoes laying around without worrying that he would reprimand her. He could work on a jigsaw puzzle on the dining room table without fear that she would carelessly lose a piece.

This love-hate thing went on for years and their apartments took on their respective personalities. Her tiny apartment was like one of her flea market stands; sunny and bright, with every chachke, figurine, piece of costume jewelry and silver cigarette box prominently displayed on small tables. Beautifully framed paintings and photographs hung in tastefully arranged groups on every wall. In the bedroom, clothes were piled high on the bed, in the closets, in the bathtub. Her apartment door was always wide open, the sound of Turkish music and the wonderful smells of Turkish food wafting freely down the long hallway.

His apartment in Silver Spring was frugal, unadorned, functional; everything in its place. The last time I visited him there I sat at the dining room table while he cooked his fabulous chicken wing *Tas Kebab*. I noticed there was a five dollar bill thumb-tacked to the wall next to me. When I asked him about it, he said he had finally beaten her at Gin Rummy and kept this bill on the wall as a way to constantly remind her of that fact.

![Photo of grandchildren on a porch]

Figure 113: Beti and Zeki adored their grandchildren. Here are 9 of the 10 in 1995. Left to Right: Clay Conger, Ceylan Conger, Idris Mokhtarzada, Zeki Mokhtarzada, Isaac Buckley, Haroon Mokhtarzada, Gabriel Conger, Yahya Mokhtarzada, and Turhan Buckley. Unfortunately, this photo doesn't include the eldest grandchild, Homeyra Mokhtarzada. It's hard to get all 10 of them together in one place!

GRACE

My parents did us the honor of both living well and dying well.

Zeki had been undergoing dialysys for more than five years. Each time he went, he came home completely exhausted. Despite his protestations to the contrary, it became clear that Zeki could no longer care for himself. We moved his things into the basement of Ilhan's house where a small apartment had been set up. She had five children then, and he thoroughly enjoyed every one of them.

Then one day Zeki announced he would not go to dialysis anymore. We begged him to continue. We talked about a heart surgery that might help his symptoms. He stopped us in our tracks with ferocious eyes. With one hand gesturing down an imaginary road, he would say *Ben yolcuyum!* (I am on my way!). I called my half-brother *Turhan Ağabey* in Istanbul and told him he should come to the USA to "help dad's morale." He was there within a week. The two men, now 87 and 67, lived together quietly in that one-room basement apartment. They got up in the mornings together, made breakfast together, played cards together, father and son. For a couple of months it seemed that Zeki was indeed feeling better. One day he woke up, made his bed, ate breakfast and then went up to lay on the couch in Ilhan's living room. The kids were running around and I'm sure he heard them laughing as he took his last breath. He died with his eyes open.

I wondered where he had gone. Had he finally seen the vast, infinite, timeless, glorious Creator, Allah, God, Adonai, Tanrı? As much as he hated religious dogma, Zeki had always been a believer. He had said God's gifts were everywhere you look; each beautiful day, each new grandchild. He nurtured God's creations; baby rabbits, fine horses, flowers in the garden. He had retained a child-like wonder, always taking the time to marvel at the iridescent shine of a beetle's shell, the perfection of a soap bubble, the majesty of a lone tree in a field, the vastness of the ocean. Even life's tragedys were met with that same sense of wonder. illness and death were greeted with a calm submission to God's will.

He had been close to death before. In the late '80s I received word that my father had suffered a heart attack and was taken to the Intensive Care Unit at Holy Cross Hospital. Fearing the worst, I ran through the ER, shaken and crying. I rushed past nurses to find him sitting up in bed within a glass-enclosed cubicle. Contrary to my worst fears, he was smiling with mild embarrassment, the I.V. taped to his arm, oxygen nibs tucked into his nostrils, a spoonful of Jell-O jiggling in his hand.

He was surely aware that the strange calmness of the scene confounded my expectations, because when I sat next to him he shook his head quickly side to side – a Turkish way of asking, "What's going on with you?" When I couldn't answer, he understood. He told me not to be afraid of death, and then described his own father Hüseyin's passing.

"I was sitting by his bed, " Dad told me. "and my father was laboring with each breath. Then his eyes opened wide. He placed his open hand on his chest, and in great surprise he sighed, '*Allah!*' He then closed his eyes and was gone. Can you imagine what he saw, Beyhan? How wonderful it must have been - that it would cause him to say, Allah?" I stared at him, feeling shaky but safe, comforted that the moment I feared most, the moment of my own death, might actually turn out to be beautiful. "I'm not afraid of dying," he said. "*Allah büyük* (God is big)." His smile assured me.

Sometimes when I see something amazing I take a mental photograph of it and pray my memory will serve me late in life so that I can revisit the great moments. When I think of my father, I often go back to one of those photographs, one of those moments. I was in my late thirties and the family had gone to an amusement park. The weather had been hot, overcast, and drizzling rain all day. Undeterred by the rain, we decided to ride the roller coaster. We all piled in except my father who preferred to watch. He was almost 80 and had no interest in that kind of thrill. As the train of cars made the wide turn heading for the long ramp up to the top, I looked back to where we left my father. Suddenly the sun came out and everything wet seemed to sparkle and glitter. I spotted my father standing alone, the umbrella held over his head shimmering in the sunlight. Like a statue newly arrived from some long ago place and time, he stood calmly in his own shade while everything around him quivered with light. I pondered the scene as the clackety car started its steep ascent. I turned my eyes and traced the track ahead up to the sky and suddenly realized I was in for a hell of a ride and it would be without him.

My mother still had plenty of life in her. She was strangely detached from the events surrounding my father's death and the funeral itself. She had already compartmentalized, and stubbornly fixed her eyes on the present day. She couldn't have been happier when I started dating Bruce, a Jewish doctor. We tried to make her understand that he was an epidemiologist, not a medical doctor. "He does cancer research," I told her. "Prostate cancer research." She didn't really understand what a prostate is, so I told her it was something men had. Stunned, she said, "You mean he is studying the tra-la-la!?!" She used to call me every day to ask me about Bruce, warning me not to blow it, not to let him get away. At my wedding in 2002 she was the proud "Grand Dame." Having never worn a wedding veil of her own, I wondered if she would like to share mine for a photo. She was more than happy to oblige.

Beti lived her last years squeezing every last drop out of life. At the age of 78 she landed a job at the Embassy of Mauritania. Her fabulous career had seen better days; the embassy wasn't always able to make payroll or fix the leaky roof of the once-beautiful mansion housing their mission.

But she knew Mauritanians to be warm, kind people. Working in her fourth African embassy felt like coming home, and the staff definitely needed her diplomatic savoir-faire. (It was Beti, for example, who walked the new ambassador through the protocol for presenting his credentials to President G.W. Bush when he took his post in the United States.) When Beti wasn't answering the phones in French, English, and Spanish, she was writing official correspondence for His Excellency to sign. And the Mauritanian ambassador and staff were grateful to have her. They treated her like a queen, even though Mrs. Revah (as she always called herself) was walking slower and slower everyday. She was also getting very thin and her skin had turned a distinctly yellow hue.

She was close to 80 years old when she finally allowed us to take her to the doctor; the first doctor she'd seen in 40 years. (Beti firmly believed that if she went to a doctor she would die.) After our physician examined her, Mom sat in the waiting room while I got the news. It was a tumor the size of a football; pancreatic cancer. "How long?" I asked. "A year, six months?" No. "Two weeks, three weeks?" I pressed. "Maybe three weeks."

We didn't tell Beti. Honestly, if you knew my mom you would know the news would have killed her. The excessive bile her body was producing would soon make her too confused to understand what was happening, and then she'd gradually descend into a coma from which she would not recover. So my siblings and I agreed to make her last days happy. We told her she had a very bad urinary tract infection, "thank God". We gave her a multi-vitamin every day and told her it would make her feel much better. Accustomed to spending one night a week at Çaya's house, she didn't object when we suggested she stay there until she "recovered." So for three weeks, 'round the clock, one of us was with her. She rested on the couch in Caya's sunroom looking at the flowers in the backyard. Çaya's daughter Ceylan entertained her while Çaya's husband Herbie did all the heavy lifting and kept things calm. I arrived in the mornings to bathe her and drive her to work. (Yes, she still went to work.) The kind people at the embassy went along with the ruse. They welcomed her at the door , brought her coffee, and expected very little of her by way of productivity. Kemal picked her up in the afternoons to bring her home.

Her many, many friends came to visit. They brought flowers and wished her a quick recovery from her infection. Her hairdresser friends brought cards and they played poker together, laughing and gossiping. A steady stream of relatives and old friends came for tea. Beti basked in the warmth of the many well-wishers hovering around her.

Yes, I believe that on some level she knew what was happening. I was driving her to work one morning and turned on some of the Turkish dance music she loved. She waved her hand in the air as if she were dancing. She gazed at the sky, and sighed. And then wistfully, as if almost asking permission, she smiled and said, "I do not want to die."

One Tuesday morning I was bathing her, and as I shampooed her hair I realized how small she had gotten. Her head was tiny and fragile in my hands. She looked up at me and said, "God rewards people who are kind to their parents." That morning, when I dressed her for work, she asked to sit down for a moment. I suggested the unthinkable. "Maybe just this once we can call the embassy and tell them you're not coming in today. You can go tomorrow." She then spoke the words I thought I would never hear pass through her lips. "Yes, maybe I will not go to work today."

The next day she gently slipped into a coma. A day later Mehmet's wife Bonnie sat with her, polishing her nails. My niece Homeyra noticed there was no sound of her breathing. As she stood over her, Homeyra realized that Beti was gone. Bonnie knew it, of course, but decided to paint the last nail before putting her hand down.

Beti lay there throughout the morning as family members came to say their goodbyes. Niso arrived and said Kadish. Someone placed a rose in her hands and we finally pulled the sheet over her face.

The pretty Jewish girl's funeral was as unique and accepting as she was. Her casket was carried from the hearse on the shoulders of her son, her Muslim son-in-law, her Christian son-in-law, her Jewish son-in-law and the grandsons she was so very proud of. No one had ever seen a Middle Eastern funeral like this one. Younos said a few prayers from the Kuran in front of her plain pine coffin. Then he translated the Arabic into English. Jewish family members said Kadish. And when the Muslim family members lined up to pray, Jews joined them, shoulder to shoulder, kneeling and bowing as the Kuran (Qur'an) was recited. Looking through the crowd one could see yarmulkes and head scarves. People shared stories about how wild and irrepressible she was. Someone spoke of how they had once gone to Atlantic City and seen her there. They were riding up the escalator, leaving the casinos at 1:00 in the morning when they saw Beti coming down, getting ready for a night of gambling. I think the comment was, "and she was all dolled up."

We laid Beti next to my father at Norbeck Memorial Park and someone giggled that Dad had just rolled over in his grave when he realized she was coming. We kidded that she would confound and frustrate him through eternity. But in our hearts we sensed she would keep him good company. After she was lowered into the ground, we all took turns with the shovels, filling up the grave, as is our custom. Then we gathered around her. Family (young and old), friends (old and new), stood side by side to honor Betina and to lay her where she would finally rest.

Beti and Zeki left behind an impressive legacy. There are four children, ten grandchildren, and eight great-grandchildren. They are Fulbright scholars, Harvard Law School graduates, members of the Foreign Service, PhD's, Master Architects, business leaders, entrepreneurs, artists, chefs, mothers, fathers, sisters and brothers. My parents, the runaway love birds, took their wild, passionate, crazy ride together for 52 years. They were one of those lucky couples who enjoyed the rarest of God's gifts; a true love.

Cultural Issues and Turkish Etiquette

Turkish culture, like most traditional cultures, is surprisingly homogenous. Everyone essentially has the same cultural sensibility and conducts himself within the confines of a commonly accepted code of behavior. But one is hard-pressed to define a singular, common heritage or tradition here in the USA where many diverse communities from around the world add their own particular flavor to the proverbial melting pot. In this kind of cultural "stew," traditions and norms tend to sink to the bottom while change and individuality rise to the top. As long as you're not hurting anyone, and you're not a jerk, you can pretty much dress the way you like, hang out with whomever you like, do and say what you like. Not so in the Middle East where every aspect of your behavior is dissected and scrutinized for possible intentions and hidden meanings.

Here in the USA there's less chance of screwing up a social exchange because you can mean what you say and say what you mean. In the Middle East, when it comes to delicate situations, one rarely says what one means, at least verbally. Your mouth may smile and speak affirmatively while your body is saying something completely different. That way, if you're called out, you have plausible deniability. My point here is that body language in the Middle East is the way one speaks when verbal communication is deemed inappropriate. Unfortunately for immigrants, the intricate and rich body-language commonly understood in Middle Eastern society is lost on most Americans; falling on "deaf ears," if you will. I'll give you some examples of this later. At the same time, Americans often unwittingly give off body signals that a foreigner is hearing loud and clear. Without even knowing it, a person who doesn't speak body language can actually be shouting a competing message from the one he is speaking with his mouth. Imagine how stressful it can be trying to figure out which message to hear, and which to ignore.

When you're raised in America by "Old World" parents, you become a cultural schizophrenic, a split-personality of sorts. You are Turkish at home and American out in society. My parents didn't much care that the rules of proper Turkish etiquette they were teaching us at home had nothing to do with our outside American world. What they had learned is what they taught us. In the same why I share what I learned from them with you. And though Turks certainly have no expectations that Americans accept Turkish values, keeping these rules in mind might simply help you better understand the Turkish sensibility. Perhaps they will help you avoid accidentally insulting Turks you meet in your travels and maybe even bring you closer to your new Turkish friends.

EATING DECORUM

Sweets and pastries are always readily available in a Turkish home for the casual caller and unexpected friend. Guests, by Middle Eastern convention, expect and enjoy a warm, enthusiastic welcome at any time of day. I am not surprised that Turkey is known for its Oriental hospitality because in our house a guest was always welcomed, no matter the time or circumstance. If someone came during dinner, everyone would rush around setting another plate, pulling up a chair, pouring a glass of water. If there were not enough chairs, one of us would get up pretending to be finished so that the guest could sit down.

Some claim that this decorum is somehow ingrained since it has been deeply rooted by centuries of custom. People have often commented that my own children, born and raised here in the United States, have somehow inherited it. That's just silliness. Courtesy and decorum were drilled into us as very young children. And I drilled it into my children using very much the same admonishing tone and glances my mother and father used on me.

Table manners were non-negotiable. A table cloth was always required, as was a fork on a folded napkin to the left of each plate, as well as a knife on the right. My son Tory knew how to use a fork and knife by the time he was two years old. Though our sons complained bitterly about the formality surrounding meals at home, they ultimately came to appreciate the training when they saw how some of their friends ate.

I also taught my children the Eastern custom of politely refusing when someone they are visiting offers them something to eat. They were taught to not accept until they were asked a second time, to make sure the offer was sincere and to not give people the impression that they were underfed paupers. My sons always complained how frustrating it was for them to go their friends' houses for dinner. The mother would offer them food which they would politely decline, to demonstrate their excellent breeding. Unfortunately, she would take them at their word, and not offer the food a second time. The poor guys would come home hungry and confused.

Actually, in our house, we weren't even allowed to ask a guest if he or she would like something to drink. I remember Beti invited my high school music teacher Mr. Hansen and his wife for dinner. They had just arrived and been seated in the living room with my solicitous parents. My father signaled me to serve something cold to drink. Hoping to impress

Mr. Hansen with how very mature I was, I politely asked, "Would you like something to drink?" You'd think I had committed a capital offense. My father winced, and with his eyes directed toward the plant near him, (which had suddenly become very interesting somehow), exasperatingly whispered, "*Sorulmaz, kız. Kalk getir!*" (One doesn't ask, girl. Just get up and bring it!) My father assumed that any proper guest would obviously refuse if asked. To this day I wonder what Mr. Hansen would have responded.

DON'T ACT HUNGRY

In Turkey, showing too much anticipation or eagerness for food is considered poor manners. After all, breaking bread together is more about communion and talking than it is about food. If you act too hungry it gives the impression that you are either poor and don't get enough to eat, or that you're a glutton. It's also considered impolite to complain about being hungry, since so many people in the world are starving. It's also best not to act too impressed with the food. Yes, you should be grateful, and compliment the cook for her efforts, but it's considered childish to make a big deal out of it. Now I know that when you're with friends and a lovely dish comes out of the oven, you'll say "yum" and look forward to tasting it. I think that's normal. But if someone declines to eat part of a shared dish, like cake or pizza, don't shout, "That's OK. It just means more for me!" In any polite society, that is not funny.

SERVE FOOD IN THE RIGHT ORDER

To serve food Turkish style, be aware that the order in which people are served is important. The order is based on age, status, and whether or not you are a family member. The oldest guest, for example, would be served first. If there is an elderly couple, the husband gets served first. The guest should then politely refuse the first service, asking the host to offer it to the elder of the family. The family elder should then kindly refuse and insist that the guest receive it first. Obviously, the exchange is not about food; they are honoring and complimenting each other with respect and deference. Ultimately one of them wins out, and everyone feels warm fuzzies. The "winner's" wife should then be served, even if she is younger than others at the table, because she is included in her husband's status. When it comes to serving two people of the same age and family relationship, the one with the most education would win out. And in that case, his or her spouse would then get served, as well. If you are served first, please consider refusing the plate or trying to pass it on, as a sign of humility, an admired trait in Turkish culture. I mentioned earlier how direct verbal communication sometimes feels harsh to Turks. Instead, one employs a highly developed sub-layer of communication using seemingly innocuous actions to express displeasure. In this case, if you are at a dinner and end up being served after the teenager next to you, you might want to think about what you might have done to insult the host.

Buffet lines have similar protocol regarding who eats first. My siblings and I always prided ourselves on how we would wait at the end of the line so that the elders could get their food first. Politely deferring your place in line to someone shows that you are a selfless person, kind, with good breeding. I can't tell you how many times we kids finally made it to the food, only to find that other kids had rushed to the front and had grabbled up more than their share of the best desserts or *böreks*, leaving none for us. We chalked it up to their uncouth barbarism.

BASIC RULES FOR A GUEST AT DINNER

Here are some simple rules, dear reader, for when you are invited to dinner at the home of a Turkish or Middle Eastern family:

1. When food is placed on your plate, it's okay to glance at it and say thank you, but for God's sake don't dig in! At home, we never started eating until everyone had been served. Also, the guest started first.

2. Don't be the slightest bit impatient as other people's plates are being filled. If your meal is getting cold, too bad. Again, you're not there for the meal.

3. While you're waiting, try to make pleasant conversation. You can offer to help with service. When I was a child, men never helped in the kitchen, and women were expected to help the hostess. Of course this is changing, but many hosts would still be mortified if their male guest stood up to help in the kitchen. If you're a first time guest, allow the host to be attentive. (If the host doesn't allow you to help, sit down.) But you're great friends and have been a guest in the home before, feel free to playfully scoot the host out of the way as you help clear the table or do dishes. It's actually a good way to bring a friendship one step closer.

4. Do not serve yourself, unless the hostess insists. As children, if we were invited to dinner somewhere, we wouldn't dare serve ourselves, nor would we ask for anything. We would graciously accept whatever the hostess offered us, and so should you. If she forgets to give you water, too bad. If you want just a little more rice to go with the meat you got, too bad. As kids, even if we were dying of thirst, we were expected to sit quietly and wait until the hostess saw that our glass needed to be

filled. Luckily, Turkish/Eastern hosts keep a watchful eye on the comings and goings of food on the table. She will notice when all your rice is gone, and will either attempt to put more rice on your plate, or discretely ask a family member to do so.

5. If you want more of a particular dish, you need only look around the table a bit and allow your eyes to rest on it. Since all the family members are required to be vigilant in their duties to be hospitable and friendly, someone will notice the glance and offer you some. Try it! You'll see.

6. Also, remember that it is more appropriate to compliment the chef than the food itself. In Turkey, one says *Elinize sağlık* (health to your hands). A Turkish hostess would, more often than not, deflect the compliment and the credit with the simple response *afiyet olsun*, (may it be satisfying to you). More often than not, Turkish cooks will even add that phrase to the end of a written recipe, since it is almost like offering the food itself!

How to Tell When You've Been Insulted

I used to tell my husband that the best insults are wasted on Americans because they rarely know when they have been insulted. Here's my favorite example. My father's *muhallebi* (a type of rice pudding)was famous in our family. This dessert is labor intensive and requires loving care to prepare properly, so it was only served on special occasions. Obviously it was popular, so everyone was careful to take only a small portion. Well, almost everyone. Year after year, one of the in-laws would see my father enter with the large platter in his hands, and rush to the dessert line, exclaiming, "Yum, it's that pudding stuff!" And while others were still eating the meal, this person would heap at least a fourth of the *muhallebi* on his plate for himself and his family. This would enrage my father so much that he would threaten to not to make it anymore. "Why should I put in all this effort, just so this bum can eat half of it himself?" he would say. But Zeki Bey relented when we explained that the rest of us would suffer with no *muhallebi* because of one person's selfishness. So my father came up with a wickedly clever solution. At the next festivity, he arrived with not one, but two platters of *muhallebi*. He was still in his coat, laying the platters down on the buffet table when this fellow eagerly approached, looking like a kid in a candy store, but not in a cute way. "Wow, you made two!" he exclaimed. At which point my father responded, "Yes, I know how much you eat, so I made one just for you." "Gee thanks!" was the response. The guy happily indulged, with no clue that he had been insulted. My father's victory.

Obviously, this particularly subtle insult that my dad so beautifully served up reflects years and years of training in the delicate art of social interaction. Most insults are much easier to recognize, and avoid. Here are some of the most obvious:

"No" is a No-No

In the Middle East, it is considered very harsh to say the word "no." When someone offers you something, you cannot just say "no", or "no thank you" because it comes off as a rejection of the person as well as the offer. Instead, you might place your palm on your chest, and softly bow your head to one side and smile slightly. This means that you are satisfied and have no need of anything. When you shop in Turkey and ask the store owner if they have such-and-such, they won't say "no." They will respond with a head bow and the word *malesef* (unfortunately). When a wife asks her husband if he wants to go to the movies, he may simply pause before replying, to show his discomfort with having to decline her offer. She will quickly offer him an escape from this potential conflict by saying something like, "maybe you're a little tired today," at which point he can agree with her and thank her for understanding his needs. It's a centuries-old win-win strategy.

Indirectly to the Point

If you grew up in our family, and wanted to let your girlfriend know that you were mad at her, you would never just call her up and say, "I'm mad at you." Much too direct and hurtful. There are so many other ways to make the point without being confrontational. You might, for example, decline an invitation to her home with a lame excuse. Or perhaps you would sit near her with your back slightly turned to her. Perhaps your hello kiss would be too cool, and your eyes wouldn't meet. Perhaps you would hand her something but be looking in another direction instead of at her face. Perhaps you wouldn't put it in her hand at all, and instead flop it down on the table near her. I can tell you my mother got into plenty of arguments with waitresses who had inadvertently put down a plate or glass too brusquely. And, of course, there's the most brutal of all; not talking to her beyond the basic "hello" and "goodbye." My father used this one on me frequently to express his displeasure. When I was 16 we went a month without speaking. It was only because he was leaving on a trip that I was forced to submit. We were all saying goodbye to him at the airport and he had kissed everyone goodbye except me. My mother whispered to me, "Go kiss you father's hand." This act of kissing someone's hand and putting it to your forehead is a sign of respect and also submission. I didn't even think twice about it. I went to him and reached for his hand. Surprisingly, he gave it to me, which he was normally too humble to do. I kissed it and put it to my forehead. As I stood up, he lightly slapped me. Then he kissed me. Crying, he turned, and boarded the plane.

What did you call me?

A person can be insulted if you call him by his name. In most countries in the middle east, we refer to one another by title or position. As children we were taught to call Ilhan *abla* (older sister). Uncles were *amca* or *dayı*, depending on whether or not they were uncles by blood or by marriage. My aunts in America are Jewish, so, by family tradition, we refer to them as *tant* from the French word. Had they been Muslim, Tant Ida (my mother's sister) would have been Ida *Teyze*, and Mati (my mother's sister-in-law) would have been Mati *Yenge*. In fact it would have been perfectly fine to call her just *Yenge*. On the streets of Istanbul one approaches strangers with the same familial designations. Older women are called *Teyze* (aunt) or better yet *Teyzeciğim* (my dear aunt). Alternatively, men would be referred to as *Amca* (uncle).

The structure of the language itself assists in the status stratification process, providing formal and informal forms for the word "you." Similar to the Spanish *tu* versus *ustedes*, you in Turkish is *sen* and *siz* respectively. Though children may be addressed more often by their names alone; the word *kardeşim* (younger sibling), is employed frequently, especially to little boys on the street. In Afghanistan, the patriarch of Ilhan's family had the highest title I've heard yet. He was called *Kaka Jan Kelan*, loosely translated as "dear great uncle."

If you do address someone by their name and do not want to add the title, it is customary to add "dear" to the name. In Turkish I would be *Beyhancığım*. For people you don't know, always try to use *Bey* (sir) after the name when addressing a man, and *Hanım* (lady) for a woman.

Basic Body Language

As I mentioned earlier, body language like slight shifts in body position or a failure to meet someone's eyes communicates volumes. In Afghanistan, for example, it plays a critical role in communicating deference to status. One always rises, for example, when an elder walks into the room. But one gesture that I always found dear is when you beckon for someone. Here in the USA, you hold out your hand, palm up and move your pointer finger towards you a few times. Moving a single finger is a strange gesture in Turkish culture. Instead, you would beckon someone by holding out your hand, palm down, and curling all your fingers in slightly, and just once. This movement comes with an ever-so-slight nod of the head, so that the gesture looks more like a request than a command. Without the nod, the gesture reads as arrogant. Speaking of arrogance, Ilhan once refused to see a doctor because the first time she met him, he put his feet up with the soles of his shoes facing her.

The body language of Turks trails far behind Afghans or Iranians in terms of the subtlety of their social cues. Having lived in Afghanistan for ten years, Ilhan can tell you that Afghan body language had been raised to the level of fine art. In Kabul, when an elder entered a room, everyone stood up. When the elder then prepared to sit down, everyone would essentially lower their bodies slightly, as if to sit down, but hover over their seats for as long as it took for the elder to take his seat. If this person were to get up to leave the room, everyone would again rise.

In much of the Middle East, it is considered rude to enter a room before someone of higher status. My sister's mother-in-law and I negotiated one particular door for almost a whole minute before she finally pushed me through ahead of her. Ilhan promptly admonished me for letting her mother-in-law win that particular tussle. Ilhan showed me that when you sit, your feet must be drawn up very close to your chair. Your posture should be somewhat constricted so that even though you are sitting up, you don't appear to be trying to take up more space than your status warrants. She was able to send me signals across a room with the tiniest most innocuous cues. Just by looking down near my feet I could tell that she was warning me that my legs were out too far. By smiling at me and then strangely gazing toward her sister-in-law, she let me know that I had neglected to ask how she was doing, and about her family.

Palavra and the Collision of Languages

I remember one family gathering when everyone was sitting around the table listening to my mother tell a story about her latest escapade. Her brother, Onk Niso stretched out his arm and ran his other hand back and forth along it. Everyone laughed. I asked him the significance of the gesture and he said, "*palavra*." I asked him what he meant. He said, "You know what *palavra* is, right? It means 'talk' in Spanish." Of course I knew that. But I still didn't get the significance of the gesture.

"When we used to go to the barber in Turkey," he explained, "they had a heavy leather strap to sharpen their razor. They would run the razor back and forth along the strap like this." He repeated the motion. "And you know how people talk and talk at the barber? I am showing you how your mother does that kind of *palavra*." Everyone laughed, especially her.

The collision of languages was so common in our family we never noticed it was unique. When my mother talked with her Jewish relatives, you would hear Spanish and Turkish peppered with French, Greek, Hebrew, and English. If you dug deeper, you could even discern the old Arabic and Persian words in the Turkish. My mother would recount a story in Turkish to Ida who would respond in disbelief with "*Ay que me morier ayo no!"* (Ladino for "Oh, that I die, but no!") Sometimes, she'd even slip in some 15th Century Christian lingo; *"Ay Dio Santo Piadoso"* (Oh God, Holy, and Merciful)! She would often hold her hand to her chest and abbreviate that particular exclamation with just *"Atyo!"*

The Jews in my family felt perfectly comfortable saying customarily Muslim phrases like *MashAllah* and *InshAllah,* (Thank God and God Willing). If my mother saw a person with an affliction, for example, she'd turn away whispering, *"Allah Korusun,"* (may God protect us.) It should come as no surprise then, that many Turkish Sephardic recipes have names that are also linguistically inclusive. Look at the name of the dish, *Köfte de Prasa.* The word *Köfte* is Turkish for the oval-shaped patty so common in the Middle East. *Prasa* is a misspelling of the Turkish word *pırasa* or "leeks." And there, in between these two Turkish words is the little Spanish *de,* meaning "from."

A collision of languages and cultures continued when our family came ot the USA. To this day the women in our family do the cooking and serving. As a teenager I objected vehemently that the girls had to do all the work preparing the meals and picking up the table while the boys watched TV in the other room with the men. I remember feeling particularly resentful during Passover Seder because my cousins Sami and Silvio, and even my own brother Kemal sat there with their smug grins while we girls dutifully stood next to them pouring water onto their hands and offered them the drying towel during the ritual handwashing.

These days I am ambivalent about the traditional sex roles. On some level, I feel comforted by the custom. While I'm grateful that I have been able to accomplish so many things that were traditionally denied women, (playing NCAA basketball, getting a black belt, playing in a rock and roll band, becoming an architect), I also feel gratified fulfilling the "womanly" role my father had wanted so badly for me.

I especially feel this way when I look over at my husband Bruce reading the Hagadah. He's wearing his yarmulke, head in the book. His eyes are tired from working all day. He's still wearing the tie he put on 14 hours ago. He's hungry. I feel like he takes care of so many things in our home; the children, the repairs, the mortgage, the dogs, and he still has an infinite capacity for kindness and gentleness for us. Is it really too much for me to offer him warm water to wash his hands so he doesn't have to get up? Isn't it worth the smile on his face when I offer him his first bite of food after a long day and a long Seder? Am I not allowed to feel happy about being able to do this for him? I can be an architect again in the morning, but for this moment, I am happy to be a good wife.

The Gypsy

My grandfather Kemal once told me "You are a gypsy just like your mother." It was meant as an insult. To him, a gypsy was someone who charmed and swindled people out of their money, who lived one place after another, and who could tell the future and read palms. Gypsies wore lots of cheap jewelry, acted like they had a sixth sense, and cast spells and curses. I thought a lot about Granpapa Kemal's comment that day, and how cruel it was to say something like that to me. But then I came to a wonderful realization. He was right; Beti was a gypsy!

She was really good at reading fortunes - either by reading your palm or your *fal* (grounds from your coffee cup). That's because Beti was a terrific con-artist. She could run a scam with the best of them. Beti crashed more parties, high-end affairs, movies, concerts, operas, embassy functions and lectures than anyone I know. With four children in tow, she routinely and artfully snuck us into places like the Uptown Theatre and the Kennedy Center by laying out any variety of cons. We unreservedly followed her lead, and played whatever role she needed from us at that particular moment. We would pretend, for example, that my father was inside waiting for us with the tickets. Or we would pretend that she couldn't speak English, and that we had actually been inside but that she had confused the exit with the bathroom.

One time, we all managed to sneak into a packed house at the Uptown Theatre. All except Beti, that is. While we were happily taking our seats, she had hit a snag at the front door, namely the theatre manager, obviously a stickler for protocol. A man and his pregnant wife sitting near us immediately understood our dilemma and gave us one of their ticket stubs. I took it out, along with mine, and approached the manager who was arguing with my mother. Pretending to have been looking for her everywhere, I said, "*Anne*, (Mom) where have you been!? I told you we were on the upper level. Here's your ticket." I handed her the stub and she took it with, "Oh, I got confused." (I love the way my mom could lay on the "poor little old lady" routine.) I put my consoling arm around her and began to maneuver toward the theatre. The manager tried to stop me, "Wait a minute, wait a minute! Where is her ticket?" My mom presented the stub. After a moment of bewilderment, he stammered something like, "but this ticket... but this one... Oh NEVER MIND!" He shooed us in, either because he just wanted to get us out of his hair or because he felt we deserved a reward for our Oscar-caliber performances. When we finally got to our seats, Beti was very grateful to the couple who gave us their ticket stub. She handed the husband $10.00, the cost of a ticket, to buy a present for their new baby. What goes around comes around.

Beti's talent in reading *fal* was rooted in her ability to read people. In a heartbeat, she could size up a person's nationality, trustworthiness, gullibility, energy level, station in life, intelligence, and sex life.

She also read palms. She would sit people down, gazing intently into their hand. If she didn't instantly get a fix, she would cast out bait, tid-bits of information to see what kind of reaction she got from the person or her friends nearby. From that "tell," my mother could then hone in on what this person needed to hear. I can't tell you how many people were completely taken in by her charm and dazzling performance.

But don't get me wrong; Beti had a clean heart. She didn't take advantage of people... much. Sure, we snuck into places, but there was no way she could have afforded paying for all of us. And she really didn't see the harm.

Perhaps you've heard of Marian Anderson. She was the African-American contralto who in 1939, having been denied access to Constitution Hall, sang on the steps of the Lincoln Memorial on Easter Sunday to a crowd of 75,000 spectators. Well, the Kennedy Center was hosting a reception for Ms. Anderson to commemorate her lifetime achievements, and my mother Beti, already well into her seventies, decided to go.

Mom was in her "bag lady" phase at that time. She always carried a couple of shopping bags with toiletries, a change of clothes, Turkish magazines, homemade pastries and *börek* wrapped in aluminum foil, billfolds with pictures of all her grandchildren, knitting needles and yarn, and a variety of small boxes of costume jewelry and perfume to give as gifts. It's not that she was homeless; she just hated being alone, so she always slept in one of our houses. She would be at Çaya's one night, Tant Mati's the next, etc. She also occasionally took the afternoon bus to Atlantic City, gambled all night, slept on the bus back to D.C. and arrived the next morning to her job at the Tunisian Embassy.

Short in stature, with swollen ankles overflowing her off-brand designer shoes, she walked with a sort of determined waddle. Her hands displayed a different ring on every finger, and her beautiful "ash blond" hair was always elegantly swept up with a ribbon clip she had bought at the corner CVS. Her face was always made-up; although looking like her eye liner had been applied either hastily or without a mirror while riding on a moving metro train.

So here comes Beti, waddling down the red-carpeted Grand Hall of the Kennedy Center to see Marian Anderson. She lays down her shopping bags at the reception table. A swift reconnaissance and she notes that the staff are busily checking names of VIP's and guests on their lists. She confidently approaches and states her name, Berta Revah. As the security people vainly search, she pretends to be annoyed, and then spots her "friends" inside. Waving happily at someone whom I'm sure was terrifically confused, she hurriedly thanks the poor folks at the desk and slips in. Afterwards, she gloats to us that she did indeed meet Ms. Anderson, and that she even curtsied as she shook hands with her. She also said the food at the Kennedy Center was delicious.

Epilogue

I often wonder how things might have turned out had Zeki and Beti never brought us here to the United States. They could have lived comfortably in Turkey on his generous pension. My father had been happy there. Proud, self-assured, with a good income and a young family, Zeki had really made something of himself in Turkey. He could have looked forward to a long retirement surrounded by friends in tea houses playing *tavla*, going to soccer matches, fishing along the Golden Horn, watching the ferries come and go. He probably would have had a deep relationship with his first sons as well as their children. As an old man Zeki Bey would have been afforded great respect, and his grandchildren would have kissed his hand before climbing onto his lap in search of the chocolates he always kept in his coat pocket.

But let's not forget that Beti was 17 years younger than Zeki. A traditional home life with a retired husband while she was still in her thirties would have felt suffocating. She loved excitement and change. She may have gotten tired of him and tried to leave. Then the cards would definitely have been stacked in his favor; all the courts would have given him custody of the children. And there was always the issue of her legal status as the "other woman."

But the truth is, they came to America because Zeki wanted to. My father had always chafed at the yoke of unreasoned religious doctrine. He always felt that Turkey was too conservative, felt too oppressive, unyielding. He saw how Americans were free to be themselves, choose their own careers, choose their own wives, speak their mind. America didn't seem to have the heavy bureaucracy, the red tape and stamped forms that made everyday life in Turkey feel so heavy. Zeki wanted to feel light after 16 years of carrying so much baggage. There was the abandoned wife and children, the disdainful father, the contemptuous mother-in-law. There were always questions about the pretty Jewish girl. He could never be free from the burden of their scandal.

To Zeki America was opportunity - the big land with big ideas and big cars. He could be anonymous there, his own man. He could make a fresh start and have to answer to no one. But Beti wasn't so keen on the idea. In Turkey she had the best of both worlds, career and family. Her work at the Embassy of Mexico was appreciated. Sex roles were clear then, and it was understood that working women also had responsibilities at home. So Beti was never expected to work too hard or too late. And she came home to maids and nannies. The gardener greeted her, the door man had picked up groceries. We children were never alone and when she came home she found us clean and fed. And there were neighbors and friends who helped each other, supported each other.

In America, Beti and Zeki had to dive into their jobs, just to make ends meet. She had no support at home and was unappreciated at work. For working women in America, gender was actually a liability. My parents saw that Americans worked really hard, and worked a lot. Maximum productivity trumped esprit de corps, and both my parents came home every night exhausted. During the first few years Beti wanted to go back to Turkey. But Zeki was living the dream; he owned a home. He owned land, a backyard with fruit trees. He had a car in the driveway. *Hayırsız Zeki* had finally become *Hayırlı*.

As part of the diplomatic corps that inhabited the capital of the greatest country in the world, Beti finally found her niche. Ambassadors and presidents, kings and shahs were attending one gala after another, with their entourages of family and staff at their beck and call. Beti was thrilled to be awakened in the middle of the night by a telephone call from "His Excellency" needing something or other.

The higher she climbed up the social ladder, the lower Zeki felt. He preferred simple, down-to-earth people, and had little in common with elite diplomats or the well-heeled American Turkish Association crowd. His dream was fading. The pride Zeki had felt owning his own home evaporated when her gambling debts forced him to sell the house and move the six of us into a small apartment in the Maryland suburbs. He became a cab driver, and though the Diamond Cab he drove (#823) was kept immaculately clean, and he drove it with a chauffeur's cap, he knew in his gut he was only a hack. He would end each day counting coins from tips, occasionally talking about how he had been robbed by a gun-wielding youth.

Zeki found very few Turkish friends and they were mostly like him, satellites in orbit around the central clique of poetry-reading, concert-attending, mini-skirt wearing Washington Turks. He was the only Muslim in the extended family my parents gradually assembled in America. He politely wore a yarmulke on Passover, and sometimes even went to the

Caya, Kemal, and Beyhan with nanny in Ankara 1956

synagogue. But seeing women there wearing jewelry and expensive hats irritated him; he could not square the image with his understanding of worship. Of course he was comparing the synagogue to the sober formality and modesty he had experienced in mosques. Yet another stark reminder that these were not his customs, his religion, his people.

The cultural disconnect worked both ways. My mother felt suffocated seeing Muslim women hiding themselves from the public, or walking meekly behind their husbands. Perhaps it reminded her of the humiliation her mother had endured with an oppressive husband.

Their relationship, though still passionate, began to fray. The good-hearted jibes at each other's religions which used to elicit laughter were now delivered harshly. But religion was not the issue. Somehow, neither one of them could see that she was helplessly drawn to the very limelight he assiduously avoided. The bottom line is that he was a traditional man with old-world values, hopelessly in love with a young, vivacious superstar who had caught life by the horns and intended to ride it wild and hard.

Zeki had lost his own mother in infancy, and had been spurned by mother figures throughout his childhood. Beti was the girl of his dreams until she became the neglectful mother of his children. Then she was only a painful reminder of his own unmet needs. She was habitually late coming home, leaving us without dinner until 10:00 in the evening. Breakfast was a paper box of cereal, the sandwich in our lunch boxes a square pat of butter rudely slapped between two slices of Wonder Bread. With an empty refrigerator greeting us after school, we made do with ketchup-carrot sandwiches and olives.

Finding the house in disarray, children unfed, and no woman at home was too much for the Turk. Their relationship, though still passionate, became toxic. Nightly arguments ended in tears. One night, during a particularly nasty quarrel, he roused us from our beds. Gathering us up in his arms, he nuzzled his face into our cheeks and fervently promised to never leave us. Up until that moment, I had never thought such a thing was even possible.

Threatened by the attention she received, and unable to leave, my father became passive-aggressive. I can't tell you how many times they would dress up for an event, and at the last minute he would change his mind and refuse to go. With eyes swollen from crying, she would go out into the night, forced to make a grand entrance on no one's arm. But Beti would not be conquered. The more he tried to control her, the more she remembered her father and gathered her resolve. Out there was freedom, joy, life. She would go to the party, calling his bluff, going it alone.

Being irrelevant had been the final blow to his manliness. My father's longing for the Ottoman Empire took him first to Afghanistan and then back to Turkey. But he couldn't rebuild the life he had before Beti. His second son Orhan had died without ever really knowing him. Though he was loved in Turkey, he had no "status" in his family, no position. He had not built the life a Turkish man builds, with family and lifelong friends. There was no one he knew at the tea houses. So, I think it was a demoralized Zeki who finally returned to America to put together the pieces of the life he had left behind with Beti. But this time, it was very definitely on his terms. And the "New Arrangement" I talked about earlier, with him living in his own apartment, renewed his sense of self. He became the center of his life, and allowed Beti to orbit him, but only at a safe distance. And she understood this. She didn't like it, and tried several times to move in with him.

Once he came home and found her sitting in his living room. She had conned the apartment manager into letting her in by telling the woman that Zeki had not answered his phone in days and that she was frightened that something had happened to him. Once in, Beti convinced the manager to let her wait for Zeki. His anger upon finding her sitting in his favorite chair melted away as she charmed him, delighting him with the story about the con that got her in. Then she smiled at him flirtatiously and reminded him that he would never be able to get rid of her. She convinced him to let her cook dinner for him, and he agreed as long as she promised to sauté the onions long enough before adding the vegetables. She convinced him to play cards with her. And then she beat him at cards and took his money. Then she convinced him to let her spend the night. And so it went.

And now you know why we laughed at her funeral when someone quipped that Zeki had turned over in his grave when Beti was finally laid to rest next to him.

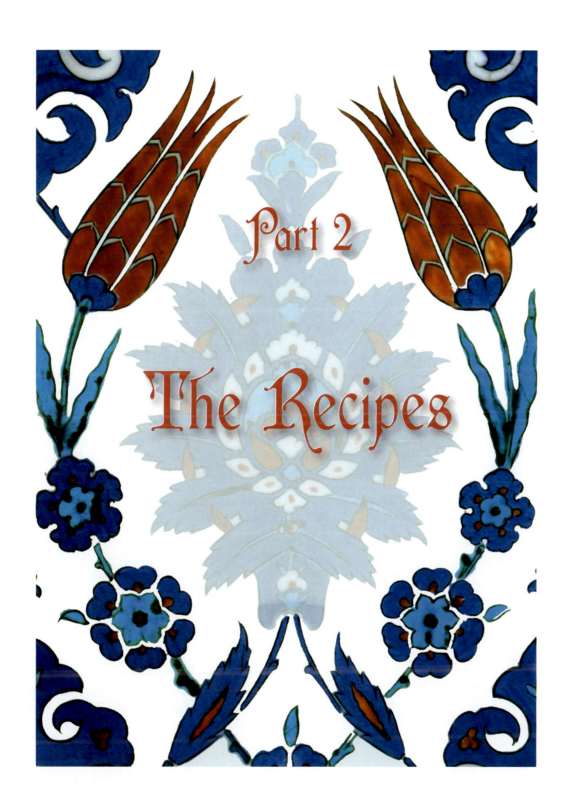

Part 2

The Recipes

Turkish Ingredients

Common to both sides of the family are the ingredients that were available for cooking. Both Turkish and Judeo-Turkish cuisine are rich in a wide variety of seasonal vegetables, often flavored with meat, and a full range of spices. Below are the main vegetables (and their Turkish names) used in the recipes of this book.

ARTICHOKE (Enginar)

Part of the daisy family, the artichoke is a thistle-like plant with tough, green leaves and large, blue/purple flowers. Used mostly in the Aegean and Istanbul, artichoke is usually prepared in "olive oil" dishes as a meze or appetizer.

BEETS (Pancar)

From the spinach family, the original species of beets grows wild along the shores of the Aegean and Mediterranean. Its substantial leaves are sometimes used to wrap fillings, while the intense red root is often pickled.

CABBAGE (Lahana)

A plant in the mustard family, cabbage is a fall and winter vegetable. The flat, wide leaves are ideal for wrapping around fillings, but are also used in other main dishes and soups. Kale, or "black cabbage" (kara lahana) is very popular in the Black Sea region. Red Cabbage is only used in salads, while White Cabbage is used for pickling.

CARROTS (Havuç)

Carrot is actually the root of a plant in the celery family. Both stalks and leaves are used as an ingredient in soups, bean dishes, and meat dishes to add flavor and color.

CAULIFLOWER (Karnıbahar)

Part of the mustard family, cauliflower has cabbage-like leaves. The part we eat is the dense mass of developing flower buds. It is cooked with tomato sauce and ground meat, and is mostly used in western Turkey.

CELERIAC OR CELERY ROOT (Kereviz)

Celery root is part of the celery family, with leaves that look like robust parsley. The large, yellowish root is just plain ugly, but it's also delicious. Most popular in the west and in Istanbul, it is cooked in a meat dish as well as cold as meze.

CUCUMBER (Hıyar, Salatalık)

A member of the squash family, cucumber is eaten on its own or used in pickles and salads. Although it is raised throughout Turkey, various varieties are preferred in different regions, each with its own flavor.

EGGPLANT/AUBERGINE (Patlıcan)

Turkish food is loaded with this member of the nightshade family which thrives in moist soils and hot weather. Eggplant appears in pilav, salad, kebab, pickles and even jams. When buying eggplant, make sure the black or purple skin is firm and tight, with no dark spots. The stems should be fresh and green. If the flesh is to be pureed, using round "globe" eggplant is fine. Otherwise, look for Italian eggplant which is smaller and less bitter.

GARLIC (Sarımsak)

Garlic, a bulb-forming plant of the lily family, popular in Turkish cooking for its dense aroma and flavor.

GRAPE LEAVES (Asma Yaprağı)

Aegean and Mediterranean cooks pick fresh grape leaves from their yards. After cleaning them, they blanche the leaves in water which has either salt or lemon added to it. The leaves are then packed in brine and stored for as long as six months. Jars of grape leaves packed this way are available in most markets here in the U.S. Opened jars keep as long as a year in the refrigerator.

LEEKS (Pırasa)

Leeks are from the lily family, and are used in both "olive oil" dishes and meat dishes. The white to pale green stems look like a large scallion, and have a taste similar to sweet onion.

LETTUCE, ROMAINE (Marul)

This vegetable from the daisy family has broad crisp leaves and is used in salads dressed with olive oil, lemon and fresh dill. It is also used for the Sephardic Passover Seder.

OKRA (Bamya)

A member of the mallow family, okra should be picked when young, because the pods toughen as they mature. In Turkish cuisine it is used both fresh and dried in meat and "olive oil" dishes.

ONIONS (Soğan)

Onion in Turkish simply means "bulb" and actually applies to many different plants in the lily family. The common kitchen onion is one of the fundamental vegetables in Turkish cooking.

PARSLEY (Maydanoz)

In Turkish cuisine parsley leaves are used more as a flavoring herb than a vegetable. Parsley provides aroma and color to cooked dishes as well as salads.

PASTIRMA (Pressed Meat)

Pastırma is highly seasoned, air-dried, cured beef. It is sold in Mid-east markets thinly sliced, and is served as a cold-cut with Kahvalti, cooked in eggs, or as a topping for pizza. From the Turkish "bastirmak" (to press) the name comes from Turkic nomadic horsemen of Central Asia who preserved meat during their long rides by placing slabs of it in the side-pockets of their saddles, where it would be pressed by their legs as they rode. Pastırma is prepared by salting the meat, then washing it with water and letting it dry for 10-15 days. The blood and salt is then pressed out of the meat which is then covered with a cumin paste called çemen made of crushed cumin, fenugreek, garlic, and hot paprika. The meat is then thoroughly air-dried.

PEPPERS (Biber)

The edible part of this member of the nightshade family is the seed pod, which is green when unripe and red when ripe. Peppers are raised almost everywhere in Turkey, in many varieties, names, and shapes. The skins of Turkish peppers are thinner than those of the bell pepper commonly found U.S. grocery chains, but homegrown peppers here often offer the same thin skin.

POTATOES (Patates)

This member of the nightshade family is grown for its edible tubers which are rich in Vitamin C and B6.

SPINACH (Ispanak)

Probably originating in Central Asia, this plant with edible leaves is cooked alone or with ground meat. It is also used in dishes with eggs and as a filling in börek.

TOMATOES (Domates)

Tomatoes have a major place in Turkish cooking, used fresh in salads and for flavor in many cooked dishes. It's hard to believe, that this member of the nightshade family entered Turkish cuisine only about 100 years ago. Originating in South and Central America, tomatoes are technically a fruit. I believe you haven't really tasted tomato until you've had one in Turkey.

ZUCCHINI, SQUASH, AND PUMPKIN (Kabak)

A plant in the same family as melons and cucumbers, squash comes in many varieties in both summer and winter. Zucchini, an oblong, light green and lightly fuzzy squash, appears in a great many dishes. The pear-shaped winter or Butternut Squash are used mostly for sweets.

Grains and Beans

CRACKED WHEAT (Bulgur)

Bulgur is used for making various pilav and soups (medium grain), vegetable kebabs, and in salads (fine grain).

FAVA BEANS (BROAD BEANS) (Taze Bakla)

In summer, fresh fava beans are cooked in olive oil and served with yoghurt and dill as a meze. Frozen fava beans or lima beans are a good substitute.

FILO DOUGH (Yufka)

This paper-thin dough appears in many Turkish pastries, both sweet (baklava), and savory (borek). It can be bought fresh in Middle Eastern markets or frozen in most grocery stores. Always allow refrigerated yufka to warm to room temperature in its box for at least two hours before using. Frozen yufka will need to be thawed overnight in the refrigerator.

FILO DOUGH - SHREDDED (Kadaifi)

Kadaif is similar to yufka except it is shredded. The dough, (made with flour, milk, and water), is poured through a fine sieve onto a hot steel plate in long thin strands, making it somewhat crispy. Kadaif is primarily used for syrupy desserts. Like yufka, kadaif needs to be brought to room temperature 2 hours before using.

Seeds and Herbs

CILANTRO (Kişniş)

Cilantro is actually fresh coriander, and is widely used in the southern and eastern parts of Turkey. It can be kept fresh up to a week in the refrigerator if the leaves are covered with a plastic bag and the stems are placed in a jar of water.

BLACK CARAWAY SEEDS (Çörek Otu)

Also called Nigella, these small black seeds have an intense fragrance and are sprinkled on breads, böreks, and rolls before baking. Do not confuse them with black sesame seeds.

MINT LEAVES (DRIED) (Kuru Nane)

Dried mint is used more than fresh in Turkish cooking. But Turkish dried mint is much more flavorful and aromatic than what we can typically buy here. If you can't find dried mint leaves in Middle Eastern markets, organic dried mint from some place like Whole Foods is a good substitute.

RED PEPPER FLAKES (Kırmızı Acı Biber)

Red pepper imparts aroma, heat, red color and a subtle pepper flavor to many Turkish dishes. Known as Maraş, Gaziantep, and Urfa peppers, for the regions in which they are grown, each type of red pepper flake has its own distinctive flavor. The heat of the pepper varies from very hot to sweet. Don't be afraid to use Turkish red pepper because it is more flavorful than it is hot. Ground red pepper found in the U.S. is a good substitute.

SEMOLINA (İrmik)

Made from durum what, semolina is a yellowish color and sold either coarse or fine in most Middle Eastern grocery stores. It is usually the basis for dried products such as couscous (North Africa), and bulgur. It is also mixed with sugar, butter, milk, and pine nuts to make helvah.

SESAME SEED (Susam)

Sesame seeds are one of the oldest seeds used in the culinary world. The cream-colored, distinctly oily and flavored seeds are sprinkled liberally over pastries, böreks, and breads.

SUMAC (Sumak)

These dried and crushed red berries from the Sumac tree are sprinkled over grilled meats and salads for a slightly lemony, sour taste. The sumac you find in Middle Eastern markets is NOT the poisonous kind.

TAHINI (Tahin)

Made from sesame seeds which are roasted and ground into a paste, tahini is used to make hummus as well as a confection called halvah (helva in Turkish). Women of ancient Babylon ate helva to prolong youth and beauty, while Roman soldiers ate the mixture for strength and energy. In Turkey, tahin is stirred together with pekmez (a molasses-like syrup which was used as early as the 11th century by Oğuz Turks) to make a dish called tahin-pekmez. This calorie-dense and highly nutritious dip for bread is served at breakfast or as dessert, especially in the cold winter months.

OLIVE OIL (zeytinyağı)

A major component of the Mediterranean diet, olive oil is the only vegetable oil eaten freshly pressed from the fruit. Leaving the oil as a natural juice preserves the olive fruit's taste, aroma, and vitamins. Olive oil's health benefits are due to both its high content of both mono-unsaturated fat and antioxidants. It's known to offer protection against heart disease by controlling LDL (bad) cholesterol levels while raising HDL (good) cholesterol.

In terms of flavor, the less the olive oil is handled, the closer it is to its natural state, the better the oil. Olive oil comes in four grades, which are used for different purposes:

EXTRA VIRGIN – The highest (and most expensive grade) of olive oils, extra virgin olive oil is the least processed oil since it is the juice from the first pressing of the olives. It is extracted without using heat (a cold press) or chemicals, and has no "off" flavors. Extra virgin also has the lowest acidity and the greenest color. Use it for seasonings, marinades, dressings, and to drizzle on top of foods before serving.

VIRGIN – This grade comes from the second pressing and is also cold pressed. It has a more pronounced olive flavor and a higher acidity. This is the grade to use for cooking.

PURE – This second press oil undergoes some processing, such as filtering and refining. Yellow, and with less flavor, it is fine to use for sauces and soups.

EXTRA LIGHT – The least expensive grade of olive oil, this oil undergoes considerable processing and only retains a very mild olive flavor. This is the oil to use for frying and sautéing.

Judeo-Spanish Cooking

ADAPTATIONS:

Certain adaptations have crept into Turkish Sephardic cooking to maintain Jewish dietary laws. In particular, margarine (a vegetable oil) replaces butter (a dairy food) whenever meat is included in the dish. So in the Turkish Sephardic kitchen, margarine or olive oil is used to sauté onions and meat. In meat borek, margarine is spread on the filo leaves rather than butter. Sepharads obviously forego using yogurt as a garnish for the many meat and kebab dishes. But a delightful substitute for yogurt, the lemony/egg sauce called agristada, can be used as a sauce for little meatballs called köfte or as a topping for fish. When meat kebabs are served with rice (pilav) a little sumac can impart a little lemony tang, as well.

In Judaism, foods that are neither meat nor dairy are called pareve (also parevine). This means that they also contain no meat or dairy derivatives, have not been cooked or mixed with any meat or dairy foods, and were not prepared using instruments which had been used to prepare meat or dairy foods. Because pareve foods are essentially "neutral" they can be eaten together with either meat or dairy foods.

Common pareve foods are fish, fruit, vegetables, nuts, grains, un-processed juices, and eggs. But, eggs must be checked for blood spots which means fertilization has occurred. Dark chocolate might be pareve; milk chocolate definitely is not. Also, bread made with whey is also not pareve.

CUAJADO:

A type of savory baked Sephardic dishes called cuajado are made from a combination of cheeses with lots of eggs, a little matzo-meal for binding, and large amounts of grated fresh vegetables (like spinach, zucchini, eggplant, leek or tomato). The texture is something like a savory bread pudding; soft but not mushy, with the cheese forming a slightly hardened crust.

We always served Cuajado (meaning coagulated or having curds) dishes after the Passover Seder because they can be made ahead of time and really taste best when they're just warm or at room temperature. For times other than Passover, you can use bread or mashed potato as a binder, depending on the vegetable.

Cuajado shouldn't be confused with cuajada, which is a rennet custard traditionally made from ewe's milk. (Ewe!)

FRITADA:

Fritada means "a fried thing." It is actually cuajado that's made on top of the stove in a skillet. It's very similar to Spanish tortilla except that it has cheese. In fact, during the Inquisition the cheese in fritadas and cuajados marked them as distinctly Jewish. Preparing or eating either one – especially during Shabbat - was enough evidence for someone to be tossed into prison.

Soups and Sauces

Kara Lahana Çorbası
Collard Greens Soup

Collard greens are part of the cabbage family and very close to kale. They're nutritious, full of disease-fighting antioxidants, and delicious. Collard greens reach their peak flavor in the winter months, which is why this healthy, hearty soup is a winter specialty of Trabzon. In the Black Sea region this soup is served hot with freshly-baked cornbread. Try dipping your cornbread into the broth for the ultimate Black Sea comfort food experience.

INGREDIENTS:

½ c. dry Pinto, Cannellini or Northern beans
1 large bunch fresh Collard Greens (about 5 cups)
    (Kale or Cabbage are good substitutes)
3 Tbsp. Vegetable Oil (Canola or Olive)
2 Tbsp. Butter, divided
½ large Onion, peeled and chopped
2 Tbsp. Cracked Corn or Bulgur
½ tsp. Red Pepper (Cayenne)
½ tsp. Sugar
1 Tbsp. Salt
2 large Potatoes, peeled, cut into small pieces
3 Tbsp. Corn Flour
8 c. Hot Water or Broth

❖ The night before, place beans in a small pot with 3 to 4 cups of water. Bring to a boil, then turn off heat and allow beans to soak uncovered overnight.

❖ Wash collard greens well, throwing out any old leaves or dry tips. Slice leaves into strips about ¾ inches wide. (Areas with thicker stems should be sliced a little thinner.) Then cut slices crosswise into bite-size pieces and set aside.

❖ Set a pot or kettle of 6 to 8 cups of water to boil.

❖ Heat oil and one tablespoon butter in another large pot. Add onions and sauté over high heat for about ten minutes, stirring frequently until onions are tender and translucent.

❖ Add collard greens to pot. Rinse and drain beans. Add to the pot. Cook covered over medium-high heat for about 5 minutes, stirring once or twice so that ingredients don't stick to bottom.

❖ Stir in cracked corn or bulgur, red pepper, sugar and salt.

❖ While stirring, add enough HOT water to cover ingredients (about 8 cups). Simmer covered over medium-low heat until beans are tender, about 30 minutes.

❖ Stir in potatoes. Cover pot and simmer again until potatoes are tender, about 15 minutes.

❖ Place corn flour into a small bowl and slowly add about ½ cup water, stirring constantly to prevent lumps. Gradually introduce spoonfuls of soup into this small bowl until corn flour is nicely dissolved. Gradually stir corn flour mixture into pot of soup.

❖ Simmer another ten minutes. Serve soup hot with cornbread or your favorite bread. *Afiyet olsun.*

COLLARD GREENS SOUP **147**

Tavuk Çorbası - Terbiyeli
Chicken Soup with Egg and Lemon

A steaming bowl of homemade chicken soup is a primal comfort food. This classic recipe is made with an egg and lemon sauce (*terbiyeli*) which makes the broth creamy smooth yet surprisingly light. I use only a fresh young chicken (not frozen); its meat is always amazingly tender and juicy. If you like a thicker soup, feel free to add more flour to the *terbiyeli* sauce mixture. You can also make a heartier version of this soup by adding a cup of vermicelli, rice, noodles, or chopped potatoes 20 minutes or so before serving. My mother used to garnish her soup with chopped parsley. You can also use red pepper, or for a really beautiful presentation, try the topping of sizzled butter, paprika, and mint found in the *Ezo Gelin* soup recipe on page 150.

BROTH

INGREDIENTS:

1 whole Fresh Young Chicken (4-5 lbs.)
1 large Onion, peeled and halved
2 Carrots, ends removed, peeled
2 stalks Celery, rinsed
5-6 sprigs fresh Parsley, rinsed, divided
Salt

TERBIYELI (LEMONY-EGG) SAUCE

1/4 + 1/8 c. Flour (1 Turkish Coffee Cup)
2 small Lemons, divided
Yolks of 2 Eggs
Salt (or Chicken Bouillon Flavoring)
Ground Black Pepper

❖ Remove giblets from inside chicken cavity. Rinse them and chicken thoroughly under running water. Make sure all blood is removed and water runs clear. (Wash off all surfaces that touch raw chicken with soap and water!)

❖ Place chicken and giblets, onion, carrot, celery, 4 sprigs parsley, 2 tsp. salt, and 16 c. water into a large pot. Bring to a boil.

❖ Skim off foam which forms on top with a sieve. When foam subsides, cover pot and reduce heat. Slowly simmer chicken for 2 to 2½ hours, or until very tender and meat falls away from the bone.

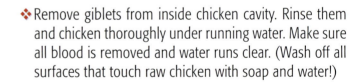

❖ Carefully lift chicken from pot and place on a large plate or cutting board.

❖ Pour remaining broth through a sieve into another large pot. Discard drained vegetables. Rinse empty pot and set aside.

❖ Separate the meat from the bones, cutting or tearing it into pieces small enough to fit on a spoon. Set aside.

❖ To prepare sauce, place flour in cleaned pot. Slowly add broth, a few spoonfuls at a time, stirring constantly with a whisk to prevent lumps. Continue to stir until flour has dissolved and all the broth has been added.

❖ Add cut chicken pieces to broth and slowly bring liquid to a boil. Meanwhile, in a medium-sized bowl, beat egg yolks together well with juice of one lemon.

❖ Little by little, add some broth to this egg mixture, stirring constantly with a whisk or fork. When mixture is quite liquid, pour back into soup pot, stirring well. Continue to heat for only 3 to 5 minutes, before turning off heat and serving.

❖ Season soup to taste with salt (or chicken bouillon), pepper and more lemon. This soup can be thick or thin depending on your preference. If it's too thick, add water.

❖ Chop remaining parsley sprig and sprinkle some over each bowlful of soup as garnish before serving. *Afiyet olsun.*

EZO GELIN ÇORBASI
Red Lentil and Bulgur Soup

Serves 10-12

In most Middle Eastern cultures the rocky relationship between bride and mother-in-law is infamous. Like stereotypical Jewish mothers, Turkish mothers are known to consider their precious sons too good for any woman. Their relationship with their daughters-in-law can be particularly acrimonious when the two live under the same roof (a common arrangement in Turkey). Tension between a new bride and her mother-in-law is so entrenched in Turkish folklore that songs are written about it, crimes are committed because of it, and even food is inspired by it.

Not to be mistaken for "Wedding Soup," this delightful red lentil and bulgur soup is named after a raven-haired beauty named *Ezo*, born in the village of *Dokuzyol* in 1909.

The girl had been unlucky in love. She left her abusive first husband only to be taken to live in Syria with her second. She suffered not only from homesickness, but also from the relentless criticism of her new mother-in-law.

The *gelin* (bride) is said to have created this soup to try to appease the old bat. After bearing 9 children, *Ezo* died of tuberculosis. Her life (and soup) have since become an integral part of Turkish folklore and weddings. Today, brides are served this soup on the eve of their nuptials, along with sage advice on how to wisely navigate and nurture the all-important relationship with the in-laws.

2 Tbsp. Virgin Olive Oil
2 Tbsp. Butter, unsalted
1 large Onion, finely diced (¾ cups)
¾ tsp. Cumin
4 cloves Garlic, minced
2 Tbsp. Tomato Paste
1 medium Tomato, peeled, seeded and chopped fine (about ½ cup)
2 Tbsp. Paprika
½ tsp.Turkish Red Pepper (or ground red pepper)
1½ c. dried Red Lentils, picked through, rinsed, drained
¼ c. long-grain white Rice
6 c. Chicken Broth, unsalted (or water)
¼ c. Bulgur
1 Tbsp. Dried Mint
1 Tbsp. Salt
1 tsp. Ground Black Pepper

TOPPING

3 Tbsp. Unsalted Butter
1 Tbsp. Dried Mint
½ tsp. Paprika
Salt and Pepper
Lemon wedges or Yogurt, optional

❖In a large heavy pot, heat olive oil and butter over medium/high heat. Add onion, cumin, and garlic. Sauté several minutes until onions are translucent.

❖Stir in tomato paste, and then quickly add tomato, paprika, and red pepper.

❖Add lentils, rice, and stock. Cover pot and bring to a boil. Reduce heat to low and simmer for 30 to 35 minutes, stirring occasionally, until rice is cooked and lentils have blended into the stock.

❖Stir in bulgur and 1 Tbsp. mint. Season with salt and pepper. Simmer for another 10 to 20 minutes, stirring occasionally. (Soup thickens quickly, so add a little water periodically, as needed.)

❖Topping: Just before serving: Melt butter in a small saucepan over low heat. Add 1 Tbsp. mint and paprika. Stir mixture until it sizzles. Remove from heat. Immediately ladle soup into individual bowls and drizzle a little topping over each serving. Serve at once with lemon wedges or yogurt. *Afiyet olsun.*

CACIK
Cold Yogurt Soup

On hot summer evenings, my mother would stir ice cubes into this bright, refreshing soup and serve it in small bowls set next to our dinner plates. *Cacık* (pronounced juh-jik) is similar to Greek Tzatziki, but less thick. Speaking of which, I never understood why the Greeks call this dish *Tzatziki* until I actually went to Greece and saw a magazine with a picture of Antzelina Tzoli and Brad Pitt. That's when it dawned on me that there is no "J" sound in Greek.

INGREDIENTS:

1 lb. Yogurt, plain and very cold
2 cloves Garlic, minced
Salt
1 tsp. fresh Dill, rinsed, chopped (or ½ tsp. dried)
1 to 2 Tbsp. Olive Oil
1 Cucumber, peeled, and grated or chopped fine

❖ Stir yogurt in a medium-sized bowl with about a cup of cold water.

❖ Stir in garlic, salt to taste, dill, and oil.

❖ Stir in cucumber. Add enough water to give it a soup-like consistency. Chill at least an hour before serving, or stir in 2 to 3 small ice cubes to serve immediately.

❖ To Serve: garnish with a little more dill along with a small drizzle of olive oil over the top.

Cacık is also wonderful when eaten with grilled meats. Of course, this isn't Kosher, but the Jewish side of my family wasn't very strict about mixing meat with dairy, perhaps because meat with yogurt is ubiquitous in Ottoman cuisine. You might also enjoy *cacık* as a sauce on rice or macaroni!

AGRISTADA
Egg and Lemon Sauce

Agristada refers to a family of light, creamy sauces and soups made with egg and lemon juice mixed with broth, and then heated to thicken. *Avgolemono* is its Greek name and *Terbiyeli* the Turkish. Sephardic Jews often use it with meat dishes in place of milk-based sauces to adhere to the laws of kashrut. Agristada is a refreshing condiment or sauce for vegetables like artichoke, warm dolmas, chicken, meatballs, or fish as shown here. It's also a delightful sauce for pasta!

INGREDIENTS:

2 Eggs
2 Tbsp. Extra Virgin Olive Oil
2 Tbsp. All-purpose White Flour
2 c. Chicken Broth, divided
1 Lemon (zest and juice)
Salt and Ground Black Pepper to taste
1 Tbsp. Fresh Parsley, rinsed, drained, chopped fine

❖ Beat eggs with oil in a small bowl until well combined.

❖ In another small bowl, mix flour with enough chicken broth (about 3 Tbsp.) to make a smooth paste. Slowly add mixture to eggs as you whisk ingredients together.

❖ Gradually add remaining chicken broth and 2 Tbsp. lemon juice, stirring constantly to combine.

❖ Pour mixture into a 2-quart saucepan and stir constantly over medium heat until it thickens enough to coat the back of a spoon. Season to taste with salt and pepper.

❖ Serve warm (not hot) poured directly over chicken or vegetables, garnished with long pieces of lemon zest and parsley. *Afiyet olsun.*

YOGURT
Tant Mati's Recipe

Serves 10-12 as Condiment

Yogurt is a staple of the Turkish diet.

It is offered as a condiment with eggplant and kebabs; mixed with water and salt as a refreshing summer drink called *ayran*; mixed with grated cucumbers and minced garlic as a cold soup called *cacık*, and even as a dessert when mixed with mashed bananas, chopped fruit, honey or just plain sugar.

Back in the late 1950's, yogurt was unfamiliar to most Americans. By the 1970's though, it could be found in major grocery stores, usually as single-serving sized pudding with fruit on the bottom. Up until the 1980's, the best way to get good plain yogurt in America was to make it yourself. Tant Mati still makes her own, a process which is surprisingly easy once you have a good starter batch (*maya*). Mati's son Sami and his wife Ann were kind enough to share Mati's famous recipe, complete with some unconventional but very Turkish instructions.

You will need 5 kitchen towels, 1 non-metal bowl, and 1 lid for the bowl, (or a kitchen plate to cover it).

1 Pint Whole Milk (2 cups)
1 Pint Half & Half (2 Cups)
3 Tbsp. Yogurt Starter (*Maya*) (Buy natural plain yogurt with active culture, (bulgaris bacteria) or use some yogurt you have previously made.

❖ Combine milk and Half & Half in a saucepan. Warm over medium heat until just before froth rises and milk begins to boil (185°F).

❖ Quickly remove pot from heat and cool milk down to 110° (or the highest temperature at which you can dip your little finger in and count to ten. It should sting.) If the milk is much cooler or hotter than this, the yogurt will fail.

❖ Meanwhile stack four towels on the counter, half of each one overlapping in the center, and each facing a different direction (like the petals of a flower).

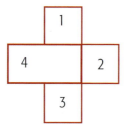

❖ Place a glass (or any non-metal) bowl in center of towels.

❖ When milk cools to proper temperature, pour into bowl. Place starter yogurt into milk at the edge of the bowl. Give a quick stir. Cover with lid or plate.

❖ Fold ends of four towels up and over top of lid/plate. Lastly, fold a fifth towel in half and place on top of bowl with its corners draping down.

❖ Leave covered bowl in warm spot over night or for at least 8 hours. (Traditionally the yogurt would be placed in the oven where the pilot light would keep it warm. Even though there are no more pilot lights, Mati still places hers inside the oven to keep it away from drafts.)

❖ When yogurt has set, it will look like creamy custard. Store in refrigerator where it will keep for a week. Make a new batch every four days (using your own *maya*), to ensure a constant supply. *Afiyet olsun.*

If you just leave milk sitting around for a few days, it will not turn into yogurt. That's because the texture and characteristic tang of yogurt comes from fermentation of lactose made possible by a bacteria. Of course this was not known 4,500 years ago, which is when cultured milk products were first used. We know that Medieval nomadic Turks were eating it. The Bible even mentions Abraham serving soured milk to three angels. Ancient physicians of the Near and Middle East were pre-scribing yogurt or soured milk for stomach, intestine, and liver ailments, as well as to stimulate appetite. Yogurt has also been used for preserving meat during summer months. Persian women used it as an anti-aging treatment; the fat in the milk nourishes and hydrates the skin while the lactic acid acts as a natural alpha-hydroxy acid. (Another reason for marinating meat in it; it's a natural tenderizer!)

The earliest yogurts were probably spontaneously fermented by wild bacteria. There is a Bulgarian legend about a young shepherd who watched over his flock in the mountains. The boy's goats produced so much milk he didn't have enough cans to hold it. So he made a sack from a lamb's skin and put the milk in it. The next morning he found it had turned into yogurt. Of course, we now know this happened because of bacteria in the sack.

Actually, it was the unusually long lifespans of Bulgarian peasants that led to our current understanding of yogurt and its benefits to human health. In 1903 a Russian biologist named Ilya Ilyich Mechnikov hypothesized that the microflora of Bulgarian yogurt neutralize intestinal poisons that cause early aging. He believed that regular consumption of yogurt was responsible for the large number of Bulgarians who lived past 100 years.

In 1905 the Bulgarian scholar Dr. Stamen Grigorov found that a small rod-shaped bacterium he called *Lactobacillus Bulgaricus* (named after Grigirov's homeland), caused the lactose in milk to turn into lactic acid, causing the milk to ferment and curdle into yogurt. L. Bulgaricus is one of those "good" micro-bacteria that naturally lives in the human body, usually in the gastrointestinal tract and vagina. It helps promote the growth of other beneficial bacteria, helps maintain a healthy immune system, and may help our bodies maintain healthy choles-terol levels, and even curb the proliferation of pathogenic micro-organisms in the gut. Though it makes up only a small portion of all gut flora,

L. Bulgaricus is important because it helps our bodies break down the enzymes we eat. By breaking down lactose and con-verting it to lactic acid, this particular bacterium helps people digest dairy. That's why people who are lactose intolerant can often tolerate yogurt.

By 1919, a Jewish entrepreneur from Ottoman Salonika named Isaac Carasso was mass-producing yogurt. He owned a small business in Barcelona named *Danone* (little Daniel) after his son. The brand later became known in the U. S.A. by its American name: Dannon.

In fact, yogurt was first introduced to Americans in 1929 by Armenian immigrants in Andover, Massachusetts. Sarkis and Rose Colombosian started Colombo and Sons Creamery and delivered Colombo Yogurt around New England in a horse-drawn wagon inscribed with the Armenian word *madzoon*. Since Turkish was the *lingua franca* among immigrants (the main consumers at that time), the word *madzoon* was changed to the Turkish name *yoğurt*. How crazy is that?

It was Dannon who brought the "Yogurt with added fruit jam" from Europe to the United States in 1947. Its popularity was en-hanced in the 1950's and 60's when it was marketed as a health food. In 1993 Colombo Yogurt became mainstream when it was sold to General Mills.

You are going to be frustrated when I tell you how to say **yoğurt** in Turkish because that "g" with the little "u" on top is a little tricky to explain. But here goes.

In older Turkish the letter ğ is a "voiced velar fricative." See? I told you you'd be frustrated. But fear not! Let's give my sister Ilhan a call.

CAN YOU SAY YOGURT?

"Hi Ilhan. What is a voiced velar fricative?"

Notice the strange way we start phone conversations in our family. Really not so strange, given that Ilhan holds a Ph.D. in Linguistics. In fact we often talk about the world of language in our family. We've always been fascinated with the origin and evolution of words. English, after all, is our second language. Our parents each spoke five languages. We kids are bi, tri- and quadri-lingual (last time I looked). Every time we got a new nanny we seemed to learn another language. Plus, that ğ is particular close to my heart since it's in my maiden name, Çağrı.

Ilhan explains voiced velar fricative:

"Well, velar means the part of your mouth that makes the K and G sounds. Velar sounds are articulated with the back part of your tongue pressing against your soft palate. Say "ka" a couple of times and you'll feel it in the roof of your mouth."

While she's telling me this I am quietly saying kuh, kuh, guh, guh, noticing the back of my tongue compressing against my palate.

"Do you see how the Ka gets blown through your mouth after the air is momentarily stopped?" she asks. "That's what fricative means; the sound is produced by constricting air flow at the place of articulation."

"Uh-huh…" I'm trying to appreciate this mechanism; stopping the air, and then letting the consonant explode through when I release the air. I've been doing velar fricatives since I was in infant and never noticed how complicated it is.

Hoping she'll be impressed that I've done my homework, I ask her what it means when the velar fricative is "elided."

*"It means the sound disappears." She pauses.
"Look, let's take the word "yoğurt.""*

Can you believe it? She's honed in on exactly the word I was thinking about. Without me even telling her! She interrupts my celebration;

"We don't say the guh in "yoğurt." I mean, the Turks in the Balkans still do, but not in Turkey. The 'elided' G sound disappears. Ok," she backtracks, "it almost disappears. You lose the G but its place is held between the back vowels O and U."

I say it a couple of times to see if it sounds right; yo-urt, yo-urt. "But in old Turkish," I ask, " they used to say a very soft G, making it 'gh,' right?"

"Yes," she says. "Gh" is a little bit like the French "R," which is velar. Merci, au revoire, etc."

I'm getting it. I practice being French and saying "yo-rurt."

"Some eastern dialects in Turkey still say the consonant G in that position, (yo-gurt), and in some villages it is still pronounced "gh" (yo-rurt), but in major cities, standard Turkish dialect, it is elided and pronounced yo-urt."

"Well why don't we say it like that here in America?" I ask. "Why do we pronounce the G?"

"Well, English doesn't have the French R, so the "gh" sound is out. And it would be strange to say "yo" and then "urt," she says. "That's because in English there are very few words or syllables that start with the U sound. Look how Americans say Uygur. They can't say "ooy-gur." Have you ever heard how they say it? They say 'wee-gur.' The only word that starts with that U sound is 'oops.' In English it feels much more natural to just put the hard G back in and say 'yo-gurt,' so that is what has evolved."

I get it. Ilhan is a genius.
Bruce says "oodles of noodles" to me. We smile.

Ilhan Merih Cagri, PhD. 2008

Culture Clash around Yogurt

When you're a bi-cultural couple, you can never predict or prepare for those times when you interpret the same event so differently from your spouse you wonder if you were both there at the same time. Bruce and I experience these "cultural dis-connects" quite a bit. He's a Jewish guy from the midwest, and I'm a Jewish-Muslim from the Mideast. You see the problem.

Shortly after we were married, I had prepared a nice dinner and placed a tub of store-bought plain yogurt on the table. Bruce, wanting to be helpful, stirred it up. If you know anything about Turks, you will have just gasped with horror, which I did. It took me some time to articulate Bruce's faux pas. Can you guess what it is?

I explained to Bruce that in Mediterranean culture, making yogurt is a bit of an art. Tant Mati makes the best yogurt in our family; it's not only creamy, but also firm with a lovely froth on top. When she brings her bowl of yogurt to the table, people actually marvel at it. We admire it and remark on its thick consistency as we place a dollop on top of eggplant or on the side of our plates. Stirring up a bowl of yogurt, as Bruce had done, is a no-no because it essentially robs the diner of this eating experience as well as the chance to compliment the chef on her skills.

Believe me, Bruce has never stirred yogurt again. Some time later, however, he made the grievous error of taking some yogurt from the wrong part of the serving bowl. You see, it is polite to carefully remove yogurt from around the sides of the bowl so as not to spoil the beautiful center, and so that the liquid which forms when yogurt is "broken into," is restricted to one place. I admit I may have been a tad over-zealous in my admonition that his spoon had entered perilously close to the center of the bowl. You may ask, how it is that my husband is still with me. How can he put up with endless rules which, to his mind, I seem to arbitrarily invent just for kicks?

Luckily, Bruce is a well-traveled man who really appreciates other cultures. Even though he hates the liquid that forms after yogurt has been disturbed, he would hate being accused of boorish behavior even more. Also, I married a saint; or in Bruce's case, a "mensch."

Food Mold

Mati tells me that yogurt keeps for one week. My father, on the other hand, insisted it never goes bad; just more sour. I remember he would simply spoon out the parts of the yogurt that had turned a blue or reddish color (mold) and would eat the rest. Then again, Zeki Bey grew up in Turkey during WWI. My daughter Shanie is traumatized by food mold because she once ate a slice of yellow cake mistakenly believing it was marble cake. She's so worried about mold she is forever sniffing food from the refrigerator to see if it is still fresh. I think we have grown accustomed to throwing out food that is perfectly good, just because we don't know the rules, and don't want to risk getting sick. So here are some important rules:

Regarding mold in dairy products:

1. When you see moldy food, don't sniff it. You don't want it to go into your lungs.
2. If food is covered with mold, put it into a small paper bag or wrap it in plastic and throw it out in a covered trash can that animals can't get into.
3. Clean the refrigerator or pantry with soap and water at the spot where the food was stored.
4. Check nearby items the mold might have touched. Mold spreads quickly in fruits and vegetables.
5. If it tastes or smells "wrong," don't eat it!

When to Use, When to Toss:

Hard Cheeses can be saved, as long as the mold is cut off. Because the cheese is hard, the mold generally can't penetrate deep into it. Cut off at least 1 inch around and below the mold spot (keep the knife out of the mold itself so it will not cross-contaminate other parts of the cheese). After trimming off the mold, cover the cheese in fresh wrap.

Soft Cheeses (such as cottage, cream cheese, crumbled, shredded, and sliced cheeses of all types) should be thrown out if it contains mold. Foods with high moisture content can be contaminated below the surface. These cheeses can be also be contaminated by the knife, so use only clean knives to cut.

Yogurt and Sour Cream - Creamy dairy products like yogurt can easily spread mold and should be discarded if any of it is moldy.

Are Any Food Molds Good for You?

Yes, molds are used to make certain cheeses. Blue veined cheese such as Roquefort, Blue, Gorgonzola, and Stilton are made by introducing certain mold spores. Cheeses like Brie and Camembert have white surface molds. These molds are safe to eat.

Nohut Salatasi
Humus

This chickpea and garlic spread is ubiquitous in the Middle East as a meze, dip, sauce, or side dish. Homemade humus is a lot less expensive than store-bought, and you can fine-tune the ingredients to your preference. This traditional recipe calls for dried chickpeas, so if you want to use canned garbanzos instead, skip the first three steps in the directions below. Also, blending the ingredients in a food processor will save a lot of time and effort.

INGREDIENTS:

1½ c. Dried Chickpeas
½ c. Tahini (ground sesame paste)
2 cloves Garlic, minced
Salt
1 Lemon
½ c. Olive Oil + 2 Tbsp. for Garnish
Paprika or Red Pepper as garnish
2 sprigs fresh Parsley, rinsed, drained, chopped (as garnish)
1 Tbsp. Pine (Pignola)Nuts

❖ Soak chickpeas overnight (or for at least 8 hours) in a large bowl with enough water to cover.

❖ Rinse beans and bring to boil with plenty of new water in a large covered pot. Reduce heat and simmer 45 to 60 minutes until tender. Rinse and set aside to cool.

❖ Removing skins is almost as addictive as popping bubble wrap! Hold individual chickpea between thumb and forefinger. When you gently squeeze, the chickpea will shoot out, so aim it at a bowl! Discard skins.

❖ Purée skinned chickpeas in a food processor. Add garlic and salt. Blend thoroughly.

❖ Stir 3 to 5 Tbsp. lemon juice and ½ c. olive oil together in a cup, and slowly add to chickpea mixture as you continue to pulse in the food processor. Adjust stiffness of humus by adding spoonfuls of water until it is a soft spread.

❖ To serve, carefully remove humus from food processor and place in a serving platter. Spread evenly. Scoop out a shallow concave area or trough in the middle.

❖ To garnish, you can simply pour a couple of teaspoons olive oil into the shallow area and sprinkle a little paprika on top. For something a little more jazzy, try the garnish below.

Jazzy Garnish

Sauté pine nuts in 2 Tbsp. olive oil in a small saucepan over medium-high heat until nuts turn golden. Stir in a couple of dashes red pepper or paprika and continue to sauté until oil sizzles. Drizzle mixture into shallow area scooped out of humus. Garnish with a few black olives, lemon wedges, or fresh parsley.

Humus can be served with a meal, as a meze before the meal, or as an hors d'oeuvre surrounded by wedge-shaped pieces of Pita or Flat bread. *Afiyet olsun.*

Eggplant Purée
Preparing the pulp for eggplant purée dishes

My father used to say that a proper Turkish wife knows 40 ways to prepare eggplant. Many eggplant recipes begin with grilling or roasting unpeeled eggplants to imbue the pulp with a deep, smoky flavor. The eggplant is then peeled and the pulp puréed before it is incorporated into the dish. Here's how to prepare the purée from two globe eggplants (about 1½ lbs.):

❖ Eggplant tastes best grilled over charcoal, but I have had great success simply broiling it in the oven. Pierce 2 large eggplants several times with a fork and place them on a cookie sheet inside the broiler close to flame.

❖ Roast eggplants, turning them over every 10 minutes with large tongs. (You want the skins to brown and char). Continue to roast until eggplants flatten out and become very mushy. Remove from heat and set aside to cool enough to handle.

❖ Cut off stem end. Carefully peel away skin. Spread eggplants open and remove and discard large bundles of seeds. Place remaining flesh/pulp in a bowl of room-temperature water with 2 tsp. salt to draw out bitterness. Set aside for 15 to 20 minutes.

❖ Drain eggplant in colander. Rinse. Drain again, squeezing excess liquid out between hands or by pressing against inside of sieve. Pat flesh dry with paper towels. Place in a medium-sized bowl and whisk a few times with a fork to break up long strands (or pulse a couple of times in a food processor). Pulp is now ready to be used.

Alternatives:
Tant Ida sometimes sidesteps the roasting process, preferring to cook the eggplants in the microwave instead. She pierces them and cooks them on a "baked potato" function until they are very mushy, (about 20 minutes).

Of course, if you're short on time, or just don't want to deal with puréeing your eggplants, you can buy jars of grilled eggplant purée in your local Mid-eastern market. Note that store-bought purée can be a little too salty, so adjust salt in your recipe accordingly.

EGGPLANT PURÉE - FOUR WAYS

Here are four delicious examples of eggplant dips and sauces which you can make after preparing the eggplant purée on the previous page. Tant Ida taught recipes 2, 3, and 4 to her granddaughter Brielle Dana, who kindly shares them with us.

Serves 8

1. Baba Ganoush (Eggplant Dip)

3 cloves Garlic
½ c. Tahini (sesame seed paste)
Juice of 2 large Lemons
Salt
Fresh Parsley, chopped as garnish
1 Tomato, skinned and chopped fine

❖ Crush garlic and ½ tsp. salt together in a mortar and pestle. Scrape this paste into a medium-sized bowl.

❖ Stir eggplants into bowl. In a separate bowl, stir Tahini and lemon juice together. Gradually add to eggplant, stirring continuously. Salt to taste. Chill before serving.

❖ Transfer to serving bowl. Garnish with parsley and chopped tomato.

2. with Sauce Bechamel

Very similar to Turkish *Beğendi*, this creamy sauce has a warm, smoky flavor. Sephardim use it only on vegetables, while Muslim Turks also enjoy it with meats and chicken.

¾ stick Butter, (6 Tbsp.)
½ c. All-Purpose White Flour
2 c. Whole Milk
1 c. Mozzarella Cheese, grated
½ tsp. Salt

❖ Melt butter in a small pot over low heat. Stir in flour and whisk 2 minutes until smooth. Slowly stir in milk, cheese and salt. Stir together until consistency is like a loose custard. Stir in puréed eggplant and whisk vigorously until well-blended. Serve hot.

3. Kalavasucho Style

This version of eggplant is cheesy and scrumptious, like an eggplant quiche, but without the crust.

2 eggs
1 c. Mozzarella Cheese
½ c. Grated Parmesan Cheese, divided
Dash of Salt and Pepper
½ c. All-Purpose White Flour
Oil to grease pan

❖ Place puréed eggplant in medium-sized bowl. Stir in whisked eggs, Mozzarella, half the Parmesan, salt, pepper and flour.

❖ Grease a quiche or pie plate.

❖ Spread mixture in dish. Lightly brush a thin coating of oil on top and sprinkle remaining Parmesan cheese. Bake at 375° for about 40 minutes. Top should be golden. Serve warm.

4. Patlican Salatası (Eggplant Meze)

½ c. Whole Plain Yogurt
3-4 cloves Garlic, minced
juice from ½ Lemon
1 Turkish coffee cup Olive Oil (about ¼ cup)
1 tsp. Salt

❖ Pulse puréed eggplant in food processor to break up any clumps.

❖ Stir together with yogurt, garlic, lemon juice, oil and salt in a medium-sized bowl. Chill before serving.

KAHVALTI
Turkish Breakfast

orget sugary cereals, pancake, and pastries! Turkish Breakfast is a cornucopia of savory and sweet flavors eaten in bite-sized portions with a basket of fresh baked bread (*ekmek*) and a full-flavored, steaming hot cup of tea. Typically, you'll find eggs (usually hardboiled), peeled and sliced tomatoes and cucumbers, olives, sliced meats, thick cream and honey, fabulous preserves like quince, rose petals, or sour cherry (*vişne*), sharp cheeses like Feta or Kasseri (*kaşer*) and then some fresh sliced watermelon, cantaloupe or honeydew.

In our house Sunday was the day for extravagant *Kahvaltı*. Aunts, uncles, cousins, and often neighbors would gather for a mid-morning meal that typically lasted three to four hours. Putting on this major production was no easy feat.

It always started the same way; we kids would be rudely awakened at the crack o' dawn with the sound of blaring *à la Turka* music of the *Zeki Müren* vein. Beti and Zeki would be in over-drive preparing the house for guests. We girls would indignantly wrap *şile-bezi* scarves around our hair, ready for housework, while Kemal put on his shoes.

My mother emerged from the kitchen only long enough to delegate chores with boot-camp efficiency; "You, the bathroom. You, vacuuming. You the silver." The arguments would start. "No, not the silver! I did the silver last week!" "You do it better than I do!" No fair!" "Somebody get the phone!" "Why are you in my room?" "Why does this weird Turkish music have to be so loud?"

For my brother, it was errands; "Kemal, run upstairs and ask Mrs. Brozovitch if she has any eggs." "But I just borrowed sugar from her!" "Never mind, she eats here enough." It's no wonder he jumped at any chance to walk the dog. It would take him two hours to go around the block.

As the time for guests to arrive approached, tensions were so high a simple question like "Where is the *faraş* (dust pan)?" could evoke a teeth-baring threat on your life. "May God not give you the punishment you so deserve!" My mother's archaic Turkish epithets were inspired. "I will tear you apart by your legs!" We knew she was too slow and fat to be able to do that, so we laughed off her threat with typical teenage hubris. Besides, she was elbow deep in filo-dough and my father was glued to the stove stirring a temperamental cheese sauce for his scrambled eggs and preparing piles and piles of perfect pancakes.

With children all bathed and dressed, it was finally time to set the table. A crisply-starched linen table cloth was gingerly opened and placed across three tables placed end-to-end. Then came the mismatched china and polished silverware, a teaspoon and butter knife carefully placed beside each plate. A small glass for orange juice sat near each knife. A teacup and saucer next to it, with the cup handles all pointing to 4:00. A cloth napkin was gently folded and placed under each fork.

Then came the lovely assortment of dainty dishes and bowls with artfully-presented meats, jams, cheeses, and olives. Slices of deep burgundy-colored *Pastırma* (a heavily-seasoned smoked beef in a thick layer of paprika and garlic) were carefully arranged on a platter. The Kasseri (*kaşer*) cheese was cut into finger-long sticks and fanned out on a small dish. A glass box-like container held *Feta* (goat cheese), half-immersed in water to reduce its salt content. Fresh cut watermelon slices were placed near it. A few spring onions lay across a plate of wedged tomatoes and sliced cucumbers. *Tarama*, a caviar spread, was spooned evenly into a shallow dish and garnished with three olives placed gingerly in a row across the top. A delicate glass bowl filled with black olives was topped with a drizzle of olive oil and a sprinkle of dried oregano for just the right panache.

As guests arrived, the *börek* would be taken out of the oven, cut into single-serving squares and arranged in a mound on a round platter in the middle of the table. Jellies were spooned into glass bowls, each with its own tiny serving-spoon dipped tantalizingly into its syrup. Several loaves of hard-crusted bread were sliced thick and laid in a loose pile on a cloth napkin in the bread basket.

Guests and family arrived. With kisses on both cheeks, and warm greetings accomplished, everyone found their seat, elders at one end, children at the other. Tea was poured into each cup; first through a sieve from the small pot of concentrated tea leaves, followed with enough steaming hot water from the larger pot for the desired concentration.

Having been seated, we all finally had the chance to stop for a moment and admire all that had been prepared. Glances of satisfaction and pleasure were exchanged around the table as Beti offered a quick speech about how we should all appreciate the opportunity to be together again. One particular Sunday morning in the early seventies, she proudly announced that in America, *Kahvaltı* was actually called "brunch." "It is halfway between breakfast and lunch," she explained. This was a most fascinating and posh revelation. "Brunch," we repeated to one another with feigned British accents, admiring the word as if our social status had suddenly been elevated. From my father came the prayer, in gratitude. "Thanks God," without fanfare. And as all the dishes and foods began to circulate, animated conversations and laughter washed away the tension and bruised egos from earlier.

I should mention that the standard American pancake somehow made its way onto our traditional *Kahvaltı* menu. Watching my dad eat his famous pancakes was a thing of beauty. He faithfully copied an early 60's TV commercial, arranging 5 pancakes in a neat stack on his plate. He'd butter each one, and masterfully slice the pile into 6 perfect wedges. He'd then pour a generous amount of heated syrup along the cut lines. He defied us to enjoy pancakes as much as he did, deftly lifting a whole wedge with his fork and inserting it as a single enormous mouthful which he relished dramatically. After he swallowed, we'd hear mm-mm-mm-mmm as he gazed at the ceiling, sucking all remnants of the buttery sweetness from his lips.

Figure 114: Passover Seder at our home in 1966. A 3-Bedroom apartment in Langley Park, Maryland was plenty of room for four immigrant families to get together. From left to right: Onk Niso (Nesim Revah), Granpa Kemal (Kemal Revah), Tant Mati (Matilda Eskenazi Revah), Zelda Altıntaş, Vaso and Poppy, (two sisters from Greece who were friends of the family), Sami Revah, Viktorya Altıntaş (Zelda and Ester's mother), David Plihal, Esther Altıntaş Plihal standing next to my father Zeki Bey. To Zeki's left are Ilhan Çağrı, Çaya Çağrı, and Berta Revah (Beti). Seated in front of Ester are Sara Revah, little Viki Plihal sitting on my lap, and my brother Kemal Çağrı next to the flowers.

Passover

The Sephardic Passover Seder

Passover is the "telling" or haggadah of the liberation of the Israelites from slavery in Egypt, as told in the book of Exodus. The Seder, the ritual feast that marks the beginning of this holiday, is based on the Biblical verse which commands Jews to re-tell the story of how God took our people out of Egypt. It reminds us that every Jew in the world personally benefitted from this event. In Israel, the Seder is observed only on the first night of Passover; in the Diaspora communities, Jews hold Seder a second night, as well.

The photo to the right shows the Sephardic Seder Plate placed at the head of the table. Clockwise from top left you can see *Charoset* (a sweet brown paste of chopped raisins and dates), *Maror* (or *marul* in Turkish for romaine lettuce), *Karpas* (celery leaves), a hard boiled egg, vinegar or salt water, and a roasted lamb bone. The Sephardic Seder differs from Ashkenzi. For the bitter herbs which symbolize the harshness of slavery, European Jews use horse radish as opposed to our romaine lettuce. Sephardic *charoset* is made of

chopped raisins and dates rather than the chopped apples and nuts used by the Ashkenazim.

At our Seder, each person at the table read parts of the Haggadah aloud to the family. The youngest children were always being given plenty of praise for their reading skills. Special blessings, rituals, and Passover songs were included, as well as the drinking of wine. Though four cups of wine are called for, we rarely drank more than a couple of sips.

Our Seder was always done in a unique mix of four languages; Hebrew, Ladino, Turkish, and English. The family sat at a very long table, or series of tables, with the elders at the head and the youngest at the end. As year's passed, my sister Çaya and I often complained that we didn't seem to be "moving up" at the table, either because guests including rabbi's and visitors from Turkey got preferential seating or because we weren't married yet. Marriage was a serious status boost. It got my younger cousin Suzy a prime spot near the head of the table while she was still in her late teens.

About a half hour before the end of Seder, foods which had been prepared ahead of time were drizzled with chicken or meat broth and placed in the oven to warm. Immediately after the last prayer, the women quickly made their way to the kitchen to plate the assorted *cuajados* and *fritadas* to serve to the elders, men and children.

While the women were up, the children played the customary "egg game" where each person chooses an egg and raps it sharply onto another person's egg to see which one breaks. The last uncracked egg wins. (Don't forget to have salt and pepper on the table for the eggs!) First came the soup (Tant Mati's specialty), followed by fish, the *albondigas* (patties with vegetables and beef), the *fritada* made of spinach and cheese, and finally the main course, a very tender roast or brisket. This was accompanied by a crisp salad and peas with dill. Dessert was *burmuelos* (matzo fritters sprinkled with sugar) and *Gato de Pesah* (Passover Cake). Notice that *Gato* is the Ladino spelling for the French "gateau."

I recently prepared the entire Passover meal for the very first time. Though my parents and elders were sorely missed, I was comforted by the familiar aromas and flavors. It felt good to continue the traditions which were so important to them. Still, it's bittersweet to finally be at the head of the table; the elders I had so eagerly wanted to impress with my presence are no longer there. It occurs to me that they realized the same thing when they first made it to the head of the table. Of course they did.

TYPICAL SEPHARDIC PASSOVER DISHES

Hard-Boiled Eggs
Chicken Soup
Ida's Fish
Albondigas De Pirasa
Albondigas de Patates
Fritada de Ispanaka
Kalavasucho (see page 216)
Brisket or Pot Roast
Peas with Dill
Salad
Matzo
Burmuelos
Gato de Pesah
Red Wine

Albondigás de Pırasa

Leek Meatballs
Makes 20-24

The meal following the Sephardic Passover Seder always includes a variety of succulent vegetable and beef patties which are prepared days ahead and are then warmed up in the oven during the Seder. My favorite of these dishes is *Albondigas de Pırasa* (Spanish for "balls of" and Turkish for "leeks"). They're made with a seasoned ground beef and leek mixture formed into patties and fried. Variations on this dish include substituting spinach, mashed potatoes, or eggplant pulp for the leeks. My aunts shape the potato patties round instead of oval so you can tell them apart from the leek ones.

INGREDIENTS:

6 medium Leeks
¾ lb. Ground Beef
2 tsp. Salt
¼ tsp. Ground Black Pepper
1/3 c. Matzo-Meal or Matzo Cake Flour
4 Eggs, divided
Vegetable Oil for pan frying
Additional Matzo-Meal or Flour for dredging
1/3 c. Chicken Broth (For heating during Seder)

❖ Cut off heads and ends of leeks (leaving some green) and remove toughest outer leaves. Cut into 1-inch slices. Submerge in cool water and wash meticulously to remove sand or grit.

❖ Boil leeks in a large covered pot, with enough water to cover, for 20 to 25 minutes or just until tender. Don't overcook or they'll become mushy.

❖ Drain well and allow to cool. Squeeze leeks between palms to remove as much water as possible. Then chop very fine and set aside. (I don't recommend using a food processor to chop leeks; they become slushy.)

❖ Place meat, salt, pepper, matzo-meal and 2 eggs in a large bowl and knead well with hands for at least four minutes. Add leeks and continue to knead until mixture is thoroughly blended. Add more Matzo-meal if mix is too wet to form into patties.

❖ Have a small bowl of water nearby when you are ready to form patties. Moisten hands and grab about 1/3 cup of mixture and pat it into a flattish, oval patty about ½-inch thick, rounding the ends. Set aside on aluminum foil. Repeat with remainder.

❖ Heat ½-inch deep oil in a large skillet over high heat. Meanwhile set out a shallow bowl with two whisked eggs, a wide plate with Matzo-meal for dredging, and a baking sheet with paper towels spread across it for soaking up excess frying oils.

❖ Test oil temperature by carefully flicking a tiny drop of water into it. It should sizzle. Dredge each patty; first in flour and then in egg. Gingerly place into hot oil. Continue with 4 to 5 more, and fry until they turn a deep golden brown (about 3 to 4 minutes). Gently flip over, brown other side, and drain on paper towels. Fry remaining patties.

(Here's a frugal tip from Ida's mother in law Sultana Dana; if you find you're running out of egg, but don't need enough to warrant cracking a new one, stir a little water into the remaining egg to stretch it. In Sephardic cooking, we waste nothing!)

❖ When *albondigas* have cooled, remove paper towels from under them and place baking sheet in freezer for at least 3 hours. Place them into a large freezer bag and store in freezer until needed.

❖ Thaw patties in refrigerator on the day of Passover. Twenty minutes before the end of the Seder, arrange patties in an oven-proof casserole dish. Pour chicken broth over top, cover, and warm inside 350°F oven 15 to 20 minutes until all the broth has evaporated. *Afiyet olsun.*

Fritadas de Ispanaka
Spinach and Cheese Fritters

Juicy morsels of spinach and cheese, *Ispanak Fritada* is one of the easiest Passover recipes and tastes a lot like spinach quiche. I make it the afternoon of the Seder, and cook it while I also have the brisket or roast cooking in the oven. This dish will keep in the refrigerator for the entire week of Passover. But don't just make it for the holidays; you can substitute bread crumbs or moistened stale bread for the matzo to make this nutritious side-dish anytime of the year.

INGREDIENTS:

2 lbs. frozen chopped Spinach (three 10 oz. boxes)
1 c. Matzo-meal
3 Eggs
1 c. Kasseri or Parmesan Cheese, grated, divided
   (any sharp, hard cheese can be used)
Salt
¼ tsp. Ground Black Pepper
4 Tbsp. Vegetable Oil , divided
½ c. Vegetable broth

❖ Boil frozen spinach in a medium-sized saucepan with a little water until it is soft. Drain in a sieve, and then squeeze between palms to remove as much excess water as possible. Place into a large-sized bowl.

❖ Add matzo-meal, eggs, 3 tablespoons oil and ¾ c. cheese.

❖ Amount of salt needed depends on sharpness of the cheese you use, so taste mixture before adding salt and pepper.

❖ Blend ingredients together well with your hands, adding water as needed to be able to work the mixture into what Tant Mati calls "a big mush."

❖ Place mixture into a Grease an 11-inch x 15-inch or equal size oven-proof casserole dish with a tablespoon of oil. Add spinach mixture and level with your palm until it is flat all the way across.

❖ Sprinkle remaining cheese on top for color and crunch. Bake for about 45 minutes at 350°F. Top should be a little browned. Allow to cool uncovered.

❖ Cut *fritada* into small squares and loosen them in the casserole dish with a spatula. This will make it easier to serve after the Seder. Cover with aluminum foil and set aside until evening.

❖ About 20 minutes before the end of Seder, drizzle vegetable broth evenly over *fritada*, cover with aluminum foil and warm in 350°F oven until broth is absorbed. Arrange pieces nicely in a serving platter to serve. *Afiyet olsun.*

HAROSET PARA PESAH
Passover Charoset

Serves 12 for two nights

The foods of our Passover Seder are symbolic. They link us in an unbroken chain of generations to the very first Seder. *Haroset*, for example, is deliberately made to look like the dark-colored mortar used by the enslaved Jews to build the clay brick store-houses and supply centers for the Pharoahs of ancient Egypt. Handling *haroset*, spooning it onto Matzo (similar to how mortar was trowled onto bricks), is a tactile reminder of the agony of this back-breaking work.

The word *haroset* (spelled many ways, including charoset, charoseth, haroseth) comes from the Aramaic *charoses*, a food made of various fruits, nuts (usually almonds and/or walnuts), ginger, cinnamon, occasionally honey, and either wine or grape juice. The variety of *haroset* recipes reflect the many Jewish communities which, over time, modified the blend to suit local cultures, climates, and the availability of certain ingredients.

In Turkey, there are regional, cultural, even familial variations in *haroset* recipes. Turkish Jews of Romaniote descent (Jews who have been living in Turkey since the Roman destruction of the Second Temple in Jerusalem in 70 C.E.) have their versions of it. The Turkish Sephardic Jews like my family (descendants of Jews expelled from Spain and Portugal in 1492 and 1497 respectively) have their versions, as well.

Here are two Sephardic recipes for *haroset*. The first comes from the wonderful book *Sefarad Yemekleri*, an important collection of authentic Sephardic recipes put together in 1985 with the help of the Elderly Assistance Association in Istanbul. The second version is Tant Mati's.

TRADITIONAL TURKISH SEPHARDIC HAROSET

1 c. Raisins, black, soaked overnight in water
1 c. Dates
1 Orange
1 Apple, peeled and cored
Sugar (optional to taste)

❖ Place soaked raisins in a medium-sized saucepan.

❖ Remove and discard date seeds. Add dates to pan.

❖ Grate colored surface of orange peel and add this zest to pan. Remove and discard bitter white rind from orange. Slice remaining fruit and add to pan.

❖ Cut flesh of apple into small pieces, and add to pan.

❖ Boil ingredients together with ½ cup water until soft.

❖ Drain liquid and purée *haroset* in food processor to a mud-like consistency.

TANT MATI'S HAROSET

For as long as I can remember, Tant Mati has made this basic haroset for both Tant Ida's table and her own. I think she prefers a simple recipe because it doesn't make much sense to embellish this symbolic food with delicious flavors when it is meant to signify sadness, labor, and pain.

24 oz. Raisins
5 tsp. Sugar
1 Apple (peeled and grated)

❖ Soak raisins in water 20 minutes or until they are soft.

❖ Boil raisins and grated apple pulp in small saucepan with sugar for five minutes.

❖ Drain and purée in food processor to a mud-like texture.

Dos Gatos para Pesah
Two Cakes for Passover

Each cake serves 8

Walnut Passover Cake

This quick and easy cake for Passover is made with Matzo Cake Meal, which is more finely-ground than basic Matzo-Meal.

INGREDIENTS:

6 Eggs
1¼ c. Sugar
1¼ c. Matzo Cake Meal
Juice and zest of one Orange
1 c. Walnuts, pulverized in food processor
2 Tbsp. Vegetable Oil, to grease pan
Confectioner's Sugar

❖ Preheat oven to 350°F.

❖ In medium-sized bowl, mix eggs well with sugar. Gradually add cake meal. Stir in juice and zest of orange, and walnuts.

❖ Pour mixture into a greased 9-inch round cake pan and bake for about 30 minutes. (Stick a toothpick into center to test for doneness. It should come out clean.)

❖ Allow cake to cool before removing from pan. Place cake on a serving dish and dust with confectioner's sugar. (Hint: For a smooth dusting, first pour some sugar into a sieve and then tap side of sieve held over cake.)

Carrot Passover Cake with Almonds

This moist, delicious Passover cake requires no Matzo at all. Separating the eggs and beating the whites into a foam makes it light and fluffy. Really!

INGREDIENTS:

4 Eggs, separated
1 c. Sugar, divided
1 Lemon, rind and juice
½ lb. Blanched Almonds, pulverized in food processor
½ lb. Carrots, rinsed, peeled, and grated
pinch of Salt
Confectioner's Sugar

❖ Whisk egg yolks together in medium-sized bowl. Add 2/3 c. sugar, ¼ tsp. lemon rind and 1 Tbsp. lemon juice, nuts and carrots. Stir ingredients together well and set aside.

❖ Preheat oven to 350°F. Beat egg whites and a pinch of salt in a very clean, dry, medium-sized bowl for several minutes until it forms stiff peaks. Blend in 1/3 cup sugar.

❖ Gently fold egg white mixture into carrot mixture just enough to blend ingredients. Do not overmix.

❖ Place into a greased 7-inch to 8-inch spring-form cake pan and bake for 45 minutes. Check for doneness by sticking toothpick into center of cake. It should come out clean.

❖ Allow cake to cool, and remove from pan. Place cake on a serving dish and dust with confectioner's sugar. (Hint: For a smooth dusting, first pour some sugar into a sieve and then tap side of sieve held over the cake.)

Beating Egg Whites

About Rice

White rice is the name given to milled rice that has had its husk, bran, and germ removed to prevent spoilage and to extend the storage life of the grain. We buy our rice in 10 lb. burlap sacks from the Mideast market. My father taught me to wash it in a large bowl of water by rubbing it together between my palms. Doing this removes any stones and chafes away much of the starch that makes it sticky.

I've never understood why making basic rice seems to be so challenging to American cooks. I was making rice for the family by the time I was eight years old. At that time Uncle Ben's was running a commercial showing a graphic of rice going through a "high-tech"machine that scraped the sides of each grain. They called it "Converted Rice." The ad worked on my mother and she bought the stuff. It tasted awful. My brother Kemal called it "Uncle Ben's Perverted Rice." TV also advertised Instant Rice for "perfect rice, every time." Was making rice really such a problem? Then there was frozen rice that you could boil in its own pouch. And of course, Rice-a-Roni, the "San Francisco Treat" in a box, a little bit of rice, a few spices, and a whole lot of salt. We were always amused that all these products were meant to make rice more manageable or more appetizing. In the end, these ads only fueled the notion that making basic rice was both difficult and somehow unsatisfying. No wonder there wasn't much rice on Americans plates; certainly not the copious amounts found on ours at almost every meal. We had rice three or four nights a week and never worried that it was going to be less than perfect. That's because we always stuck to the fundamentals.

RULES FOR RICE:

1. Never open a pot of steaming rice. It will instantly disturb the balance of moisture in the pot and your rice will come out sticky and mushy. If you keep the heat at the very lowest temperature you can cook rice much longer than required and it will still be fine.

2. Remember the 1 : 1½ : 1 ratio. For every 1 cup of rice use 1½ cups of water and 1 tsp. salt. The amount of butter or oil can vary with personal taste.

3. Cold rice/hot water or hot rice/cold water. The difference in temperature accelerates the absorption of water into the rice. If you boil your water first, you should add room-temperature rice. Conversely, some recipes call for sautéeing rice with onions or pignola nuts before adding water. In this case the rice will be quite hot, so the water you pour over it should be room temperature.

4. Stickiness according to Region. A little stickiness is not necessarily a bad thing. In fact, the further East you go, the more sticky the rice is. The Chinese are able to pick up mouthfuls of their sticky rice with chopsticks. Quite different from the Basmati rice served in places like India, Iran, and Afghanistan where the rice is thin and long grained. If the grains are not distinct and separated from one another, the rice is considered a failure. Ilhan mastered this rice while living in Afghanistan for ten years. Her rice is pristine and fluffy and she often receives the very Afghan compliment that you can "count each grain." With five children and a very large extended family, Ilhan customarily makes enough rice to feed 15-20 people. She serves it using a large slotted spoon to lift and fluff it before casting it onto a very large platter as a light, airy mound. Of course chopsticks are of no use in Afghanistan, where rice is typically eaten in small morsels scooped up onto the four fingers of the right hand and then pushed into the mouth with the back of thumb. My father never got accustomed to Ilhan's rice, and often complained, "What's the matter with your rice? It doesn't stick together!" Turks prefer short grained rice and serve it more wet, more buttery. Turkish cooks often serve rice in little mounds made by pressing it into individual portion-size glass bowls and then flipping the bowl over onto the plate. The mound is then garnished with spices and chopped herbs.

5. Rice can be cooked and then kept covered over very low heat for hours before serving. When you do this, the rice at the bottom of the pot becomes crunchy and golden. This crust (referred to as Ta'deeg or "bottom of pot" in Farsi) is actually considered the best part of the rice, and in much of the Middle East, is prepared and served as its own separate dish.

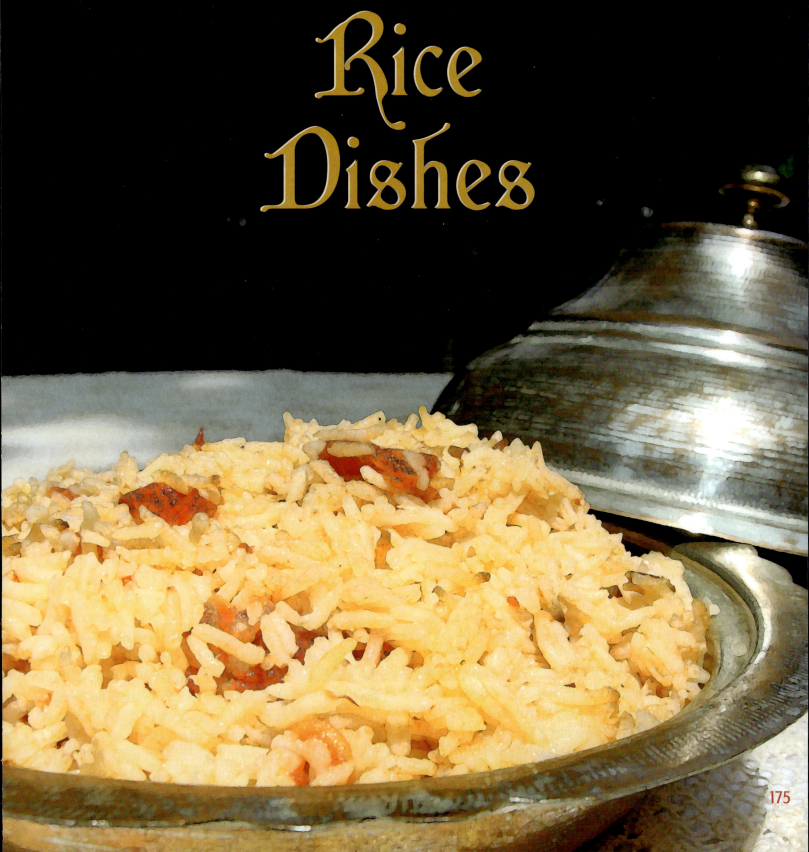

Rice
Dishes

İÇ PILAV
Rice with Currants and Pine Nuts

İç Pilav literally means "Inside Rice." That's because it's so flavorful and aromatic it's often used as a filling to stuff tomatoes, green peppers, grape leaves, and even mussel shells. Vegetables stuffed with rice are playfully called *yalancı* (liar or fake) *dolma* because they're not stuffed with meat filling, which is always more expensive.

About this recipe. My dad lived simply, almost spartan-like. At the end of his life he had accumulated few material possessions. All the more reason I cherish the two items I received when he passed away. One is his sewing box, a treasure-trove of old thimbles, spools, ancient needles, buttons salvaged from every

shirt he threw away, zippers from every pair of pants. The box is fashioned from a round cookie tin which he lined with scraps of grey velvet. His name is carved on the lid.

The other item I received is my father's trusted cookbook. Written in 1974, Ekrem Muhittin Yegen's famous *Yemek Öğretimi* remains a mysterious tome which I can barely decipher with my weak Turkish. My father referred to this book often. Tant Mati apparently did, too, because this *iç pilav* is the traditional one found in that book. Of course there are a few important modifications which give this robust and fabulous rice the exact flavors I remember from childhood.

INGREDIENTS:

¼ c. Dried Black Currants
2 c. Long-grained White Rice
8 Tbsp. Unsalted Butter, divided
1 medium Onion, chopped (½ cup)
1/3 c. Pignolia (pine) Nuts
1 medium Tomato, skinned and chopped (or 1/8 c. tomato paste)
1 tsp. Ground Cinnamon
1 tsp. Allspice
1 tsp. Sugar
1 Tbsp. Salt
1 tsp. Ground Black Pepper
3 c. Chicken Stock or Water
¼ lb. Chicken Liver, cut into ½" cubes
2 tbsp. Fresh Parsley, (washed, chopped)
¼ c. Fresh Dill, (washed, chopped)

❖ Soak currants in warm water for 20 minutes. Drain and set aside.

❖ Rinse rice in a medium-sized bowl with plenty of cool water. Rub rice between your palms to help loosen the starch. Exchange water with fresh water and repeat. Drain and set aside.

❖ Melt 6 Tbsp. butter in a heavy, large pot over medium-high heat. Sauté onions, stirring with a wooden spoon, until they are translucent. Add pine nuts and continue to sauté until nuts turn slightly golden and give off a mild aroma.

❖ Add rice and sauté 10 minutes more. Stir constantly.

❖ Stir in tomato, cinnamon, allspice, sugar, salt, and pepper.

❖ Stir in chicken stock, a little at a time. (Do this carefully because the mixture will sizzle and sputter.) Immediately stir in currants and bring to a boil. Cover pot and reduce heat to very low. Cook gently until water is absorbed, approximately 40 minutes. (Do NOT open the lid during cooking!)

❖ Sauté chicken liver in 2 Tbsp. butter until outside is browned and inside remains slightly pink. Set aside.

❖ Once water of rice is completely absorbed (check to make sure there is no liquid in bottom of pot), add parsley, dill, and chicken liver. Blend ingredients, cover pot again, and cook at least ½ hour more over very low heat.

❖ Serve warm or use as filling. *Afiyet olsun.*

DOMATESLI PILAV
Rice with Tomatoes

Serves 4-6

INGREDIENTS:

2 c. White Rice, medium grain
6 ripe Tomatoes (or one 14 oz. can tomato sauce)
4 Tbsp. Butter
3 c. Boiling Water
2 tsp. Salt
½ tsp. Ground Black Pepper

❖ Rinse rice by placing it in a medium-sized bowl with plenty of cool water. Rub rice underwater between palms to help loosen starch. Exchange water with fresh and repeat. Set aside, allowing rice to soak in water as you prepare tomatoes.

❖ Cut tomatoes in half and grate all but skin. Discard skins.

❖ In a saucepan or kettle, bring 3 c. water to boil.

❖ Melt butter over medium heat in a large pot which can be tightly-covered. Sauté tomatoes, uncovered, in butter for 3 to 5 minutes.

❖ Drain rice well and add to pot of tomatoes. Sauté 2 to 3 more minutes to blend flavors.

❖ Add boiling water, salt and pepper. (If using canned tomatoes, consider reducing amount of salt). Stir rice, cover pot and bring water back to boiling temperature. Immediately reduce heat to very low and cook for 40 to 50 minutes. (Resist opening lid during cooking!)

❖ Drape a couple of sheets of paper towel over pot (under lid) and simmer another 20 minutes over very low heat. Gently fluff with a fork before serving. *Afiyet olsun.*

Dereotlu Pilav
Rice with Dill

Serves 4-6

INGREDIENTS:

2 c. White Rice, medium grain
4 Tbsp. Butter
1 medium Onion, chopped fine
2 tsp. Salt
3 c. Chicken or Beef Broth, unsalted (or water)
8-10 sprigs fresh Dill Weed, rinsed, drained, chopped

❖ Rinse excess starch from rice by placing it in a medium-sized bowl with plenty of cool water. Rub rice between palms to help loosen starch. Exchange water with fresh and repeat. Set rice aside to soak in water.

❖ Melt butter over medium-high heat in a large pot which can be tightly-covered. Add onion and sauté uncovered for 10 to 15 minutes until tender and translucent.

❖ Drain rice well and add to pot. Add salt. Continue to sauté with wooden spoon for 5 to 7 minutes over medium-high heat.

❖ When rice is hot, carefully add broth. Give mixture a quick stir and bring water back to boil. Immediately cover and reduce heat to very low. Cook for 40 minutes.

❖ Set aside 1 Tbsp dill weed for garnish. Lift cover of rice and stir in remaining dill as you fluff rice with a fork.

❖ Drape a couple of sheets of paper towel on top of pot (under lid) and simmer another 20 minutes over very low heat. Gently fluff with slotted spoon as you transfer to platter. Garnish with dill before serving. *Afiyet olsun.*

Salad

PIYAZ
Summary Bean Salad

Serves 8

Beans play an important role in the Turkish diet because they're full of nutrients, inexpensive, easy to store, and delicious to eat. Aside from providing cholesterol-lowering fiber, folate, manganese, vitamin B1 and important minerals, beans also provide a virtually fat-free high quality protein when combined with whole grains. Happily, there are many delicious bean recipes to choose from. No picnic, for example, is complete without *piyaz*, a colorful and robust summer bean salad. Make it a day ahead of time so that the flavorful juices have plenty of time to soak into the beans. In this recipe I also give you some basic tips on how to prepare summer vegetables for salads.

INGREDIENTS:

½ lb. (1 c.) Dried Beans (Roman, Cannellini, Pinto, Navy)
¾ c. White Vinegar, divided
1 large Onion, (peeled, halved, sliced into very thin crescents)
½ bunch Fresh Parsley
3 large Tomatoes
1 Cucumber
2 small Green Peppers
18 Black Olives
Salt
¼ c. Olive Oil
3 Eggs, hard-boiled and cooled

❖ Soak beans overnight in enough water to cover.

❖ Drain beans and transfer to a large pot with fresh water at a level 2 inches above beans. Bring to a boil over high heat. Reduce heat and simmer beans until tender but not crumbling (about 1 to 1½ hours). Remove pot from heat and allow beans and water to cool.

❖ Drain beans in colander and transfer to a shallow bowl. Stir in ½ c. vinegar and a dash of salt. Cover and set aside, allowing beans to soak 2 to 3 hours.

❖ Drain vinegar and transfer beans to a shallow serving platter.

❖ Sprinkle 1 tsp. salt on onions in a small bowl. Crush them in hands a few times to squeeze out bitter juices. Rinse, drain, and add to beans

❖ To prepare parsley, rinse in plenty of cool water to remove sand. Pat or spin dry. (Don't chop parsley too fine. Turks enjoy it as a vegetable as well as a spice. For recipes where parsley is eaten uncooked, use only the leaves, pinching them from the stems before chopping.) Add chopped parsley into bowl and mix ingredients well before spreading beans out evenly in serving platter.

❖ To prepare tomatoes, remove area around dark stem on top, as well as small dark nib at bottom of each tomato. (This is easily done by first cutting tomatoes in half and then cutting unwanted areas free with a paring knife.) Slice tomatoes into wedges (eighths for small tomatoes), and arrange around edge of platter.

❖ Peel cucumber. Cut off ends. Cut in half longways, and then cut each one longways again into three wedges. Cut away seeds from each wedge. Turn wedges 90° and slice into cubes. Arrange around platter.

❖ Rinse green peppers. Cut off tops. Slice in half lengthwise. Remove ribs and seeds, and then slice each half into strips. Turn strips 90° and slice into tiny cubes. Arrange around rim of platter, as well.

❖ Arrange olives around perimeter.

❖ To prepare dressing, whisk 2 tsp. salt, ¼ c. vinegar, and olive oil together a few times with a fork in a small bowl. Drizzle over salad. Cover and chill at least 4 hours.

❖ Just before serving, slice hard-boiled eggs into wedges and arrange around perimeter of platter. *Piyaz* is served cold. *Afiyet olsun.*

PATATES SALATASI
Potato Salad

Serves 8

When I tasted my friend *Nermin Alıçlı's* potato salad while visiting her summer home in Anamur, Turkey, it brought to mind the family picnics of my childhood. Washington, D.C. is beautiful in April, and every spring my parents took us on all-day outings to see the pink Cherry Blossoms. (More than three thousand of these trees, commissioned by Lady Bird Johnson, festoon the Tidal Basin where the white marble Jefferson Memorial sits elegantly on the water.) Beti would lay blankets out and we'd laze around all afternoon, feasting on traditional Turkish picnic fare; *börek, piyaz, köfte*, and this refreshing potato salad. Unlike heavy, mayonnaise-laden potato salad, the dressing here uses only olive oil and lemon juice, which gives it a light, bright, clean flavor.

You can garnish this salad with wedges of hard-boiled eggs and black olives and dried mint for a true picnic experience!

INGREDIENTS:

2 Large Potatoes
6-7 Scallions
½ Bunch Fresh Parsley, rinsed, dried, chopped
1 Large Tomato
5 Tbsp. Extra Virgin Olive Oil
Juice of ½ Lemon
1 tsp. Ground Sumac (optional)
½ tsp. Salt
⅛ tsp. Ground Black Pepper

❖ Boil potatoes in skins until tender but not too soft, about 45 minutes.

❖ Meanwhile, chop scallions. To do this, cut off about ¼ inch from top and pull outermost layer of skin up, over top, and off. Hold scallion under cool running water and run your fingers along stem to pull off any slippery film. Repeat with remaining. Lay them side-by-side on a wood cutting board, and holding them together firmly with one hand, slice bunch finely with sharp knife. Turkish cooks use not only the sweet white part, but much of the green stalk, as well. Feel free to use as much of the stalk as seems crisp and juicy. Place scallions in medium-sized bowl.

❖ Add parsley.

❖ Peel tomato (optional), chop into small cubes, and add to bowl. (Removing tomato skins is not always convenient but good Turkish cooks take the time to do it. A quick method is shown on page 201.)

❖ To make dressing, whisk olive oil, lemon juice, sumac, salt, and pepper together in a small bowl. Set aside.

❖ When potatoes are cooked, drain in colander and allow to cool. Peel with sharp paring knife. (Once you've cut the skin, you can gently run the knife along the surface to easily tease off remaining skin.)

❖ Chop potatoes into small cubes no larger than your thumbnail. (Do this carefully since the potatoes are easily smashed).

❖ Place potatoes in a large bowl and toss gently with half the dressing. Allow to cool completely.

❖ Add chopped vegetables and remaining dressing to bowl. To blend without smashing the potatoes, use your fingers to gently lift and toss ingredients together.

❖ Serve chilled. Salad which has been stored in fridge should be gently tossed again before serving, to revive flavors. *Afiyet olsun.*

PANCAR SALATASI
Pickled Beet Salad

INGREDIENTS:

2 Bunches Fresh Beets (approximately 8 beets)
4 cloves Garlic
¼ c. Apple Cider Vinegar
4 tsp. Sugar

*P*ickled beets are served chilled as a side dish. I love them because they have a refreshing bright flavor and provide a beautiful color to the plate. (The gorgeous deep red juice has been used for millenia as a natural dye for carpets and other textiles.) Serve chilled as a side to your favorite summer fare.

Beets will stain! Beets make an excellent dye for oriental carpets because they stain everything a deep beautiful red. Use stainless steel spoons instead of wood, and make sure to quickly wash off any surfaces that come into contact with this vegetable, including your sink and dish towels.

❖ Rinse beets well in cool water.

❖ Cut off very bottom of root, and very top, just below stems. Remove leaves from stems. (You may want to set them aside for re-use because beet leaves, like grape leaves, are wonderful for wrapping around beef or rice fillings. See page 232.)

❖ Tant Ida uses both the root and stems in her beet salad. (Remember; nothing is wasted in Middle Eastern cooking!) Rinse stalks, too. Slice lengthwise into thin sections, and then again crosswise a few times.

❖ Place whole beet roots and stalks in a pressure cooker with enough water to barely cover. Boil beets under pressure for 45 minutes. Release pressure either by allowing pot to cool naturally or by holding it under running water. (If you are unsure about how to use a pressure cooker, see page 213).

❖ Check beets with a fork for doneness. Fork should be able to pierce root with very little resistance.

❖ Allow beets to completely cool. Remove skin (It should peel off very easily).

❖ Slice beets into ¼-inch slices and place into a casserole dish which can be covered and stored easily in the refrigerator. Keep stalks generally together in the dish.

❖ Peel garlic cloves and add whole to dish.

❖ Whisk vinegar with sugar in a small bowl until sugar is dissolved. Pour over beets, making sure garlic is immersed in liquid.

❖ Cover and chill at least 4 hours before serving. Stir occasionally. Like most Turkish foods, beet salad tastes better the next day. *Afiyet olsun.*

TARAMA SALATASI
Carp Roe Caviar Spread

Serves 8 as aperitif or meze

In elementary school, our teacher once asked the class what we had eaten for breakfast. Little Johnny announced he had eaten eggs and toast. Little Jane had pancakes. My sister Çaya and I proudly stated that we had eaten caviar. We were reprimanded for "exaggerating."

The truth is we often did eat caviar for breakfast. Perhaps it wasn't the expensive Russian kind, but we often spread salty *tarama*, or "carp roe," on our toast instead of jelly.

Back in the 1960's, Middle Eastern stores carried only the plain, bright orange roe, and my mother would mix it with softened butter to make a tangy spread. Then in the 1970's you could find ready-made *taramosalata*, which

tastes reasonably good and comes in handy when you are short on time. But this home-made version of tarama which I learned from Tant Ida is far superior in flavor and texture.

Blending oil, lemon and bread with plain roe creates a rich, smooth caviar spread that you can serve to dinner guests with an *aperitif*, (small alcoholic beverage before dinner), or as a *meze*. If you're lucky, there might even be enough left over to spread on your breakfast toast!

Ida Dana (Tant Ida) 1941

5 to 6 slices day-old or stale Baguette Bread

½ c. plain Carp Roe Caviar (bright orange)

Juice of 1 Lemon

1 c. Vegetable Oil

The nice thing about making your own tarama is that one jar of plain roe can make up to four jars worth of ready-made spread. That's quite a savings considering both types cost about the same at the market.

❖ Soak bread in bowl of cool water for 5 minutes.

❖ Gently peel away crust and discard.

❖ Firmly squeeze bread between your palms to remove all water, and place in a medium-sized bowl.

❖ Add tarama to bowl.

❖ With a mixer set on high, whip together tarama and bread as you gradually and alternately add a little oil and lemon. Mix until ingredients come to a spreadable consistency like mayonnaise. (Do not use a food processor or tarama will be too watery).

❖ Transfer to shallow serving platter and garnish with black olives and/or lemon slices and a sprig of parsley. Tarama will remain fresh in the refrigerator for up to a week. To keep it longer, top it with a head of olive oil. *Afiyet olsun*.

Zeytinyaği Fasülye Pilaki

Bean Salad with Olive Oil

Serves 8 as meze

This popular summer meze has a warm, slightly sweet flavor and just a touch of lemon to give it a delightful lift. When served on its own with fresh bread, this bean dish makes a healthy and very satisfying lunch. Like all Turkish olive oil dishes, *pilaki* is best served cold or at room temperature, and should get a fresh spritz of lemon juice just before eating.

There was a time when most people bought large amounts of fresh beans in the summertime, podded them, and kept them in the freezer for winter use. Fresh beans are always the tastiest, but hard to find year-round. That's why my mom used dried beans which she soaked in water overnight.

INGREDIENTS:

2 c. (1 lb.) Dried Northern or Navy Beans
(Pinto, Roman or Cannellini beans are good substitutes)
2 medium Carrots
1 large Onion
2 large Tomatoes (or 14 oz. can sauce)
1 medium Potato
½ c. Olive Oil
7-8 Cloves Garlic, peeled, whole
1½ tsp. Salt
4 tsp. Sugar
1 tsp. Paprika
2-3 c. boiling hot Water
1 Lemon, divided
3 sprigs Fresh Parsley, rinsed, coarsely chopped

❖ Soak beans in water over night. Drain. Place in large pot with fresh water to level 2 inches above beans. Bring to boil. Skim off gases, reduce heat and simmer 20 minutes. Drain and set aside.

❖ Meanwhile, here are some tips on cutting the vegetables:

Carrots: Scrape skin off carrots with knife edge. Remove ends. Cut each carrot in half widthwise, and then carefully lengthwise. With flat side down, line up carrots next to one another and slice them together into slices about 1/8-inch thick. Chop again into tiny cubes.

Onions: Cut off top and bottom of onion. Cut in half lengthwise and remove outermost peel. Lay onion flat-side down and slice thin widthwise. (To avoid cutting myself, I slide the blade down the back of my fingers, keeping my fingertips tucked under.) Slice again in opposite direction into tiny pieces.

Tomato: Cut top off tomato and grate the cut side only. Discard remaining skin. Should be about 2 cups.

Potato: Peel and rinse potato. Set aside in cool water until ready to use. Then cut in half, lay flat side down and slice into 1/8-inch thick slices. Turn slices and cut agin into perpendicular direction into tiny cubes.

❖ Heat olive oil in a heavy pot. Sauté onions and carrots over medium heat for about 15 minutes until onions are translucent.

❖ Add whole garlic cloves and continue to sauté another minute.

❖ Stir in tomatoes and sauté another 5 minutes until tomato darkens.

❖ Stir in salt, sugar, and paprika. Add drained beans, potato and enough HOT water to cover beans in 1 inch of water. Bring to boil and then reduce heat to medium low. Cover and simmer 1to 1½ hours, adding small quantities of water if needed. There should always be some sauce in the pot.

If using pressure cooker, heat until contents are under pressure and cook 10 minutes. (The exact time will depend on the size and quality of the pressure cooker.) Allow contents to cool slowly at room temperature before opening. Cook more if texture is too hard.

❖ To serve, sprinkle with juice of half lemon and garnish with parsley. Serve alongside hearty bread and remaining lemon cut into wedges. *Pilaki* can be stored in fridge up to 5 days and, like many Turkish dishes, tastes best the day after cooking. *Afiyet olsun*.

RUSS SALATASI
Russian-Style Potato Salad

Serves 4

Here's a rich potato salad made with chopped carrots and peas. Oddly enough, Sephardic Jews from Bulgaria call it Russian Salad, while Turks call it *Amerikan Salatasi!*

4 Medium Potatoes
3-4 carrots
½ c. Frozen Peas
4-5 Gherkin Pickles
Juice of ½ Lemon
¾ tsp. Salt
¼ tsp. Ground Black Pepper
1 c. Mayonnaise, divided
2 sprigs Fresh Parsley (rinsed, trimmed, as garnish)

❖ Boil potatoes in skin for about 45 minutes until soft. Meanwhile, peel and boil carrots until they too, are tender (about 30 minutes). Set aside to cool.

❖ Meanwhile steam or boil frozen peas in water for about 10 minutes. Drain and allow to cool.

❖ Peel potatoes and chop into small cubes. Place in large bowl. Chop carrots into tiny cubes and add to bowl.

❖ Chop pickles into tiny cubes and add to bowl.

❖ Add remaining ingredients plus ¾ cup mayonnaise. Toss mixture gently until ingredients are blended.

❖ Transfer to an attractive serving dish, and arrange in a mound. Spread ¼ c. mayonnaise over top, as if you were spreading a thin layer of frosting over a cake.

❖ Garnish with something green; I didn't have parsley sprigs for this photo, so I used peas! Serve chilled. *Afiyet olsun.*

ÇOBAN SALATASI

Peasant or Shepherd Salad

Serves 4-6

Likened to Greek salad, this classic blend of summer vegetables is best when tomatoes are at their peak. I use only locally grown tomatoes because they have the sweet, robust flavor this salad is known for. Tangy and crispy, *çoban salatası* is delightful with grilled fish or meats. I love having leftovers of it as a light lunch with a hearty bread. I use the bread to soak up the delicious juices in the bottom of the bowl. In fact, leftover *çoban salatası* in a blender is the basic recipe for Gazpacho!

INGREDIENTS:

4 Large Tomatoes, rinsed, skinned, coarsely chopped
2 Large Cucumbers, peeled, seeded, coarsely chopped
1 Medium Green Pepper, seeded, coarsely chopped
1 Small Red Onion, peeled, finely chopped
¼ c. fresh Parsley, rinsed, trimmed, chopped
1 Tbsp. fresh Dill, chopped (or ½ tsp. ground dill)
½ tsp. Dried Mint
1/3 c. Extra Virgin Olive Oil
Juice of 1 Lemon Juice (about ¼ cup)
10-12 Kalamata or Greek Olives
¼ lb. Feta Cheese, added just before serving
2 tsp. Ground Sumac (optional)

❖ Place all ingredients except cheese into a medium-sized bowl and toss well. Cover and refrigerate for at least half an hour.

❖ Before serving, toss one last time, and either crumble feta cheese on top, or arrange sliced portions of cheese around the perimeter of the bowl. *Afiyet olsun.*

HAVUÇ SALATASI
Carrot Salad

Carrot Salad is a wonderful summer side dish. It has a bright, refreshing flavor, a crisp texture, and is just plain beautiful. The deep orange color makes any meal look happier. Use only the freshest ingredients, especially the lemon.

INGREDIENTS

4 large Carrots, rinsed, peeled, and coarsely grated
3 sprigs fresh Parsley, rinsed, drained, divided
½ c. Extra Virgin Olive Oil
Juice of 1 Lemon (about ¼ c.)
10-12 Kalamata or Greek Olives

❖ Trim 2 sprigs parsley and chop fine. Place into medium-sized bowl with carrots.

❖ Add olive oil and lemon juice over top. (Be mindful lemon seeds don't fall in.) Toss well. Cover. Chill at least one hour.

❖ Before serving, toss one last time and transfer to a serving bowl. Arrange olives decoratively around perimeter. Add a sprig of parsley on top as garnish. *Afiyet Olsun.*

DOMATES SALATASI
Tomato Salad

Serves 4-6

*M*ake this zippy, beautiful salad in the heat of summer, when tomatoes are their most ripe and juicy.

INGREDIENTS:

3 large ripe Tomatoes
1 Small Red Onion, sliced very, very thin
5 tsp. Salt, divided
½ tsp. dried Oregano
¼ c. Extra Virgin Olive Oil
Juice of 1 Lemon (about ¼ c.)
10-12 Kalamata or Greek Olives (optional)

❖ Peel the tomatoes as shown on page 201. Chop coarsely and set aside in a medium-sized bowl.

❖ Place sliced onion in a small bowl and sprinkle 1 Tbsp. salt over it. Allow to stand 5 minutes.

❖ To remove bitterness from onion (killing the onion), firmly squeeze salt and onion together with your hand, squeezing again and again until juices seep out and onion becomes very soft and wet. Rinse onion with plenty of fresh water. Drain, and squeeze out excess water. Add to bowl of tomatoes.

❖ Add oregano and 2 tsp. salt. Toss ingredients gently with hands to distribute onions and seasonings.

❖ Add olive oil and lemon juice. Toss again - this time with a metal spoon. Garnish with olives, if you like. Serve immediately or cover and chill in refrigerator. Whenever you serve this salad, have bread nearby, to soak up the yummy juices in the bottom of the bowl! *Afiyet olsun.*

MARUL SALATASI
Romaine Salad

This is one of the easiest salads you can make, and it's a refreshing, tangy compliment to almost any main course. Because there is no salt, it stays crisp and fresh for days. Buy unpackaged Romaine lettuce with no brown on the ends of the leaves.

INGREDIENTS:
- I head Romaine Lettuce
- 1 bunch Scallions
- ¼ c. Extra Virgin Olive Oil
- Juice of 1 Lemon (¼ c.)
- ½ bunch fresh Dill, rinsed, drained, chopped, divided
- 1 Avocado (optional)

❖ Lay head of lettuce on its side and cut off and discard 1 to 2 inches from the leaf ends so that only crisp part of leaves remains. Cut off and discard white "core-end" of leaves, so that only tender green leaves remain. Slice lettuce width-wise into 1-inch slices. Rinse in large bowl of fresh water to remove any sand. Drain, spin or pat dry and place in large serving bowl.

❖ Chop off tops of scallions (usually ¼-inch will suffice) and pull outermost layer of skin up, over top, and off. Holding onion under cool running water, run fingers along stem to pull off any slippery film. Repeat with remaining. Hold bunch together firmly on cutting board and cut into ¼-inch slices. Use as much of green stalk as seems crisp and juicy (at least 2/3 of the way down). Add to bowl.

❖ Add olive oil, lemon juice, and half the dill. Toss well. Cover and allow to chill at least one hour.

❖ Before serving, add avocado slices (optional) and toss one last time. Garnish liberally with remaining dill. *Afiyet olsun!*

YOĞURTLU HAVUÇ
Carrots in Yogurt Sauce

arrots with yogurt is a healthy, low fat meze that is delicious on its own, but often accompanies seafood, grilled meats, and *Rakı*, a Turkish Anise-flavored hard-alcohol drink. Some people like to add sautéed onions and mayonnaise to the traditional recipe, to make it richer. But I prefer this light yogurt/garlic sauce because it lets the natural sweetness of the carrots shine through.

INGREDIENTS:

6 or 7 large Carrots, rinsed, peeled, grated
5 Tbsp. Olive Oil, divided
1 lb. plain Yogurt
5-6 cloves Garlic
¾ Salt, divided
¼ tsp. Dried Dill (garnish)
2 tsp. Paprika (optional)

❖ Simmer carrots in 3 Tbsp. oil in a covered large skillet over low heat for 10 to 15 minutes, stirring occasionally. When carrots are soft, set aside to cool.

❖ Crush garlic and ½ tsp. salt together in a mortar and pestle to make a rough paste. Whisk together with yogurt and ¼ tsp. salt in a medium-sized bowl. You may add up to ¼ c. water to bring sauce to consistency of mayonnaise.

❖ Add carrots and blend ingredients. Transfer to serving platter. Cover and chill at least two hours before serving to distribute flavors.

❖ Just before serving, garnish with dill. Alternately, you may place 2 Tbsp. oil in a small pan with paprike and stir over medium heat until oil sizzles. Quickly drizzle over carrots and yogurt before serving. *Afiyet olsun!*

VEGETABLE
DISHES

Basic Vegetable Techniques

Chopping Onions (And Why They Make You Cry)

Onions are full of vitamins C, B1 and B6, and lots of potassium, phosphorus and fiber. Some say they lower bad cholesterol, relieve hypertension and minimize blood clots. Onions, like their cousins garlics, chives, and leeks, absorb sulfur from the earth, and it's the sulfur which helps form molecules called amino acid sulfoxides.

Why the chemistry lesson?

Because when you chop into an onion you break open a number of cells which release an enzyme (Lachrymatory-factor synthase) into the air. This enzyme converts the sulfoxides into an unstable acid (sulfenic acid) which becomes a gas that floats up and irritates your tear ducts. In essence, the acid reacts with moisture in your eyes, creating a very mild form of sulphuric acid... which makes you cry.

There are many suggested methods for peeling onions without crying, like placing a cutting board across the sink, in front of the running water, or putting the onion in the freezer for ten minutes before peeling. I think the two best habits to get into are to chop the onion quickly in a well-ventilated area, and to keep all the unchopped onion portions cut-side-down on your cutting board. This will minimize the release of enzymes into the air.

Here's the fastest way to chop onions:

1. Chop off both ends of onion.

2. Cut onion in half length-wise.

3. Peel skin off each half. Lay halves cut-side-down on your cutting board. Discard cut ends and skin to reduce amount of acid in the air.

4. Slice each onion half into ¼-inch slices in one direction, holding onion together as much as possible.

5. Turn onion 90° and hold together as you chop slices in other direction.

6. Lay remaining small end down on its flat side to chop last bits.

CHOPPING GREEN PEPPERS

Carefully cutting crisp vegetables like cucumbers, onions, and peppers will help you create dishes that look as good as they taste. Knife skills are not rocket science; they just take a little practice and an appreciation for precision. Make sure you use a good sharp knife, and a wood cutting board.

Here's how to chop a green pepper. Wash the pepper, cut off the top, and pull out the pulp and any extra white fiber from inside. Slice off the bottom, as well. Slice pepper in half lengthwise, and then slice each half into strips. Turn the strips perpendicular, and slice them into tiny squares.

SKINNING
TOMATOES

A sure sign of a good cook is attention to detail; including not only flavors, aromas, and colors, but textures, as well. Some textures can be off-putting; the fuzzy peel of peaches, the rubbery friction of zucchini peels, or the sliminess of okra come to mind. In the best Turkish kitchens, the tough skin of tomatoes is always removed before preparing food; whether the tomato is to be chopped for a salad, cut into wedges and placed aside cheeses and olives at Kahvalti, or disolved in a rich stew. Fear not! Skinning a tomato is easy. Slice a small "X" in the bottom of the tomato. Stick a fork in the top and hold it in boiling water for 30 seconds or until the skin splits. Quickly dunk it in ice water for 15 seconds. The skin should peel right off.

Zeytinyağli Pirasa
Bet's Leeks and Carrots in Olive Oil

Serves 6-8

Leeks have long been treasured in Europe and the Mediterranean for their subtle, sweet flavor. They are a member of the onion, scallions, and garlic family and look like giant spring onions. Native to the Mediterranean area and Asia, leeks have been cultivated for more than 3,000 years. The white and light green portions are best to eat, while the dark green leaves can be used in soup stocks for flavor.

This recipe is one of my all-time favorites. The leeks come out amazingly tender and sweet, bathed in a lovely lemony sauce of rice, lemon, and carrots. It is eaten cold.

Leeks are easy to make if (and this is a big if) you can find good ones at the grocers. Look for a bunch of three; very white and firm, about 1½ to 2 inches in diameter. They should not be dry or browning on the outer layers.

Most importantly, look for leeks that are clean of sand and grit. Farmers are able to grow a longer white base (the most tender part) by stacking dirt around the plant as it grows, to keep more of it from sunlight. Since leeks grow in layers, sand and dirt accumulate deep inside the plant. So leeks must be rinsed well. There's nothing worse than preparing a beautiful dish of leeks only to throw them out after biting into grit! So before you buy, carefully pull back a layer or two of the green stalks. A little sand is normal, but if you see mud caked between the leaves, don't buy them. Leeks from places like Whole Foods tend to be clean and grit-free.

3 Leeks
2 Carrots
1 tsp. Salt
1 Tbsp. Sugar
2 Tbsp. Rice
Juice of 1 Lemon
½ c. Olive Oil

❖ Cut off root end as well as last third of green end of leeks. Discard.

❖ Cut into 1 to 1½-inch slices, and soak in a large bowl of cold water. You can use slices of the green stalk, but only if the slice hangs together.

❖ Swish slices around in cold water over and over again until all traces of sand and grit are gone. Exchange water as needed. Be meticulous.

❖ Peel carrots and slice very thin.

❖ Place leeks, carrots, salt, sugar, rice, 1 c. water, lemon juice and olive oil together in a large pot. Lightly toss ingredients.

❖ Cover pot and bring to boil.

❖ Immediately reduce heat to very low and simmer without stirring for 45 minutes to 1 hour. Check water level occasionally to maintain enough steam to cook the vegetables.

❖ Test leeks to make sure they are very tender; the white slices should seem to melt in your mouth. The water should be essentially gone, leaving behind a gooey, lemony sauce in the bottom of the pot. Remove pot from heat and allow to cool.

❖ Gently turn pot over onto a serving platter. Try not to disturb leeks too much on platter because they will be very tender. Allow carrots, rice, and sauce from bottom of pot to drizzle on top of leeks in platter.

❖ Serve cool with hearty bread and lemon wedges. *Afiyet olsun!*

IMAM BAYILDI (The Imam Swooned)
Stuffed Eggplant in Olive Oil

Serves 6-8

This famous eggplant dish achieved its notoriety not only from its delicate flavors, but also from its unique name. According to legend, *Imam Bayıldı* (the Imam swooned) when his wife served him a delicious dish of stuffed eggplant smothered in olive oil. What remains unknown is whether he fainted because the dish was so delicious, or because olive oil was so expensive!

INGREDIENTS:

6 Italian Eggplants (about 2 lbs.)
¾ Virgin Olive Oil, divided
2 large white Vidalia Onions, sliced very thin
12 cloves Garlic, finely chopped
1 bunch Fresh Parsley, rinsed, drained, chopped
2 large Tomatoes, peeled, chopped
Salt
2 tsp. Sugar
1 c. Canola Oil
3 small Italian Green Peppers (The skin of bell peppers is typically too thick for this dish unless they're homegrown.)

✡ *Imam Bayıldı* is served cold, on its own plate, as a meze or appetizer. Serve with a nice rustic bread.

❖ Leaving stems of eggplants intact, peel skin off each eggplant in thin alternating lengthwise strips. (Exposing some pulp will help draw out bitterness when eggplant is soaked in salted water).

❖ Cut a deep slit lengthwise into each eggplant, being careful not to cut all the way through and avoiding ends. Place eggplant in a large bowl of cold water with 2-3 Tbsp. salt. Set aside for at least 30 minutes.

❖ To prepare filling, heat up ½ cup olive oil in a deep skillet over medium-high heat. Sauté onions 10 minutes or until they are translucent. Add garlic and parsley. Sauté 3 minutes more. Add tomatoes, 2 tsp. salt, and sugar. Sauté 2 more minutes. Stir in ¼ c. water. Cover, reduce heat to low, and simmer for 5 minutes. Remove from heat, uncover, and allow to cool.

❖ Heat oven to 350°F.

❖ Rinse eggplants in cool water. Drain, firmly squeeze out excess water, and pat dry. Wash and drain peppers. Slice in half lengthwise. Set aside.

❖ Heat Canola oil in a deep skillet to temperature hot enough that a drip of water sizzles when dropped in. Fry eggplant until lightly browned on all sides and sagging when you lift them. Remove with tongs or slotted spoon and drain on paper towels.

❖ Turn off heat. Fry green peppers in oil for 2-5 minutes, depending on thickness. Drain on layers of paper towel.

❖ Arrange eggplants side-by-side in an oven-proof casserole dish, slit-side up. Using two spoons, gently tease apart slits and sprinkle inside of each eggplant with dash of salt. Stuff each eggplant with filling. Lay a strip of green pepper over top. Pour ½ cup water and ¼ cup olive oil around eggplants in dish. Loosely cover with foil and bake for 45 minutes to an hour.

❖ Allow eggplant to cool to room temperature before serving. *Afiyet olsun.*

ZEYTINYAĞLI ENGINAR

Artichoke Bottoms in Olive Oil

Artichokes are often served whole as an impressive-looking first course. My mom typically steamed them for about 45 minutes with a little lemon juice in a pot of shallow boiling water. We ate them by pulling out individual leaves, dipping the base of each leaf into melted butter, and then pulling it through our teeth to get the tender meat at the base. The discarded leaves accumulated in a bowl in the center of the table. When we reached the hairy choke at the center (which looks like the closed head of a thistle) we never imagined that the best part, (the saucer-shaped artichoke "bottom") lay hidden just underneath.

In this recipe, tender artichoke "bottoms" are filled with delicately seasoned vegetables. It is served as a *meze* or appetizer. Like other mezes made with olive oil (*zeytinyağlı*), this one is served to each guest on a separate, smaller plate so that it doesn't mix with later courses which might contain animal fat.

1 (14 oz.) Bag Frozen Artichoke Bottoms
(found in most Middle Eastern markets)
2 Lemons, divided
½ c. plus 1 Tbsp. Virgin Olive Oil, divided
1 Large Onion, finely chopped
1 Medium Carrot, peeled and chopped into tiny cubes
1 Medium Potato, peeled and chopped into tiny cubes
¾ c. Frozen Baby Peas
1 Tbsp. Sugar
1 tsp. Salt
2 Tbsp Fresh Dill, rinsed, trimmed, and chopped
1 to 2 c. Hot Water, divided

Artichoke (*enginar*) comes from a species of thistle cultivated by the Greeks and the Romans. It is a nutritional powerhouse, packed full of nutrients and vitamins. Most importantly, it's good for the liver. Artichoke reduces cholesterol production, expels sluggish cholesterol and stimulates bile to help break down fat. Artichoke concentrate (known as Cynarin) is used to treat kidney failure, gout, arthritis, poisoning and intestinal infections. Artichoke also contains insulin, and is therefore recommended for diabetics.

❖ Thaw frozen artichokes in a bowl of cool water with juice of 1 lemon.

❖ Sauté onions in olive oil in a large skillet over medium heat until they are translucent. Add carrots and continue to sauté a couple of minutes. Add potatoes. and continue to sauté another couple of minutes. Stir in peas and ¼ cup hot water. Immediately remove from heat. Spread vegetables out evenly to cover bottom of skillet.

❖ Remove artichoke bottoms one by one from water. Holding a half lemon in one hand, firmly rub lemon juice all over each artichoke before laying them, bowl-side down, on top of vegetables in skillet.

(I remember when my niece *Gülcan* taught me this recipe. We got the giggles when she instructed me to "massage" the little artichokes with lemon. But that does seem to be the best word for it, so, yes, massage lemon all over the artichoke.)

❖ When all the artichokes are arranged in the skillet, sprinkle sugar, salt, and a little more than ¾ cup hot water. Drizzle 1 Tbsp. olive oil over the top.

❖ Simmer covered over low heat about 10-15 minutes until tender. Check water while cooking, adding boiling water a little at a time as needed. Allow artichoke to cool to room temperature before serving.

❖ To serve, gently arrange artichokes, bowl-side up, in a serving platter. Fill each one with vegetables. If there are vegetables left over, you can serve them as a side dish. Garnish with chopped dill. *Afiyet olsun*.

KEREVIZ / APYO
Celery Root in Olive Oil, Bet's Version

This vegetarian recipe, tender celery knob and carrots in olive oil, is light, lemony and slightly sweet. It is a wonderful summer *meze*. Meze's are something like appetizers. Served both hot or cold, they're eaten before the main course - alone or with other mezes. Mezes made with olive oil (*zeytinyağlı*), like this one, are served to each guest on a separate, smaller plate, so as not to mix with later courses which might contain animal fat.

ABOUT CELERY ROOT OR CELERY KNOB:

When you buy celery root at the grocery store, it looks hideously ugly and most grocery stock boys don't even know what it is. But the look of this under-appreciated root belies its delicate flavor. *Kereviz* is always a favorite of my guests who find it both tender and surprisingly refreshing. Don't forget a hearty bread to soak up the lemony juices!

1 Handful All-purpose White Flour
2 Lemons, divided
2 Celery Roots or Celery Knobs
3 Carrots
½ c. Olive Oil
1 tsp. Salt
2 tsp. Sugar

❖ Fill a large bowl with water. Stir in a small handful of flour and one of the lemons which has been quartered and slightly squeezed. (Yes, lemon peel and all.)

❖ To prepare root, cut in half, top to bottom. Lay flat side down on cutting board. Using a sharp knife, cut away bottom of knob and all rough skin. (Flesh should be milky white. Areas of cream-colored veining are fine but if flesh is brownish with dark brown marbling, it will be stringy and tough. I would take it back to the grocer.)

Cut root into slices about the width of your index finger. Large pieces may be cut in half again. Place slices in lemony water to prevent from turning brown.)

❖ Peel carrots. Slice into thin (1/8th-inch) slices and add to water.

❖ Stir together 1/3 cup water, olive oil, salt, sugar, and juice of other lemon in a medium-sized pressure cooker. (You can lay a strainer over the pot to keep lemon seeds from falling in.)

❖ Lift celery root and carrots from bowl of water with your hands, a few at a time, allowing water to drain through your spread fingers. Place into pressure cooker. (For directions on using a pressure cooker, see page 213.) Stir ingredients gently to distribute oil and spices.

❖ Cover and cook under pressure over medium heat until bobbin begins to rock. Reduce heat to medium-low (there should be a slow, steady *phish-phish-phish* sound) and cook another 15 minutes, or until celery knob is very tender.

❖ Serve chilled with lemon garnish. *Afiyet olsun.*

CELERY KNOB IN OLIVE OIL

PORTAKALLI ZEYTINAĞLI KEREVİZ
Celery Root in Orange Sauce

Serves 8

Celery knob (*kereviz*) is a root that looks like a lumpy, brown softball. Surprisingly, the flesh of the root has a delicate flavor that goes especially well with citric sauces. In this recipe, taught to me by my talented niece *Gulcan Dolcan*, the celery knob is cooked with baby onions in a sauce of olive oil, fresh orange juice and lemon. Tell me your mouth isn't watering right now!

Like many Turkish *meze* (appetizers), this dish is prepared in olive oil and served cold. As such, it's important to serve it separately from meat dishes to keep the different juices from mixing together. So serve this dish to each guest on its own small plate, before the main course, with a nice bread to soak up the juices.

INGREDIENTS:

1½ Lemons, divided
24 Baby Onions, peeled
¼ c. Olive Oil
2 -3 Celery Knobs (don't buy huge ones; they lose flavor as they get bigger)
2 Oranges
2 tsp. Salt
2 Tbsp. Sugar
2 Parsely Sprigs as garnish

❖ Rub the cut side of a half lemon around the inside of a medium-sized bowl. Squeeze remaining juice into bowl. Fill bowl with a few cups of cool water and give it a quick stir. Set aside.

❖ To prepare root, cut in half, top to bottom. Lay flat side down on cutting board. Using a sharp knife, cut away bottom of knob and all rough skin. (Flesh should be milky white. Areas of cream-colored veining are fine but if flesh is brownish with dark brown marbling, it will be stringy and tough. I would take it back to the grocer.) Cut root into slices about the width of your index finger. Large pieces may be cut in half again. Place slices in lemony water to prevent from turning brown.

❖ Sauté onions in olive oil in a large pot over medium heat until they soften a bit, about 10 minutes. Be sure to stir consistently so that they do not brown. Turn off heat.

❖ Rinse whole oranges. (Turks rinse all fruit before cutting, including watermelon and citrus fruit.) Slice in half and squeeze out juice into a small bowl. Do same with one lemon. (Be careful to keep seeds and pulp out of bowl.)

❖ Left celery knob out of bowl with hands, allowing water to drain through open fingers. Lay slices gently into pot with onions.

❖ Add orange/lemon juice, salt, sugar and 1 cup water, stirring gently to blend ingredients evenly. Arrange celery root so that all slices will be submersed in juices as they cook.

❖ Set heat on high. When juices begin to boil, cover the pot and reduce heat to low. Simmer until celery root and onions are quite tender but not falling apart when pierced with a fork. (Cooking time varies with ripeness of root.)

❖ Allow to cool. To serve, then turn contents of pot over onto a shallow serving platter and garnish of parsley sprigs.
Afiyet olsun!

Kuru Fasülye
Roman Beans in Tomato Sauce

Serves 8 as meze

When Tant Ida and Onk Leon were first married, they lived, as most Turkish couples do, with his parents. Leon's mother, Madam Dana, taught Tant Ida everything she knows about cooking. Ida says her mother-in-law would get up at 5:00 every morning and have three dishes prepared by the time the rest of the family got out of bed. In fact, Ida didn't actually cook herself until she and Leon moved to the United States in the early 60's with their children Silvio and Suzy.

This is one of Onk Leon's favorite dishes. It appears on Ida's dinner table at least once a week and every Rosh Hashanah. *Kuru Fasülye* can be prepared with a variety of beans, including navy and pinto beans, and is made in a pressure cooker to reduce the cooking time.

INGREDIENTS:

2 c. Dried Roman Beans, soaked overnight in water
(Fresh or canned beans don't need to be soaked.)
2 large Onions, chopped fine
½ c. Vegetable Oil
2 Chicken Bouillon Cubes
1/3 c. Tomato Sauce
1 tsp. Salt
1½ tsp. Sugar

THE PRESSURE-COOKER STORY:

Cooking under pressure is a bit like playing music; sound is very important. You want to "tune" the heat level so that the bobbin (regulator on top) rocks slowly, with a gentle "phish phish phish" sound. When you turn off the heat under the pressure cooker, you must wait until the rocking stops (and the pressure bobbin drops) before opening the lid.

My mother had a terrible accident with a pressure-cooker when I was just a toddler. She had been making pea soup and had inadvertently twisted open the lid before the pressure had been fully released. The contents of the pot flew straight up into the air and fell back down on the back of my poor mother's neck. My sister Çaya remembers my father frantically patting Beti's neck with a cold wet washcloth. From then on, every time a pressure cooker was used in our house, we kids were sternly warned to not open it.

QUICK DE-PRESSURIZATION: Remember that food in the pressure-cooker actually continues to cook for a while during de-pressurization. If you ever need to open the lid quickly, here's a nifty trick. Carefully hold the hot pressure-cooker tilted slightly in the sink and run cool water over half the lid, keeping it away from the pressure regulator on top. Once you see that the air vent has dropped and no more steam (or sound) escapes when you jiggle the regulator, you can twist open the lid.

❖ Sauté onions in oil in uncovered medium-size pressure-cooker over medium-high until soft and translucent. Turks describe this step as sautéing the onions until they have "fainted" (*bayılmış vaziyete getirmek*). We also say *soğanları öldürmek* or "killing the onions!"

❖ Stir in bouillon cubes until they dissolve. Stir in tomato sauce, salt, and sugar.

❖ Drain beans and stir into pot with enough water to cover beans by 1 inch.

❖ Close lid of pressure-cooker and continue to cook over medium-high heat until the bobbin (pressure regulator) begins to rock. Reduce heat to achieve a slow rocking, and cook 20 minutes.

❖ To prevent over-cooking you need to cool the pot quickly. Remove it from heat and hold it slightly tilted in sink, allowing cold water to run over half the top (see photo above). When pressure has dropped, remove lid and check water level. If there is too much water, you can let some evaporate by continuing to cook beans uncovered for a few minutes. If there is not enough water, gently stir in a little more.

❖ Serve hot with rice for a high-protein, satisfying meal. *Afiyet olsun, mutluluk dolsun.* (Enjoy your meal, and may happiness fill you.)

ROMAN BEANS IN TOMATO SAUCE

MERCIMEK KÖFTESI
Refreshing Lentil Patties

Lentils are tiny, disc-shaped legumes full of protein, iron, and cholesterol-reducing fiber. They can be stored for years in your cupboard, and are easy to cook because they don't have to be soaked overnight.

The perfect alternative to meatballs, *Mercimek Köfte* are zesty, tender patties of lentils and bulgur, mixed with greens and seasoned with a paste made of onion, tomato and wonderfully aromatic spices. These patties are packed with flavor, and are served cold. This dish is eaten with the hands, each *köfte* nestled in a cool, crisp blanket of Romaine lettuce.

INGREDIENTS:

2 c. Dried Red Lentils (14 oz.)
1½ tsp. Salt
1 c. Bulgur (#1 or very fine)
    (found in any Mideast market)
1 Onion (large, chopped very fine)
¾ c. Extra Virgin Olive Oil
4-5 Tbsp. Tomato Paste
1 tsp. Ground Cumin
1/8 tsp. Ground Red Pepper (Cayenne)
1/8 tsp. Ground Black Pepper
1-2 heads fresh Romaine Lettuce
4 Spring Onions, rinsed, drained
½ Bunch Fresh Parsley, rinsed, drained
Juice of 1 to 1½ Lemons

❖ Pick through lentils and remove any stones. Place in large pot with exactly 4 cups water and 1½ tsp. salt. Cover pot, bring water to boil, and then reduce heat. Simmer about 20 minutes or until water is soaked up.

❖ Stir bulgur into pot, cover, and immediately remove from heat. Set aside to cool. If you're in a hurry to cool off the pot, set it in a sinkful of cool water. If the weather is cold, place covered pot outside to cool. (Don't put it in the fridge. Turkish cooks believe that placing hot foods in the fridge will ruin the refrigerator. I'm not sure that's true, but large pots of hot food in the fridge can warm up other foods, which could lead to bacteria.)

❖ Meanwhile, sauté onion and oil in a large skillet over medium-high heat for at least 10-15 minutes, stirring occasionally, until onions are translucent.

❖ Reduce heat to medium, and stirring continuously, add tomato paste. Sauté 5 minutes until paste turns darker. Stir in cumin, red pepper and black pepper. Remove from heat

❖ Add sauce to pot of cooled lentils and stir vigorously with a wooden spoon or spatula until ingredients are well-blended. Taste and season for salt. Cover and allow to cool.

❖ Pull apart leaves of Romaine lettuce. Rinse, drain, and set aside.

❖ Chop spring onions and parsley. Add to pot, along with lemon juice. Using your hands, blend ingredients together, trying not to mash them too much.

❖ Arrange individual lettuce leaves as a bed in a serving platter, with the dark green ends of leaves pointed toward the ends of the platter.

❖ Place a small bowl of cool water near platter and pot of lentils. With one hand, grab a small palmful of lentils. Squeezing lightly, bounce it inside your palm to form an oblong-shaped pattie. Blunt the ends. Gently place pattie (*köfte*) on top of leaves. Continue with remainder of lentils, nestling the patties side by side or tucked inside individual smaller leaves. Loosely cover platter. Cool on counter top.

❖ To serve, place platter at center of table. Since these *köfte* are eaten with the hands, invite your guests to tear off a piece of lettuce and nestle individual *köftes* inside it. Don't be surprised if your guests eat three or four of them! *Afiyet olsun!*

KABAK KALAVASUCHO
Zucchini and Cheese Pie

Zucchini and cheese pie is a typical Sephardic dish of the *cuajado* variety. *Cuajado* is a Ladino term for "coagulated or having curds" and refers to a number savory baked dishes made from cheeses combined with lots of eggs, a little flour or matzo-meal for binding, and large amounts of grated fresh vegetables. They're often made with spinach, eggplant, potatoes or leeks (as in this recipe). The texture is something like a savory bread pudding; soft but not mushy, with cheese forming a slightly hardened crust.

We always serve *Cuajado* dishes during Passover. They are served slightly warm or at room temperature, which means they can be made ahead of time and kept in a warm oven or on the counter during the Seder, and served immediately after with little fuss.

INGREDIENTS:

6 Medium Zucchini
2 eggs
¼ c. Flour or Matzo meal
½ c. Cottage Cheese
½ c. Shredded Mozzarella or Gruyère Cheese
½ c. Grated Kasseri or Parmesan Cheese, divided
2 Tbsp. Fresh Dill, chopped
Salt and Pepper
3 Tbsp. Vegetable Oil
Oil to grease pan

❖ Peel zucchinis lengthwise. If you want to make *Kaşkarikas* with the peels (recipe on next page), remove the skin in thick strips and set aside.

❖ Grate all the zucchini pulp. Placing small amounts of grated zucchini in your hand, gradually squeeze out as much water as possible from squash before placing it in a large bowl.

❖ Add eggs, flour (or Matzo-meal), mozzarella and cottage cheeses, half the kasseri, dill, salt and pepper.

❖ Mix ingredients well and divide equally into two greased 8-inch pie pans or one greased 9x13 oven-proof casserole dish.

❖ Sprinkle with remaining kasseri cheese. Drizzle oil on top and bake at 350°F for 40-45 minutes or until brown. (Smaller baking dishes will require a few minutes longer, since the *Kalavasucho* will be thicker.)

❖ Serve *Kalavasucho* as a side dish, or with salad as a protein main course, similar to "macaroni and cheese." *Afiyet olsun!*

KAŞKARIKAS

Little Zucchini Peels

*Açın halini tok bilmez,
hastanın halini sağ bilmez*

**A satiated man knows not hunger,
nor a healthy man disease**

Waste was shameful in our house, especially when it came to food. The pulp, seeds, or even skins removed from vegetables used in one dish made their way into other meals. Such is the case for *kaşkarikas*, a quick and very nutritious side-dish made from the peels of zucchini squash. Tant Mati told me that her mother Sultana would reserve the peels from the several pounds of grated squash pulp she used in her zucchini *börek* and sauté them in a little oil and tomato to make this *kaşkarikas*.

Recycling food stuffs is very common in Turkey, especially because most Turkish dishes taste better the day after they are prepared. Juices from a roast or the carcass of a roast chicken make great stocks for soups. Vegetable peels, stems, and ends add depth to soup stock. Mold can be cut off hard cheeses, and the rest eaten. Dry bread can be soaked in water to thicken meat dishes or purees.

For my parent's generation, survival depended on frugality, especially during the first World War. My father as a six-year-old was once sent out to buy a loaf of bread for the family dinner. Too hungry to resist, he nibbled at the end of the loaf. One bite led to another, and he came home empty-handed. He was greeted with harsh punishment from his step-mother.

Survival also depended on an enterprising (*açık göz*) mind-set. In Istanbul at the turn of the century, children like my father roamed the cobblestone streets plundering for scraps

INGREDIENTS:

6 Medium Zucchinis, (You will separate the peels from the pulp; using the peels for this recipe, and the pulp for Kalavasucho.
1 Large Tomato, chopped (or ¼ c. canned Tomato Sauce)
½ bunch Fresh Dill (or 1 tsp., dried)
Juice of 1 Lemon
¾ c. Olive Oil (or vegetable oil)
1 tsp. Salt
¼ tsp. Black Pepper
½ tsp. Sugar

❖ Rinse squash well, and with a knife or large peeler, peel zucchinis lengthwise, leaving some of the flesh with the peel.

❖ Cut strips into 1 to 2-inch pieces.

❖ Combine peels and other ingredients in a medium-sized saucepan, and simmer covered for 15-20 minutes. The peels should be *al dente*. If you prefer to use a medium-sized pressure cooker, cook under pressure for only 5 minutes. Cool before serving. *Afiyet olsun!*

---

and junk to make their toys. He and his friends would catch bumble bees, pull off their wings and tie them to old thread spools. They would watch the bee pulling the spool around like a horse and cart. The friends made soccer balls out of crumpled wads of newspaper wrapped with string. They made pirate hats out of folded newspapers. Zeki always regretted using the top of a tin can as a Frisbee. The lid flew across the street and struck a child in the forehead, slicing the boys skin and causing a good deal of bleeding.

Late in life, my father still enjoyed eating leftover spaghetti with a simple sauce of butter and sugar. Yogurt stirred into leftover rice was a perfectly reasonable lunch. Bread was precious. He'd revive dry bread by wiping it with a wet hand. He'd scrape char off burnt toast with a butter knife. We tore stale bread into small pieces and threw it outside for the winter birds. The value of bread was so ingrained I still kiss it and place it to my forehead before throwing it out.

The lessons of poverty permeated my father's life. I often saw him pick up stray nuts, bolts, and tiny springs off the street; booty which would then become part of a makeshift TV antenna or rabbit cage. Wire clothes hangers came in handy for auto repairs and plumbing. He'd remove and save buttons and zippers from old clothes, re-use old cloth for new outfits, and tear up whatever remained for household rags. He patiently darned his socks, pulling the frayed heel over an ancient little gizmo that looked like a wooden egg with a handle. He taught me to weave the thread over and under to recreate fabric where it had been worn away. I think of those lessons often and try to keep them relevant to my life today.

LITTLE ZUCCHINI PEELS

MÜCVER
Zucchini Fritters or Latkes

Serves 8

Summertime, when squash is plentiful, is the perfect time to make delicious fritters (or latkes) of grated zucchini, onions, and cheese. These fried goodies make the kitchen smell so yummy I've never been able to finish cooking a batch without someone sneaking off with one behind my back. *Mücver* are best served warm, but are also delicious at room temperature. Prepare them a day ahead and pack them easily for a picnic!

Converting Turkish recipes into English can create unique measuring units. Here, for example, I say 4/5 cup flour because it's roughly equal to the Turkish *bardak* (glass) called for in the original Turkish recipe. Two Turkish coffee spoons (*kahve kaşık*) of pepper translates to roughly one American teaspoon. If you ever need to translate a Turkish recipe, you can refer to the chart of Turkish measurement equivalencies which appears on page 342.

INGREDIENTS:

2 lbs. Zucchini
2 Large Onions, grated
1 /3 lb. Feta Cheese, broken up
4 Eggs
1 tsp. Ground Black Pepper
2 tsp. Salt
4/5 c. White Flour (or Matzo-meal for Passover)
2 Bunches Fresh Dill, chopped, divided
4/5 c. Vegetable Oil

❖ Peel zucchini and cut off ends. (If you want to recycle the skins for *Kaşkarikas* (previous recipe) allow peel to remain somewhat thick and set it aside.

❖ Grate zucchini and place in large colander.

❖ Taking small amounts of squash between your hands, squeeze as much water as possible from it before placing it in a large bowl. Continue with remaining squash.

❖ Add onion, cheese, eggs, pepper, salt and flour to the bowl. Add dill (setting aside a couple of tablespoons for garnish) and mix ingredients together well. Batter should be somewhat watery but still hold together.

❖ Heat oil in large frying pan to temperature hot enough that a droplet of water sizzles.

Frying is an art. The amount of heat will depend on how many patties you fry at a time, as well as the thickness of the batter. Each side should take 2-3 minutes to reach a golden-brown color, so adjust your heat accordingly.

❖ Carefully lay heaping tablespoonfuls of batter into pan, starting with just one or two fritters to adjust the heat. Do not crowd the fritters. Fry each one until the bottom is golden brown. Gently turn it over and brown the other side.

❖ Remove fritters from oil with a slotted spoon and place on a couple of layers of paper towel to soak up extra oil.

❖ Arrange on a serving plate, placing them in rows, each one slightly over the next, or in a circle. (If you are not serving immediately, allow to cool uncovered so they stay crisp.)

❖ Sprinkle with remaining fresh dill before serving. *Afiyet olsun!*

AYŞE FASÜLYE
Green Beans in Olive Oil

Serves 8

Whenever we're invited to dinner, I ask the hostess what I can bring. Nine times out of ten I'm asked to make *Ayşe Fasülye*. It's actually a green bean salad of sorts; eaten cold as a side-dish or *meze* (appetizer). My Grandmama Sara used to make it but my mother perfected it by adding just a touch of oregano to deepen the flavor. Her *Ayşe Fasülye* was so good, in fact, that many in our family call it *Beti Fasülye* instead.

This dish is quick to prepare and can be kept in the fridge for up to five days. As a leftover, I enjoy eating it for lunch with a nice rustic bread to soak up the wonderful juices.

INGREDIENTS:

2 lbs. Fresh Green Beans
   (or frozen whole or Italian-cut)
2/3 c. Virgin Olive Oil
2 medium Onions, chopped
2 medium Tomatoes, chopped
1½ tsp. Salt
1½ tsp. Sugar
¼ tsp. Dried Dill Weed (or ¼ bunch fresh, chopped)
¼ tsp. Dried Oregano

❖ If using fresh beans, rinse and drain them, and then snip off both ends. Cut each bean in half crosswise so that they're about 2½ to 3 inches long. Set aside.

❖ Sauté onions in olive oil in a large pot over medium high heat until tender and translucent.

❖ Add tomatoes. Continue to sauté a minute or two more.

❖ Add green beans, salt, sugar, dill, oregano and 1 cup water. Lightly stir ingredients together. Cover and simmer, without stirring, over low heat for 45 minutes to an hour until beans are very soft, . (You'll know when they're done when water is gone and only oil remains in the bottom of pot.)

❖ Allow to cool. Turn contents of pot over onto a serving platter. (Try not to disturb ingredients so that the small pieces of tomato and onion from the bottom of the pot end up on top of the beans in the platter.)

❖ Generously garnish with dill for flavor and color before serving. As with most Turkish food, you will find these beans taste even more delicious the next day. *Afiyet olsun!*

KIZARMIŞ PATLICAN
Fried Eggplant with Yogurt and Tomato Sauce

Serves 6

My mother and all my aunts knew how to fry eggplant. They knew the secrets to removing the bitterness and to keeping the eggplant light and not greasy. As a kid, I didn't know these things were even an issue! I just knew that the sound and aroma of eggplant sizzling meant that dinner was going to be special.

Here's the most common fried eggplant dish, served with a fresh tomato sauce and a delicious yogurt-garlic sauce on top. *Patlican* keeps for several days in the refrigerator and can be served as a wonderful *meze* or refreshing side dish.

EGGPLANTS

2 medium size Globe Eggplants (1 to 1½ lbs)
2 Tbsp. Salt
2 c. Vegetable Oil, divided
2 Eggs, whisked (optional)
6 Medium Italian Green Peppers (or 2 Bell Peppers)
6 Sprigs Fresh Parsley, rinsed, drained, trimmed

❖ Cut stems of eggplants. Peel half the skin off lengthwise in alternating strips (like stripes).

❖ Cut eggplants crosswise into ½-inch thick slices. To draw out bitterness, soak eggplant for at leat 20 minutes in a large bowl with salt and about 8 cups cold water. (Place a plate on top of eggplants to keep them submerged.)

❖ Meanwhile, prepare tomato and yogurt sauces.

YOGURT-GARLIC SAUCE

1 2/3 c. Whole Plain Yogurt
¼ c. water
2-4 Cloves Garlic, minced
1 tsp. Salt

❖ In a small bowl, whisk sauce ingredients until very smooth. Cover bowl and refrigerate for at least 15 minutes to allow garlic flavor to blend with yogurt.

TOMATO SAUCE

2 Tbsp. Virgin Olive Oil
3 Cloves Garlic, minced
2 Large Tomatoes, peeled, seeded and finely chopped, (or 1 ½ c. chopped canned tomatoes)
1 tsp. Salt

❖ Heat olive oil in a sauce pan. Sauté garlic for about a minute, stirring with a wooden spoon until soft, but not brown. Stir in tomatoes and salt. Reduce heat, cover and simmer until mixture dissolves into a purée. Set aside.

The first time I made this dish it was an oily disaster! The slices of eggplant drank up all the oil in the pan; obviously too greasy to eat. I called Tant Ida who told me the trick she learned from her mother-in-law Sultana; she simply dredges the eggplant slices in a plate of two whisked eggs before frying. Tant Mati concurred that she, too, dredges eggplant in egg to keep it from soaking up too much oil. Mati then noted that my mom's preference (frying without egg), is the "classic" Turkish method and that mom always complained when she saw Mati using egg. We reminisced about how much my mother loved to eat greasy foods and how she certainly didn't worry about her weight!

THREE THINGS TO REMEMBER TO REDUCE OILINESS IN FRIED EGGPLANT.

1. The salt water we soak the eggplant in does more than pull the bitterness out; it also wicks moisture out, leaving the eggplant thirsty for oil. So, when you remove the eggplant slices from the salt water, rinse them well in a bowl of fresh water so they will not soak up as much frying oil.

2. Pat and squeeze the slices dry before frying to reduce the amount of steam they give off. (Steam makes them cook unevenly.)

3. The oil temperature should be maintained at about 350-365°F. We never used thermometers for cooking, but make sure the oil is hot enough for there to be bubbles around the eggplant as they cook. A splatter guard with a fine mesh screen is also a good idea when frying.

FRYING THE EGGPLANTS:

❖ Remove eggplants from saltwater with slotted spoon, and firmly pat dry with paper towels. Rinse and dry green peppers, as well.

❖ Heat 1½ cups oil in a frying pan over high heat until a haze forms above it. (It is important for oil be hot enough - about 350-365° F - or eggplant will be too greasy.) Test temperature by carefully dipping a piece of eggplant into it. If the oil sizzles, it is ready for frying.

(continued on next page)

FRIED EGGPLANT WITH TOMATO SAUCE

❖ Pat each eggplant slice completely dry with paper towel. (If you want to use egg, whisk eggs in a shallow bowl and dredge each slice of eggplant before frying.) Carefully lay three or four slices into skillet, making sure not to crowd them. Fry about 5 minutes each side until lightly browned. Oil temperature will vary depending on how many eggplant you fry at a time. If the eggplant are browning too quickly or conversely, not sizzling around the edges, modulate heat accordingly.

❖ Remove browned eggplant slices from oil, and drain on paper towels.

❖ Add more oil to pan as needed, but remember to heat to proper temperature again before adding more eggplant slices.

❖ Meanwhile, remove seeds and extra white filaments from inside green peppers, and slice into rings or segments.

❖ When all eggplant slices are fried, turn off heat and add green peppers to the pan. Turning them over with tongs or a fork, fry for about 10 minutes until softened. Drain on paper towel, as well. You may also want to remove their skins with a sharp knife. Allow vegetables to cool.

❖ To serve, arrange eggplants on a serving platter. Pour tomato sauce over top. Arrange peppers decoratively around eggplant. Garnish with sprigs of parsley. Serve with small bowl of yogurt-garlic sauce. (Yogurt sauce served separately gives guests the option of not eating it if meat is also served with the meal).

❖ Serve at room temperature, and make sure there is hearty bread nearby to scoop up those yummy sauces! *Afiyet olsun.*

MINCING GARLIC:

Removing the skin from garlic is actually quick and easy, once you know the trick. Place the garlic clove on a cutting board. Place a broad knife on the clove and with the heel of your hand press firmly down until the garlic crunches. The cracked skin will now be easy to remove. You can then chop up the garlic by hand, or better yet, invest in a garlic press to mince it. It's inexpensive, and once I finally bought one for myself, I found I really used it a lot.

FRIED EGGPLANT WITH TOMATO SAUCE + MINCING GARLIC

Lima Beans in Olive Oil

*M*y husband Bruce hated lima beans his whole life, until he tasted them cooked "Turkish Style." Now Lima Beans in Olive Oil is the dish he requests more than any other. Serve them cold, always with yogurt and bread, as a *meze* or a side dish.

INGREDIENTS:

2 medium Onions, chopped

2/3 c. Virgin Olive Oil

2 medium Tomatoes, peeled (optional) and chopped

2 lbs. Frozen Lima Beans

1½ tsp. Salt

1½ tsp. Sugar

½ tsp. Dried Dill Weed (or ¼ bunch fresh, chopped)

❖ Sauté onions in olive oil in a large pot over medium-high heat until tender and translucent (about 10 minutes.)

❖ Add tomatoes. Sauté a minute or two more.

❖ Add remaining ingredients and 1 cup water. Stir. Cover and simmer over low heat (without stirring) for 45 minutes to an hour. Beans are done when they are soft, all the water is gone and only oil remains. Allow to cool.

❖ Turn contents of pot over onto a serving platter, trying not to disturb ingredients. Allow small pieces of onion and tomato from bottom of pot to settle on top.

❖ Garnish with dill. These lima beans will keep in the fridge for 5-6 days. *Afiyet olsun!*

ZEYTINYAĞLI BAKLA
Fava Beans in Olive Oil

Serves 8

ava Beans (Broad Beans) are large, floppy beans that show up at your grocer's in the springtime. They're high in fiber and iron, and have so much protein they have been called the "poor man's meat." Shelled fava beans (found in the freezer of Mideast markets), are often used to make a savory, robust purée. In this recipe which my mother showed me many years ago, fresh fava beans are served cold with yogurt. My niece *Gülcan* recently showed me how her grandmother (my father's first wife *Zehra Hanım*), prepared it. It's ironic that both my father's wives (one Jew-ish, the other Turkish, who had never seen each other cook), prepared fava beans in almost identical ways. The main differences? *Zehra Hanım* added flour directly into the pot, whereas mom used it only in the lemony water. Also, mom added half the dill before cooking and the rest as garnish, whereas *Zehra* added it only after cooking. The common denominator here is that both my father's wives apparently knew how he liked his fava beans!

INGREDIENTS:

3 Tbsp. Flour, divided
1 Lemon, divided
2 lbs. Fresh Fava Beans, rinsed and drained
1 large Onion, cut in half, sliced very thin
2 Tbsp. + ½ c. Olive Oil, divided
2 Tbsp. Sugar, divided
1 Tbsp. Salt
½ bunch Fresh Dill, chopped, (or 1 Tbsp. dried)

❖ Whisk together 1 Tbsp. flour and juice of ½ lemon in a large bowl of water. Set aside.

❖ De-vein fava beans by cutting off ends and then paring off the stringy spine along each side of pod. Cut widthwise into pieces at least 2" long. (Don't worry if beans fall out of the pods.) Place pods and beans into lemony water.

❖ Place 2 Tbsp. olive oil into bottom of a medium-sized pressure cooker. (Heat should be off). Lay one third of the onions into oil.

❖ Using your hands, lift up about a quarter of the fava beans from water, allowing the water to drain between your fingers, and lay over onions in pressure cooker.

❖ Sprinkle another 1 Tbsp. flour over beans, and then 1 Tbsp. sugar on top.

❖ Layer another third of onions, and then remaining fava beans. Sprinkle 1 Tbsp. flour and 1 Tbsp. sugar. Sprinkle salt on top.

❖ Lay remaining onion into pot. Drizzle ½ cup olive oil and ½ cup water over contents.

❖ Lift pot and jiggle it to distribute smaller ingredients. Do NOT stir.

❖ Cover. Set heat on high and cook under pressure until bobbin starts to rock. Reduce heat to medium low. (The bobbin should rock about 10 times in 5 seconds.) Cook ten minutes. Remove from heat.

❖ Cool the pressure cooker under running water as shown. When pressure bobbin has completely dropped and pressure is dispersed, open lid.

Optimally, there should only be oil left in the bottom of the pot, but every pressure-cooker is different. If there is water remaining, you can continue to simmer *bakla* uncovered over low heat until water evaporates. But take care not to let beans become too soft or mushy.

❖ To serve, turn over entire contents of pot onto a serving platter, trying not to disturb ingredients. Serve cool, with a garnish of dill sprinkled on top and a little yogurt on the side. *Afiyet olsun!*

FAVA BEANS IN OLIVE OIL 229

Lahana Dolmasi
Stuffed Cabbage Rolls

Serves 6

In 1978, when my mother was in her mid-fifties, she had a lovely little apartment in Bethesda. One Saturday afternoon I stopped in to visit her and found her making yummy stuffed cabbage rolls while singing along to her favorite *à la Turka* records. Here's her recipe.

INGREDIENTS:

2 tsp. Black Currants
7 medium Onions, chopped fine
½ c. + ½ c. Olive Oil, divided
¾ c. Rice
2 Tbsp. Pine Nuts
1½ tsp. Sugar
1 tsp. Salt
1 tsp. Ground Allspice
1 tsp. Black Pepper
1 large Tomato (diced) (or 1 tsp. Tomato Paste)
1 large head Cabbage
1 c. Hot Water
2 Lemons, divided

The Filling:

❖ Soak currants in a small bowl of hot water.

❖ Sauté onions, rice, and pine nuts in a large skillet with ½ cup olive oil over medium-high heat, stirring frequently, until onions are tender and translucent and pine nuts are light golden brown, (about 10-15 minutes).

❖ Stir in sugar, salt, drained currants, allspice, pepper, and tomato. (If you are using tomato paste, stir it up in a small bowl and gradually stir in ¾ cup of water until it becomes a sauce. Then add to pot.) Blend ingredients, cover, and simmer over low heat for 30 minutes.

PREPARING CABBAGE LEAVES:

❖ Rinse cabbage and cut off knob. Carefully insert a long, pointed knife deeply into bottom, (to center of the cabbage), and work it around core. Continue to loosen core until you can pull it out. Discard core.

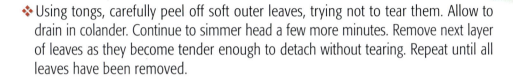

❖ Simmer cabbage head in large pot of boiling water for 10-15 minutes or until outermost leaves are tender and pliable. (The end closest to the core can still be a little stiff, since it will be removed when you roll the leaves.)

❖ Using tongs, carefully peel off soft outer leaves, trying not to tear them. Allow to drain in colander. Continue to simmer head a few more minutes. Remove next layer of leaves as they become tender enough to detach without tearing. Repeat until all leaves have been removed.

❖ Line bottom of a heavy pot with any torn leaves or ones that are too small to roll.

WRAPPING DOLMA:

❖ Spread open a leaf on a cutting board, with core end closest to you. Cut off stiff spine at bottom. Place 2 heaping tablespoons filling near core-end of leaf. (Amount of filling can be adjusted to size of each leaf.)

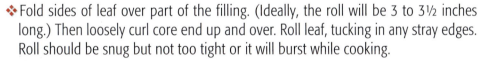

❖ Fold sides of leaf over part of the filling. (Ideally, the roll will be 3 to 3½ inches long.) Then loosely curl core end up and over. Roll leaf, tucking in any stray edges. Roll should be snug but not too tight or it will burst while cooking.

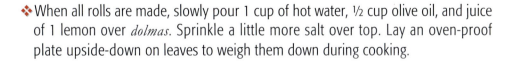

❖ Arrange rolls side by side in pot on top of bed of leaves, with seam down. You may lay the second layer of rolls on top of first.

❖ When all rolls are made, slowly pour 1 cup of hot water, ½ cup olive oil, and juice of 1 lemon over *dolmas*. Sprinkle a little more salt over top. Lay an oven-proof plate upside-down on leaves to weigh them down during cooking.

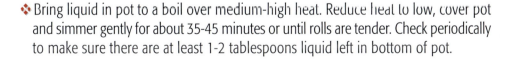

❖ Bring liquid in pot to a boil over medium-high heat. Reduce heat to low, cover pot and simmer gently for about 35-45 minutes or until rolls are tender. Check periodically to make sure there are at least 1-2 tablespoons liquid left in bottom of pot.

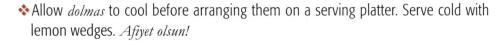

❖ Allow *dolmas* to cool before arranging them on a serving platter. Serve cold with lemon wedges. *Afiyet olsun!*

YALANCI YAPRAK SARMASI

Grape Leaves Stuffed with Rice

Grape leaves wrapped arounf a well-seasoned rice filling is the epitome of Turkish cuisine. They have all the characteristics one looks for in Turkish food, a delicate blend of flavors, surprising depth of flavors from the warmth of rice to the zing of lemon to the sweet surprise of currant. Textures in this single dish alone range from tender (rice) to chewy (leaf) to crisp (the crunch of the roasted pine nut). And finally, there is the presentation, lovely, cerfully wrapped morsels, glistening from a coating of olive oil, with a promise of a delightful zing from the lemon garnish.

I've tried grape leaves at quite a few restaurants and venues, but none have had quite the same taste as the ones I grew up with. I am so happy to share this recipe and a funny little story on the next page about grape leaves.

INGREDIENTS:

3 Tbsp. Black Currants
¾ c. plus 2 Tbsp. Extra Virgin Olive Oil, divided
5 Medium Onions, finely chopped
3 Tbsp. Pine Nuts
1 c. Long Grain Rice, rinsed, drained
2 small Tomatoes, chopped (optional)
2½ c. Boiling Hot Water, divided
3 Tbsp. Fresh Dill chopped (or 1 tsp. dried)
3 Tbsp. Fresh Mint (or 1 Tbsp. dried)
½ tsp. Cinnamon
1/8 tsp. Allspice
Pinch of Clove
Pinch of Nutmeg
Salt
1 Tbsp. Sugar
2 Lemons
1 (16 oz.) jar Grape Leaves
Lemon Wedges for Garnish

The Grape Leaves Story:

When I was nine or ten, the six of us lived in a three-bedroom apartment in Hyattsville, Maryland with our dog, a gorgeous, muscular boxer named Joe. One day, my mother was asked to prepare grape leaves (*dolma*) for a party at the Turkish Embassy. She worked well into the early morning hours to carefully wrap 300 pristine rolls and placed the pot full of dolmas on the stove before leaving for work. My father, before leaving the house, wedged a large plywood board in the kitchen doorway to make sure Joe couldn't get in.

When I arrived home from school that afternoon, I opened the door and was puzzled that Joe had not greeted me with his customary body slam. I called him and there was no response. Walking past the kitchen I noticed a strange, greenish slime coating the white vinyl floor. Upon closer inspection, I spotted two lonely *dolmas* in the middle of the kitchen floor. How odd that Joe hadn't grabbed them up, since he efficiently gobbled up every crumb within reach. My sister Çaya noticed the now-empty pot on the stove. It was then that I found the pot cover under the kitchen table. Suddenly the unthinkable dawned on us. We turned to each other with a look of "Holy Shit!"

I called the dog several times before his nose and then his face guiltily appeared from around the corner of the bedroom hallway. His body followed, distended belly sagging. He wandered drunkenly toward me, leaning on walls for support. His eyes looked sheepish, submissive. The intensity of the stale flatulence that wafted behind him was staggering. Yes, he had feasted mightily, but even the voracious Joe could not finish those last telltale *dolmas*.

We immediately called my mother at work to report this incident.

She was speechless for the first and only time. She simply listened and slowly hung up the phone. Odd, I thought.

That evening, my father was a man on a mission. When he entered the apartment, the dog sensed his peril and threw himself under the liquor cabinet; a pitiable and purely symbolic attempt at avoiding the inevitable. My father's eyes were red with rage. He didn't shout at the cowering animal; he more or less pressed incredulity and logic from between his tight lips. "Fifty cents a day? Fifty cents a day to feed you? I haven't eaten 298 dolmas in my life! In my LIFE!" The dog escaped from his hiding place and ran past my father toward the bedrooms, the "*Eau de Dolma*" adding further insult to my father's injury.

Dad caught up with the dog in the narrow hallway announcing that the mongrel would be going back to the animal shelter. Horrified, I fell to the floor and wrapped my arms around my best friend, begging my father not to send him away. My sister Çaya, just one year older than I, assumed an impressive attorney pose and began her closing argument; "How could you do that to this poor child? Take away the animal she loves so much?"

My father paused briefly, and then promptly dismissed her plea. He then turned to find something - anything - with which to hit the dog. Joe quickly high-tailed it into my bedroom. An airborne wooden chair just missed him as he slid inelegantly under the bed.

I don't know why my parents didn't get rid of Joe after this episode. A dog was a dog. Maybe they felt sorry for him. Or me. Maybe the embassy party was successful despite the 300 missing stuffed grape leaves.

PREPARING THE FILLING:

❖ Soak the currants in warm water about 15-20 minutes.

❖ Heat ¾ c. olive oil in a large pot over medium heat. Sauté onions in oil, stirring frequently until they've fainted (are translucent). Add pine nuts and sauté until light golden color. Add rice and continue to stir until another 10 minutes.

❖ (At this point, my mother would add 2 small tomatoes, cubed and mashed, and stir for another 5 minutes. Since traditional grape leaves recipes do not include tomatoes, I have excluded this step.)

❖ Carefully add 1 ½ c. boiling water to the rice. Add dill, mint, cinnamon, cloves, allspice, nutmeg, 1 tsp. salt, sugar, juice of 1 lemon, and currants. Mix well, bring to boil, cover and lower heat to very low. Cook 20 minutes until the water has been absorbed. Remove from heat and allow filling to cool.

(continued on next page)

PREPARING THE LEAVES:

❖ Remove grape leaves from jar by gently twisting and rocking them back and forth. loosen a bit, and boil in water for two minutes to soften leaves and to remove some of the brine. Using a slotted spoon, remove and rinse one at a time under running water. With a sharp knife, cut out the small, protruding stem from base of each leaf. Drape leaves, one-by-one, over edge of a colander to drain. Line bottom of large heavy pot with any torn ones.

WRAPPING THE LEAVES:

You will roll the filling inside the leaves so that they are 1¼ to 1½ inches in diameter. This will take a little practice, so don't worry if the first few are not beautiful. You will quickly get the hang of it.

❖ On a dinner plate, lay out a single leaf, veiny-side up, with stem toward you. Spoon a heaping tablespoon of filling onto leaf, just above stem. Fold end nearest you just over the filling. Fold two sides over filling, and gingerly roll leaf up (away from you) into a small cylinder. Roll should be firm but not too tight, since rice will swell during cooking and may cause roll to burst.

❖ Arrange *dolmas* snugly on bed of leaves in pot, seam-side down so they don't unravel while cooking. Lay them side-by-side, and then one layer on top of the other.

PREPARING THE SAUCE:

❖ Stir 1 c. HOT water, ¼ tsp. Salt, 2 Tbsp. Olive Oil, and juice of 1 Lemon together in a small bowl. Pour sauce over dolmas.

❖ Cover rolls with any remaining leaves, and place a small oven-proof plate upside-down over them to weigh them down as they cook.

❖ Bring liquid to a boil over medium-high heat. Cover pot, reduce heat to low and continue to simmer for 50 minutes until *dolmas* are tender. There should be no more than 1-2 tablespoons of juice left in pot. (Check water level periodically; if water evaporates before rolls are tender, add a few tablespoons hot water as needed.)

❖ Remove pot from heat and allow *dolmas* to cool in pot. Remove plate and arrange dolmas on a serving dish. Cover and refrigerate.

❖ Serve chilled, garnished with lemon wedges. *Afiyet olsun!*

GRAPE LEAVES STUFFED WITH RICE FILLING

AVAS CON ISPINAKA
Beans with Spinach

K nown in Turkish as *Kuru Fasülyeli Ispanak*, beans with spinach comes from the Sephardic side of my family. It's an inexpensive, vegetarian dish that's especially nutritious when served with rice. You can prepare it in a pressure cooker if you're short on time, but if you cook it slowly (1½ - 2 hours over low heat), you will find it has a more hearty texture and a better balance of flavors.

INGREDIENTS:

1c. Dried Canellini or Navy Beans
3 Boxes (10 oz.) Frozen Chopped Spinach
1½ c. Hot Water
3 Chicken Bouillon Cubes
1/3 c. Olive oil
1 tsp. Tomato Paste
1½ tsp. Salt
¼ tsp. Black Pepper

❖ Place beans in large pot with 8 cups boiling water. Boil 3 minutes. Remove from heat, cover, and soak overnight.

❖ Defrost frozen spinach. Drain. Also rinse and drain beans.

❖ Dissolve bouillon cubes in 1½ c. hot water to make a broth.

❖ In an un-covered pressure cooker, sauté tomato paste in olive oil for a minute or two over medium heat.

❖ Stir in broth and beans. Without stirring, distribute spinach on top of beans. Sprinkle salt and pepper. Add water so that there is enough to just cover contents.

❖ Cover pot and cook over high until pressure bobbin begins to rock. Reduce heat as needed for a steady rock. Cook under pressure for 20 minutes. Remove from heat and cool quickly under running water (see page 213).

❖ Uncover and check water level. If it is soupy, allow extra water to evaporate off over low heat, without stirring, until sauce is thick like chili. Serve warm. *Afiyet olsun!*

ZEYTINYAĞLI BAMYA

Okra in Tomato Sauce and Olive Oil

Okra originally came to the Ottoman Empire via Africa. It's been in the USA since the 1700's and is most popular in the south where it is known as "gumbo." Some people find the gooey texture of this little vegetable a bit strange; (okra's texture makes it a great thickener in soups and stews). But I love the flavor, especially when it is cooked as shown in this side-dish recipe from my mom.

You can use either fresh or frozen okra. If you are buying fresh, choose baby okra or ones that are no longer than 3 inches, or they will be too tough. Do not wash them until you are ready to cook them. Fresh okra can keep in the fridge for only 2 to 3 days.

INGREDIENTS:

1 lb. Fresh Okra (or frozen whole Okra)
2 medium Onions
1 Turkish Coffee Cup Olive Oil (¼ c.)
Juice of ½ Lemon
c. Tomato Sauce
½ tsp. Salt
1 tsp. Sugar

You can prepare this dish in a regular heavy pot or in a pressure cooker. The pressure cooker requires much less cooking time (15 minutes instead of 45) but it's difficult to control, so okra may come out too soft.

FRESH OKRA:

If you are using fresh okra, rinse, drain, and pat dry with paper towel so they don't become sticky. Cut off only stick-like stem. With a paring knife, carefully shave off tough outer shell of top in a conical shape. Be careful not to cut top off completely or pulp will ooze out during cooking. Clip off the very tip at small end.

FROZEN OKRA:

Frozen okra requires no preparation. Simply thaw package enough to separate okra from one another.

❖ Peel onions and cut in half longways. Lay on flat side and slice into very thin slices. Sauté in olive oil in a large pot (or uncovered pressure cooker) over medium-high heat until translucent.

❖ Stir in tomato sauce and continue to sauté until sauce condenses and becomes thick (5 minutes).

❖ Spread okra out evenly into pot.

❖ If you are using a regular pot: add 1 cup water, lemon juice, salt and sugar. Stir only once, to distribute ingredients. Bring to a boil. Cover and reduce heat to low. Simmer 35 to 45 minutes (depending on size of okra) until okra are very tender. Add water as needed during cooking to prevent sauce from drying out.

If you are using a pressure cooker: add lemon juice, salt, and sugar. Stir only once, to distribute ingredients. Cover and cook under pressure over medium heat for 15 minutes. Cool pressure cooker quickly so that okra doesn't continue to cook after heat is turned off (see page 213).

❖ Turn pot over onto serving dish, disturbing ingredients as little as possible. Serve warm or cool as side dish. *Afiyet olsun!*

ZEYTINYAĞLI BIBER DOLMALAR
Stuffed Peppers with Rice Filling

Serves 8 to 10

How can I describe this amazing dish? It's a hot summer day and you're craving something robust yet refreshing for lunch. Think of fresh green peppers, just in season, stuffed with a fabulous filling of rice, sweet onion, currants, olive oil, and dill. Imagine cutting this *dolma* in half and eating it cold, with a spritz of lemon. The filling is full of surprises; the occasional crunch from a roasted pine nut, a bite of sweetness from a black currant. And you had better have a hearty bread nearby because I guarantee you will want to soak up every drop of the juices on your plate.

In fact, I have some of these *dolma* in my fridge from a couple of days ago, made with peppers from our garden (better than store-bought because the skins are thinner). I can't wait to finish writing this recipe so I can go in there and eat some!

PREPARING THE RICE FILLING:
This filling can be used to stuff a variety of vegetables, including grape leaves, cabbage leaves, and tomatoes.

INGREDIENTS:

1 c. Short or Medium Grain White Rice
3 Tbsp. Black Currants
4/5 c. Olive Oil
7 Onions, finely chopped (about 6 cups)
4 Tbsp. Pine Nuts
2¼ tsp. Salt
2¼ tsp. Sugar
2 tsp. Ground Black Pepper
1 large Tomato, chopped
½ Bunch Fresh Parsley
1/2 Bunch Dill (chopped)
2 Sprigs Fresh Mint (chopped) (optional)
1 Lemon (for garnish)

❖ Place rice in a medium-sized bowl with enough hot, (not boiling) water to cover. Set aside 20 minutes to cool. Place currants in small bowl warm water. Set aside.

❖ Heat oil in a large skillet. Add onions, pine nuts, and salt. Saute over medium-high heat for 10 to 15 minutes, stirring often until onions are translucent and pine nuts are a golden color.

❖ Meanwhile, rub rice between your palms to remove excess starch. Drain. Rinse a couple of times in fresh water. Drain thoroughly.

❖ Add rice to skillet and stir until rice is hot, but not browning (about 10 minutes).

❖ Stir in sugar, black pepper, tomato, and drained currants. Add enough boiling water to cover the rice (about ¾ c.). Give mixture a quick stir, bring to boil, cover and cook over very low heat for 15 minutes.

❖ Separate 2 sprigs parsley from bunch and set aside for garnish. Chop remaining parsley and dill. Stir into filling. Loosely fluff rice onto a wide serving dish to cool and allow steam to evaporate.

PREPARING THE PEPPERS:

INGREDIENTS

16-20 Small Green Peppers (2 per person)
5 Small Tomatoes (or 1 large)
½ c. Olive Oil
½ tsp. Salt
½ tsp. Sugar

❖ Cut a hole around stems of peppers. Remove seeds and white filament. Rinse. Drain upside-down in colander.

❖ To make the tomato caps, rinse tomatoes, cut off and discard tops and bottoms. Cut into quarters and remove seeds. Set aside.

❖ Stuff peppers with rice mixture, but don't overfill. Cap each one by pressing a piece of tomato firmly into top of filling. Arrange peppers side-by-side in a large pot. Place a second layer on top of first if necessary.

❖ Stir salt, ½ c. water, oil, and sugar in a cup and pour over peppers. Place a plate turned upside-down on top of peppers to weigh them down during cooking. Bring mixture to a boil. Reduce heat to low. Cover pot and simmer 30-40 minutes, or until all the water evaporates.

❖ Allow to cool. To serve, arrange peppers on a platter. Garnish with lemon wedges and parsley sprigs. Some people like to squeeze lemon on their *dolma* just before eating because the acidic flavor is a nice contrast to the warm flavors in the filling. *Afiyet Olsun!*

Börek

BÖREK
Savory Pastry made with Filo

Serves 12 as Side Dish or Meze

What is *börek*? It's a savory puff pastry made with layers of Filo dough (*yufka*) filled with a variety of fillings. (Recipes for meat, cheese, and spinach fillings are provided on the next few pages.) Always delicious, always satisfying, *börek* is an exciting side-dish for almost any menu. And when you bake one, it fills the house with an aroma similar to pizza or fresh-baked bread. I have never met anyone who didn't love *börek* after taking the very first bite.

Filo dough (available in your grocer's freezer) comes in a box of about 20 paper-thin sheets. To make *börek*, the sheets are brushed lightly with butter and layered. The filling is placed between the middle layers. An egg glaze provides a deeper color and thicker crust, whereas a mixture of egg, yogurt or milk makes the pastry more moist with a richer flavor. Garnishes, including parmesan cheese, sesame seeds, or black Nigella seeds, provide color and a hint of flavor.

Don't be afraid to work with Filo; it's a very forgiving ingredient! Even if sheets tear, you can just patch them together and brush the seam with a little butter; no one will ever notice! The process of layering is not complicated, and with a little practice, you can construct a *börek* in about 15 minutes. The most important thing to remember about constructing *börek* is to work quickly to keep the filo dough from drying out. If you must leave it momentarily, lay a sheet of wax paper or a moist towel over all exposed *yufka*.

The instructions on the following page show how to set up your work space and make basic *börek* by layering sheets across an entire baking dish. *Börek* can also be made to look like little cigars, triangles, or "bird's nests" as shown on page 246).

SETTING UP THE WORK SPACE

Preparing your "work space" so that everything is close-at-hand will simplify the process of layering the filo. Once I prepare the filling and melt the butter, I lay out a newspaper to protect the table from grease. I set a large casserole dish directly in front of me and alongside that, the room-temperature filo dough, still in its box. (Do NOT open the sheets of filo dough until your "work space" is set up and you have generously buttered the bottom and sides of your baking dish.)

Being left-handed, I like to keep the dough to the left of my baking dish. You may wish to reverse this. The bowl of prepared filling sits near the filo with a large tablespoon. The saucepan of melted butter and a pastry brush sits directly above the casserole dish to minimize drips.

The process is fairly basic; you will begin layering individual sheets of dough lightly in the baking dish, and brushing/drizzling butter on each sheet, making sure to butter edges to keep it from sticking to the sides of the dish. Don't worry about completely covering each sheet with butter; whatever areas don't get buttered on one layer can be buttered on the next. But, as my mom insisted, be sure to amply butter the edges and corners to keep them from burning. Important note: Once you take the filo from its package, you must work rapidly to prevent the dough from drying out. (If you must stop working for more than 10-15 seconds cover un-used sheets with wax paper or a moist towel.)

CONSTRUCTING BÖREK:
(Read the following directions completely before starting.)

❖ Remove filo from box and unroll onto large sheet of wax paper. Lift top sheet and gently lay into greased baking dish as if you're making a wrinkly bed. Wrinkles are good; they leave room for air which makes the pastry nice and puffy. So allow sheets to buckle and wrinkle as needed to keep edges inside the dish.

❖ With your pastry brush, lightly spread a little butter on the sheet. (There are about twenty sheets in a box of filo, so gauge amount of butter per sheet accordingly.) To keep pastry light and airy, do not press down too much with your pastry brush. Continue layering and buttering until you have done nine sheets.

(continued on next page)

❖ Lay out 10th sheet, but do not butter. Cover pile of un-used filo sheets with wax paper or moist towel.

❖ Gently spoon out filling over entire pastry, avoiding edges. Pre-heat oven to 350°F.

❖ Continue layering remaining filo sheets. Butter top sheet evenly, but do NOT pour remaining butter over *börek*; some butter should remain in saucepan for egg glaze.

❖ Separate egg. Stir egg into saucepan of remaining butter. Brush entire top of börek with egg glaze, making sure to coat corners and edges of individual pieces.

❖ I prefer to cut before to cut the *börek* into serving-size pieces before it is baked. (Cutting the pastry is much easier if you first place it in the freezer for 10 minutes to harden the butter.) Cut with a sharp knife into about 20 servings. Cut all the way through so that pieces will separate easily from one another after baking.

❖ Glaze or garnish pastry (refer to specific *börek* recipes on following pages for a variety of delicious glazes and garnishes) and place in middle rack of oven. Bake uncovered 35-40 minutes or until golden brown.

❖ To serve, re-cut pastry, arrange individual pieces on serving platter in a loose pile. *Börek* can be served warm or at room temperature. Re-heat in toaster oven only; the microwave will make it mushy. *Afiyet olsun!*

SEPARATING EGG YOLK FROM ALBUMIN

Gently crack egg over a small bowl,* being careful not to break yolk. Allow yolk to rest in one half of shell as you pull away other half and allow albumin (egg white) to drip out. Transfer yolk to other half shell, allowing remaining egg white to drip out.

(*You can save egg whites for a delicious low cholesterol omelet!)

PEYNIRILI BÖREK
Cheese-filled Börek

Cheese filling is the easiest filling to make for *börek*. It's a simple mixture of feta cheese, cottage cheese, parsley and egg.

PASTRY:

INGREDIENTS:

2 Sticks unsalted, sweet cream Butter (16 Tbsp.)

1 16. oz. Box Filo Dough (#7 is thicker, easier to handle without tearing, #4 is more delicate.) *Thaw frozen filo un-opened on counter for at least 8 hours before use. If filo has been stored in refrigerator, set it un-opened on counter for at least 2 hours before use.*

FILLING:

INGREDIENTS:

½ lb. Turkish, Greek, or Bulgarian Feta Cheese

8 oz. Small Curd Cottage Cheese
(to reduce saltiness of the Feta cheese)

3 Eggs, divided

1 Bunch of Fresh Parsley, rinsed, drained, trimmed and chopped rough

GARNISH:

½ c. grated Parmesan Cheese

❖ Melt butter in a small sauce pan over very low heat.

❖ Prepare filling: Crumble feta cheese with your fingers or a fork in a medium-sized bowl so that there are no pieces larger than a pea. Stir in cottage cheese, two eggs, and parsley until ingredients are blended. Do not over stir. Set aside.

❖ Prepare pastry: Follow directions for constructing either Pan *Börek* (page 243) or Bird's-nest *Börek* (page 247).

❖ Garnish: Sprinkle Parmesan cheese evenly over pastry.

❖ Bake 35-45 minutes or until golden brown. Allow to cool 10 minutes before separating and lifting individual pieces with metal spatula.

❖ Arrange pieces on serving platter. Serve warm or cold, with plain yogurt. *Afiyet olsun.*

ETLI KUŞ YUVASI BÖREK FILLING
Meat-filled Bird's Nest Pastry

Meat-filled *börek* is my family's favorite. A little heartier than cheese *börek*, it's a delicious meze and also a satisfying lunch when served warm with yogurt and a salad. You can, of course, use this meat filling and construct a pan-style *börek* (as shown on page 242).

PASTRY:

INGREDIENTS:

2 Sticks unsalted, sweet cream Butter (16 Tbsp.)

1 16. oz. Box Filo Dough (#7 is thicker, easier to handle without tearing, #4 is more delicate.) *Thaw frozen filo un-opened on counter for at least 8 hours before use. If filo has been stored in refrigerator, set it un-opened on counter for at least 2 hours before use.*

FILLING:

2 Lbs. Ground Lamb or Beef

2 Tbsp. Olive Oil

I small Onion, chopped

3 Garlic Cloves, minced

2 Medium Tomatoes, peeled and chopped, (1 c.)

¾ c. coarsely chopped fresh Parsley leaves

Salt

Ground Black Pepper

GLAZE:

1 Egg Yolk

¼ c. Grated Cheddar Cheese, garnish (optional)

❖ **PREPARE FILLING:** Sauté onions in olive oil over medium-high heat in a large skillet until translucent. (In Turkish we say "until the onions have fainted.")

❖ Add garlic and meat. Sauté until meat is browned.

❖ Add tomatoes, parsley, salt and pepper to taste. Stir well. Reduce heat, cover, and simmer until juices are re-absorbed, about 15 minutes. Set pan aside to cool.

❖ **CONSTRUCTING THE BIRD'S NESTS:** Melt butter in a small sauce pan over very low heat. Set up work space as shown on page 243.

❖ Lay out one sheet of filo on a sheet of wax paper, short side facing you. Cover remaining dough with wax paper to prevent drying. Brush a little butter on half of filo sheet closest to you. (Let's call this half the bottom half.)

❖ Fold top half toward you and lay it over bottom half. Brush butter over top half.

❖ Gently spoon about one rounded tablespoon filling along bottom edge of sheet. (To determine how much filling to use for each sheet, think of it this way; You have about 20 sheets of filo in the box. Draw an x in the skillet with a spatula to divide filling into four equal parts. Each of these parts is enough filling for 5 bird's-nests.)

❖ Turn up edge closest to you (top and bottom halves together) over filling. Gently roll *börek* away from you like a carpet or tube. The tube should be snug but not tight. Preheat oven to 350°F.

❖ Tuck one end of tube in slightly, and wrap tube sideways into a loose coil. Do NOT wrap too tight or coil will rip apart.

❖ Slightly twist tail end of tube and tuck it under coil as you place it into a shallow, greased oven-proof casserole dish or baking pan. Brush top of coil and exposed end lightly with butter before beginning next coil. Continue to lay coils side-by-side in pan. (It's okay if they touch one another, but avoid squeezing them into pan too tightly.) Don't use all the butter; 3 to 4 Tbsp. should remain in saucepan for glaze.

❖ **PREPARE GLAZE:** When all coils have been wrapped, stir egg yolk into remaining butter in saucepan. Brush over individual nests. To garnish, sprinkle Parmesan cheese evenly across top.

❖ Bake uncovered for about 25-30 minutes or until golden colored. Use a spatula to remove them from the pan and arrange on a platter to serve. *Afiyet olsun.*

ISPANAKLI BÖREK FILLING
Spinach Börek Filling

Serves 12 as Side Dish or Meze

My sister Çaya used to sell this yummy spinach-filled *börek* at her coffee house, The Café Monet. Every Friday evening Beti and her friend Fortune Sadak met at the Café to make tray after tray of the pastry dubbed *Beti's Börek*. It quickly became a favorite of the Kensington lunch crowd and the many kids who came into the café for a warm, satisfying after-school snack. Prepare the filling and then follow directions on page 242 to construct Pan *Börek* or page 247 for the individually constructed Bird's Nests.

FILLING:

3 Lbs. fresh chopped Spinach (or 1 lb. box frozen)
¼ c. Virgin Olive Oil
¼ c. unsalted, clarified or melted Butter
I small Onion or ½ c. Scallions, chopped
1 c. Mozzarella Cheese, grated
½ c. Cottage Cheese
¼ c. Parmesan Cheese
2 Eggs
Salt to taste
¼ c. Flour (optional)

PASTRY:

2 Sticks unsalted, sweet cream Butter (16 Tbsp.)
1 16. oz. Box Filo Dough (#7 is thicker, easier to handle without tearing, #4 is more delicate.) *Thaw frozen filo un-opened on counter for at least 8 hours before use. If filo has been stored in refrigerator, set it un-opened on counter for at least 2 hours before use.*

BUTTERY SPREAD:

¼ c. Sweet Cream Butter, melted
1/3 c. Milk
¼ c. Virgin Olive Oil
1 Egg

GLAZE AND GARNISH:

2 Egg Yolks
¼ c. Milk
¼ c. Grated Parmesan Cheese, garnish (optional)
Sesame or Nigella Seed, garnish (optional)

INGREDIENTS:

❖ **PREPARE FILLING:** Cook spinach in boiling water for about 15 minutes until wilted. Drain, squeeze firmly between hands or press against side of sieve with back of spoon to remove water. Set aside.

❖ Heat olive oil and butter in a large skillet over medium-high heat. Add onion and sauté until translucent. Add spinach and sauté two minutes. Set aside to cool.

❖ Add the filling cheeses, 2 eggs, pinch of salt, and flour (optional) to cooled spinach mixture. Set aside.

❖ **PREPARE BUTTERY SPREAD:** Spinach *Börek* tastes better when you enrich the butter spread with oil and egg. Melt butter in a small saucepan over very low heat. Slowly stir in milk and olive oil. Remove from heat and allow to cool slightly. Whisk egg in a small bowl and stir into saucepan, whisking constantly to prevent egg from curdling.

❖ **PREPARE PASTRY:** Follow directions ofr constructing either Pan *Börek* (page 243) or Bird's-nest *Börek* (page 247).

If you have constructed pan-type *börek*, you may cut it either before or after baking. To cut before baking, place in freezer 10 minutes to harden butter. (This will make cutting easier.) Cut pastry into 12 to 24 pieces, depending on how large you want the individual servings.

❖ **PREPARE GLAZE:** When pastry is ready for glaze, whisk egg yolks and milk into butter remaining in saucepan. Brush glaze over entire *börek*, especially over edges and exposed corners.

Sprinkle with garnish and bake uncovered at 350°F for 30 to 35 minutes or until golden brown. *Afiyet olsun!*

SPINACH-FILLED BÖREK

BÖREKITAS DE BERENJENA

Crescent Pastries Filled with Eggplant and Cheese

Makes 18 to 20

*F*amily occasions aren't complete until Tant Ida arrives with these delightful moon-shaped pastries. The crumbly crust gives way to a fabulous filling of grilled eggplant and cheese. A true Sephardic tradition (referred to in Ladino as *Burmuelos*), *Börekitas* are Tant Ida's specialty and a family favorite. No matter how many she makes, they all seem to disappear as soon as she puts them on the table.

Börekitas are also versatile; you can fill the pastry with mixtures of cheese, meats, vegetables, and even fruit fillings. You can also freeze and store them unbaked for months!

FILLING

INGREDIENTS

- 2 to 3 Fresh Globe Eggplants (2½ lbs.) or 16 oz. Bottled Eggplant Purée
- 1 c. Shredded Mozzarella Cheese
- ¼ c. grated Parmesan Cheese
- ½ tsp. Salt

DOUGH

INGREDIENTS

- 1½ c. Vegetable Oil (or 5 Turkish Coffee Cups)
- 1 tsp. Salt
- ½ c. grated Kasseri Cheese (*Kaşer Peyniri*)
- 4 to 5 c. All-purpose White Flour
- ¼ c. grated Parmesan Cheese (topping)

❖ **PREPARE FILLING:** Roast eggplants following directions for Eggplant Purée on page 160.

Place eggplant pulp in a small bowl and blot dry with paper towel to remove excess moisture. Add Mozzarella, ¼ c. Parmesan cheese, and ½ tsp. salt. Blend well. Set aside.

❖ **PREPARE DOUGH:** Spread a sheet of parchment paper on cookie sheet and set aside. (If you plan to bake the *börekitas* at a later date, clear a level place in your freezer large enough for the cookie sheet.)

Pour oil into a medium-sized bowl. Stir in ¾ c. water, 1 tsp. salt, and Kasseri cheese.

Stirring constantly with one hand, gradually add about 4 to 4½ cups flour, a little at a time until there is just enough to hold mixture together in a very loose and squishy ball. Do not overmix; the dough should be very soft and wet. Tant Ida always says; "it should feel like your earlobe."

(Dough must be kept cool to prevent it from losing its consistency. To do this, place bowl of dough inside a larger bowl of ice water, or if you prefer, keep half of it cooled in the freezer while forming *börekitas* with the other half.)

Pour about ½ c. pile of flour off to the side on a large flat wood work surface.

❖ **CONSTRUCT PASTRIES:** Pinch off a large walnut-sized piece of dough. Pat it once into pile of flour. Flip it over and pat again. Roll quickly between palms and lay ball on work surface. Use fingers to press ball into a disc shape about ¼ inch thick and 3 to 3½ inches in diameter. (It doesn't have to be beautiful.) Spoon 1 tsp. eggplant filling into center of disc.

Now here comes the fun part. With flour on your fingertips, delicately peel up edge of disc and pull it completely over filling, allowing it to droop over the other side. (Ida is a "pro" at this, and you will be, too with a little practice.)

To make *börekita* fluffy, you must NEVER touch the top! Tuck upper edge underneath while puffing up bottom edge to form a continuous seal. While you are doing this, gently coax pastry into a pudgy, crescent shape. Lift pastry either with fingers (or quickly thrust a metal spatula under pastry to scoop it up), and lay onto parchment paper with enough room for each pastry to expand during baking. Continue with remaining dough.

❖ **BAKE:** Sprinkle pastries with Parmesan cheese topping. Bake at 400°F for the first 30 minutes, then reduce heat to 350°F and bake another 15 minutes or until light brown.

(To freeze uncooked *börekitas* for baking at a later date, place uncovered baking sheet of pastries into freezer until they are completely frozen. Cover with foil or transfer to freezer bag until ready to cook. *Afiyet olsun!*

BETI'S QUICK BÖREK

A quick version of Cheese Börek

Here's a "working woman's" variation on cheese *börek*. My mother employed a couple of shortcuts to the basic recipe to help you make a yummy *börek* in a hurry.

INGREDIENTS:

2 Sticks unsalted, sweet cream Butter (16 Tbsp.)
1 16. oz. Box Filo Dough (#7 is thicker, easier to handle without tearing, #4 is more delicate.)
Thaw frozen filo un-opened on counter for at least 8 hours before use. If filo has been stored in refrigerator, set it un-opened on counter for at least 2 hours before use.
1 box (No. 7) Filo Pastry (20 sheets)
¼ lb. Feta Cheese
½ lb. Cottage Cheese, small curd
3 Tbsp. Fresh Parsley, rinsed, drained, trimmed, chopped
6 Eggs, divided
Dash Black Pepper
¾ c. Milk
2 to 3 Tbsp. Plain Yogurt, well-stirred

❖ Melt butter in a saucepan over very low heat. Spread a few tablespoons butter on bottom and sides of large oven-proof casserole dish (about 11-inch x 14-inch).

❖ Break up feta cheese with fingers or a fork in a medium-sized bowl. Add cottage cheese, parsley, 3 eggs, and dash of pepper. Mix thoroughly.

❖ Stir milk, and yogurt into the saucepan of butter. Add 3 eggs and whisk ingredients together thoroughly. Keep warm on *very* low heat until work space is set up to construct *börek*, (see page 243).

CONSTRUCTING THE PASTRY:

❖ Lay two sheets of filo loosely into bottom of baking dish. Spread about 2 Tbsp. butter mixture lightly over filo sheets with pastry brush. Continue to layer and butter, two sheets at a time, until you reach center (5 layers of two sheets each). Do NOT spread butter over 10th sheet.

❖ Pour cheese mixture over *börek* and spread evenly without pressing too hard. Lay two more sheets over filling and continue butter and layer until all the filo is used.

❖ Brush 2 to 3 Tbsp. butter mixture over top layer until completely coated; no dry spots. Drizzle remaining butter mixture from saucepan around sides and corners of baking dish to seal *börek*.

❖ Bake at 350°F for about 35 minutes or until golden brown. (Since this quick *börek* is not cut into servings before baking, it will be very puffed up coming out of the oven. It will flatten as it cools. *Afiyet olsun!*

KIYMALI ARNAVUT BÖREK
Homemade Börek with Ground Beef Filling

Serves 8

INGREDIENTS:

1 large Onion, sliced thin and finely chopped
¾ c. Canola Oil, divided
1 lb. Ground Beef or Lamb
2 tsp. Salt
½ tsp. Ground Black Pepper
4 Tbsp. Tomato Sauce
½ bunch fresh Parsley, rinsed, trimmed, chopped
6½ c. All-purpose Flour
1½ c. Warm Water

One afternoon in the summer of 2011, my niece *Gülcan* came to visit from Istanbul. A terrific cook in her own right, *Gülcan* learned her top-notch culinary skills from her grandmother, who happens to be my father's first wife *Zehra Hanım*. My niece was kind enough to make *Arnavut* (Albanian) *börek* from scratch for us. She showed us the traditional method of making filo dough using a long skinny rolling pin called an *oklava*. My son Tory still raves about the this version of *börek* and describes it as "a crispy satisfying crunch, mellowed by a savory, meat filling, seasoned with intense spices." That says it all!

❖ **FILLING:** Sauté onions in 2 Tbsp. oil in a large pot over medium-high heat 10 to 15 minutes until translucent.

Add meat. Break it up with spatula as you continue to sauté for 5 minutes. Cover pot to allow meat to give off juices and then re-absorb them (about 5-10 minutes).

Stir in salt, pepper, tomato sauce and parsley. Sauté 3-5 minutes. Cover, remove from heat, and set aside.

(continued on next page)

ARNAVUT BÖREGI

❖ Preparing Filo Dough *(Yufka)*:

Using hands, blend ½ c. oil, warm water and flour together in a large bowl until it can be gathered up. Place on clean surface which has been dusted with flour. Knead with heel of palms, gradually adding more flour as needed to create a soft dough the consistency of your ear lobe. Total kneading time is about 5 minutes.

Shape dough into a loaf (about the size of pound cake). Cut loaf in half. Divide eac half into 10 equal size parts, and roll each into a ball (twenty balls total).

Brush 2 Tbsp. oil in bottom and along sides of a large baking dish. (Homemade *börek* is normally made in a round baking pan or *tepsi*, like the 15-inch diameter one shown here. They can be found at most Middle Eastern markets.

Dust work surface with about ½ tsp. of flour and pat top and bottom of first ball in it. Dust a rolling pin with flour. Roll ball of flour into a flat disc, alternately rolling and turning the disc 90° to maintain its circular shape. When disc is about 6-inches in diameter set it aside. Dip fingers in a small bowl of oil, and spread a thin layer on top of disc.

Roll out 8 more discs, spreading oil on top of each one and layering them one on top of the other. Roll out 10th disc and lay on top of pile. Do not oil. Instead dust top of pile with flour.

Using rolling pin or *oklava*, roll out entire pile to circular shape slightly larger than diameter of the *tepsi*.

❖ Assembling Börek:

Lay pile into *tepsi*, turning up sides. Press bottom and sides into pan.

Drain meat filling by pressing it against side of pot to squeeze out extra juices. Spread meat evenly in *tepsi*.

Repeat directions for rolling out remaining dough. Top half of dough should be slightly SMALLER than diameter of *tepsi* in order to fit inside it. Lay top half gently over filling.

Turn edges of bottom layer over top layer, pinching edges to lock in filling.

❖ Baking Börek:

Bake in center of 400°F oven for 45 minutes to one hour until top is browned. (In Turkey this color is known as "pomegranate red.") Remove from oven and flick small amounts of cool water on top of pastry with fingers to keep it from drying out. Serve warm. *Afiyet olsun.*

Meat Dishes

In Turkish cuisine, there is a wonderful variety of beef and lamb dishes. If you cut it into chunks, marinate it and grill it over a charcoal fire, it is called *Izgara Kebabı*.

If you stew it with vegetables in a heavy clay pot, you've made *Güveç*.

Grind the meat and mix it with spices to make *Köfte*. *Köfte* can take the form of meatballs that are baked or pressed onto skewers and grilled. A more exotic dish, *Tandır Kebap*, (similar to Indian *Tandoor*), is traditionally a whole lamb slow-cooked in a brick oven or in a six-foot deep pit oven.

Chicken, fish and other meats are also plentiful in Turkish cuisine, and are usually cooked with spices, seasonal vegetables and light sauces which enhance the meat without overpowering it.

When Napolean III's wife Empress Eugénie visited *Topkapı* Palace, she fell in love with a dish called *Hünkar Beğendi*, smoky, creamed eggplant served under chunks of beef. She sent her chef to the vast palace kitchens to write down the recipe. The Head Chef, however, was not about to give up his secrets. He protected his recipe from the French chef, managing a cloaked insult at the same time. The Turk politely pointed out that a "true" chef cooks by instinct and not by exact recipes.

I readily admit I am not a "true" Turkish chef; I like having recipes written out like blueprints so I can accurately re-create the flavors of my childhood. That's why you, dear reader, are more fortunate than Empress Eugénie; I am happy to share the recipe for *Hünkar Beğendi* with you on page 262.

ARNAVUT CIĞERI
Lamb's Liver with Onion Garnish (Albanian Style)

In the U.S.A. we often disregard organ meats like liver, kidney, brain, tripe, and tongue because they are high in cholesterol or because we have simply forgotten how to prepare them. But in Turkey, meat is expensive, and very little of a slaughtered animal is allowed to go to waste. Hence many delicious recipes have been developed for organ meats. I love the strong flavor of liver, especially when it's coupled with a traditional garnish of sweet onions and parsley. *Arnavut Ciğer* is best served immediately after frying, but you can also have it cold as a meze.

INGREDIENTS:

2 small Onions
Salt
1 lb. Lamb's Liver or Veal Liver
Canola or Vegetable Oil for frying
1 c. Flour
1 tsp. Ground Red Pepper
¼ c. Fresh Flat Parsley, rinsed, trimmed, chopped fine
½ tsp. Ground Sumac, for garnish (optional)

❖ Cut onions in half lengthwise. Then slice very, very thin. Stir together with 1 Tbsp. salt in a small bowl. Set aside 30 minutes.

❖ Meanwhile, rinse liver under running water to remove any blood. Cut into "bird's head" size pieces, cutting away any veins. Set aside in a sieve to drain.

❖ Heat about ½ inch oil in a heavy skillet over medium-high heat until a light haze forms above it or a tiny drop of water sizzles in it. Meanwhile, mix flour, ½ tsp. salt, and 1 tsp. red pepper together in a deep bowl or medium-sized plastic bag.

❖ The "lazy" way to cook liver is to dredge all the pieces together in flour and fry them all at once. This method causes the liver to stick together when cooking, with clumps of wet flour left between unevenly cooked pieces of meat. That's not good.

Here's the right way: Toss about a third of the lamb in flour to coat. Using a small sieve, lift individual pieces, shake off excess flour, and carefully place into skillet. (Adjust heat periodically; oil should sizzle slightly around edges of meat; If oil is too hot and sizzles "angrily," the outside of the meat will burn before inside is properly cooked.)

Fry liver 1 or 2 minutes until lightly browned. Remove with slotted spoon and drain on paper towels. Before frying next batch, skim and discard any flour remaining in hot oil. Fry remaining liver in similar fashion.

❖ Squeeze onion slices firmly and repeatedly with hands until they are juicy and soft, but not stringy.

Rinse well under running water. Drain and squeeze until no more water drips out.

Toss together in a large bowl with parsley and ¼ teaspoon salt until well mixed. I like to add ground sumac to the garnish for color and a slightly lemony flavor.

❖ To serve, mound liver in center of a serving platter. Arrange onion mixture on or around it. Serve at once. *Afiyet olsun.*

ŞIŞ KEBAB

Lamb Shish Kebab

We can thank Central Asian nomads for *Şiş Kebab*. These medievil, horseback-riding warriors crossed vast regions of the Steppe with little to eat other than the animals they took with them. Having no cooking utensils to speak of, they would slaughter a lamb and skewer pieces of it onto their beloved swords. The meat would then be grilled over a communal fire. The flat "sword-like" stainless steel skewers still used in Turkey work great for keeping the meat from spinning as you turn it over while grilling.

LAMB OR BEEF MARINADE:

This naturally acidic marinade of lemon and onion is a delicious way to tenderize the meat before grilling. Blend ingredients in a shallow, medium-sized dish.

INGREDIENTS:

1 Onion (grated)
½ c. Olive Oil
¼ c. fresh Lemon Juice
1 tbsp. Vinegar
2 tbsp. Oregano
1 tsp. Black Pepper
2 tsp. Salt

Chicken Shish Kebab

Serves 8

CHICKEN MARINADE:

Thyme and garlic give this chicken marinade a warm, earthy flavor. Blend ingredients in a shallow, medium-sized dish.

INGREDIENTS:

1 Onion (grated)
½ c. Olive Oil
¼ c. fresh Lemon Juice (2 small lemons)
3 cloves Garlic (minced)
2 tsp. Thyme
½ tsp. Black Pepper
1½ tsp. Salt

CONSTRUCTING KEBAB

2½-3 lbs. fresh Lamb Shoulder or Thigh, or Chicken Breast
2 Large Onions
2 large Green Peppers, chopped into 1 to 1½-inch cubes
30-40 Cherry Tomatoes (or 6-8 small tomatoes, quartered)

❖ Trim away any fat from meat. Cut into 1-inch cubes. Add to marinade and blend well with hands. Refrigerate 5-8 hours, stirring at least once during this time.

❖ Halve onions and remove layers of inner third (smaller pieces are difficult to skewer). Cut outer layers into 1 to 1½-inch squares

❖ Rub a little marinade on skewer so meat will slide off easily after grilling. Alternately thread ingredients onto skewers, leaving at least 2 inches of skewer exposed on each end.

❖ Grease grill. Place skewers over flame side-by-side, not touching one another. Grill over medium-high heat, 1½ minutes each side. (The meat has four sides!) If using coals, grill with lid off. For gas, cook with lid on. Do not overcook or meat will be dry. *Afiyet olsun.*

HÜNKAR BEĞENDI
Stewed Beef over Creamed Eggplant

Serves 8

Serve this exotic dish, also known as *Sultan's Delight*, to special guests. They will not be able to resist these tender, bite-sized pieces of stewed meat served on a bed of smoky, puréed eggplant.

CREAMED EGGPLANT (*beğendi*)

INGREDIENTS:

3 lbs. Globe Eggplants (3 large)
3 Tbsp. Lemon Juice
3 Tbsp. Salt
1 c. Milk
2 Tbsp. Heavy Cream
4 Tbsp. Butter (¼ cup)
¼ c. All-purpose White Flour
4 oz. Kasseri or Parmesan Cheese, grated (½ c.)

MEAT

INGREDIENTS:

1 Medium Onion, diced (about ¾ cups)
4 Tbsp. Butter (¼ cup)
3 Tbsp. Olive Oil
3 lbs. boneless Lamb or Stewing Beef, cut into 1-inch cubes
4 Cloves Garlic, minced
2 tsp. Tomato Paste
4 Medium Tomatoes, peeled, seeded, diced
  (or 2½ cups canned diced tomatoes)
½ tsp. Dried Thyme
1 tsp. Dried Oregano
1½ c. Meat Stock or Water
2 tsp. Salt or to taste
⅛ tsp. Black Pepper
⅓ c. Fresh Parsley, rinsed, drained, trimmed, chopped

❖ To Prepare Meat: Sauté onions with butter and oil in a heavy pot over medium-high heat until translucent. Add meat and garlic. Continue to sauté until meat is browned all over.

Stir in tomato paste, tomatoes, thyme, oregano, and stock. Season with salt and pepper. Bring to a boil. Reduce heat, cover, and simmer 1½ to 2 hours or until meat is tender and most of water is absorbed.

❖ To Prepare Eggplant: Using a skewer, pierce eggplants deeply several times to allow steam to escape while broiling. Place eggplants on a cookie tray into broiler, about 5 inches from heat source. Grill for 10 minutes. Turn over with tongs. Repeat until eggplant are charred all over and have collapsed (about 20 to 30 minutes).

Meanwhile, blend lemon juice, 3 cups water, and 3 Tbsp. salt in a large bowl. Set aside.

When eggplants are cool enough to handle, remove and discard skin and seeds. Place pulp in bowl of lemon water to suck out bitterness and to keep pulp from turning brown. Let stand for 10 minutes.

Gently press pulp through a large strainer using back of a wooden spoon to squeeze out water.

❖ To Prepare Cream Sauce: Melt butter over low heat in a small saucepan Stirring with a wooden spoon, gradually add flour and cook gently for about 1 minute.

Using a wire whisk, slowly stir in milk and cream, stirring constantly to prevent lumps. Heat until warm.

Stir in eggplant pulp and cheese, whisking briskly to break up long strands of pulp. Cook for 4 minutes, whisking until mixture is smooth and creamy. Cover and set aside until meat is very tender and ready to serve.

❖ To Serve

Spoon eggplant onto center of serving plates and arrange meat on top of it. Ladle some sauce from pot on top of meat. Garnish with chopped parsley. Serve immediately with hearty bread. *Afiyet olsun!*

THANKSGIVING TURKEY
Beti's Recipe

Thanksgiving is a difficult holiday for Turkish kids. For years we were the brunt of endless Turkey jokes; *"You're from Turkey? Gobble Gobble! Ha!"* Or the more clever; *"We were so Hungary for Turkey with Greece on China. Are you Finnish with your plate yet? Ha Ha Ha."* The dumbest question we ever heard is *"Do you celebrate Thanksgiving in Turkey?"*

"... No, Thanksgiving was a feast enjoyed by Pilgrims and Native Americans before the white man decimated millions of indigenous peoples, displaced them, and ultimately destroyed their traditional way of life." Always a conversation stopper.

So here's a morsel of delicious irony. During the heyday of the Ottoman Empire, exotic foods were collected from all over the world to be tested and tasted in the kitchens of the Sultan. One of these foods was a uniquely ugly Mexican bird that was brought to India, and became known in Constantinople as "Hindi." The bird became popular throughout the Ottoman Empire, the "land of the Turks." Hence, when the funny bird arrived on tables in Europe and the New World, it was called, you guessed it, the turkey.

But of course, this wasn't the reason our family celebrated Thanksgiving. Quite simply, we took part in almost every American holiday. We went "trick-or-treating" every Halloween. Each year we sat on blankets at the base of the Washington Monument to watch the Fourth of July fireworks diplay. On Christmas we decorated our tree, just like all the other Muslim/Jewish kids, or so I thought. For us, it was all part of Americana, which my parents embraced and enjoyed. Thanksgiving dinner was no exception, complete with cranberry sauce, sweet potatoes, and pumpkin pie. Here's Beti's famous chestnut stuffing. You can't tell me this isn't the best stuffing you've ever tasted!

One 25 lb. Turkey
2 c. fresh Mushrooms, chopped
2 lbs. fresh Chestnuts
½ bunch fresh Dill
1 Stick Butter or Margarine (8 Tbsp.)
4 Sticks Celery
1 Green Apple, chopped
1 Red Apple, whole
1 bunch fresh Parsley
1½ Tbsp. Salt
1 Tbsp. Black Pepper
Plain Stuffing Croutons (enough for 16 lb. bird)
1 Egg
4 c. Warm Water
All Purpose Flour (for gravy)

❖ Prepare chestnuts by cutting a shallow slice lengthwise down front of each one.

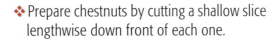

Boil chestnuts in medium-sized pot with enough water to cover, for one hour. Set aside to cool.

Peel away shells and skin. Place in large bowl.

❖ Rinse celery stalks. Cut away leaves and dark green sections. Chop remaining stalk and add to bowl.

❖ Rinse and dry parsley. Remove larger stems. Chop remaining and add to bowl. Repeat with dill.

(continued on next page)

❖ Cut away flesh of apple from core. Chop and add to bowl.

❖ Wash and peel away skin from mushrooms. Cut off extraneous stems. Chop mushrooms. Add to bowl.

❖ Add croutons, softened butter, salt, pepper, and egg.

❖ Blend ingredients together well with hands, gradually adding 3 cups warm water.

❖ Rinse turkey inside and out to remove any blood.

❖ Pat dry and stuff with filling from bottom and top end.

❖ Plug bottom with whole apple so that the bird will retain moisture.

❖ Wrap aluminum foil around the wing tips and ends of drumstick to prevent them from burning.

❖ Pour 1 cup water into bottom of pan. Roast 1 hour at 400°F. Reduce heat and continue to roast (at 350°F), basting occasionally until turkey is thoroughly cooked, with a minimum temperature of 180° taken deep in the thigh. (See Meat Roasting Chart on page 341. The stuffing must be a minimum temperature of 165° to make sure there are no living bacteria.)

❖ To make gravy, pour remaining juices from bottom of roasting pan into a large skillet over low heat. Gradually stir in small amounts of flour and continue to gently stir until gravy thickens up. If it gets too thick, add small amounts of water as you stir.

Afiyet olsun!

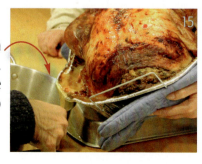

KUZU PIRZOLASI
Grilled Lamb Chop

Serves 4-6

Lamb. Grilled. Juicy. Yummy. Enough said.

INGREDIENTS

2 lbs. Lamb Chop or Shoulder
1 Tbsp. Olive Oil
1 tsp. ground Oregano
Salt to taste
Black Pepper to taste

❖ Tenderize lamb by pounding (beating) it with a mallot on a wood cutting board (avoiding the bone), until each lamb chop is about ¼ inch thick. Place on a plate.

❖ Spread oil over each chop, sprinkle with half the oregano, salt, and pepper. Flip chops over and repeat.

❖ Grill for 3-5 minutes each side over charcoals or in broiler, (medium -high heat). Cut into one of the chops to check for doneness. Do not overcook! They should be pink inside.

❖ Serve with rice or fried potatoes.

RULOS DE BERENJENA
Beef-filled Eggplant Rolls

These cute little morsels of delicately seasoned *köfte* wrapped in fried eggplant are a Sephardic specialty in Turkey. Brightly-colored toothpicks keep the rolls from unraveling in the oven and give this dish a festive look. This recipe comes from Tant Ida's granddaughter Brielle who watched Ida make it, and astutely jotted down the recipe! Traditionally the rolls of eggplant are topped with a small piece of cut tomato and green pepper. Ida came up with the idea of placing a cherry tomato on top as a shortcut and to give it a little extra flair. I kinda like it!

INGREDIENTS:

2 Long Globe Eggplants
Salt
1 Onion, grated
¼ Bunch Fresh Parsley, rinsed, trimmed, chopped
1 lb. Ground Beef
¼ tsp. Pepper
¼ tsp. Cumin
¼ c. Bread Crumbs or Matzo-meal
4 to 5 Eggs, divided
1 c. Vegetable Oil
1 Green Pepper
24 Cherry Tomatoes

❖ Remove half the skin from eggplants by peeling in alternating strips lengthwise. Slice eggplant lengthwise in long, thin (3/8-inch) slices. Place slices in a bowl with enough water to cover and 3 Tbsp. salt. Set aside for 15-20 minutes (so the salt can draw out the bitterness of the eggplant).

MEAT FILLING:

Place onion and parsley in medium-sized bowl with ground beef, 1 tsp. salt, pepper, cumin, breadcrumbs (or Matzo) and 2 eggs. Blend well with hands, kneading mixture to tenderize meat as the ingredients are distributed throughout. Set mixture aside.

FRYING THE EGGPLANT:

Remove eggplant slices from salted water. Rinse and drain in colander.

Heat oil in a large pan to medium-high heat. (A drop of water should sizzle.)

Whisk together 2 eggs and place in a shallow dish.

Twist eggplants to squeeze out water. Pat dry with paper towels.

Dredge eggplant slices, two or three at a time, in egg before laying them carefully in hot oil. Fry a couple of minutes until bottom is golden brown. Flip with tongs to cook other side. Place slices on paper towels to soak up any extra grease.

When all the eggplant slices are cooked and draining, turn off heat. Cut green pepper into approximately 1" x 1 ½" pieces, (at least one for each of the eggplant slices) and fry in oil. Set aside on paper towel, as well.

ROLLING THE EGGPLANT:

Count the number of eggplant slices to estimate amount of meat required for each roll. Divide meat accordingly. (for example: if you have 20 eggplant slices, divide meat into quadrants. Then divide each quadrant into 5 equal balls.)

Place ball of meat onto end of eggplant slice. Roll eggplant over meat. Place a piece of green pepper on roll. Pierce a cherry tomato with toothpick and thread toothpick through pepper and eggplant roll to secure it shut.

Place rolls side-by-side in a 9 x 13 x 2 oven-proof dish. Sprinkle tops of eggplant rolls with a little salt and sugar. Drizzle ¼ c. water over top to prevent it from drying out. (If you have a fresh tomato laying around, grate it and drizzle its juices and pulp on top of the rolls instead of plain water.) Bake at 350°F for 25 minutes or until meat is cooked. Serve warm. *Afiyet olsun!*

Tas Kebab - Tavuk Kanadi
Stove-top Chicken Wings

Serves 4-6

Chicken wings are tender tasty, and inexpensive.

So why do they only show up on the table as "buffalo wings" in sweet barbecue sauce?

Not here! *Tas Kebab* chicken wings are savory, robust, and so tender they almost melt in your mouth. My father loved this delectable dish so much he would hum to himself while cooking it. In fact, this is one of the few dishes my mother allowed us to eat with our hands. Yes, it's literally finger-licking good! And at the end of dinner, we would laugh at the theatrical way my dad smacked his lips, as if he were trying to suck up every last bit of succulent flavor.

INGREDIENTS:

3 lbs. Chicken Wings (about 14)
4 Tbsp. Butter
1½ c. Onion, chopped
2 cloves Garlic, minced
1 Tbsp. Salt
1 tsp. Pepper
1 tsp. Paprika
1 Tbsp. White Flour
2 c. Tomatoes, grated
½ tsp. Sugar
1 Bay Leaf

❖ If you buy the wings whole, cut off and discard tips and cut each wing at the main joint to separate it into two pieces. (Sometimes this will already have been done for you by the grocer, and the chicken will be sold as "buffalo wings.")

❖ Sauté wings with butter in a large pot over high heat for 5-8 minutes until it turns yellowish. Stir often to prevent meat from sticking to bottom of pot. Add onions and continue to sauté until onions are translucent. Add garlic, salt, pepper, and paprika.

❖ Stir in flour, and then immediately, but gradually, stir in tomatoes. Stir in 1 cup water, sugar, and bay leaf.

❖ Bring mixture to a boil. Reduce heat to low and simmer covered for an hour, stirring periodically. Monitor water level to make sure there is enough for a thick sauce. Serve warm over rice, and have plenty of napkins on hand! *Afiyet olsun!*

TAVUK OTURTMASI

Baked Chicken with Vegetables

Serves 6-8

This "all-in-one" meal is the perfect comfort food for winter nights. The aroma of the chicken baking in the oven makes the whole house smell so nice that people will be milling around in the kitchen long before dinner. Bring the casserole dish straight from the oven to the table and watch everyone's mouths water. It happens every time.

INGREDIENTS:

12-14 Chicken Thighs with skins, rinsed, drained
1 Large Onion, chopped
2 Tbsp. Vegetable Oil
Salt
Ground Black Pepper
1 tsp. Dried Oregano
8 Medium Potatoes
3 Large Carrots
½ lb. Frozen peas
1¼ c. Tomato Sauce, divided
¼ tsp. Sugar (to balance bitterness of tomato)

❖ Sauté onion and chicken with vegetable oil in a large pot over high heat until chicken is yellow on all sides. Stir in 1 Tbsp. salt, ¼ tsp. black pepper and 1 tsp. oregano. Continue to sauté, stirring often to prevent chicken from sticking to bottom of pot.

❖ Meanwhile peel and quarter potatoes, placing them in a bowl of cold water to prevent drying out. Peel carrots, cut into thick slices and set aside.

❖ Once thighs are golden colored, add ¼ c. tomato sauce and sauté 5 more minutes. Pour into an oven-proof casserole dish (about 9x13), distributing thighs evenly. Drain potatoes and arrange around chicken. Distribute peas and carrots, as well.

❖ In a small bowl, mix 1 cup tomato sauce, sugar, 1 tsp. salt, ¼ tsp. pepper and ¾ c. water. Pour evenly over chicken and vegetables.

❖ Cover tightly with aluminum foil. Place on cookie sheet to prevent spills, and bake at 350°F for 1½ hours or until meat readily falls away from bone. Allow to cool 10 minutes before serving with rustic bread. *Afiyet olsun!*

KIYMALI ISPANAK
Spinach with Ground Beef

The Mediterranean Diet is healthy because its dishes are often primarily vegetables, with only a small amount of red meat incorporated for flavor and fat. Here's a nutritious spinach dish that is incredibly easy to prepare and really satisfying. With an almost "porridge" consistency, it goes great with a dollop of yogurt on top, similar to the way one puts sour cream into a bowl of chili. The contrast between the soothing flavors of hot spinach and the tang of the cool yogurt is so delicious my mouth waters just thinking of it. No wonder I grew up loving spinach!

INGREDIENTS:

1 Kilo Fresh or 16 oz. Frozen Spinach, chopped
5 Tbsp. Butter or Margarine
1 Large Onion, finely chopped
1 lb. Ground Beef
Salt and Pepper
¾ c. Tomato Sauce
1 palmful (2 Tbsp.) Uncooked Rice
Yogurt as garnish

❖ If you are using fresh spinach, remove stems, rinse well, and then drain in colander. Boil spinach leaves for 5 minutes in a large pot. Rinse with cool water and drain. Squeeze spinach in your hands to remove excess water. Chop and set aside.

❖ Sauté onion in butter in a large pot over high heat for 5 minutes. Add ground beef, breaking it up into small pieces with a wooden spatula. Stir in 1 tsp. salt and 1/8 tsp. pepper. Cover pot so that beef can give up its juices and then re-absorb them. Stir once or twice during this process so that meat does not stick to bottom of pot.

❖ Once beef has soaked up juices, add spinach, ¾ c. water, 2 tsp. salt, tomato sauce, and rice. Stir ingredients together, cover, and simmer over medium heat for 30-40 minutes or until spinach is very tender. Check water level periodically to make sure mixture remains saucy. Serve warm in a bowl with yogurt and rustic bread. Like most Turkish dishes, this one tastes best the day after cooking. *Afiyet olsun!*

DOMATESLI TAVUK

Chicken Thighs in Tomato Sauce

Turks are known for their hospitality. This is why we had guests come for brunch or dinner at least once a week, including our High School teachers, stray foreigners with no family, neighbors, even strangers mom may have met on the street.

Preparing food for all these extra mouths could get pretty expensive. That's why this easy chicken recipe is a favorite; it's not only delicious, but you can buy large packages of frozen chicken thighs on sale at a terrific price.

Now don't turn up your nose at dark meat; it's much more tender and flavorful than white. And buy it with the skin and bone; it just tastes better. I always buy organic meats. You can really taste the difference between Halal/Kosher/Organic chicken and the poultry you buy at large grocery chains.

INGREDIENTS:

12 -14 Chicken Thighs (with skin and bones)
1 Large Onion, chopped
2 Tbsp. Vegetable Oil or Butter
1¼ c. grated Tomatoes or Tomato Sauce
1 Tbsp. Salt
¼ tsp. Black Pepper
1 tsp. Sugar
1 tsp. Dried Oregano

❖ Rinse chicken to make sure any residual blood has been removed. Allow extra water to drip off.

❖ Place onion and chicken thighs in a large pot with the vegetable oil or butter. Sauté over high heat, stirring often to prevent chicken from sticking to bottom of pot.

❖ Once onions have "fainted" (become translucent) and the thighs are golden colored, add tomatoes and sauté 2-3 more minutes.

❖ Add 1 c. water, salt, pepper, suger, and oregano. Stir to distribute spices. Bring to boil. Cover pot and reduce heat to low. Simmer for 1½ hours until thigh meat readily falls away from bone. Monitor the water level to make sure there is always sauce in bottom of pot. *Afiyet olsun!*

HINT ABOUT LEFTOVERS:

Conserve any leftover sauce. You can add vegetables and water to it for a quick and delicious soup!

TAS KEBABI
Stewed Lamb or Beef

Serves 6-8

Tas kebab is literally "roasted meat in a bowl."

Imagine succelent, tender chunks of lamb or beef, beautifully seasoned with thyme and oregano, covered in a thick, aromatic gravy.

Now imagine tenderly laying this delightful concoction over a hot bed of rice.

Now put aside your tablemanners and weight-loss plans, because you're gonna want to use a tablespoon to slurp up every bite of this savory delight!

INGREDIENTS:

2 lbs. Stewing Lamb or Beef
2 Tomatoes
4 Tbsp. Butter
1 Onion, chopped
2 cloves Garlic, minced
2 Tbsp. Flour
4 Tbsp. Tomato Sauce
2 c. Hot Water
1½ tsp. Salt
½ tsp. Ground Black Pepper
½ tsp. Dried Thyme
1 tsp. Dried Oregano
2 Bay Leaves

❖ Rinse meat under cold running water to remove any blood. Cut away fat and tendons (anything white), and cut into small *kuş başı* (bird's head) sized pieces. Set aside.

❖ Skin tomatoes. (See page 201 for easy directions for this optional step). Chop tomatoes and set aside.

❖ "Anger" the butter in a heavy pot. I know that's funny, but in Turkey, you don't simply melt butter before browning meat in it; you heat it up to a sizzle (*Yağı kızdır*). So "anger" the butter over medium-high heat.

❖ Add meat and stir frequently over medium-high heat until all sides are seared. Remove meat from pot with a slotted spoon and set aside.

❖ Sauté onions and garlic in remaining juices in pot for 10-15 minutes or until onions become translucent. (If you are using very lean meat and don't have enough juice in the bottom of the pot, add a couple more tablespoons butter to sauté the onions.)

❖ Stir flour into a small area in the pot until it is dissolved and has no lumps. Gradually stir in tomatoes, tomato sauce, and hot water. (If you don't have tomato sauce, substitute 2 Tbsp. tomato paste, and add an additional ½ c. hot water.)

❖ Stir in salt, pepper, thyme, oregano and bay leaves.

❖ Re-introduce meat to pot. Stir ingredients well and bring to boil. Cover and reduce heat to low. Simmer 1½ to 2 hours until meat is very tender. (Check water periodically to make sure there is always liquid to prevent scorching and also to provide a few tablespoons of sauce for each serving.)

Hint: The sauce should have the consistency of gravy. If it is too watery, place a bit more flour in a small bowl and gradually introduce spoonfuls of the meat juice into it while stirring. Once it is a smooth paste, you can stir this mixture back into the pot and distribute it evenly. The sauce will soon thicken.

❖ Serve hot over rice with rustic bread. *Afiyet olsun!*

PATLICAN OTURTMASI
Beef Stew and Eggplant Casserole

This is a rich eggplant dish with many layers of robust flavor. The name *Patlıcan Oturtması* literally means "seating of the eggplant" and refers to how the fried eggplants are laid out in the bottom of the casserole dish before the meat topping is poured on top of it and baked. This recipe comes from my niece *Gülcan Çağrı Dolcan* in Istanbul, a terrific cook who honed her culinary skills in the kitchen of her grandmother *Zehra hanım*, my dad's first wife. *Gülcan* prepares her stewing beef a little differently than I normally do; rather than searing the meat in butter, she browns it all by itself in a covered pot first, and only after it releases and re-absorbs its juices, does she add butter, onions and spices. I was dubious, but it works!

INGREDIENTS:

4½ lb. Globe Eggplants (Aubergines)
2 lbs. Stewing Lamb or Beef
2 Tbsp. Butter
2 small Onions, finely chopped
1 medium Green Pepper, chopped (see page 201)
3 Tbsp. Salt, divided
4 medium Tomatoes, skinned (see page 201) and chopped
1 c. Vegetable Oil

❖ Cut ends off eggplants. Peel alternating slices of skin. Cut into quarters long ways, and then slice quarters into ¾-inch pieces, or *küçük küçük* (little little) as we say in Turkish. To remove bitterness, place eggplant in a large bowl. Add 2 tablespoons salt and enough water to cover. Lay a heavy plate on top of eggplant to keep it submerged. Allow to soak at least 30 minutes.

❖ Rinse and drain meat to remove any blood. Cut it into small "bird's head" size pieces. Place in a large pot, cover, and cook over medium heat, (no oil) until meat gives up its juices and then re-absorbs them (20-30 minutes). Pay attention that bottom doesn't get scorched during this time.

❖ Add butter, onions, and peppers along with 1 Tbsp. salt. Sauté over medium-high heat until onions are translucent.

❖ Add tomatoes. Stir, cover, and simmer over medium-low heat 45 minutes. Add water periodically as needed.

❖ Meanwhile, heat oil in a large frying pan over medium-high heat. Drain bitter brownish water from eggplant. Squeeze eggplant between paper towels before gently placing several pieces at a time into frying pan. Fry eggplant, constantly turning pieces to prevent burning, until soft. Drain on paper towels to remove excess oil, and arrange (seat) in a large oven-proof casserole dish.

❖ When meat is tender, spread it and its sauce evenly over the eggplant. Bake at 350°F for 30-45 minutes. Serve hot with French fries or rice. Whenever I serve eggplant I always have a little yogurt or *cacık* (page 152) on the side; a cool, bright flavor for a little contrast.

Yaz Türlüsü
Beef Stew with Summer Vegetables

Serves 6-8

Ester Altıntaş Plihal was a beautiful woman, inside and out. Ester had married a Muslim Turk but was widowed when she arrived in the USA from Istanbul with her adorable son David (born Atilla), whom she loved more than life. Ester and David were so much a part of our lives, we knew her only as our real aunt and David our real cousin. It remains that way today.

Intelligent, inquisitive, spiritual, and pioneering, Ester drove a gray Volkswagen Beetle and was politically progressive long before it was cool. She looked like Petula Clarke and happily sang the song "Downtown" for us with little prompting. She was the first Turkish person I ever met who actually listened to children. I was astounded the first time she kept adults waiting to give me time to finish my sentence. She was kind and took time to explain things. Ester had wanted nothing more than a "real family" here in the US. Happily, she fell in love and married the handsome navy captain Richard Plihal and left a legacy of not only three children, (David, Viki, and Jak), but nine beautiful grandchildren, as well.

One summer morning I happened to visit her just as she was making *türlü*, a hearty stew of layered vegetables slow cooked in a meat sauce. I am happy to share her recipe with you.

About Türlü

Türlü is made on the stove in a heavy 5-6 quart pot. The meat is cooked first, The meat is cooked first, until it's tender.The vegetables are then layered over it; the ones requiring the most cooking time placed closest to the bottom. The stew is then cooked all together. (Like most Turks, Ester never wasted food. Rather than stewing new beef, she would often use pot roast left over from another meal to make *türlü*. She would simply cut up the pot roast and place it in the bottom of the pot before layering the vegetables. She would then pour pot roast juices on top before cooking. Delicious!)

INGREDIENTS:

2 lbs. Stewing Beef, trimmed of fat, cut into "birds head" size pieces (1-inch cubes)
6 Tbsp. Butter or Margarine, divided
3 medium Onions, divided
3 Tbsp. + 1½ tsp. Salt, divided
½ c. Tomato Sauce
1 medium Globe Eggplant (about 1 lb.)
½ lb. fresh Green Beans
2 medium Zucchini Squash (about 1 lb.)
3 Large Tomatoes, cut into ¼-inch thick slices
1 lb. Potatoes, peeled and cut into 2-inch cubes
1 lb. Frozen Okra (small, whole)
¼ lb. Green Peppers, seeded and sliced
1 tsp. Sugar
¼ tsp. Black Pepper

❖ Sauté 2 Tbsp. butter, meat, and 2 chopped onions over medium-high heat in a medium-sized pressure cooker, but NOT under pressure. Cover, without pressure bobbin, and cook just long enough for meat to give off its juices and then re-absorb them (about 15 minutes).

❖ Stir in ½ tsp. salt, tomato sauce and ¼ cup water. Bring to a boil. Reduce heat to medium-low, cover and cook (under pressure this time) for 25 minutes. Allow pot to release all its pressure before opening.

(continued on next page)

❖ While meat is cooking, peel skin of eggplant in alternating strips for a striped effect. Cut off ends and cut eggplant in half lengthwise. Cut crosswise into 2-inch cubes and place into a bowl of generously salted (about 2 Tbsp.) water for at least 20 minutes.

❖ If you are using fresh green beans, rinse and drain them. Cut off ends. Cut crosswise into pieces about the width of two fingers (2 inches) and set aside.

❖ Peel squash. Cut into quarters lengthwise. Remove and discard seeds. Cut into slices about the width of two fingers (2 inches) and set aside.

❖ Peel and quarter potatoes. Set aside in bowl of water to prevent from drying out. (You can also use whole baby potatoes which only need to be rinsed.)

❖ If you are using fresh okra, rinse and pat dry. Using paring knife, cut away tough skin from cone-shaped cap. Place fresh okra in water with 1 Tbsp. salt. Set aside. (Frozen okra requires no preparation but should be thawed enough to pull them apart.)

❖ Now the layering: lift meat from pressure cooker and evenly distribute it in bottom of a large heavy pot. Retain juices.

Scatter green beans evenly over meat.

Scatter green pepper next. Then potatoes.

Drain eggplant. Rinse and drain. Layer it on top of potatoes.

Drain and rinse fresh okra and layer it on top of eggplant.
(Or simply layer frozen okra on top of eggplant).

Lay squash over okra.

Lay tomatoes over squash.

Finally, lay slices of onion on top.

❖ Sprinkle vegetables with 1 tsp. salt, sugar, and black pepper. Slice 4 Tbsp. butter into small pats and distribute over vegetables. Pour any remaining juices from meat over vegetables.

❖ Bring mixture to a boil. Cover, reduce heat to very low and simmer for 1 to 1½ hours. Add water periodically, as needed, to maintain a couple of inches of liquid in bottom.

❖ Serve warm with rustic bread. This dish will keep in the fridge up to a week.
Afiyet olsun!

BEEF WITH SUMMER VEGETABLES

ETLI KABAK

Zucchini with Ground Beef

Sometimes I don't have time to make real stuffed zucchini (recipe on page 286). Here'a short-hand version that may not have a dramatic appearance, but the flavors are all there!

INGREDIENTS:

2 lbs. Zucchini, (4 large)
1 lb. Ground Beef or Lamb
1 Large Onion, finely chopped
2 Tomatoes, skinned (optional), chopped
¼ c. Tomato Sauce
¼ c. medium-grain white Rice
2 Tbsp. Butter
3 cloves Garlic, minced
½ c. Fresh Dill, rinsed, trimmed, drained, chopped
½ c. dried Mint Leaves
2 tsp. Salt (divided)
Ground Black Pepper to taste

❖ Heat butter in large pot. Sauté meat and onions over medium-high heat for about 5 minutes. Add garlic, 1 tsp. salt, and pepper. Continue to sauté until meat is browned and onions are translucent.

❖ Stir in tomatoes, tomato sauce, rice, ¾ cup water, dill (reserving a little for garnish), and mint. Simmer covered 10 minutes over medium-low heat.

❖ Meanwhile wash and peel zucchini. Cut off both ends and slice into pieces the width of two fingers.

❖ Add zucchini to pot. Add 1 tsp. salt. Toss ingredients well to spread sauce on all the zucchini.

❖ Cover pot and cook over high heat for 5 minutes. Then reduce heat to medium-low and simmer 45 minutes to an hour. Check to make sure there is always a little liquid in bottom of pot.

❖ To serve, garnish with a little more dill and serve with yogurt and a fresh hearty bread. *Afiyet olsun.*

ALBONDIGÁS AGRISTADA
Meatballs in Egg-Lemon Sauce

Serves 6

Everyone loves this traditional Sephardic recipe. Succulent, juicy meatballs bathed in a lemony-egg sauce. Oh boy. Doesn't that make your mouth water?

Albondigá, the Ladino word for meatball, is derived from the Arabic *al bundaq* meaning "round." My mom's sister Ida Dana learned this dish from her very talented mother-in-law Sultana. Nicknamed Suzan, Sultana was a marvel in the kitchen and taught Ida practically everything she knows about cooking. How lovely then, that Ida taught the recipe to her granddaughter Brielle Dana, Sultana's great grand-daughter. And now Brielle kindly shares it it with you!

By the way, Ida named her daughter Suzy after her mother-in-law. Unlike the Ashkenazim of Europe, Spanish (Sephardic) Jews have no problem naming their children after living relatives. In fact, it's considered an honor.

INGREDIENTS:

MEATBALLS:

1 lb. Ground Beef
1-2 Tbsp. bread crumbs or Matzo-meal
1 medium Onion, grated
5 sprigs fresh Parsley, chopped
1 Egg
½ tsp. Salt
½ tsp. Cumin
¼ tsp. or sprinkle Black Pepper
¼ c. Vegetable Oil

SAUCE:

½ c. Flour or Matzo-cake flour
2 Eggs
Juice of 1 Lemon
½ tsp. Salt
1/8 tsp. Sugar

To Make Meatballs:

❖ Place ground beef in a medium-sized mixing bowl with bread crumbs, onion, parsley, egg, salt, cumin, and pepper. With wet hands, blend ingredients together, punching mixture down and working it very well to tenderize meat and blend spices thoroughly .

❖ Wet hands again and roll small meatballs inside your palms (about the size of a walnut). Place in a large skillet.

❖ Add ½ cup water, vegetable oil, and a dash of salt. Cover skillet, leaving room for a little steam to escape. Cook meatballs 15 minutes over medium-high heat.

WALNUT

Sauce:

❖ Combine flour and ½ cup water in a medium-sized bowl.

❖ In another small bowl whisk together eggs, and add to flour mixture.

❖ Stir in lemon juice, salt and sugar. Set aside.

❖ When meatballs are cooked, remove them one-by-one from skillet and place in a shallow serving platter or bowl. Leave juice in skillet.

❖ Stir ½ cup water into juices in skillet.

❖ Transfer a few large spoonfuls of juice into bowl of egg sauce. Do this gradually to prevent curdling.

❖ Slowly stir entire bowl of egg sauce into skillet. Simmer sauce over very low heat for 2 to 3 minutes, stirring continuously as sauce thickens. Turn off heat and continue to stir slowly until desired thickness is achieved. If sauce becomes too thick, add water.

❖ Pour thickened sauce over meatballs and serve immediately. *Afiyet olsun!*

REHEATING: When you re-heat leftovers of dishes made with *agristada* (egg and lemon) sauce, you must be careful not to curdle the sauce. Always heat the food very slowly over very low heat, stirring the sauce around as best you can. If sauce starts getting lumpy, immediately remove pan from heat and allow to cool a bit before continuing.

KADIN BUDU KÖFTESI

Woman's Thigh Köfte or Rice and Meat Patties

These scrumptious *köftes* (patties) are named "Woman's Thigh" because of their incredibly smooth texture. The first time I made them for my husband, he couldn't believe they were made with meat! Enjoy them with a bright garnish of onion, parsley and sumac.

GARNISH:

1 Onion
2 Tbsp. Salt
1 tsp. Ground Sumac
¼ bunch fresh Parsley, rinsed, chopped

MEAT PATTIES:

½ c. medium grain white Rice
1¼ c. Oil, divided
2 medium Onions, chopped fine
2 lbs. Ground Lamb or Beef, divided
2-3 slices of stale Baguette Bread
¾ bunch fresh Parsley, chopped
1½ tsp. Salt
1/8 tsp. Ground Black Pepper
7 Eggs, divided
2 c. Flour

INGREDIENTS:

❖ The garnish is prepared first. To extract bitter juice from onion, slice very thin and place into small bowl. Add salt and squeeze onion firmly again and again in your palm for at least two minutes until it is very soft and watery.

❖ Rinse thoroughly in fresh water and drain, squeezing out as much excess water as possible.

❖ Stir together with sumac and parsley. Set aside in small serving bowl.

❖ Rinse rice in cool water, drain, and place in a medium-sized pot with 2 cups cold water. Bring to a boil over hight heat. Reduce heat to low. Cover and simmer for 15-20 minutes. Drain rice well in sieve. Set aside to cool.

❖ Heat ¼ cup oil in a large skillet. Add onions and sauté over medium-high heat until tender and translucent. Add half of meat (1 lb.). Sauté until browned. Allow to cool thoroughly before placing in a large bowl.

❖ Allow bread to soak 5 minutes in cool water. Remove crust and discard. Squeeze remaining bread firmly between hands to remove excess water. Place in bowl with meat.

❖ Add remaining meat, cooked rice, parsley, salt, pepper and 3 eggs to bowl. Knead well with hands. Cover and store in refrigerator for 30 minutes so seasonings can blend.

❖ Dampen hands with water and shape meat into oval patties about the size of approximately two walnuts, and place on wax paper. Meanwhile, heat 1 c. oil in a skillet over medium-high heat.

❖ You will dredge each *köfte* in flour and egg before frying, so pour some flour into a shallow bowl and place it near the skillet. Whisk remaining four eggs well and set aside in a shallow bowl.

❖ To fry, dredge a patty in flour, and then in egg, before gently laying it into frying pan. (Oil should be hot enough to sizzle.) Add four or five more *köftes*. Fry for about four minutes or until bottoms are browned. Flip carefully with tongs, and brown other side. Remove *köftes*, arrange on serving platter. Repeat for remaining meat mixture.

❖ Serve immediately, alongside small bowl of onion garnish and some extra ground sumac. *Afiyet olsun!*

WOMAN'S THIGH KÖFTE 285

ETLI KABAK DOLMASI
Meat-filled Zucchini Squash

Here's a side-by-side comparison of a traditional Turkish dish and its Sephardic modification. The Jewish version was taught to me by my "sort of aunt" *Fortune Sadak*. Due to Jewish restrictions regarding eating dairy with meat, there are slight variations between the Sephardic and traditional Turkish recipes. The Sephardic version calls for oil instead of butter, and is served without yogurt. Bread or matzo-meal as well as egg are used for binding the meat. The squash is stood up in the pot to cook, and the tomato is part of the meat filling rather than part of the sauce.

The squash itself is prepared the same way for both recipes:

❖ Peel and rinse zucchini. Cut off and discard stems. Cut squash in half crosswise. Using a vegetable peeler or apple corer, scoop out pulp, leaving at least 1/8-inch thick shell. Set aside.

❖ When filling meat into each zucchini, allow a little room for rice to expand during cooking. Also, after stuffing the squash, make small meatballs with any remaining meat and throw them into the pot, as well.

FILLING: TRADITIONAL OTTOMAN VERSION

INGREDIENTS:
2 lbs. Zucchini, (6-8 small)
½ bunch Fresh Parsley, rinsed, drained
1 lb. Ground Beef or Lamb
2 large Onions, finely chopped
2 Tomatoes, skinned and diced
1 Tbsp. Tomato Paste
1/3 c. medium-grain White Rice
2 Tbsp. Butter
3 Cloves Garlic, minced
½ c. Fresh Dill, rinsed, drained
½ c. Ground Mint
Salt and Pepper to taste

❖ Cut off and retain stems of parsley and dill. Chop leaves and place in a large bowl.

❖ Add meat, onions, tomatoes, tomato paste, rice, 1½ c. water, garlic, parsley, dill, mint, salt and pepper. Knead with hands for at least 5 minutes to tenderize.

❖ Stuff zucchini with meat filling.

❖ Lay a bed of parsley and dill stems in bottom of a heavy pot. Stand stuffed *dolmas* snugly and upright in pot. Dot each with a thin pat of butter.

❖ Stir ½ teaspoon salt into 1 c. water and pour gently over zucchini.

❖ Spread a sheet of wax paper over *dolmas*. Place a plate upside-down over paper to weigh vegetables down. Cover pot and bring to boil. Reduce heat to medium-low and simmer 45 minutes to an hour or until tender when poked with a fork. Check water level periodically to maintain a small amount of liquid in bottom of pot.

❖ Serve with yogurt. *Afiyet Olsun!*

FILLING: SEPHARDIC VERSION

INGREDIENTS:
2 lbs. Zucchini (6-8 small)
½ bunch Fresh Parsley, rinsed, drained, chopped
1 bunch Fresh Dill, rinsed, drained, chopped, divided
2-3 slices White Bread
    (or ¼ c. Matzo-meal or bread crumbs)
1 lb. Ground Beef or Lamb
1 Egg
1 Medium Onion, grated
1 Tbsp. medium-grain White Rice
¾ tsp. Cumin
2 medium Tomatoes, divided
2 Tbsp. Vegetable Oil, divided
Salt and Ground Black Pepper

❖ Rinse, drain, trim and chop parsley and dill leaves.

❖ Soak bread in water for 5 minutes. Tear away crust and discard. Squeeze remaining bread well and place in a large bowl. (If using Matzo-meal, add 2 Tbsp. water.)

❖ Add meat, egg, onions, rice, parsley, dill (reserving 1 tsp.), cumin, 1½ tsp. salt, and ¼ tsp. pepper. Knead with hands for 5 minutes. Stuff zucchini with meat filling.

❖ Spread half of tomato in bottom of a large skillet. Sprinkle a dash of salt, pepper and ½ tsp. dill. Drizzle 1 Tbsp. of oil on top. Lay zucchinis side-by-side in skillet. If you have too many zucchini, use two skillets.

❖ Spoon remaining grated tomato on top. Sprinkle a dash of salt, pepper, and remaining dill. Drizzle oil on top and a few tablespoons water around zucchini's. Cover. Simmer over medium-low heat 45 minutes or until tender.

❖ Place cooked squash side-by-side in oven-proof casserole dish. Bake uncovered at 350°F for 15 minutes to "refine" the texture. Serve warm. *Afiyet Olsun!*

PIŞKADO (À LA TANT IDA)

Tant Ida's Fish with Vegetables

Serves 8

Holiday dinners at Tant Ida's house invariably began with a small serving of this fish recipe as the first course. It's a flaky, moist fish topped with a light and flavorful sauce of vegetables sautéed in olive oil. Since Ida's elaborate dinner parties routinely included twenty five or more guests, she took advantage of modern shortcuts whenever possible, including using frozen chopped vegetables to prepare this sauce.

INGREDIENTS:

¼ c. Olive Oil

2 large Onions, chopped

1 c. fresh of frozen Red and Green Peppers, chopped

2 large Tomatoes, diced (or one 14.5 oz. Canned)

¼ c. Tomato Sauce, canned

1 Tbsp. Dried Parsley

1 tsp. Salt

¼ tsp. Ground Black Pepper

2 lbs. Fresh White Fish, filleted
(Cod, Haddock, Halibut, Flounder, Turbot, Tilapia)

❖ Preheat oven to 350°F.

❖ Sauté onions in oil in a medium-sized pot over medium-high heat until translucent (10-15 minutes).

❖ Add peppers and sauté 2 minutes more.

❖ Stir in tomatoes, tomato sauce, parsley, salt and pepper. Reduce heat and simmer uncovered for 10 minutes.

❖ Meanwhile, cut fish into serving-size pieces. Rub a small amount of oil on bottom of each piece and arrange on a cookie sheet.

❖ Spoon vegetable mixture over each piece of fish.

❖ Bake uncovered 20 minutes. Serve immediately. *Afiyet olsun!*

PIŞKADO CON AGRISTADA (À LA TANT MATI)

Fish with Lemon/Egg Sauce

Sephardic Jews often use a creamy egg/lemon sauce called *Agristada* instead of milk-based sauces to adhere to the laws of kashrut. This fish recipe is one of the most traditional Agristada dishes and is served as a first course. Tant Mati calls this recipe *à la şaka* (in jest) because it's a simplified, flour-free version of the true Agristada Sauce from page 153. This dish is traditionally made with Orange Roughy, but since Roughy is over-fished these days, use any other white fish.

INGREDIENTS:

1½ lbs. White Fish, filleted, washed, patted dry, cut into 6 serving pieces
4 Tbsp. Vegetable Oil
Juice of 2 small Lemons, divided
2 Eggs
Salt
Fresh Parsley, chopped, as garnish (optional)

❖ Heat vegetable oil and juice of one lemon in an extra large skillet over medium heat.

❖ Arrange fillets so that all parts of fish are in contact with skillet bottom. (You can use two smaller skillets by adding only half the ingredients in each pan.)

❖ Sprinkle salt over fish and allow to simmer 5 minutes until fish is opaque around the edges.

❖ Gently flip fish over and drizzle juice of other lemon on top. Add small amounts of water as needed so that there is always enough juice in skillet to almost cover fish.

❖ When fish is opaque and flaky, remove from pan and arrange on a serving platter. (Thick filets take longer to cook. You may flip fish over again if other side needs more time, but avoid over-cooking or fish will dissolve.)

SAUCE:

❖ Remove pan from heat. Stir in 4 Tbsp. water and allow to cool a minute.

❖ Meanwhile, whisk eggs in a separate bowl. Add a dash of salt. Gradually whisk into skillet juice.

❖ Stir constantly over medium heat and until sauce thickens to consistency of mayonnaise (about 5 minutes).

❖ Pour sauce over fish and serve immediately. (May also be eaten cold, and keeps in fridge 3-4 days.)*Afiyet olsun.*

ETLI YAPRAK DOLMASI
Grape Leaves Stuffed with Meat

Serves 6

S ucculent and savory, stuffed grape leaves are so festive and delicious they will always wow your guests. My friend Dean once came for dinner and asked me where I had bought the stuffed grape leaves. When I answered that I had made them, he was incredulous. "Yeah right, Bey," he laughed. "You rolled each one of these little things just for me." You should have seen the look on his face when he realized I had done just that!

LEAVES AND SAUCE FOR POT

- 1 (8 oz.) Jar Grape Leaves, (about 40)
- 3 Tbsp. unsalted Butter
- 1 Tbsp. Tomato Paste
- 2 c. Beef Stock or Water

FILLING

- 1 lb. Lean Ground Beef or Lamb
- 1 medium Onion, grated
- 3 cloves Garlic, minced
- 1 Tbsp. Tomato Paste
- 1 medium Tomato, peeled and chopped, (2/3 cup)
- ½ c. white Rice
- 2 Tbsp. fresh Dill, finely chopped (or 1 tsp. dried)
- ¼ c. fresh Parsley, finely chopped (or 1 Tbsp. dried)
- ½ tsp. Red Pepper
- 1½ tsp. Salt
- ¼ tsp. Black Pepper

INGREDIENTS:

- ❖ Place all filling ingredients in a large bowl. Knead well with hands to blend thoroughly. Cover and refrigerate.

- ❖ Gently tease grape leaves from jar, being careful not to tear them. Drain. Poach leaves in 2 quarts of boiling water for two minutes to soften them up and to remove brine. Using a slotted spoon remove them, one-at-a-time, from the pot. Rinse each one under running water. Pinch off any small, protruding stems from base of each leaf. Smooth out folds, and drape leaves, one-by-one, over edge of a colander to drain.

- ❖ Line bottom of a heavy pot with a few of the torn leaves.

- ❖ Lay out a leaf, vein-side up, with stem-end closest to you. Place 2 Tbsp. of filling at stem-end. (Adjust amount of stuffing based on size of each leaf.)

- ❖ Fold stem end over filling. Then loosely fold sides up and over. Roll up leaf, tucking in stray edges. (Do not roll too tight, or it will burst while cooking.) Lay roll seam-side down on bed of leaves inside pot.

- ❖ Roll remaining leaves and place side-by-side into pot. They should be snug. Dot each one with butter.

- ❖ For sauce, stir tomato paste in a small bowl to loosen it. Slowly stir in stock or water. Spread out any remaining leaves on top of rolls. Place an oven-proof plate on top of leaves to weigh them down during cooking.

- ❖ Cook over medium heat until liquid begins to boil. Cover, reduce heat, and simmer gently for 1 hour 15 minutes, or until rolls are tender. Check periodically to make sure there is some juice left in bottom of pot.

- ❖ Serve hot, with some of the juice spooned over top of rolls. Provide yogurt on the side for those who may like it. *Afiyet olsun!*

Etli Nohut
Chickpeas with Beef

This is my all-time favorite chickpea recipe. It's a yummy comfort food perfect for cold weather. My half-brother Turhan taught me how to make it. He would toss large chunks of fresh onion and tomatoes (as well as *way too much* black pepper!) into the pot just before serving. Canned chickpeas are fine, but dried ones have a richer texture, and you'll be able to control the salt better.

INGREDIENTS:

2 c. Dried Chickpeas (or 4 c. canned)
½ tsp. Baking Soda (only if using dry beans)
1 lb. Lamb or Beef
2 c. Tomatoes, skinned, chopped
   (or 1½ c. canned Tomato Sauce)
3 large Onions, chopped
4 Tbsp. Butter
3 tsp. Salt, divided
½ tsp. Sugar
½ tsp. Red Pepper, or to taste
1 c. Hot Water

❖ Rinse and drain dried chickpeas and place in large pot. Cover with water and soak for at least 12 hours.

❖ Add 1 tsp. baking soda and enough additional water to a level about 1 inch above chick peas. Simmer over low heat until tender but not falling apart, about 20 minutes. Monitor temperature; froth from gas drawn out of peas may boil over quickly. Skim off froth with large spoon. (Don't add salt yet. Cooking chickpeas in salt toughens the skin.)

Remove pot from heat, and stir in 2 tsp. salt. Set aside. (For canned chickpeas, simply rinse, drain, and add only 1 tsp. salt.)

❖ Rinse meat under cold running water to remove any blood. Trim away fat and tendons (anything white). Cut meat into small pieces (Turks say the size of a "bird's head" or *kuş başı*.) Set aside.

❖ Skin tomatoes (see page 201) (optional). Chop and set aside.

❖ Sauté onions and butter in a large pot over medium-high heat for 10-15 minutes or until translucent.

❖ Add meat. Cover and cook , stirring occasionally, until meat gives off its juices and then re-absorbs them. Check occasionally to avoid scorching bottom of pot.

❖ Stir in tomato. Reduce heat to medium, and sauté 2-3 minutes. (If you only have tomato paste, use 2 Tbsp. paste dissolved in ¾ c. hot water instead).

❖ Add 1 c. hot water to pot. Stir in 1 tsp. salt, sugar, and red pepper. Simmer on low heat until meat is very tender, (1 to 1½ hours). Check water level periodically, adding small amounts as needed to maintain a stew-like consistency.

❖ When meat is tender, drain chickpeas and stir into pot. Add water if needed. Cover and simmer for 15 minutes over medium-low heat.

❖ Serve warm over rice, with *cacık* (page 152) or yogurt. *Afiyet olsun!*

POT ROAST

When I'm having special guests and want to serve a meal with several courses, I offer this delectable, succulent pot roast. It's so tender and juicy it almost melts in your mouth. Serve it in slices with rice, and generously lather the flavorful sauce on top of both. A crisp salad on the side gives a bright contrast to the mellow flavors on the plate.

INGREDIENTS:

1 large Onion, chopped
2½ lbs. Boneless Chuck Roast
¼ Vegetable Oil
4 cloves Garlic, chopped
2 tsp. Salt
½ tsp. Ground Black Pepper
½ c. Tomato Sauce
1 c. fresh or canned tomato, diced
1 pinch Sugar
3 Bay Leaves

294   MEAT DISHES

❖ Sauté onions and meat in oil in an un-covered pressure cooker over high heat until all sides of meat are seared.

❖ Add garlic and sauté a couple of minutes more.

❖ Add salt, pepper, tomato sauce, tomatoes, sugar, bay leaves, and ½ cup water. Turn meat over a few times in pot to distribute juices and seasonings all over it. Bring to boil.

❖ Cover, reduce heat, and cook under pressure for 45 minutes. (If you're worried about cooking with a pressure cooker, see page 213). Remove pot from heat and wait until pressure bobbin drops before opening lid of pressure cooker.

❖ Using two large forks, lift meat from pot in one piece and place on a large cutting board. (Boards with a groove to catch juices is best). Trying to keep the roast together as much as possible, cut meat into thin slices. (Go ahead and taste it. You know you want to!)

❖ When entire roast has been sliced, carefully return meat (in one piece, if possible) to pressure cooker. Lift juices and onions from bottom of pot and spoon over top of meat. Adjust salt to your taste. (If meat is too salty, add a peeled, quartered potato to pot to soak up salt.)

❖ Cover pot with a different lid so that NO PRESSURE will build up, and simmer ingredients over low heat at least 30 minutes until meat is very tender. Check periodically to maintain plenty of juices in bottom.

❖ To serve, carefully arrange slices in a shallow bowl or platter. Discard bay leaves. Generously spoon contents in bottom of pot over meat. Add as much juice as you like. Serve warm. *Afiyet olsun!*

HINT: The juices remaining in the pot are a fabulous stock for soups! Just throw in any extra vegetables you have laying around, add water and salt as needed. Simmer until vegetables are tender.

HASAN PASHA KÖFTESI
Meatballs Stuffed with Mashed Potatoes

Serves 6

Typical Turkish Turban (worn by Mehmet Ali Pasha - Auguste Couder)

A mashed-potato turban on a meatball head? Yes! This bold, flavorful dish is a tongue-in-cheek homage to a "bigger than life" 18th century pasha named *Cezayırlı Gazi Hasan Paşa*. A former slave, comrade of the Barbary Coast pirates, and heroic naval commander, *Hasan Paşa* even had a pet lion. Consider this muscular dish "meat and potatoes" Turkish style.

MEAT PATTIES

INGREDIENTS:
- 2 slices of stale Baguette Bread (or rusk)
- 1 lb. lean Ground Beef
- 1 small Onion (½ cup) grated
- 2 cloves Garlic, minced
- ¼ c. fresh Parsley, finely chopped
- 1 Egg
- ¼ tsp. Red Pepper
- ½ tsp. Paprika
- 1 tsp. Ground Cumin
- 1 tsp. Salt or to taste

POTATO PURÉE

INGREDIENTS:
- 3 medium Potatoes, peeled, quartered
- ½ c. Milk
- 1 Tbsp. unsalted Sweet Cream Butter
- 1 clove Garlic, minced
- 1 Egg, whisked
- ½ tsp. Salt or to taste

TOMATO SAUCE

INGREDIENTS:
- 1½ Tbsp. unsalted Sweet Cream Butter
- 2 tsp. Tomato Paste
- 1¼ c. Tomatoes, chopped
- 1 c. Beef Stock or Water
- 1 tsp. Salt or to taste
- ½ c. Grated Kasseri or Parmesan Cheese

Preparing the Köftes (meat patties):

❖ Soak bread in cold water for 5 minutes. Remove and discard crust. Squeeze out excess water from bread and place in medium-sized bowl.

❖ Add meat, onion, garlic, parsley, egg, red pepper, paprika, cumin, and salt. Moisten hands and knead for 2 minutes to tenderize meat and blend ingredients together thoroughly. Cover bowl and refrigerate at least 30 minutes so that seasonings can blend together.

Preparing the Potato Purée

❖ Place potatoes in a large saucepan with lightly salted water. Bring to a boil over high heat. Reduce to simmer for 25 minutes or until tender.

❖ Heat milk in a small saucepan until just warm. Set aside near stove to keep warm.

❖ Sauté butter and garlic in a medium-sized pot over low heat for about a minute until butter has melted. Add potatoes and mash. Stir in ½ tsp. salt and whisked egg. Remove from heat. Gradually add milk while stirring, adding enough for potatoes to become smooth but still firm enough to be able to form into peaks.

❖ Preheat oven to 375°F. Moisten hands and shape meat into 12 equal-sized balls (*köftes*) about the size of an egg. With your fingers, dig a well into the center of each *köfte*, forming it into a bowl. Arrange bowls in an oven-proof baking dish. Bake uncovered 25 minutes.

❖ Remove baked *köftes* from oven and reduce temperature to 350°F. Stuff each *köfte* with potatoes. Allow potatoes to mound high on *köftes* to look like a sultan's turban on a meatball head. Isn't this funny!?! (If you're inspired, squeezing potatoes through a star-shaped pastry tube makes for a very elegant presentation!)

Preparing the Tomato Sauce

❖ Melt butter over medium heat in a small saucepan. Stir in tomato paste. Stir in tomatoes and stock and bring mixture to a boil. Boil for 3 minutes, stirring constantly until ingredients are well-blended.

❖ Spoon sauce carefully between *köftes*. Sprinkle grated cheese on top of potatoes. Bake uncovered for 35 minutes, or until cheese is slightly browned.

❖ To serve, arrange two *köftes* in center of each serving plate. Spoon sauce around them and serve immediately. *Afiyet olsun!*

MEATBALLS STUFFED WITH MASHED POTATOES

Çerkez Tavuğu
Circassian Chicken Salad

Serves 6-8

This *meze* (or appetizer) is a specialty of the Caucuses and the Black Sea region. Think of it as light chicken salad with a creamy spread of crushed walnuts instead of all that mayonnaise!

Çerkez Tavuk is usually served warm or at room temperature. Try it mounded at the center of a ring of rice. Or for informal occasions, lay a bed of romaine lettuce leaves in a serving platter and mound the chicken on top. Your guests will enjoy spooning individual portions of chicken inside cool leaves of crispy Romaine lettuce and eating them with their hands.

CHICKEN

INGREDIENTS:

1 Fresh Young Chicken for boiling (about 3½ pounds)
2 Carrots, rinsed and cut into four pieces each
1 large Onion, quartered
1 Celery Stalk, rinsed and cut into four pieces
¼ bunch Fresh Parsley
2 c. Walnuts, chopped
3 slices of stale White or Baguette Bread (or rusk)
2 cloves Garlic
2 tsp. Salt
¼ tsp. Ground Black Pepper
Red Pepper to taste

GARNISH

1 tsp. Ground Paprika
2 Tbsp. Olive Oil or Butter
Romaine Lettuce (optional)

❖ Rinse chicken, removing any giblets. Place in large pot with carrots, onion, celery, parsley and 8 c. water. Bring to a boil and skim foam off top. Reduce heat to medium. Cover pot and lightly boil until chicken is tender, about one hour. Carefully lift chicken from water and set aside to cool. Strain and reserve stock. Discard vegetables.

❖ Remove all skin and bones from chicken. Cut or tear meat into small pieces (about 1-inch long) and set aside in a medium-sized bowl.

❖ Finely chop walnuts in a food processor until almost pulverized.

❖ Remove and discard crust from bread. Soak remainder in a cup or two of chicken stock. Squeeze with hands to remove excess liquid and add to walnuts in food processor. Add garlic, salt, and pepper. Process mixture again until blended.

❖ Gradually add 1 cup of stock, ¼ cup at a time, and continue to process until mixture becomes a spreadable paste like mayonnaise. Add more stock as needed for proper consistency.

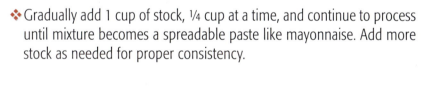

❖ Place half of contents of food processor into bowl with chicken. Blend well. Transfer chicken to a shallow serving platter and arrange in a mound. Spread remaining paste over it as if you're frosting a cake.

❖ For garnish, heat olive oil (or butter) and paprika in a very small saucepan over low heat until oil turns reddish. When it just begins to sizzle, remove from heat and allow pepper to settle. Drizzle over chicken before serving. Serve warm or cold. *Afiyet olsun!*

Yoḡurtlu Kebab
Grilled Kebabs with Tomato and Yogurt Sauces

My favorite barbecue dish! Grilled, succulent beef kebabs are laid on a bed of warm pita bread, and then topped with three mouth-watering sauces. You'll love the layers of flavor in this dish, and the way the juices soak into the bread; delicious down to the last bite. To grill the kebabs, you will need 12 flat skewers which are at least ¾" wide to keep the meat from falling off when you turn them. If you don't have skewers, just shape the meat into oval patties (*köftes*) and grill individually.

Kebab Ingredients:

4 -5 slices of day-old Italian or Baguette Bread
2 lbs. lean Ground Beef
½ small Onion, grated (about ¼ cup)
4 cloves Garlic, minced
2 Eggs
½ tsp. Red Pepper
1 Tbsp. Paprika
1 Tbsp. Ground Cumin
¼ tsp. Sugar
1½ tsp. Salt
¼ tsp. Ground Black Pepper
½ bunch Fresh Parsley, finely-chopped, divided
12 small (6 to 8-inch diameter) or 6 large Pita Breads,
    cut into 1 to 1½-inch squares

Yogurt Sauce

1½ c. Yogurt (plain)
4 cloves Garlic, minced

Tomato Sauce

1½ Tbsp. Olive Oil
4 large Tomatoes, peeled (see page 201) and chopped
    (or 2½ c. canned diced tomatoes)
½ tsp. Salt
¼ tsp. Pepper

Garnish

3 Tbsp. Butter, (unsalted, sweet cream)
1 tsp. Ground Paprika
½ tsp. Red Pepper (optional)

❖ Soak bread in cold water for 5 minutes. Remove and discard crust. Squeeze out excess water from remainder, and place in a large bowl.

❖ Add meat, onion, garlic, eggs, red pepper, paprika, cumin, sugar, salt and ground black pepper. Add parsley, reserving 1 Tbsp. for garnish. Moisten hands and knead for at least 2 minutes to tenderize meat and to blend ingredients together very well. Cover bowl and refrigerate for about 30 minutes so that seasonings can be absorbed.

❖ To prepare yogurt sauce, whisk garlic, yogurt, and salt together a medium-sized bowl. (Add a little cold water if it's too thick to spoon easily.) Cover and chill ½ hour to give garlic time to distribute its flavor.

❖ To prepare tomato sauce, heat olive oil in a small saucepan over medium heat. Stir in tomatoes. Season with salt and pepper. Sauté until consistency is a lumpy purée. Cover and reduce heat to lowest setting to keep warm.

❖ With moistened hands, divide chilled meat into 12 equal servings. If using skewers, wrap meat tightly around blade, keeping it at least 3 inches from either end. (If you have no skewers make 24 oval-shaped patties instead.) Lay skewers on a sheet of aluminum foil so it won't stick when you pick it up to put on the grill.

❖ Wrap cut-up pita bread in a large sheet of aluminum foil. Place on a free area of grill, not too close to heat source, to warm up.

❖ Place skewers on grill, about 5 inches above heat source. Grill about 4-5 minutes each side, depending on thickness of kebab.

❖ Remove bread and divide equally on 6 serving dishes. Remove kebabs from skewers. Cut into large pieces and arrange each serving on top of pita bread on each serving dish.

❖ Generously spoon tomato sauce over meat and bread. Then drizzle some yogurt sauce on top.

❖ Quickly melt butter over medium heat in a small saucepan. Stir in paprika, remaining parsley, and a little red pepper if you like. Drizzle this garnish on top of yogurt sauce on each serving dish, and serve immediately. Oh, you are going to love this! *Afiyet olsun!*

GRILLED KEBABS WITH TOMATO AND YOGURT SAUCES

Etli Biber ve Domates Dolmasi
Meat-stuffed Peppers and Tomatoes

Serves 6-8

In the summer time when vegetables are plentiful and inexpensive, my mother would often bring home large bags of green peppers and tomatoes. That's when I knew we would be making *dolma*, vegetables stuffed full of juicy beef and rice. *Dolma* takes a little time to construct, but the flavors are delectable, and the presentation is so dramatic, it's well worth the effort. The best part is that *Dolma* always tastes better the day after you cook it, and leftovers keep in the fridge for 4 to 5 days.

VEGETABLES
INGREDIENTS:
- 6 Small Green Peppers
- 6 Medium Tomatoes
- 1 Tbsp. Tomato Paste
- ½ tsp. Sugar
- 1 tsp. Salt
- 6 Tbsp. Butter

FILLING
INGREDIENTS:
- 1 Lb. Ground Beef or Lamb
- 1 Medium Onion, grated
- 4 Cloves Garlic (my mom didn't use garlic in her *dolma* but I think it gives depth to the flavors)
- ¼ c. Uncooked White Rice
- 1 Tbsp. Tomato Paste
- 2 Tbsp. Fresh Dill, rinsed, trimmed, and chopped
- 1 Tbsp. Dried Mint
- ½ Bunch Fresh Parsley, chopped fine
- 4 tsp. Salt
- 1 tsp. Ground Black Pepper

❖ Twist off any stems on tomatoes, and cut off excess stems from green peppers. Rinse vegetables and set aside in a colander to drain.

❖ Slice partially through top of each pepper, making sure to leave enough to hinge the top open without removing it completely from the bottom.

❖ Reach inside and remove pulp and seeds, as well as white filament. Reserve pulp of three peppers for filling. Hold pulp under running water to brush away seeds. Chop pulp and place in a medium-sized bowl which you will use for the filling. Rinse peppers inside and out and set aside in a large bowl.

❖ Carefully cut off top of each tomato, making sure to leave just enough to hinge top open without removing it completely. Firmly hold tomato cupped in one hand. Scrape inside with edge of a teaspoon to remove pulp and seeds from the cavity. Chop pulp and place in bowl with pepper pulp. (The tomato pulp in the filling gives tomato flavor to the stuffed peppers, while the green pepper pulp gives its flavor to the stuffed tomatoes.)

❖ To make filling, place meat, onion, garlic, rice, 1 Tbsp. tomato paste, dill, mint, parsley, 4 tsp. salt and 1 tsp. ground black pepper into bowl with tomato and pepper pulp. With your hands, knead ingredients together well.

❖ Gently press filling into peppers and tomatoes. The tops need not close completely, i.e., be careful not to overstuff or they may burst while cooking. Stuff remaining vegetables. Place dolma upside-down inside a large pot. (It is alright if tomatoes are not bearing directly on floor of the pot, as long as they are snug.

❖ Form any remaining meat filling into small meatballs and add to pot.

❖ Place 1 Tbsp. tomato paste in a small bowl and gradually stir in 1½ cups warm water. Pour over *dolmas*. Sprinkle with sugar and 1 tsp. salt. Finally, dot *dolmas* with pats of butter.

❖ Place an ovenproof plate upside-down on dolma to weigh them down during cooking. Cover pot and bring to boil. Reduce heat to medium-low. Simmer for 45 minutes to 1 hour, or until peppers are tender.

❖ To serve, ask your guests if they would prefer pepper, tomato or both. Place *dolma* in center of each plate and pour a little sauce on top. Serve warm with rustic bread. *Afiyet olsun!*

DOMATESLI YUMURTA
Fried Eggs in Light Tomato Sauce

We have two teenage sons at home, and it's usually impossible to get them to the breakfast table. But when I offer "tomato eggs," they suddenly find their appetites. Try this recipe and you'll see how a touch of tomato and a dash of basil can turn a basic egg into a supringly delectable treat!

INGREDIENTS:

2 ripe Tomatoes
2 Tbsp. Olive Oil
8 eggs
Salt
Black Pepper
½ tsp. Dried Basil, divided
1 Tbsp. grated Parmesan Cheese (optional)

❖ Rinse tomatoes and cut off tops. Laying cut end flat on grater, grate flesh of tomato. Discard skin.

❖ Sauté tomato in large skillet with olive oil over medium-high heat until it condenses into a sauce (5-7 minutes).

❖ Sprinkle a few dashes salt, pepper and half the basil on tomato sauce. Reduce heat to medium.

❖ Break eggs into skillet, trying not to break yolks. Sprinkle salt, pepper and remaining basil.

❖ Fry eggs uncovered until albumin is completely set and white but yolk is soft. Gently but quickly flip eggs over. Immediately sprinkle cheese. Fry only 30 seconds more, and remove from heat. Serve immediately. *Afiyet olsun!*

MENEMEN
Scrambled Eggs with Vegetables

INGREDIENTS:

1 Green Pepper
2½ Tbsp. Butter
½ small Onion, chopped
2 ripe Tomatoes (or ½ c. canned) peeled, chopped
1 Tbsp. fresh Parsley, washed, trimmed, chopped
6 eggs
Salt
Black Pepper
2 Tbsp. Feta Cheese (or Cheddar), crumbled, divided
1 Tbsp. Fresh Parsley, chopped (garnish)

❖ Remove stem and seeds of green pepper and cut into thin rings. Cut larger rings into half or fourths. Pieces should all be about the same size.

❖ Melt butter in a large skillet over medium heat. Add onions and sauté for 5 minutes.

❖ Add green pepper and continue to sauté until soft, but do not allow to brown.

❖ Add tomatoes and sauté a few minutes more, crushing tomato pieces into a loose sauce. (Don't rush this step. The tomatoes should be nice and soft.)

❖ In a medium-sized bowl, whisk eggs together just enough to break up large clumps. Stir in salt and pepper to taste. Add to skillet and stir gently, making sure to toss cooked egg from bottom and sides of pan to keep from burning.

❖ When egg begins to set, sprinkle in half the cheese and continue to sauté until all the liquid is evaporated.

❖ Garnish with remaining cheese and parsley. Serve immediately. *Afiyet olsun.*

SAHANDA ISPANAKLI YUMURTA
Skillet Eggs with Spinach

Makes 12 Eggs

E ver come home late and find there is nothing in the fridge to cook up for dinner? Look again. If you've got eggs and frozen spinach, you've got a nutritious and tasty meal. Fried eggs nestled in a bed of sautéed spinach and onions is a popular lunch or dinner in Turkey because it's a great substitute for meat, looks and tastes delicious, and is a terrific way to get spinach into kids. Serve hot with yogurt or *cacık* (page 152) and a hearty bread.

You can also try this dish with a side of rice, macaroni and cheese, or a cheese *börek* (page 242).

INGREDIENTS:

2 boxes chopped Frozen Spinach (10 oz. each)
  (or 2 lbs. fresh chopped spinach) 12 Eggs
4 Tbsp. Butter
2 large Onions, finely chopped
3½ Tbsp. Vegetable Oil
Salt (to taste)
Ground Black Pepper (to taste)
Ground Red Pepper (to willingness to suffer)
¾ c. Meat or Vegetable Broth
12 Eggs
¼ Paprika (garnish)

❖ Boil spinach in enough water to cover for 15 minutes. Drain and set aside.

❖ Heat butter in a large skillet over medium-high heat. Add onions and sauté 8 to 10 minutes, stirring occasionally, until onions are tender.

❖ Squeeze spinach between your palms to remove excess water. Add to skillet and season with 1 tsp. salt and a few dashes each of black and red pepper. Stirring as needed, sauté for 15 -20 minutes.

❖ Stir in broth, cover, and cook over low heat until spinach soaks up the liquid. Set aside until you are ready to prepare eggs.

❖ Using two forks, gingerly create 12 "holes" in the spinach and break an egg into each one, being careful to keep each yolk intact.

❖ Season with ½ teaspoon salt and a couple of dashes of paprika for color.

❖ Allow to cook uncovered over medium heat until egg whites are set. If top of egg whites are taking too long to set, you can cover pan, but only for one minute. Try not to let the yolk cook through. Serve hot. Afiyet olsun.

Karni Yarik
Eggplant Stuffed with Beef

6 Baby Eggplants (long thin ones are best)
Salt
¾ lb. Ground Beef
1 large Onion, grated
2 Tomatoes, divided
1 Italian Green Pepper, chopped fine
Ground Black Pepper to taste
¼ tsp. Paprika
½ tsp. Allspice
½ tsp. Cinnamon
1 Tbsp. Tomato Paste
½ bunch Fresh Flat Parsley, loosely chopped
1 c. Canola, Sunflower or Vegetable Oil to fry
4 skinny Green Banana Peppers, optional
1 c. Tomato Juice (or diluted tomato sauce)
¼ c. Boiling Water

One of my favorite eggplant recipes! *Karnı Yarık* literally means "split belly." Baby eggplants are split open, lightly fried, and then stuffed with a tasty meat filling. Yum!

❖ Trim caps of eggplants, leaving an inch of stem intact. Peel thin strips of skin off each eggplant in alternating, lengthwise strips. (Exposing some pulp will help draw out the bitterness when you then soak eggplant in salted water).

❖ Cut a deep slit lengthwise into each eggplant, being careful not to slice all the way through, and avoiding each end. Place the eggplant into a large bowl of cold water with 2 tablespoons of salt. Set aside at least 30 minutes.

❖ To prepare filling, brown ground beef and onion over high heat in a large skillet without oil or butter. (If meat is very lean, you may need to add 1 Tbsp. oil to prevent sticking.) Sauté for 8 -10 minutes, stirring occasionally, until onions are tender and translucent.

❖ Grate pulp of 1 tomato. Add to meat. Continue to sauté for 5 minutes.

❖ Add Italian pepper, 1 tsp. salt, ground black pepper, paprika, allspice, cinnamon, and tomato paste. Continue to sauté for five minutes.

❖ Stir in parsley. Reduce heat to low. Cover pot and simmer 10 minutes. Turn off heat and set aside.

❖ Heat up oil in a large skillet over medium-high heat. Drain eggplant. Squeeze each one and pat it dry with paper towel. Gently lay eggplant into skillet, three at a time. Fry, turning them over every minute or two, until they are browned on all sides and are soft inside. (Eggplants should sag a bit as you lift them out of oil.

❖ Drain fried eggplants on paper towel to soak up extra oil. Arrange in a 9 inch x 12 inch oven-proof baking dish. Leave enough room around each eggplant so you can open them up a bit to fill them.

❖ Turn off heat under skillet. Rinse skinny peppers and pat dry. Fry for 5 to 7 minutes. Set aside.

❖ Using two tablespoons, gently pull sides of each eggplant open, nudging some pulp out of the way. Fill each one with about 2 Tbsp. filling.

(Do not over-stuff. Instead, save any left-over filling. It's yummy to eat all by itself or inside an omelet or *borekita*!)

❖ Cut second tomato either into wedges or slices and lay one on top of each eggplant. (Wedges can be pressed gently into filling.)

❖ Stir tomato juice and boiling water in a small bowl. Pour around each eggplant. Lay a pepper on top of each one. Cover tightly with foil. Bake 30 to 40 minutes at 350°F.

❖ Serve warm, with eggplants arranged nicely in a serving platter. Drizzle a little sauce over each one. Serve with rice and a hearty bread. This dish is also nice with a little yogurt on the side. *Afiyet olsun!*

EGGPLANT STUFFED WITH BEEF

Izmir Köftesi
Cigar-shaped Meatballs in Tomato Sauce

Serves 6-8

Isn't this dish beautiful? And I'll bet you've never tasted *köftes (*meat patties) this succulent and pillowy-soft!

The spices in this traditional Aegean recipe give the meat patties a robust yet pleasantly refined balance of flavors. I like to make this dish in a 24-inch diameter pan called a *tepsi* (available in most mid-east markets). I bring it directly from the oven to the table, with the *köftes* still sizzling and steaming in a luscious tomato sauce.

This is a simple recipe but it takes a little time to prepare. The meat (mixed with soaked bread, egg, and spices) is kneaded for several minutes before being formed into cigar-shaped patties. The patties are then fried to sear in the juices, and then baked in a zesty but light tomato sauce.

Izmir Köftesi is often served with fried potato wedges. A nice variation is to lay peeled potato wedges in the tomato sauce alongside the *köfte* before baking. If you do this, sprinkle a little extra salt over the potatoes, and a little paprika for color, before baking.

MEATBALLS

INGREDIENTS:

- 4 -5 slices of day-old Baguette or White Bread
- 2 lbs. Lean Ground Beef
- ¼ c. Onion, grated
- 4 cloves Garlic, minced
- 2 Eggs
- 1 tsp. Paprika
- 1 tsp. Ground Cumin
- ¼ c. Fresh Parsley, finely chopped (or 1 Tbsp. dried)
- 2 tsp. Salt
- ½ tsp. Black Pepper
- ¼ c. Vegetable Oil

SAUCE

INGREDIENTS:

- 8 small Green Peppers
- 2 Tbsp. Sweet Cream Butter (unsalted)
- 1 Tbsp. Tomato Paste
- 2 c. Tomatoes, chopped
- 2 c. Beef or Chicken Stock (or water)
- 1 tsp. Salt
- Dash of Black Pepper
- Dried Sumac (optional garnish)

❖ Soak bread in cold water for 5 minutes. Peel crust away and discard. Squeeze excess water out between your palms. Place in medium-sized bowl.

❖ Add beef, onion, garlic, eggs, paprika, cumin, parsley, salt, and black pepper. Dipping your hands periodically into a small bowl of warm water, knead ingredients well for about 3 minutes.

❖ Lay out a large sheet of wax paper. With moistened hands, roll small amounts of meat mixture between your palms to form 28 to 30 flattened cigar-shaped patties. Gently blunt ends to keep them from being too pointy. Set them aside on wax paper.

❖ Heat oil in a skillet over medium-high heat. Fry *köftes* a few at a time, for about 2½ minutes each side or until browned. Arrange them nicely in a 24-inch diameter round *tepsi* or baking pan.

❖ When all patties are browned, turn off heat under skillet. Fry the green peppers (from sauce ingredients) in remaining oil for 5 to 7 minutes. Set aside.

❖ To make sauce, first melt butter in a medium-sized saucepan. Stir in tomato paste till loose. Stir in tomatoes, stock, salt, and pepper. Bring to boil.

❖ Pour sauce over patties. Arrange green peppers between them.

❖ Cover and bake at 350°F for 40 minutes. Check for doneness; meat should be brown, not pink, on the inside.

❖ To serve, bring entire *tepsi* to table. Place 3 to 4 *köfte* on each plate. Drizzle a few tablespoons of sauce over them. Provide a little dried sumac on the table. A crisp salad on the side provides a nice variation in texture. *Afiyet olsun.*

CIGAR-SHAPED MEATBALLS IN TOMATO SAUCE

Desserts

IRMIK HELVASI
Semolina Dessert (Halvah)

Serves 12

The sesame-flavored tahini halvah you find in the grocery store is nothing like homemade Turkish *helva*, a light and crumbly semolina (*irmik*) dessert served on holidays and special occasions. I love Tant Ida's *helva* and she loves how my eyes light up when she brings a warm bowl of it out from the kitchen.

Helva has a different consistency depending on where you are in the Middle East. In much of Anatolia it is more like a dense paste which is spread and pressed into a serving platter and decorated with roasted almonds. My friend *Ayla Pazarbaşihad* prepared a dish of irmik helva for a group of friends and family, and actually brought her semolina (durum wheat) with her from Turkey, saying that the semolina in the USA is not coarse enough. (She also brought her own butter, insisting that butter here foams up and separates when you melt it.) Ayla was kind enough to let me photograph her *helva* on the next page.

As you can see, my helva (shown above) is crumbly and fluffy, which is why it's served in bowls. Ayla's is a more formal version and is pressed into a 1-inch slab and sliced into small squares when served. If you would like to try her method, substitute 1½ c. water for the same amount of milk. Also, do not open the pot once towels have been placed on top. Allow the helva to cool for one hour, and then spread the mixture onto a platter. Also press almonds firmly into helva to keep them in place.

INGREDIENTS:

2 palmfuls Pine Nuts (½ cup)
1½ sticks unsalted sweet cream Butter (12 Tbsp.)
2 c. Semolina (#2 or coarser)
3 c. Milk
1½ c. Sugar
Ground Cinnamon (garnish)
2 palmfuls fresh Almond (optional)

- Sauté pine nuts in butter in a large pot over medium-high heat, stirring constantly with a wooden spoon until butter melts.

- Stir in semolina and cook for a minute or two before reducing heat to medium. Continue to stir until semolina turns a light brownish color, (about 20 minutes). Take care not to burn the semolina! If it gets too brown, it will have an unpleasant aroma and flavor.

- Meanwhile, stir milk and sugar together in medium-sized saucepan. Warm slowly over low heat.

- When semolina is golden brown, SLOWLY introduce milk to pot. Continue to stir slowly over medium heat until semolina has soaked up liquid and mixture starts to gather itself up.

- Turn off heat. Drape a couple of paper towels over the pot. Place cover of pot on top. Allow to sit for 5 minutes.

- Remove cover and paper towels, fluff up mixture with spoon, turning it over a few times to give it some air. Drape new paper towels over pot and replace cover. Allow mixture to cool again for 5 minutes.

- Repeat previous step one more time, but this time allow *helva* to cool completely.

- To serve, fluff up helva as you place it into a serving bowl. Sprinkle cinnamon over top. When this dessert is spooned into individual serving bowls, more cinnamon can be sprinkled over each person's bowl according to their preference. Serve warm or room temperature. You can microwave helva for a few seconds to warm it up before serving. *Afiyet olsun!*

ALMONDS (OPTIONAL):

- If almonds have skins, soak in a bowl of hot water overnight. Drain and soak again in hot water for 5 minutes. The peels should come right off.

- Roast almonds on a lightly greased cookie sheet at 350°F for about ten minutes.

- To serve, spread *helva* onto a platter. Press into a pleasing shape. Decorate with almonds.

SYMBOLISM AND FOOD

Weddings and holidays are not the only important occasions for cooking and sharing food. Deaths also call for certain dishes with symbolic meaning. In Turkey, neighbors prepare and send dishes to the bereaved household for three days after a death. The only dish prepared by the household of the deceased is helva. Customarily, making it is a communal effort. A good friend of the deceased begins preparing the helva while recounting fond memories. Then the spoon is passed to the next person who takes up the stirring and continues to reminisce. Usually the helva is done by the time everyone in the room has had a chance to speak and stir. This simple ceremony encourages those left behind to talk about happier times, a process which assuages their grief and strengthens the bond between them. The finished helva is then sent to neighbors and friends who honor the family by remembering and praying for the departed.

(adapted from the Turkish Cultural Foundation)

Gato Salam
Chocolate Cake That Looks Like Salami

Serves 12

For festive occasions, Tant Mati always made this delicately flavored, frozen chocolate cake (or *gateau* in French). Served in thin slices, this charming dessert looks a little like sliced salami, hence the funny name. This dessert is a family favorite and can be stored in the freezer for months!

INGREDIENTS:

2 Sticks Butter (16 Tbsp.)
6 Squares Semi-sweet cooking chocolate (6 oz.)
3 Tbsp. Cocoa Powder
6 Tbsp. Powdered Sugar
1 tsp. Vanilla Extract
2 Packages "Petit Beurre" tea cookies (400 g.)
   (available at ethnic markets and large grocery chains)
3 Eggs
1 Sheet Aluminum Foil (18 to 20 inches long)
1 Sheet Wax Paper (18 to 20 inches long)

❖ Melt butter in a medium-sized saucepan over low heat. Add chocolate squares, cocoa powder, and powdered sugar. Heat until all ingredients are melted and blended. Remove from heat. Stir in vanilla extract and set aside.

❖ Crumble cookies into very small pieces and crumbs inside a large bowl.

❖ The chocolate cshould have cooled a little by now. Whisk eggs in a small bowl and pour into chocolate. Continue to whisk briskly for about three minutes until mixture thickens to pudding-like consistency.

❖ Pour chocolate into bowl of crumbled cookies. Blend well to distribute chocolate thoroughly. Mixture should appear like dry cookie dough.

❖ Lay sheet of aluminum foil on counter. Lay sheet of wax paper over it.

❖ Empty bowl onto wax paper, centering dough long ways.

❖ Carefully lift wax paper on either side of dough. Push and mold dough inside the paper so that it forms a long triangular loaf, (similar to a large Toblerone chocolate bar). Leave about 2 inches on each end so that you can fold the ends of the paper in.

❖ Wrap wax paper tightly around the triangular loaf, folding down the top edge. Tightly wrap aluminum foil around as well.

❖ Push ends in to make a flat triangular end to the loaf. Fold ends of paper shut like giftwrap. Repeat with foil.

❖ Push sides as needed to give loaf a consistent triangular shape along its entire length. Flip it to the next side to flatten it more, and then the third. When you are satisfied with the shape, place on baking sheet or flat surface, and place level inside freezer. Freeze for at least one hour before serving.

❖ To serve, carefully pull foil and paper away from cake, but only from as much as you want to serve. Cut exposed cake into thin slices (3/8-inch), and arrange on shallow serving platter. Re-wrap remainder of cake and return to freezer.

❖ Serve immediately. And as Tant Mati would say, *Bon Apetit*.

CHOCOLATE SALAMI CAKE

Kabak Tatlisi
Butternut Squash Dessert

Have you ever walked past unfamiliar fruits and vegetables in the grocery store, intimidated by not knowing what they are, or how they might be prepared. For me, one of these strange beasts was butternut squash, a pear-shaped beige-colored gourd that shows up on produce stands every autumn.

Until my teen years I assumed my favorite Thanksgiving dessert, *kabak tatlısı*, was made from some exotic pumpkin or sweet potato drenched in syrup and then topped with chopped nuts. I would never have guessed that the heavenly concoction is actually made from this weirdly-shaped winter vegetable. Butternut squash dessert has a glorious deep-orange color, a very tender texture, and a bright flavor with just a hint of lemon. After a big Thanksgiving meal, it's a welcome alternative to heavy pumpkin pie.

Buy squash that weigh about 3-4 pounds each. Note that the more orange the flesh color, the sweeter the flavor will be.

2 Medium Butternut Squash

4 c. Sugar

2 c. Crushed Walnuts

❖ Butternut squash has a tough skin. To cut, grasp it firmly and use a sharp knife to slice it in half, width-wise. Turn halves and cut again to quarter the squash. Remove seeds* and most of the stringy pulp. (Mom actually liked the stringy part because it's the sweetest!)

❖ Slice squash in 2-inch slices. Cut away skin and pale flesh, leaving the deep orange. Cut into 2-inch x ¾-inch slices. Cut slices in half widthwise.

❖ Lay pieces in a large heavy pot, a layer at a time, pouring some sugar over each layer. Cover pot and set aside for 5 hours until contents are quite juicy.

❖ Simmer covered over very low heat for 1 hour. Do NOT stir. If you need to adjust pieces, do so carefully. Squash is done when it is tender when pierced with a fork. (It should almost "melt in your mouth.)

❖ Remove pot from heat and allow to cool.

❖ Gently arrange squash on a large serving platter. Pour any remaining juices over top and allow to cool completely. Sprinkle half the walnuts on top, reserving remainder in a small bowl near the platter so that guests can sprinkle more nuts on their individual plate if they like. Heavenly...
Afiyet olsun!

*If you like salted pumpkin seeds, try this. Rinse the squash seeds and spread them on a baking sheet to dry overnight. Sauté them for 15 minutes in a few tablespoons of salt water in a skillet over medium-high heat. Allow to dry.

MUHALLEBI
Zeki Bey's Milk and Rice Flour Pudding

This wonderful dessert is especially meaningful for me because it was my father's specialty. Yes, this "old school" recipe requires 45 minutes of constant stirring to get the milk to the correct consistency. But don't be put off! My Dad and I had some of our sweetest conversations as I sat on the kitchen counter next to the stove while he lovingly stirred the sweet milk with a wooden spatula. These days, when I make *muhallebi*, in the same pot my dad used, my son Isaac sits nearby and reads to me to pass the time.

Serve *muhallebi* on a shallow, non-white platter about 24-inches long. My father's platter is quite old and yellowed. The intricate floral decoration around the cracked, fluted edges is mostly faded. Still, every time I serve *muhallebi* in it, the pudding looks beautifully white, and someone invariably pulls me aside and says, "I remember your father always used this plate." To this day, when I make *muhallebi*, there are tears at the dessert table as we reminisce about the beautiful decorative flowers, birds, or basket-weave patterns he would create by gingerly tapping the side of a tilted cinnamon bottle held over the platter. He'd even sprinkle our names on our birthdays or wedding days. When I make *muhallebi*, people tell me it tastes just like my dad's. That makes me very happy.

INGREDIENTS

½ Gallon Whole Organic Milk
1 ¼ c. Sugar
¼ tsp. Salt
2/3 c. Rice Flour
Cinnamon as garnish

❖ Set aside serving platter. Pour milk into a large heavy pot, preferably with no rivets on inside. (They get in the way as you run your spatula along the sides while stirring.) Set heat on high. With a large wooden spoon or spatula, slowly stir in sugar and salt.

❖ While milk is heating up, place rice flour in a medium-sized bowl. Gradually add large spoonfuls of the milk into flour, stirring constantly, until you have a smooth, runny paste. Slowly, re-introduce this rice-flour paste back into pot of milk.

❖ Continue to stir milk gently for about 10 minutes. It will rise suddenly when it reaches boiling temperature, so keep a watchful eye. When it *just* begins to boil, quickly reduce heat to medium. Continuously weave spatula to keep milk moving while gently teasing it from sides and bottom of pot to prevent it from sticking. Adjust temperature slightly as needed to maintain a very lazy boil the entire cooking time.

❖ After about 30 minutes, (yes, 30 minutes!) milk will condense and become thick. Bubbles will become large and heavy. You will be tempted to pour the *muhallebi* into the serving platter at this point, but don't do it! The next 15 minutes of stirring will really pay off with a thick, rich consistency. *Muhallebi* is ready when the rim of each bubble remains standing after bubble pops. Dad described it this way; the bubbles will not pop so much as "faint." Stop stirring for a second and listen. The bubbles should make a sound like a slow whispered "paaaaahhhfff."

❖ Turn off heat. Immediately, starting near one end of the platter, tip pot over and pour mixture with one smooth pour to other end. With a soft spatula, quickly wipe the edges and bottom of the pot in one or two sweeps. (Don't be finicky about scraping the last bits into the platter; the pudding sets very quickly and you will blemish the beautiful smooth surface if you add more pudding on top. Besides, leave some in the pot for the children!)

❖ Allow *muhallebi* to cool un-covered. Decorate with sprinkled cinnamon. Serve chilled.

TRANSPORTING: To carry *muhallebi* to weddings and gatherings, Dad came up with an ingenious way to keep plastic wrap from sagging and sticking to it en-route. He'd recycle the little plastic "stools" that come in pizza boxes and place one in the middle of the pudding before tightly stretching plastic over the platter. (Judiciously sprinkled cinnamon hid the holes!)

YOĞURT TATLISI
Yogurt and Semolina Cake

Many Turkish desserts are drenched in a luscious sweet syrup after baking. Think of *Yoğurt Tatlısı* as a slightly dense, juicy cake with a lot of texture and just the right hint of orange.

Yoğurt Tatlısı is similar in flavor to its cousin *Revani* (on the following page). In fact, most people can't tell the two cakes apart. Both are made with coarse semolina (also known as farina and readily available in ethnic markets). But my *Yoğurt Tatlısı* is a little lighter than *Revani* in that it has half as many eggs, half the butter. Most importantly, it contains yogurt. If you can't find semolina, you can use Cream of Wheat cereal instead.

SYRUP:

- 3 c. Sugar,
- 1 Tbsp. Lemon Juice
- 3 c. Water

CAKE:

- 4 Eggs, at room temperature
- 1 c. Sugar
- 2½ Tbsp. Butter, softened, divided
- 1 c. Plain Yogurt at room temperature
- Shredded peel of 1 rinsed Lemon
- Shredded peel and juice of 1 rinsed Orange
- 1 c. Semolina (#2 coarse)
- 1 c.+ 1 Tbsp. All-Purpose White Flour, divided
- 1 tsp. Baking Soda
- 1 tsp Baking Powder
- 1 c. Bioling Water

INGREDIENTS:

- To make syrup, bring sugar and water to a boil in a medium-sized sauce pan. Cook at low boil for 5 minutes. (This syrup does not need to be thick.) Stir in lemon juice and set aside to cool completely.

The secret to getting the cake to soak up all the syrup is basic science; if the pastry is hot, the syrup should be cold, and vice versa. If you have just removed the cake from the oven, you should pour cooled syrup on it. On the other hand, if the cake has already cooled, the syrup should be heated before pouring it over the pastry.

- Lightly grease bottom and sides of a 12-inch square, 12-inch round, or 13-inch x 9-inch oven-proof casserole dish with ½ Tbsp. butter. Dust evenly with 1 Tbsp. flour. Shake pan to distribute flour. Tap upside-down over sink to discard extra flour. Set aside. Preheat oven to 350°F.

- In a large mixing bowl, beat eggs and sugar with an electric hand mixer for at least 10 minutes until mixture becomes a foamy, thick cream.

- Blend in 2 Tbsp. softened butter. Blend in yogurt, lemon peel, orange peel, and orange juice.

- In a separate medium-sized bowl, whisk together semolina, 1 c. white flour, baking soda, and baking powder. Add these dry ingredients a little at a time to bowl of eggs, continuing to beat on low speed until well-mixed.

- Pour batter into baking dish. Bake for 35-45 minutes or until golden brown. Cake is done when toothpick inserted in center comes out clean. Have a cup of boiling water nearby when the cake is done.

- Turn off oven. Remove cake and immediately pour boiling water evenly over it, a little at a time. Cover cake with foil and set back into oven to allow cake to absorb most of the water (at least 15 minutes).

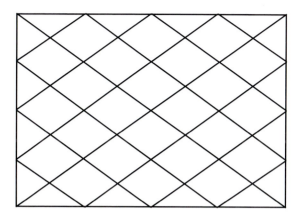

- Remove cake from oven and quickly cut into "lozenge" or diamond-shaped servings, as shown.* Immediately ladle cooled syrup over warm cake and set aside to cool uncovered for at least one hour.

- To serve, remove only individual diamond-shapes and arrange on a shallow serving platter. (Hint: kids love the smaller triangle-shaped pieces left at edges of the pan!)

- *Yoğurt Tatlısı* tastes best when served the day after it is prepared. Serve plain, dusted with confectioner's sugar, or topped with whipped cream. You can also sauté pine nuts in a little butter until golden brown and sprinkle some on top of the whipped cream before serving. Refrigerate to store. *Afiyet olsun!*

*If you have made your cake in a round cake pan, you have the option of flipping the whole cake over in one piece onto a serving platter. In this case, remove the cake from pan by placing a larger serving platter firmly over the cake and swiftly flipping both pan and platter over. Place both on counter. Gently jiggle and lift pan off of cake and platter. Immediately ladle cooled syrup over top, giving each ladle-full a moment to soak in. You can spread a thick layer of whipped cream as frosting. Note that a round cake provides fewer but bigger servings.

REVANI
Semolina Cake with Syrup

In our family, celebrations like weddings come with lots of kissing (on both cheeks), dancing to Turkish music with arms up in the air, loud laughter, and dressy clothes. And no festivity is complete without this delicious, syrupy cake.

Revani is a luscious, sweet, juicy, and somewhat dense cake with a hint of lemon. My mouth waters when I see the syrup pool onto the plate at the bottom of each serving.

Revani can be frosted with thick whipped cream (1 cup heavy cream whipped with 1 tablespoon confectioner's sugar and 1 tsp. vanilla extract). Or try sprinkling confectioner's sugar or crushed pistachios on top for a little color!

INGREDIENTS:

CAKE:

4½ Tbsp. Sweet Cream Butter, softened, divided
9 Eggs, room temperature
1¼ c. Sugar
½ tsp. Vanilla Extract
Juice of 1 Orange (about ½ cup)
Grated Rind from 1 Small Lemon
2 c. Semolina Flour (#2, coarse)
1/3 c. All-Purpose White Flour
1 tsp. Baking Soda

SYRUP:

3 c. Sugar
3 c. water
1 Tbsp. Lemon Juice

❖ To prepare syrup, bring sugar, 3 c. water, and lemon juice to a boil in a medium-sized sauce pan. Reduce heat to low boil and cook 5-10 minutes. The syrup doesn't need to be too thick. Remove from heat and set aside to cool.

❖ Lightly grease bottom and sides of a 12-inch square, 12-inch round, or 13-inch x 9-inch oven-proof casserole dish with ½ Tbsp. butter. Dust evenly with 1 Tbsp. flour. Shake pan, and then tap upside-down over sink to discard extra flour. Set aside.

❖ Separate eggs into two clean large bowls. (See page 244 for separating eggs). Set egg whites aside.

❖ Beat egg yolks, sugar, vanilla, orange juice, and lemon rind together with an electric mixer for 5 minutes or until pale yellow. Set aside. Wash and dry mixer whisks.

❖ In the other bowl, beat egg whites with a pinch of salt for at least 10 minutes until mixture forms stiff peaks. (Boring, yes. But don't stop mixing until peaks can stand firm on their own. See above.) Preheat oven to 350°F.

❖ Whisk together semolina, white flour, and baking soda. While stirring, transfer flour gradually to bowl of beaten yolks. Blend ingredients well.

❖ Gently fold egg whites into batter with wooden spoon. Gradually add softened butter. Blend well.

❖ Pour batter into baking dish and bake at 350°F about 45 minutes or until color turns a light caramel. Cake is done when a toothpick stuck into center comes out clean.

❖ Turn off oven. Remove cake and quickly cut it into 25-30 "lozenge" or diamond shapes inside the pan. (See diagram on page 323). Cutting the cake at this point exposes more surface area to soak up the syrup.

❖ Ladle cooled syrup over cake, a little at a time, to give it a chance to soak up each ladle-full. Set aside to cool uncovered for at least 2 hours before serving.

❖ To serve, remove individual diamond-shaped servings and arrange on a shallow serving platter. (Hint: kids love the smaller triangle-shaped pieces left at the edges of the pan!)

❖ Refrigerate to store. *Revani* is best when served the day after it is made. After a few days, if your cake seems a little dry, you can spoon a little water on top to refresh it. *Afiyet olsun!*

BOREKAS DE MUEZ
Walnut-Filled Tea Cookies

Purim is the Jewish holiday commemorating the day Queen Ester of ancient Persia foiled a plot by the Prime Minister to kill all the Persian Jews. *Borekas de Muez* are little nut-filled cookies that are traditionally served to commemorate this holiday. They are meant to be somewhat dry, and not too sweet since they often accompany afternoon tea or coffee. And they keep for weeks, which makes them perfect to have around for guests who drop-in unexpectedly.

By the way, in order to foil the plot against the Jews, Ester had to reveal to her husband King Ahasuerus that she was herself Jewish. It tickles me that the queen passed as a non-Jew in the Persian empire, especially because my mother did the same thing as head secretary of the Embassy of Iran here in Washington. (See page 122 for the story!)

FILLING:

¼ lb. Walnuts, finely chopped but not pulverized
1½ tsp. Sugar
1 Tbsp. Jam (any kind)
2 dashes Ground Cinnamon

PASTRY DOUGH:

3 Eggs, divided
½ c. Sugar
3/8 c. Canola or Sunflower Oil
2 Tbsp. Butter (room temperature)
Flour (about 3 cups)
Nigella Seed (optional as garnish)

INGREDIENTS:

TO MAKE FILLING

❖ Stir walnuts, sugar, jam and cinnamon together in a medium-sized bowl. Use any jam you like, but make sure you thoroughly distribute it. Set aside.

Pastry Dough

❖ Whisk two eggs in a medium-sized bowl. Stir in ½ cup sugar, oil, and butter. Stir well.

❖ Add enough flour to pull dough together, about 2½ cups. Blend with fingers until you can gather dough up into a ball. Handle dough as little as possible to keep crust flaky. Little by little, add enough flour for dough to feel (get ready for this) like your earlobe.

TOTALLY IRRELEVANT BUT FUNNY FACT:
The Turkish word for earlobe is
kulak memesi or "ear nipple."

❖ Dust a little flour onto counter or rolling surface and rolling pin. Roll out dough to about 1/8th-inch thickness.

❖ Press a large water glass upside-down onto dough and cut out as many circles as possible. (Thinner glass rim cuts better than thick.)

❖ Lift up remaining dough from around cut-out circles and set aside.

❖ Place a teaspoon of filling onto each circle. Gently turn half of circle over to cover filling. Gently pull up bottom edge as you turn down upper edge to "seal" the pastry. Lay crescents on an ungreased cookie sheet so that they do not touch on another.

❖ Gather up remaining dough, handling it as little as possible. Re-roll it out to 1/8" thickness. Repeat previous step. (Repeating process a third time will result in hard pastry. You can try if you like.)

❖ To make a glaze, separate an egg and whisk yolk in a small bowl with a touch of water to thin it a bit. Brush over each pastry and then sprinkle nigella seeds on top.

❖ Bake about 30 minutes at 350°F until tops are golden brown.
Afiyet olsun!

Turkish Coffee

In Turkey, there is no such thing as getting coffee "to go." If you tried to order take-out coffee, you would, at best, confuse the proprietor and, at worst, insult him. Coffee in the Middle East is savored either with good conversation, a game of backgammon, a cigarette, or all three. The few minutes it takes to drink a cup of coffee is the perfect chance to take a break from our routines and just savor life.

Turkish coffee is made of finely pulverized roasted coffee beans sold in small shops called *Kuru Yemisçi*. It used to be that every Turkish house had a brass, hand-cranked coffee mill for pulverizing the beans. Now it comes packaged.

When you order Turkish coffee in Turkey, you are asked how sweet you like it. It is polite and helpful to the coffee maker if you order the same level of sweetness as your co-drinkers, since each sweetness level is prepared separately.

There are four choices for sweetness:

Az Şekerli	little sugar, about ½ tsp.
Orta Şekerli	the standard amount of sugar, 1 tsp.
Şekerli	sweet, 1½ tsp.
Sade Kahve	black coffee, without sugar.

Cezve - You will need a small pot specifically designed for Turkish coffee. It has a long handle (to avoid burning your hand), and a brim for accurate pouring. A copper *cezve* distributes heat best. Size is important; use the best size for the number of servings.

Demitasse Cups - Turkish coffee is served in small, highly decorated cups that hold about ¼ cup liquid.

Turkish Coffee (Extra fine-ground coffee available in most Middle Eastern Markets)

Sugar (optional)

❖ Using your demitasse cup to measure, pour one cup of cold water into cezve for each serving.

❖ Place proper amount of sugar into *cezve*.

❖ Add one heaping, (and I mean really heaping) teaspoon ground Turkish coffee for each serving.

❖ Set heat to medium and stir ingredients very well while water heats up. In the old days Turkish coffee was heated for 15 to 20 minutes over charcoal embers, with the *cezve* frequently taken away from the fire to prevent coffee from boiling and to maximize the prized, creamy foam on top known as *kaymak*. This foam is the signature characteristic of a well-made cup of Turkish coffee.

Stop stirring but DO NOT WALK AWAY! Foam will appear around the perimeter and gradually build up inside the *cezve*. When the coffee is just about to boil, immediately remove *cezve* from heat.

❖ Pour only a little of the foam into each of serving cup, distributing it equally between cups. Return *cezve* to heat.

❖ Heat without stirring until coffee rises again. Pour equal amounts into cups, gently nudging *cezve* from side to side over each cup as you pour to keep foam evenly distributed on top.

❖ Serve immediately alongside a small sweet and a glass of cold water. (Turn page to read more about how to enjoy Turkish coffee.) *Afiyet olsun!*

HOW TO ENJOY TURKISH COFFEE

Since Turkish coffee is not filtered during the brewing process, you should wait for a minute for the coffee grounds to begin drifting to the bottom of the cup before drinking. It is customary to hold the saucer in your open palm as you sip from the demitasse cup with the other hand. Sip slowly; and drink only three quarters of the coffee; you will definitely not enjoy drinking the sediment! If you are lucky enough to be having coffee with someone who can "read" coffee sediment, you can ask them to tell you your fortune, or *fal*.

The *fal* reader will place the saucer upside-down over your cup, and deftly flip both the cup and saucer over so that none of the contents escape. The upside-down cup will be allowed to stand for a couple of minutes. She (*fal* readers are usually women) will then lift the cup and tell your fortune by interpreting the images she sees in the drips and clumps of coffee grounds inside. Mom would read the grounds in the saucer, as well.

Coffee came to Istanbul in the mid-16th century during the reign of Süleyman the Magnificent when the Governor of Ethiopia, Özdemir Pasha, brought it back from Africa. It was initially enjoyed only in the palaces and stately mansions. A ceremonial "feast for the eyes" gradually evolved around the process of drinking it, where three girls (coffee 'angels' no more than sixteen years of age) served guests tiny sips of it in ornate serving sets. In time the tradition of drinking coffee spread throughout Turkey.

Because coffee is still ceremoniously served by young girls, my father taught my sisters and me, from a very early age, the importance of being able to serve coffee and tea to guests. In Dad's mind, he was preparing us for the day a mother would come with son in tow to "look" at a prospective bride. Our role, in Dad's mind, would have been to enter the sitting room with the beverages once the guests had been seated. He imagined we would then glance up shyly, just long enough to glimpse our potential spouse.

In our minds, Dad's hopes and expectations were quaint yearnings, tragically out-of-touch with the American lives we were living in the late 1960's. Still, I could see he longed for those old days when such a scene would have moistened the eyes of everyone in the room. So, for my father's sake, I learned to walk into a room with a tray of coffee without looking down at the contents and without spilling a drop. I learned to gracefully kneel to place the tray on the coffee table. (In our house, the coffee table was for coffee.) I learned to offer it to guests in the proper order, holding the saucer in both hands, smiling as I handed it to them. Then, after having performed my daughterly duty, I would stand and glance at my father's proud and satisfied face, and greet it with the subtlest of eye rolls and a faint sigh of resignation.

You can create your own traditions around serving Turkish coffee. My husband and I enjoy our afternoon coffee served in a beautiful Limoges porcelain demitasse set given to me by my brother Turhan. While I prepare the coffee, Bruce sets up the ancient *tavla* (backgammon) set we bought in Istanbul on our honeymoon. We then turn on some very traditional Turkish music and settle into the very Turkish ritual of taunting and teasing each other about who is a better *tavla* player. Good-humored and playful conversation is as much a part of Turkish *tavla* as the game itself. I'm not sure why, but Bruce and I absent-mindedly banter in accents while we play. Our favorite alter-ego personalities emerge: the cartoon spies Boris Badenoff and his colleague Natasha, the Beverly Hill Billies, the très chic French couple, the British aristocrats, and the Baltimore corner boys. We slap the pieces down on the board and laugh uproariously, especially when double-sixes come. Playing *tavla* while sipping coffee always evokes happy memories of our travels in Turkey.

SEMOLA

Semolina Helva - Sephardic Style

My cousin Suzy Dana Menase grew up with some of this traditional Sephardic dessert always available in her refrigerator. This modest confection is made with semolina flour (similar to farina or cream of wheat) and is sort of a lighter, smoother and less sweet version of *helva* (recipe on page 314). *Semola* has a slightly spongy texture and a hint of lemon. Suzy loves it so much she takes a slice of it to work with her everyday.

INGREDIENTS

1 c. Sugar
1 c. Milk
Peel of 1 Lemon, grated
1 c. Semolina (fine)
Ground Cinnamon

❖ Using a wooden spoon, stir sugar, milk, 4 c. water, and lemon peel together in a heavy pot and bring to a boil.

❖ Gradually stir in semolina, and reduce heat to a very soft boil. Continue to stir until helva reaches the consistency of pudding.

❖ Pour into a mold, and allow to cool. Refrigerate for at least 1 hour before flipping it over onto a serving platter. Garnish decoratively with ground cinnamon. *Afiyet olsun!*

Tezpisti
Walnut Cake in Syrup

About 18 pieces

My grandmother's half-sister Rejina Gerson Alhale (or Alhalel. we're not sure about the spelling)

Often mis-pronounced Tish-Pishti, *Tezpişti* (meaning "fast cooked") is a sweet and juicy holiday nut cake with a hint of orange. It's traditionally served on Rosh Hashanah, but can be modified to serve on Passover by substituting Matzo cake meal for the flour, Matzo-meal for the bread, and simply leave out the leavening ingredient, baking soda.

Here's my cousin Viki's recipe, as she remembers her mother Rejina Alhale preparing it. Make this cake a couple of days early; it continues to absorb its sweet syrup, and tastes better and better as days go by!

SYRUP

2½ c. Sugar (1½ c. for Passover version)
2 c. Water (2/3 c. for Passover version)
2 Tbsp. juice from fresh-squeezed Lemon

CAKE

2 c. Hazelnuts or Walnuts
1 organic Navel or Valencia Orange
2-3 slices day-old baguette or white Bread (½ c.)
    (for Passover version use Matzo-meal)
5 Eggs
1 c. Sugar
½ c. Canola or Sunflower Oil
2 c. Flour (Matzo Cake Meal for Passover version)
1 tsp. Baking Powder (not used for Passover version)
1 tsp. Ground Cinnamon

INGREDIENTS:

❖ To make the syrup, bring sugar, water and lemon juice to a boil in a sauce pan. Reduce heat and simmer for 10-15 minutes. Set aside to cool.

❖ Mix walnuts in food processor until very finely chopped, almost as fine as coarse bulgur. Set aside.

❖ Rinse orange. Zest the peel, collecting zest in a small cup or bowl. Cut orange in half and squeeze juice into same cup or bowl. Set aside.

❖ Remove and discard crust from bread. Grate bread until you have about ½ cup. Set aside.

❖ Preheat oven to 350°F and grease inside of a 13-inch x 9-inch oven-proof casserole dish or cake pan.

❖ In a large bowl, whisk eggs until frothy. Gradually add sugar and continue to whisk until well blended.

❖ Using a wooden spoon, gradually stir in oil, flour, walnuts, orange, bread, baking powder, and cinnamon. Mix well so that all ingredients are blended and batter resembles cookie dough.

(If you are using Matzo-cake meal, the batter will be very thick. If it becomes unmanageable, add small amounts of water so that you can continue to blend ingredients.)

❖ Spread batter into cake pan, pressing it flat. Cut into diamond shapes. (Don't worry if batter fills into cut lines; they will serve as guidelines to re-cut after cake is baked.) Bake for 30 minutes. Test for doneness; toothpick inserted into center should come out clean.

❖ Remove cake from oven. Quickly re-establish cut lines with a sharp knife. Immediately pour cooled syrup evenly over top. Allow to cool.

❖ Cover cake with aluminum foil and let stand for at least 2 hours (overnight is better) before serving. *Afiyet olsun!*

BAKLAVA - PAN STYLE
Sweet Walnut-filled Pastry

Makes 24 servings

Luscious, sweet and buttery, *baklava* is the most famous Turkish dessert. It's made of layers of filo pastry, filled with chopped nuts and cinnamon, all drenched in a lush syrup of sugar and lemon. Don't let anyone tell you that *baklava* is a Greek dessert. The technique of layering filo emerged from the layering of flat breads cooked over fires by Central Asian nomadic Turks and was perfected in the palace kitchens of the Ottoman sultans. Greece definitely has baklava, but only because Greece was once part of the Ottoman Empire! I will admit, however that my Greek friend Amalia Levi makes a pretty mean baklava.

I like to cut it into serving-size diamonds and arrange them in a pattern on a serving platter. Cutting in a diamond pattern always leaves little triangular pices at the edges that are the perfect size for kids to just pop into their mouths as they pass by the kitchen. I like to watch them lick their fingers as they walk away.

SYRUP

- 2 c. Sugar
- 1 c. Water
- 2 Tbsp. Lemon Juice

PASTRY

- 1 Box Filo (Phyllo) Dough (If dough is frozen, it must be thawed for at least 8 hours in the fridge, and then left out on the counter for at least two hours to fully reach room temperature.)
- 2 Sticks Butter (1 c. or 16 Tbsp. or 8 oz.)
- 2 c. Walnuts, chopped uniformly
  (Mom used a mortar and pestle to chop nuts. I prefer chopping them with a sharp knife for better control. You can also pulse small amounts in a food processor once or twice, but don't pulverize them; they should be chunky. Or wrap them in a clean dish towel and hammer with a rolling pin or book.)
- 1 tsp. Cinnamon

INGREDIENTS:

❖ To prepare syrup, bring sugar, water, and lemon to boil in a medium-sized sauce pan. Reduce heat and cook at a low boil for 10 to 15 minutes. Check for doneness by dropping a tiny bit on a wood surface. It should be yellowish and feel tacky between your fingers. Set aside to cool.

❖ Melt butter slowly in small saucepan over very low heat.

❖ Assembling baklava is similar to making *börek*, so read through the recipe on page 243 before beginning. When butter has melted, brush 2 tablespoons into bottom and along sides of an 11-inch x14-inch or similar size baking pan.

❖ Lay first sheet loosely in pan, and lightly brush a little less than a tablespoon butter on top and around the edges. Take no more than 5-7 seconds to spread butter so that next layer doesn't dry out. Repeat for next nine layers. (There will be about 20 sheets of filo in your package.)

❖ When half the sheets have been layered, sprinkle nuts evenly over dough like a blanket. Sprinkle ground cinnamon over nuts. (Some people then mist a little water over walnuts to stabilize the next filo layer. I don't bother.)

❖ Layer remaining sheets of filo as before. Brush top sheet and its edges generously with a final layer of butter. (Ideally, you will have finished almost the entire saucepan of butter. If you have none left, melt a small amount more for the top. If you have too much butter left, do NOT pour all of it in on top; the dessert will be too greasy.) Set aside any left over butter.

❖ Before cutting, place *baklava* into freezer for 10 minutes. (Allowing butter to harden makes cutting the pastry much easier.) Preheat oven to 350°F. Remove from freezer and, using a sharp knife, cut into serving size pieces. (See diagram on bottom right.)

❖ Place on middle rack of oven and bake until top turns light gold, about 25 to 30 minutes. (If you do not intend to bake immediately, cover pan with plastic wrap or aluminum foil and store in freezer. Add 10 minutes to baking time to cook frozen.)

❖ Remove from the oven. Quickly run a sharp knife along cut lines, making sure cuts go down to bottom of pan. Slowly, pour syrup evenly over entire pastry.

❖ Allow to cool uncovered before serving. Sugar is a terrific preservative, so baklava can be stored at room temperature for more than a week. Just make sure it is covered so it doesn't dry out. Don't microwave it or it will become soggy. *Afiyet olsun!*

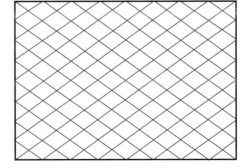

BAKLAVA - ROLLED
Sweet Walnut-filled Pastry

For formal occasions when finger food is called for, I make Tant Mati's rolled baklava. These little pastries are bite-size, and so scrumptious they disappear long before traditional desserts like chocolate cake, brownies or cookies. Most guests can't help but eat 3 or 4 of them.

It's not hard to make baklava; three sheets of buttered filo dough are rolled around a walnut filling, and then sliced diagonally to make the perfect serving size. They are then baked and drenched in sweet, lemony syrup. Yum!

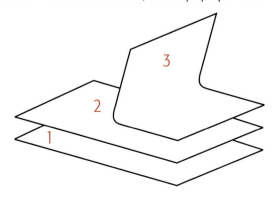

SYRUP
- 2 c. Sugar
- 1 c. Water
- 2 Tbsp. Lemon Juice

PASTRY
- 1 Box Filo (Phyllo) Dough, at room temperature (If dough is frozen, it must be thawed for at least 8 hours in the fridge, and then left out on the counter for at least two hours to fully reach room temperature.)
- 2 Sticks Butter (1 c. or 16 Tbsp. or 8 oz.)
- 2 c. Walnuts, chopped (Walnuts should be chunky. My son Tory likes to chop them with a sharp knife so the pieces are consistent in size. Mom used a mortar and pestle, where as Tant Ida pulsed small amounts in a food processor once or twice. Just don't pulverize them. You can also put nuts in a clean dish towel and hammer them with a rolling pin or book.)
- 1 tsp. Ground Cinnamon

INGREDIENTS:

❖ To prepare syrup, bring sugar, water, and lemon to boil in a medium-sized sauce pan. Reduce heat and cook at a low boil for 10 to 15 minutes. Check for doneness by dropping a tiny bit on a wood surface. It should be yellowish and feel tacky between your fingers. ⟵ Set aside to cool.

❖ Melt butter slowly in small saucepan over very low heat. Meanwhile stir walnuts with cinnamon in small bowl. Preheat oven to 350°F.

❖ Lay parchment paper into bottom of 11-inch x14-inch (or similar size) baking dish. Set up workspace as described on page 243. Remove filo dough from box and lay out next to you. Take three sheets of filo and lay them on a sheet of wax paper. (Lay another sheet of wax paper over remaining pile of filo to keep it from drying out.)

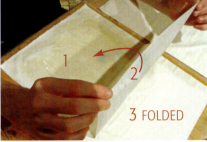

❖ Lift edge closest to you of sheets 2 and 3 and fold the sheets in half. Brush butter on exposed half of sheet 1.

❖ Fold bottom half of sheet 2 down over 1. Brush exposed half of sheet 2 with butter.

❖ Fold bottom half of sheet 3 down. Brush only bottom half of sheet 3 with butter.

❖ Lift unbuttered end of sheet 3 and fold over buttered half. Brush exposed half of sheet 3 with butter.

❖ Lift unbuttered end of sheet 2 and fold over sheet 3. Brush with butter.

❖ Lift unbuttered end of sheet 1 and fold over. Brush with butter.

❖ Gingerly lay 2 to 2½ tablespoons walnut filling in a line along bottom edge of filo. Roll filo up snugly (but not tight) around filling. Roll into log. Lay seam-side down on parchment. Brush top and ends with butter.

❖ Repeat with remaining filo laying rolls snugly side-by-side in baking dish. (There are approximately 21 sheets of filo per box, enough for 7 rolls total.)

❖ With sharp knife, cut across rolls diagonally into bite-size pieces. Brush tops again with butter. Place on middle rack of oven and bake until top turns golden brown, about 35 to 40 minutes.

❖ Remove from oven. Immediately pour syrup, slowly and evenly over entire pastry. Set aside to cool, uncovered. Sugar is a terrific preservative, so baklava can be stored at room temperature for more than a week. Just make sure it is covered so it doesn't dry out. Don't microwave it or it will become soggy. *Afiyet olsun*.

TEL KADAIFI - CEVIZLI
Shredded Filo with Nuts

This traditional and beloved Ottoman dessert is similar to baklava, except that it's made with shredded filo dough called *kadaif* that resembles a mishmash of thin wire (*tel* in Turkish), hence the name. When the nut-filled pastry comes out of the oven, it is drenched in a luscious syrup that thirstily soaks it up. The result is a dewy, delectable delight.

A wonderful variation of *kadaifi* is *künefe*, which has Syrian string cheese in the middle. The melted cheese contrasts beautifully with the sweetness and texture of the pastry! Some cooks also brown both sides of the pastry by flipping it over and baking it another ten minutes before adding the syrup. Serve *Kadaifi* warm or cold. You can add a dollop of *kaymak* (heavy cream), or whipped cream on top if you like.

INGREDIENTS:

3 c. Sugar
2 c. Water
1 Tbsp. Lemon Juice
2 Sticks Butter (1 c. or 16 Tbsp. or 8 oz.) melted, divided
1-½ lbs. Frozen *Kadaif* (Shredded Filo Dough found in freezer section of most Middle Eastern markets.
2 c. Walnuts, chopped but not pulverized
1 tsp. Cinnamon

❖ To prepare syrup, bring sugar and water to a boil in a medium-sized sauce pan. Continue boiling for 5 minutes. Reduce heat and simmer for 15 minutes. Add lemon juice and set aside.

❖ Preheat oven to 350°F. Melt butter slowly in small saucepan.

❖ Spread ¼ c. melted butter into bottom and along sides of a 13-inch x 9-inch Pyrex or oven-proof baking dish.

❖ Remove *kadaif* from box and break apart by either teasing it apart over a cookie sheet with your hands, pulsing it once or twice in a food processor, or simply slicing the entire mound of dough like a loaf of bread, into slices no more than ½-inch long. (Whichever method you choose, work quickly so dough doesn't dry out.)

❖ Spread half of shredded dough evenly in baking dish, and press down with palms of your hands.

❖ Spread nuts evenly over dough like a blanket. Sprinkle with ground cinnamon.

❖ Spread remaining dough as a second blanket. Again, press with palms. Spoon remaining butter along edges of pan and evenly across top.

❖ Bake on middle rack of oven 30 to 35 minutes until top turns a reddish-gold color. (Turks call this color "pomegranate skin.")

❖ Remove *kadaif* from oven and drain any extra butter. Carefully pour cooled syrup evenly over entire pastry, a little at a time, to give it time to absorb.

❖ Allow to cool before cutting. *Afiyet olsun!*

COOKING AS A NEIGHBORHOOD ENDEAVOR

Tant Ida and I discussed *Tel Kadaifi* while enjoying tea and chocolate biscotti's in her kitchen. She recalled that as a small girl in 1940's Istanbul, no one had an oven in their home. To bake the kadaif, her mother would send her to the local bread-maker who, for a small fee, would cook the neighborhood's pastries in his bread oven. (No wonder, then, that the oven temperature for all these pastry recipes, is invariably 350°; the temperature for baking bread!) Ida says the bread maker (*ekmekçi*) would take the pastry and instruct her to come back in an hour to pick it up.

When I first returned to Istanbul in 1970, the side streets were still full of young children, 4, 5, 6 years old, running errands for their mothers. I can still recall the clacking of their hard sandals as they scurried along the cobblestones, carrying loaves of bread, small packages from the pharmacy, or a cup of sugar from a neighbor. My own nephew Ercan was a mischievous boy, so his grandmother Zehra made sure to keep him busy with errands throughout the day. Ercan would often stop momentarily to to kick back a stray soccer ball or to watch his friends huddled around a sidewalk game of marbles, while his grandmother impatiently waited for the evening's bread.

In those days, the streets were full of horse-drawn carts full of fruits and vegetables and people hawking their wares. An *eskici* or handyman coaxed his donkey (packed high with pots and pans), along the narrow alley. A basket tied to a light rope edged down the stone facade from one of the upper floor apartments. A vendor looked up to the *ev hanım* (lady of the house), who was leaning out the window shouting instructions. He filled the basket and up it climbed. The yogurt man sang out in a deep baritone, "*Yo-uuuuuuurt! Yo-uuuuuuurt!*" A teenager came by with a broom handle balanced across his shoulders, each end draped with freshly-toasted sesame rings called *simit*. His voice rang out, "*Sim-iiiiit! Sicak, sicak sim-iiiiit!*" (Simit! Hot, hot simit!)

My sister Çaya likes to tell the story about the first time she returned to Turkey at 13 years of age. Taking a nap, she dreamt that a desperate man was wandering down the street in a confused state. In her dream his arms were outstretched and he vainly searched the streets yelling, "I don't know, I don't knoooooooow." Çaya woke up disturbed by the dream and related it to my father, who cracked up laughing. Her dream had incorporated the very real parsley vendor (*maydanozcu*) outside her window who had been yelling "*May-da-noz, may-da-noooooooz!*"

Sütlaç
Rice Pudding

S mells and tastes from childhood often make vivid lifelong impressions. One of my earliest and fondest memories is of grandmama Sara making *sütlaç* for me in her Istanbul kitchen. I remember clutching her apron, straining on tip-toes to smell the sweet milk she was patiently stirring on the stove.

Children love rice pudding. It's essentially rice cooked in sweetened milk which is thickened with rice flour. Some people add vanilla. Cooks in the sultan's kitchen sometimes flavored it with rose-water, a distinctly "acquired" taste. In modern Turkey, most patisseries have their own version of the classic recipe and serve it either hot or cold. In our family it was always served chilled. The Turkish Sephardic community also traditionally serves *sütlaç* on the joyous Jewish holiday *Sukkot*.

INGREDIENTS:

½ c. short grain white Rice, rinsed and drained well
4 c. Whole Milk (1 quart)
4/5 c. Sugar (use ¾ c. plus 4 Tbsp.)
½ c. Rice Flour
1 tsp. Cornstarch (optional)
Ground Cinnamon (topping)

❖ Bring ¾ c. water to a boil in small saucepan. Add rice, cover and reduce heat to very low. Simmer 15 minutes.

❖ Meanwhile, in a large pot, heat milk and sugar over medium-high heat. Stir frequently. Just before it boils (and rises abruptly) reduce heat to medium. Simmer, stirring slowly and constantly with a wooden spoon to keep it from scorching.

❖ To add rice flour without lumps, scoop up a cup of the milk and stir it gradually into a small bowl along with rice flour until flour is dissolved. Stir mixture back into pot.

❖ Add cooked rice to pot. Continue to simmer until milk thickens (20 minutes). You can add a tsp. cornstarch (using same method as with rice flour) to thicken pudding further.

❖ Pour pudding into small serving bowls and cool at room temperature. Chill uncovered in refrigerator at least 2 hours before serving. Sprinkle with ground cinnamon. Enjoy with loved ones. *Afiyet olsun!*

HELPFUL STANDARDS

MEAT ROASTING CHART

Meat Type	Minimum Target Temperature	Simmering Time
Poultry		
Chicken Un-Stuffed (4-7 lbs)	180° (inner thigh)	20 min/lb @ 350° (+20 minutes if stuffed)
Chicken Un-Stuffed (3-3½ lbs)	180° (inner thigh)	13-15 min/lb @ 450° (+15 minutes if stuffed)
Turkey Un-Stuffed (16-24 lbs)	180° (inner thigh)	12-15 min/lb @ 325°
Turkey Stuffed	180° (inner thigh)	See Thanksgiving Turkey Recipe
Beef (allow to rest 15 min before carving)		
Rib Eye Boneless (3 lbs)	(rare)	12-13 min/lb @ 350°
Rib Bone (4-6 lbs)	(rare)	25 min/lb @ 300°
Tenderloin Boneless (5½-6½ lbs)	(rare)	20 min @ 500° and then 8-10 min/lb @ 375°
Brisket (5-6 lbs)	(rare)	30-35 min/lb

Adapted from Rosso and Lukins, The New Basics Cookbook, Workman Publishing, 1989

PREPARATION OF DRIED BEANS

Type of Dried Bean	Soak?	Simmering Time
Chick Peas	✔	2-3 Hours
Fava or Broad Beans	✔ + Peel	2-2 1/2 Hours
Kidney or Cannellini Beans	✔	1 1/2 - 2 Hours
Lentils	no	30 - 40 Minutes
Lima Beans	✔	1 1/2 Hours
Pinto Beans	✔	1 1/2 - 2 Hours
Red Beans	✔	1 1/2 - 2 Hours
Split Peas	no	40 - 50 Minutes
White or Navy Beans	✔	1 1/2 - 2 Hour
Great Northern Beans	✔	1 1/2 - 2 Hour

Rosso and Lukins, The New Basics Cookbook, Workman Publishing, 1989

Units of Measure and Temperatures

Traditional Turkish	**Standard American**
Su Bardak (water glass)	4/5 cup 8 oz 250 ml.
Çay Bardak (tea glass)	½ cup 4 oz 125 ml.
Çorba Kapýk (soup spoon)	1 Tbsp.
Yemek Kapýk (food spoon)	1 Tbsp.
Kapýk	1 Tbsp.
Tatlı Kapýk (sweet spoon)	1 Tsp.
Çay Kapýk (tea spoon)	½ Tsp.
Kahve Kapýk (coffee spoon)	½ Tsp.
Kahve Fincan	10 Tsp. < ¼ c.
(Turkish coffee or Demitasse Cup)

Spoons	**ML**		
1/8 tsp.	½ ml	1 pinch	
1/4 tsp	1 ml		
1/2 tsp	2 ml		
1 tsp	5 ml	120 Drops	
1 tbsp	15 ml	3 tsp.	½ oz.
2 tbsp.	30 ml	6 tsp.	1 oz.

Cup	**Ingredients**	**Grams**
1 cup	Granulated sugar	200 grams
1 cup	Packed Brown Sugar	220 grams
1 cup	Sifted White Flour	125 grams
1 cup	White Rice, uncooked	185 grams
1 cup	White Rice, cooked	175 grams
1 cup	Butter	227 grams
1 cup	Almonds, slivered	108 grams
1 cup	Oil	224 grams
1 cup	Maple Syrup	322 grams
1 cup	Milk, non-fat	245 grams
1 cup	Milk, sweet condensed	306 grams
1 cup	Broccoli, flowerets	71 grams
1 cup	Raisins, packed	165 grams
1 cup	Milk, dry	68 grams
1 cup	Yogurt	245 grams
1 cup	Water	236 grams
1 cup	Confectioners Sugar	110 grams
1 cup	Cocoa	125 grams

Cups	**Tbsp.**	**ML**
1 cup	16 Tbsp.	250 ml
3/4 cup	12 Tbsp.	175 ml
2/3 cup	10 ½ Tbsp.	150 ml
1/2 cup	8 Tbsp.	125 ml
1/3	5 ¼ Tbsp.	75 ml
1/4 cup	4 Tbsp.	50 ml

Pounds	**Grams**	**Ounces**
1 Lb.	454 grams	16 oz.
1/3 Lb.	150 grams	
2.2 Lbs.	1 Kg. (1000 g.)	35.3 oz.
.44 Lbs.	200 grams	
.55 Lbs	250 grams	
1 oz.	28.4 grams	
.035 oz.	1 gram	

Lb.	**Ingredients**	**Cups**
1 lb.	Brown Sugar	3 ½ cups
1 lb.	Sugar	2 ¼ cups
1 lb.	Powdered Sugar	3 ¾ cups
1 lb.	Butter -- or any fat	2 cups
1 lb.	Grated Cheese	4 ½ cups
1 lb	Flour	3 cups
1 lb	Whole Wheat Flour	3 1/3 cups
1 lb	Corn Meal	3 ¼ cups
1 lb	Raisins	3 cups
1 lb	Pitted Dates	2 2/3 cups
1 lb	Un-pitted Dates	3 ½ cups
1 lb	Chopped Nuts	4 cups
1 lb	Onions, chopped	4 cups
1 lb.	Un-cooked Rice	2 cups (6 c. cooked)

Miscellaneous Measurements:

½ Pint	16 Tbsp.	1 Cup	8 oz.	240 ml.
1 Pint		2 cups	16 oz.	473 ml.
1 Quart	2 Pints	4 cups	32 oz.	
4 quarts	1 gallon	16 cups	128 oz.	
1 liter	4.22 cups	1.06 quarts		
1/8 liter	6 2/3 tbsp.			
8 quarts	1 Peck			
1 cm	0.39 inches			
1 inch	2.54 cm			

Oven Temperatures:

350° F	170° C
375° F	180° C
400° F	200° C
425° F	220° C

REFERENCES

Barbaro, Giosofat Travels to Tana and Persia (A Narrative of Italian Travels in Persia in the 15th and 16th Centuries) Page 106.

Benbassa, Esther. Zionism in the Ottoman Empire at the End of the 19th and the Beginnings of the 20th Century, Studies in Zionism, Vol.11 No. 2, 1990.

Bostom, Andrew G. "Under Turkish Rule, Part II" Front PageMagazine.com Friday, August 03, 2007

Brendemoen, Bernt Turcologica 50 The Turkish Dialects of Trabzon - Their Phonology and Historical Development Volime 1: Analysis p.284

Dimont, Max I. Jews, God and History, The New American Library

Divani Lugati't-Turk, 11th century Turkic scholar Mahmud of Kashgar (origins of Oghuz) and Oguz Turkish literature includes the famous "Book of Dede Korkut" which was UNESCO's 2000 literacy work of the year, as well as the Oguznama and "Koroglu" epics

Durghali, Matthew Crimean War - France in the Crimean War, Silvapages

Ekinci, Mehmet Ugur, The Origins of the 1897 Ottoman-Greek War: A Diplomatic History (a Master's Thesis) The Department of History, Bilkent University, Ankara, July 2006 http://www.thesis.bilkent.edu.tr/0003114.pdf

Ergene, M. Bahri via Osmanli Ulemasi (Ottoman Scholars) Vol. 3, p. 88 File No. 2455

Findley, Carter Vaughin. The Turks in World History. Oxford University Press, 2005. ISBN 0195177266.

Finkel, Caroline, The History of the Ottoman Empire, Osman's Dream (Basic Books 2005).

Fragner, Bret, "From the Caucuses to the Roof of the World,: A Culinary Adventure", A Taste of Thyme - Culinary Cultures of the Middle East, Sami Zubaida and Richard Tapper, Taurus Parke, 2000

Freely, John Storm on Horseback, The Seljuk Warriors of Turkey, I.B. Tauris, 2008

Golden, Peter. An introduction to the history of the Turkic peoples: Ethnogenesis and state-formation in medieval and early modern Eurasia and the Middle East, Harrassowitz, 1992.

Gurtour (http://www.gurtour.com/default.asp?section=sites&a=trabzon)

Hillenbrand, Carole Turkish Myth and Muslim Symbol – The Battle of Manzikert, Edinburgh University Press, 2007

Hostler, Charles Warren The Turks of Central Asia, Praeger, 1993

Imber, Colin. The Ottoman Empire 1300-1650, The Structure of Power Palgrave Macmillan 2002

Isichei, Elizabeth. A History of African Societies to 1870. pp. 192. Cambridge University Press. (1997).

Jackson, Peter and Lockhart, Laurence. The Cambridge History of Iran: The Timurid and Safavid Periods. Cambridge Univerity Press, (1986).

Karpat, Kemal. Studies on Ottoman Social and Political History, " The Hijra from Russia and the Balkans; the Process of Self-Definition in the late Ottoman State" Page 148 Brill 2002 (DR576 .K37 2004)

Katz, Yosef. "Paths of Zionist Political Action in Turkey, 1882-1914; The Plan for Jewish Settlements in Turkey During the Young Turks Era," International Journal of Turkish Studies, vol. 4, no. 1

Keli, Haje. Polygamy in the Muslim world and new restrictions in Iraqi Kurdistan

Kurdish Herald Vol. 2 Issue 1, February 2010 (http://www.kurdishherald.com/issue/v002/001/article08.php)

Meserve, Margaret. Empires of Islam in Renaissance Historical Thought, Presidents and Fellows of Harvard College, 2008

Mihailović, Konstantin. Memoirs of a Janissary, trans. Benjamin Stolz, p 117. (Ann Arbor: The University of Michigan, 1975), xxii

Nicolle, David, PhD. Attila and the Nomad Hordes, Osprey Military Books 1996

Necipoglu, Gulru. "The Life of an Imperial Monument: Hagia Sophia after Byzantium" p.197, 202-4. In Hagia Sophia, ed. Robert Mark and Ahmet S. C(h)akmak. Cambridge, 1992

Norwich, John Julius (1995). Byzantium:The Decline and Fall. New York: Alfred A. Knopf. pp. 413-416. ISBN 0-679-41650-1)

Perry, Charles. "The Taste of Layered Bread among the Nomadic Turks and the Central Asian Baklava," page 89, A Taste of Thyme - Culinary Culture in the Middle East, Taurus Parke 2000

Reade, William Winwood The Martyrdom of Man "Arab Spain" P 113, 1872 http://www.exclassics.com/martyrdom/martman.pdf

Ridvan Akar, The Capital Tax: An Example of Anti-Minority Politics in the Era of One Party Rule, Belge Yayinlari, Istanbul, 1992

Robinson, George. Essential Judaism – A complete Guide to Beliefs, Customs, and Rituals, Pocket Books, 2000

Rossi, Ettore, "The Rise and Fall of the Ottoman Empire" arcticle "La Sultana Nur-Banu (Cecilia Venier-Baffo), Moglie di Selim II (1566-1574) e Madre di Murad III (1574-1595)", published in Oriente Moderno, Anno XXXIII, Nr 11 (Novembre 1953), pp 433-441 evidence that Nur Banu, wife of Sultan Selim II and mother of Sultan Murad III, was Venetian Cecilia Venier-Baffo.

Roux, Jean-Paul Historical Introduction , The Turkic Peoples of the World, , Kegan Paul International , 1993 Editor- Bainbridge, Margaret

Runciman, Steven (1965). The Fall of Constantinople: 1453. London: Cambridge University Press. pp. 56. ISBN 0-521-39832-0).

Shepherd, William R. Map: The Empire of Trebizond and other states carved from the Byzantine Empire, as they were in 1265 (Historical Atlas, 1911)

Silburn, P. A. B. (1912). The evolution of sea-power. London: Longmans, Green and Co.)

St. Clair William. That Greece Might Still Be Free The Philhellenes in the War of Independence. London: Oxford University Press, 1972.

Steevens, George Warrington. With the conquering Turk: Confessions of a Bashibazouk, Dodd Mead 1897 from the collections of Harvard University

Swenson, R. Victor, The Military Rising in Istanbul 1909, Journal of Contemporary History 1970; 5 p. 171-184

Sykes, Mark The Kurdish Tribes of the Ottoman Empire. the Journal of the Royal Anthropological Institute of Great Britain and Ireland, Vol. 38, (Jul. - Dec., 1908), pp. 451-486

Toktas, S. Turkey's Jews and their Immigration to Israel http://issuu.com/suletoktas/docs/2006_turkey_s_jews_migration_to_israel. 2006

Toynbee, Arnold J., A Study of History, Volumes 1-4 by D.C. Somervel (Oxford University Press 1949) pp. 169, 175.

Wasserman, A. Cooking the Sephardic Way Sephardic Sisterhood, Temple Tifereth Isreal, Los Angeles, CA 1971

Weatherford, Jack Genghis Khan and the Making of the Modern World Three Rivers Press 2004

Williams, Brian Glyn The Crimean Tatars. The Diaspora Experience and the Forging of a Nation Leiden: E. J. Brill, 2001. 520 p.

Leiden: E. J. Brill, 2001. 520 p. Assistant professor of Islamic History at the University of Massachusetts, Darthmouth. E-mail: bwilliams@umassd.edu.

Woo, X. L. Empress Wu the Great: Tang Dynasty China, Chapter 5: Rebellions, Algora Publishing

Websites

Ahmad, Jamil. Tariq Bin Ziyad (http://www.renaissance.com.pk/marletf95.html)

Ak Koyunlu Rulers (http://tr.wikipedia.org/wiki/Akkoyunlular)

Amateau , Janet. A Recipe: POACHED FIGS / una receta: COMPOSTO DE HIGOS February 20, 2009 http://sephardicfood.wordpress.com/2009/02/20/recipe-composto-de-higos/

Amin, Hussein Abdulwaheed The Origins of the Sunni/Shia split in Islam IslamForToday.com

Andic, Fuat Farewell Homeland: Tale of Two Cities and One People 2008 www.booksurge.com

China Knowledge http://www.chinaknowledge.de/History/Tang/turks.html

Diaspora, Howard Sachar (number of Jews InSpain) http://www.simpletoremember.com/vitals/world-jewish-population.htm

Foundation for the Advancement of Sephardic Studies and Culture http://www.sephardicstudies.org/osmanlica.html

Greek point of view http://upge.wn.com/?t=ancientgreece/index9.txt

Jewish Encyclopedia http://www.jewishencyclopedia.com/view.jsp?artid=80&letter=N#ixzz0chmfgwiH

Jewish Encyclopedia http://www.jewishencyclopedia.com/view.jsp?artid=80&letter=N#ixzz0chlFp4sF

Kamen, Henry. The Spanish Inquisition, p. 17.

Mamluk History http://www.allempires.com/forum/forum_posts.asp?TID=27297&PID=628973

Nelson, Lynne The Rise of Christianity, Lectures in Medieval History http://www.vlib.us/medieval/lectures/christianity_rise.html

Radikal. http://www.radikal.com.tr/haber.php?haberno=163380.) Information on Wikipedia on Varlik Vergesi

SEPHARDIC FOOD http://sephardicfood.wordpress.com/2008/12/21/one-for-the-glossary-cuajado-uno-para-el-glosario-cuajado.

Singer ,Jeffrey A., Making Sense of Jewish Stereotypes Freedom Daily April 2000 http://www.fff.org/freedom/0400f.asp

"The Therapeutic Value of Sesame Oil by Anne McIntyre issue 81 - October 2002 Positive Health Online http://www.positivehealth.com/article-view.php?articleid=1104

Trabzon and the Ottomans (http://www.turizm.gov.tr/EN/Genel/BelgeGoster.aspx?17A16AE30572D3137A2395174CFB32E1A510106937B3F39C)

Turkish Cultural Foundation, http://www.turkish-cuisine.org/english/pages.php?ParentID=6&PagingIndex=0 (List of vegetables)

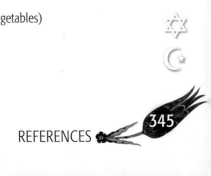

INDEX